VIJAY TENDULKAR

Five Plays

VIJAY TENDULKAR

Five Plays

Kamala
Silence! The Court is in Session
Sakharam Binder
The Vultures
Encounter in Umbugland

DELHI
OXFORD UNIVERSITY PRESS
CALCUTTA CHENNAI MUMBAI

Oxford University Press, Great Clarendon Street, Oxford OX2 6DP

Oxford   New York
Athens   Auckland   Bangkok   Calcutta
Cape Town   Chennai   Dar es Salaam   Delhi
Florence   Hong Kong   Istanbul   Karachi
Kuala Lumpur   Madrid   Melbourne   Mexico City
Mumbai   Nairobi   Paris   Singapore
Taipei   Tokyo   Toronto

and associates in

Berlin   Ibadan

© Oxford University Press 1992
Kamala is published here for the first time
Silence! The Court is in Session was first published
by Oxford University Press in 1974
Sakharam Binder was first published by Hind Pocket Books
in 1974
The Vultures was first published by Hind Pocket Books
in 1974
Encounter in Umbugland was first published by
Hind Pocket Books in 1975
This edition first published 1992
Oxford India Paperbacks 1995
Second impression 1997

ISBN 0 19 563736 4

Printed at Saurab Print O Pack, Noida
and published by Manzar Khan, Oxford University Press
YMCA Library Building, Jai Singh Road, New Delhi 110 001

CONTENTS

CONTENTS

INTRODUCTION

Vijay Tendulkar has been in the vanguard of not just Marathi but Indian theatre for almost forty years. Beginning his career as a dramatist in the mid-fifties, this prolific writer has twenty-eight full length plays, twenty-four one-act plays, and eleven children's dramas to his credit, a good number of which have been translated and produced in major Indian languages. His *Silence! the Court is in Session* earned him a place among leading Indian playwrights in the late sixties while his *Ghasiram Kotwal* won him international fame in the mid-seventies. Winner of several national and international awards and fellowships, he is both a venerated and a controversial figure in the country's theatre scene. To discuss such a figure and his equally well-known works, most of which have generated so much intellectual debate and controversy, one requires a temporal distance—a separation in time—to be able to understand and evaluate them in clear perspective. The intervening years, since the plays were written, provides us with that advantage.

Tendulkar's first major work that set him a part from previous generation Marathi playwrights was *Manus Navache Bet* (An Island called Man) (1955), which gave expression to the tormenting solitude and alienation of a modern individual in an urbane, industrialized society. His dramatic genuis was cut out for the newly emerging, experimental Marathi theatre of the time. His direct association with Rangayan at this point of his career and continuous interaction with such theatre personalities as Vijaya Mehta, Arvind and Sulabha Deshpande, Kamlakar Sarang, Madhav Vatve and Damoo Kenkre, provided new impetus for his creative faculties. Thus *Manus Navache Bet* was closely followed by a spate of plays—*Madhlya Bhinti* (The Walls Between) (1958), *Chimnicha Ghar Hota Menacha* (Nest of Wax) (1958), *Mee Jinklo Mee Harlo* (I Won, I Lost), (1963), *Kavlanchi Shala* (School for Crows) (1963) and *Sari Ga Sari* (Rain, O Rain) (1964)—which would chart the course of avant-garde Marathi theatre during the next few years. There seems to be a consistency of theme and treatment in them despite the apparently disparate nature of their subjects. In all these early plays, Tendulkar is concerned with the middle class individual set against the backdrop of a hostile society. Another distinctive feature of these plays is the absence of an easy solution. Tendulkar presents modern man in all his complexities. He portrays life as it is from different angles, without trying to moralize or philosophize in any way. Most of these works are endowed with his characteristic style of dialogue—jerky, half-finished, yet signifying more than what it says. Another implicit quality of the treatment of his subjects in all these creations is an underlying sympathy for the 'little big man' in our modern world.

With the production of *Shantata! Court Chalu Ahe* (*Silence! The Court is in Session*) in 1967, Tendulkar became the centre of a general controversy. He had already acquired the epithet of 'the angry young man' of Marathi theatre, but now he was definitely marked out as a rebel against the established values of a fundamentally orthodox society. The theatre group in *Silence!* ... which comes to perform at a village is a miniscule cross-section of middle-class society, the members representative of its different sub-strata. Their characters, dialogues, gestures and even mannerisms reflect their petty, circumscribed existences fraught with frustrations and repressed desires that find expression in their malicious and spiteful attitudes towards their fellow beings. Leela Benare, the central character of the play, is the only exception. Possessing a natural lust for life and a spontaneous *joie de vivre*, she ignores social norms and dictates. Being different from the others, she is easily isolated and made the victim of a cruel game, cunningly planned by her co-actors. During the course of this so-called 'game', which is meaningfully set in the form of a mock-trial, Miss Benare's private life is exposed and publicly dissected, revealing her illicit love affair with Professor Damle, a married man with a family, which has resulted in her pregnancy. Professor Damle is significantly absent at the trial, denoting his total withdrawal of responsibility, either social or moral, for the whole situation into which he has landed Miss Benare. During the trial, he is summoned merely as a witness while Benare remains the prime accused as the unwed mother of his illegitimate child. Interestingly, the accusation brought against her at the beginning of the trial—that of infanticide—turns into the verdict at the conclusion, principally because contemporary Indian society, with its roots grounded firmly in reactionary ideas, cannot allow the birth of a child out of wedlock. This very reversal in the attitude of the 'authorities' expresses the basic hypocrisy and double standards on which our society is founded.

The violence that Tendulkar's later plays would be associated with, already makes itself felt in this play. In the persecution of this helpless woman, a fierce psychological violence becomes evident. The latent sadism of the characters, of Sukhatme, of Mr and Mrs Kashikar, of Ponkshe, Karnik or even Rokde, surfaces during the process of the trial. In delineating these characters, Tendulkar has explored their psyches to the extent of revealing the hidden sense of failure pervading their lives—the inefficiency of Sukhatme as a lawyer, the childlessness of Mr and Mrs Kashikar, the non-fulfilment of Ponkshe's dreams to become a scientist, the vain attempts of Karnik to be a successful actor and the inability of Rokde to attain an independent, adult existence. The figure of the simple-hearted villager, Samant, is adeptly handled by the dramatist to offset the complexities of the urbane characters.

Leela Benare's defence of herself against the onslaught of the upholders of social norms in a long soliloquy, has become famous in the history of contemporary Marathi theatre. It is important to note here that Tendulkar leaves us in doubt as to whether or not Benare at all delivers the soliloquy, thus suggesting that in all probability what she has to say for herself is swallowed up by the silence imposed upon her by the authorities. In fact, during the court proceedings, on several occasions, her objections and protestations are drowned by the judge's cry of 'Silence!' and the banging of the gavel. Benare's monologue is reminiscent of Nora's declaration of independence but lacks the note of protest that characterizes the speech of Ibsen's heroine. It is more a self-justification than an attack on society's hypocrisies. It is poignant, sensitive and highlights the vulnerability of women in our society.

On the surface, Tendulkar seems to have adapted the model of naturalistic drama. But the integration of the play within a play creates an additional dimension where the demarcating line between reality and illusion is often blurred. An almost 'Pirandellesque' effect is achieved as the characters move back and forth from make-believe to naked reality. A good instance is Samant's evidence where his reading from a sensational and fictitious novel comes dangerously close to the real situation. But it is important to remember that Tendulkar's central concern, unlike Pirandello's, is not the philosophical issue involving the correlation of illusion and reality, but the relationship between individual and society. Also noteworthy is the manner in which Tendulkar uses the hackneyed courtroom drama to build serious theatre just as

Ibsen had adapted romantic drama as a receptacle for his indict-
ments of society. Like other dramatists of naturalistic plays,
Tendulkar too makes use of certain dramatic symbols in the play.
The door bolt that hurts Benare's finger at the very outset, physic-
ally locks her into the hall where her tormentors persecute her.
This incident in itself is an externalization of the 'no escape' plight
in which she finds herself in real life. There is also the green cloth
parrot and the sad lullaby that Benare sings. Both assume sym-
bolic significance at the resolution of the play.

Tendulkar has been quite often accused by critics and scholars of
appropriating ideas from Western plays and films and Indianizing
them. In the story-line of the play under discussion, critics have
seen reflections of *The Dangerous Game*, a dramatization of the
German writer Friedrich Durenmatt's novel. It is necessary to
point out here that, despite the similarity in the outline of the plot,
the objectives of the two authors are entirely different. Durenmatt
was essentially concerned with existential questions whereas the
Indian playwright is involved with social issues. It must, however,
be mentioned in this context that Tendulkar himself has admitted
to being generally influenced in his early days by Western films,
mainly the Hollywood films of the forties, and Western playwrights
like Arthur Miller, Tennessee Williams and J. B. Priestley in
particular. He has also stated on occasion that he has consciously
and unconsciously been inspired by just about everything around
him: real life experiences, hearsay, news items, films, plays and
literature in general . . . 'But the basic urge has always been to let
out *my* concerns vis-a-vis *my* reality: the human condition as I
perceive it.'

Dambadwipcha Mukabala (*Encounter in Umbugland*), written and
produced a year after *Shantata*, is a play of a completely different
nature. Indeed, it falls in a separate class in comparison with all
the other four plays of this anthology. It is essentially a political
allegory but not bereft of human dimensions. It is not difficult to
find reflections of the political situation in India of the late sixties
and early seventies in the royalist regime of Dambadwip (Umbugland). But the play is not merely topical; it unveils the essential
nature of the game of politics as also the basic craving for power in
human nature. The powerful satire that Tendulkar builds,
exposes the intricate political intrigues designed to attain positions of authority and the corruption involved in holding on to
them. Despite the distancing achieved through the creation of a
fictitious milieu, it is easy to identify the characters with political

figures who held ministerial positions in those years—the 'principled' politician who spouts moral platitudes; his antitype, a blatantly immoral character; the statesman whose face is stretched in a constant smile and who gesticulates wildly but at the same time is taciturn to a fault; the floor-crosser who pretends to be ill and sits on the fence till the eleventh hour. And of course, there is the indomitable Princess Vijaya, herself the daughter of the autocratic king, who turns the tables on her advisers and refuses to be their pawn. Tendulkar has portrayed this character with utmost care. There is a definite development in her from a headstrong, self-opinionated but politically inexperienced young princess to an intelligent yet whimsical ruler who devises her own (successful) methods of vanquishing her enemies. There is an intensely human aspect to her nature which is revealed in her highly complex, but interesting relationship with Prannarayan, the eunuch. Prannarayan's function in the plot is the same as that of a *sūtradhār* or that of a chorus. It is he who introduces the play and acts as the neutral and patient commentator throughout the action. Yet he is not a mere observer or even commentator, but a philosopher as well. In the light of his natural wisdom, the reader-audience becomes aware of the ugliness and futility of the power game. It is through his eyes that the dramatist uncovers the central concern of the play: All power corrupts.

The play has the usual three-act, multiple-scene structure, but Tendulkar uses an interesting device in the play which also acts as a jibe against the media, to which, incidentally, he was professionally attached at different stages of his life. The theatrical function of this device is to create interludes where information regarding the political feuds are provided and apparently objective observations are made on the recent developments in the political situation of Dambadwip. Tendulkar uses two masked actors, armed with outsized pens, who arrive at regular intervals mouthing hackneyed remarks set in free verse in a sing-song way. In their observations, one can hear an echo of the cynical tone of the headlines published daily in our newspapers—ultimately meaningless statements that resolve nothing but aggravate existing problems.

In proportion to the large number of plays written in Marathi, the number of political plays is comparatively small, apart from the output of Dalit playwrights. *Dambadwipcha Mukabala* is one of Tendulkar's first political plays. He would write others later, like *Ghasiram Kotwal* which would give rise to such furore. But

Mukabala has a unique freshness of treatment, unlike other political satires, a kind of objective yet human outlook, that raises it above just another topical, political play.

Gidhade (*The Vultures*), chronologically the next play to be produced (1970) and published (1971) after *Mukabala*, was actually written fourteen years before. The entirely different nature of the work underlines the astonishing range of Tendulkar's dramatic genius. After the first production of this play, Girish Karnad wrote that the staging of *Gidhade* could be compared to the blasting of a bomb in an otherwise complacent marketplace. It was with the production and publication of *Gidhade* that Tendulkar's name became associated with sensationalism, sex and violence. There ensued a long war with the censors who condemned the play as obscene and in bad taste. Conservative sections of Maharashtrian society were stunned by the open display of illicit sexual relations and scenes of violence that constituted the plot.

Today, twenty years later, it is possible to judge the play with objectivity. The play is a ruthless dissection of human nature revealing its inherent tendencies to violence, avarice, selfishness, sensuality and sheer wickedness. It does not have the redeeming humour of *Shantata*. It is intensely morbid in the portrayal of its characters and action. The decadence and degeneration of human individuals belonging to a middle class milieu is exposed through the interactions among the members of a family. Ramakant and Umakant's greed and viciousness, their father's degenerate nature, their sister Manik's gross sensuality—all add up to a naturalistic depiction of those baser aspects of human that one would like to shut one's eyes to. The beating up of the father by his own children, the two brothers' forcible abortion of their sister's child, the mutual hatred among the members of the family, underline the fundamental evil inherent in human character.

Yet there is something more in *Gidhade* than sheer violence and evil. In the character of Rama, Ramakant's wife, Tendulkar is able to create a sensitive, naturally kind and good hearted individual. She is like a helpless, submissive, tender little bird among the vultures. Her illicit relationship with her half-brother-in-law, Rajaninath, who is a bastard and an outcaste from the family, may raise a few conservative eyebrows and evoke questions of morality, but one has to admit that it is the single genuine and humane relationship in the context of the whole play. The sexual aspect of their association is merely an extension of their love which is the only redeeming feature in the morbid and claustro-phobic atmosphere of the family. Rajaninath, like Samant in *Shantata* and Prannarayan in *Mukabala*, is an observer and also a commentator. He is a poet and he too, like Rama, has a sensitive personality. Tendulkar makes Rajaninath recite three poems, at the beginning and end of Act I and at the conclusion, which add a special dimension to the play. The innate compassion of the dramatist, who remains an objective onlooker for a major part of the play, neither condemning nor judging either the characters or their actions, finds expression in the lines of these poems. His deep empathy for the victims of human viciousness flows like an undercurrent throughout the play.

Apart from Rajaninath's poems, *Gidhade* has a two-act, multiple scene structure. Tendulkar punctuates the structure with the poems, as mentioned earlier. In these sequences, he also suspends the chronological movement of the play. This gives an interesting twist to the otherwise conventional structure.

Tendulkar has said that *Gidhade* was born out of a personal crisis in his life, that it poured out of him within the short span of four days and he himself was shocked that he could give expression to so much violence. It was almost a cathartic process. Soon after writing *Gidhade*, he commented that he did not think that he could write such a play, wrought with violence and sex, again. But he did. Just sixteen months later he wrote *Sakharam Binder*. In the words of a critic, commenting on the play soon after it was produced: 'For many decades no play has created such a sensation in the theatre world of Maharashtra as Vijay Tendulkar's Marathi play *Sakharam Binder*.' It evoked even more resistance from the censor boards than *Gidhade* had.

Sakharam Binder is probably Tendulkar's most intensely nat-uralistic play. The play, as Tendulkar has stated in an interview, grew around the central character Sakharam, a book-binder, who though a Brahmin, is the antithesis of the general idealized conception of a member of that caste. Through the delineation of this character, Tendulkar explores the manifestation of physical lust and violence in a human being. What Tendulkar is able to achieve in his characterization, not only of Sakharam but also of Laxmi and Champa, is an almost total objectivity. All kinds of moralizing and judgement are avoided. Tendulkar seems keen to demonstrate the basic and essential complexity of human nature which is neither black nor white but varying shades of grey. Thus all his characters are a combination of good

and evil, weakness and strength. Sakharam, though apparently
crude, aggressive and violent, has his own laws of personal
morality. He is a man who is primarily honest and frank. This
openness of his personality becomes in itself a criticism of the
hypocrisy of the middle class. Sakharam ridicules the double
standards of the middle class. His straightforwardness in dealing
with helpless women such as Laxmi demands a certain admiration. He flaunts his virility as a make-believe to compensate for his
inner weakness and loneliness, only to discover its transient
nature later on in the play. Laxmi, on the other hand, the
embodiment of the ideal Indian woman, a maturer version of
Rama in *Gidhade*—loyal, docile, religious, hard-working, self-
effacing and tender-hearted—turns out to be wily and vicious
when her survival is threatened by the presence of Champa. After
Champa's murder she shows greater ruthlessness and presence of
mind in covering it up than Sakharam, who is totally bewildered
by what he has done. Champa, gross, sensuous, brazen on the
surface, shows strange kindness and generosity when she con-
vinces Sakharam to give shelter to Laxmi who, for all she knows,
may turn out to be her rival. Among the minor figures, Champa's
husband, Fauzdar Shinde, is a rather interesting character. There
is a touch of masochism in the way he returns to Champa again
and again to get abused and beaten. His friendly relationship with
Laxmi shows the inherent affinity between their characters. Just
as Laxmi is a counterfoil to Champa so is Shinde to Sakharam, at
least within the periphery of the play. Daud Miyan, the only other
character, is the least complex of them all. His admiration for
Laxmi and physical attraction to Champa emphasizes the fundamental nature of these two women. Daud, through his com-
ments and observations, is also able to reveal the essential
difference between the relationships which Sakharam has with
the two women.

Tendulkar weaves a matrix of intricate interrelationships
between his characters. Sakharam, who does not believe in the
institution of marriage and arranges contractual cohabitation
based on convenience with single women who have been deserted
by their husbands or have walked out on them, shows tendencies
of being religious and domesticated when in contact with Laxmi.
In his association with Champa he is transformed into a sensuous,
lewd drunkard with thoughts only of sexual enjoyment. The
presence of Laxmi and Champa at the same time has a strange
effect on Sakharam as if the two different strands in his character

come into direct confrontation, creating a psychological turmoil in him and resulting in his temporary impotence. Laxmi and Champa are also connected in an extremely complex relationship. When Laxmi returns, Champa does not visualize any possibility of competition from her for she is confident of her own sexual attractions. In fact, she pities this homeless, shelterless woman. It is the kindness of this otherwise hard-hearted woman that makes it possible for Laxmi to stay in Sakharam's house. Yet there is also a touch of contempt in Champa's treatment of Laxmi—the contempt that a stronger person feels for a weakling. The two women between themselves satisfy the different needs of the male they share—one his domestic, the other his physical demands. Laxmi develops an asexual friendship with the other weakling in the play, Shinde, as mentioned earlier, while Champa has a sexual relationship with Daud Miyan. Though Laxmi finds nothing wrong with her own association with Shinde, her moral sense is outraged by Champa's affair with Daud and she uses this opportunity to malign her rival. This brings out the latent hatred in Laxmi for Champa. Sakharam's masculinity is doubly hurt through the knowledge of Champa's physical association with Daud, since he himself can no longer satisfy her. Hence in his rage, he kills Champa.

Tendulkar is highly realistic not only in the delineation of characters and human relationships but also in the depiction of the setting in which these characters enact the drama of their lives. The locale is a mofussil town and the action takes place in a lower middle class home. The extensive stage directions, which have become more elaborate than those in either *Gidhade* or *Shantata*, help to create a vivid and detailed picture of the interior of an economically backward household. In their portrayal of this lower strata of society, Tendulkar's plays signified a definite departure from the mainstream Marathi drama that mostly dealt with the more privileged sections of society. One of the reasons why there was such a reaction against *Sakharam Binder* was its burning naturalism. Here was a raw chunk of life with all its ugliness and crudity which was more than a shock to refined and prudish middle-class audiences. Such a direct confrontation with 'vulgar' reality was difficult for them to bear.

Yet there is in this play, as in *Gidhade*, a subtle underlying tone of sensitivity and tenderness towards humanity as a whole. One can discern, if one delves into the core of the play, the seeds of basic human values. In Sakharam's playing of the *mridanga* and the joy he finds in it, in Laxmi's friendship with birds and insects, and Daud's loyalty to his friend until he is lured by Champa's attractions, in Champa's generosity towards Laxmi—the kinder aspects of human nature and its inclination towards higher values are unfolded.

This three-act play has a definite structure that is in harmony with the development of its action. As mentioned earlier, Sakharam's character is the mainstay of the plot. The first act is devoted to the delineation of the relationship between Laxmi and Sakharam, while the second act portrays that between him and Champa. The last act depicts the three-cornered association between the two women and Sakharam. There is thus a wonderful symmetry in the construction of the drama. The language used is extremely coarse, rugged, laden with abuse but at the same time crisp and colloquial. The choice of such a medium for the dialogues makes the play even more living and realistic.

Kamala (1981), another play written in the naturalistic mode, came almost a decade after *Sakharam*. The intermediary period produced two other major works, *Baby* (1975), centering around the character of a simple-minded film extra who is exploited by those around her, and *Pahije Jatiche* (The Right Type) (1976), a semi-farcical play on the theme of casteism. Besides, in 1972, he wrote that controversial play, *Ghasiram Kotwal*, which with the perspective acquired during an interval of two decades, can definitely be considered a landmark in Indian theatre. Totally novel and experimental in form, this play, set in a historical background, focuses on the power games that men engage in and the corruption, violence and sensuality in which they indulge in the process.

Though not a political play in any sense, *Kamala*, too, is a topical drama, as *Dambadwipcha Mukabala* is. It was inspired by a real life incident—the *Indian Express* exposé by Ashwin Sarin, who actually bought a girl from a rural flesh market and presented her at a press conference. But using this incident as a launching pad, Tendulkar raises certain cardinal questions regarding the value system of a modern success-oriented generation who are ready to sacrifice human values even in the name of humanity itself. The innate self-deception of this standpoint is exposed dramatically by the playwright. At the centre of the play is a self-seeking journalist, Jaisingh Jadav, who treats the woman he has purchased from the flesh-market as an object that can buy him a promotion in his job and a reputation in his professional life. He is one of those modern day individuals with a single-track mind, who pursue their goal unquestioningly. Jadav never stops to think what will happen to Kamala after this exposé. Tendulkar makes a jibe at the modern concept of journalism which stresses the sensational. For this, he uses Kakasaheb, a journalist of the old school, who runs a small paper with his own resources. Kakasaheb provides the true ideals of journalism and in contrast to these, Jadav's concept of newspaper reporting is shown in a critical light. That Kakasaheb edits a paper published in the vernacular, while Jadav's medium is English, also helps to highlight the elitist nature of the journalism practised by Jadav. By introducing Jadav's colleague into the play, Tendulkar is able to depict the true nature of the rat-race that goes on in this milieu.

But there is more to *Kamala* than this jibe at contemporary journalism. Once again, as in *Shantata* and *Gidhade*, Tendulkar explores the position of women in contemporary Indian society. Through Sarita, Jadav's wife, who is in her own way as exploited as Kamala, Tendulkar exposes the chauvinism intrinsic in the modern Indian male who believes himself to be liberal-minded. Like Kamala, Sarita is also an object in Jadav's life, an object that provides physical enjoyment, social companionship and domestic comfort. Kamala's entry into the household reveals to Sarita the selfish hypocrisy of her husband and the insignificance of her own existence. Yet, like most of Tendulkar's sympathetic women characters, she does not have the spirit to rebel against her present condition. Instead, she extends emotional support to Jadav when at the close of the play he is treacherously deprived of his job. But the dramatist also suggests that Sarita cannot unlearn what she has come to realize and at the end of the play there is a faint hope of her attaining independence sometime in the future. Kamala and Sarita are both built of the same material as Leela Benare in *Shantata*, Rama in *Gidhade* and Laxmi in *Sakharam*. The other type of woman that Tendulkar portrays is more selfish and assertive—Manik in *Gidhade*, Champa in *Sakharam*, and Vijaya in *Mukabala*.

From the formal point of view, *Kamala* has nothing new to contribute to Marathi theatre. But then, Tendulkar has always claimed that it is the content of his work that determines the forms. And it is difficult to think of any alternative structure into which the central theme of *Kamala* could be cast. But the evaluation of the role of an Indian woman within the institution called marriage, considered to be the holiest of the holy in our society, definitely provides a completely novel point of view showing that women are still mere slaves to their male owners in Indian society in the latter half of the twentieth century. One should take note here that all three female characters in *Kamala* are in some way or the other subjected by the dominant male character Jaisingh Jadav, who occupies the centre of the plot.

All the five plays included in this anthology have a direct, one-to-one relationship with reality. All of them concentrate on different aspects of the human character. All of them highlight the complexity of human relationships. Most deal with the individual placed against the backdrop of society and explore the tensions between the two. In all of them, women play significant or key roles in the plot. All the works contain a latent critique of modern Indian society, mostly middle class and lower middle class, though from different angles. Most of them follow the naturalistic model of playwriting.

Yet, despite these similarities, the plays are clearly distinct from each other. *Shantata* is a play which combines social criticism with the tragedy of an individual victimized by society. *Damdwipcha Mukabala* is primarily a political satire. *Gidhade* depicts, with a strange admixture of ruthlessness and compassion, the degeneration of a family, economic and moral. *Sakharam* explores with great objectivity the complications in human nature, two necessary components of which are sex and violence; while *Kamala* is an indictment of the success-oriented male-dominated society where women are often victims or stepping stones in men's achievements. Thus, we cannot accuse these plays of lacking in variety, despite commonalities in theme and structure.

In the 1960s four dramatists from different regions of India, writing in their own regional languages, were said to have ushered modernity into the sphere of Indian drama and theatre. They were Mohan Rakesh in Hindi, Badal Sircar in Bengali, Vijay Tendulkar in Marathi and Girish Karnad in Kannada. Rakesh's untimely death left his life's work incomplete, and Karnad has written only intermittently. Sircar, of course, has been almost as active as Tendulkar, though his plays can be divided into three distinct periods. Tendulkar, however, has not only been the most productive but has also introduced the greatest variations in his dramatic creations. Beginning from *Grihastha* (Householder) (1955), Tendulkar has travelled a long way. His two most recent works, *Safar* (Journey) (1991) and *Niyaticha Bailala* (Damn You, Fate!) (1991), and *Kanyadan* (Gift of a Daughter) (1983), another of his significant but misunderstood plays, are indicative of this variety. These variations are not only of theme but also of form—from purely naturalistic plays and stark tragedies to farces, from musicals set in traditional folk modes to absurd drama, from full length plays to one-acts. Thematically, his plays have ranged from the alienation of the modern individual to contemporary politics, from social-individual tensions to the complexities of human character, from the exploration of man-woman relationships to reinterpretations of historical episodes. But it is probably only natural that his works should have such a wide ambit when one considers the multifacetedness of his creative genius. A journalist by profession, he has penned daily columns in newspapers, started his career as a creative author by writing short stories, composed children's plays, diverged later into screenplay writing, translated and adapted novels and plays both from English and from regional languages. His creativity has a prismatic quality—myriad potentials and a multitude of colours seem to emanate from it.

The greatest quality which Tendulkar can claim as a creative writer and dramatist is an ability to simultaneously involve and distance himself from his creation. This endows his works with infinite subtlety. None of his creations are ever simplistic—like his genius they too have the same prismatic quality of giving forth new meanings as one turns them around in the light of one's understanding. Two other hallmarks of his creative self are his keen sense of humour and his intense compassion, which are sometimes difficult to detect because of their imperceptible quality.

Growth, change and activity are the three major criteria with which a person's age can be measured. By these standards, Vijay Tendulkar at sixty-four is still a young man. His multifaceted creative genius continues to experiment and explore the potentials of the dramatic genre—his primary area of creation. Theatre-lovers all over the country continue to look forward to the harvests that his fertile pen will bring forth in the years to come.

ARUNDHATI BANERJEE
Department of Comparative Literature
Jadavpur University
Calcutta

KAMALA

Translated by
Priya Adarkar

CHARACTERS

KAKASAHEB

SARITA

KAMALABAI

JAISINGH

KAMALA

JAIN

ACT ONE

Morning. A small bungalow in the fashionable New Delhi neighbourhood of Neeti Bagh. The drawing-room. Jaisingh Jadhav, a well-known young journalist working as an Associate Editor in an English-language daily, lives here.

When the curtain rises, Kakasaheb, Jaisingh's wife Sarita's uncle, is speaking on the phone. A sixtyish gentleman born in an aristocratic family, but who has lived his life simply, under the inspiration of Mahatma Gandhi.

KAKASAHEB [*On the phone*]. Hello, whom do you want? . . . Yes. This is Jaisingh Jadhav's house . . . He's gone out of town . . . He's not in Delhi, he's gone away . . . He may come back today . . . Yes, today . . . Yes phone him, please phone him . . . Tomorrow, not today.

[*Enter Sarita with breakfast.*]

SARITA [*Putting down the breakfast things on the table*]. Who was it, Kakasaheb?

KAKASAHEB. Someone. I didn't ask who. He didn't say, either. What do you want the name for? He'll phone again tomorrow.

SARITA. I have to write down each phone call.

KAKASAHEB. Well, I've just taken at least three. How many are you going to write down? If it's anyone important, they'll tell you their names. If they don't, you can happily assume they're not important.

SARITA. That's the way you see it. My husband sees it differently. If I say they didn't tell me their names he gets angry with me for not asking.

[*The phone rings. Sarita goes and picks it up.*]

Please begin, Kakasaheb. I'll be with you in a minute. [*Into the phone.*] Hello? This is Mrs Jadhav speaking. *Namaste ji.* No, he hasn't come yet . . . He didn't tell me when . . . Is there anything I can . . . Press Conference? Tomorrow evening at 6 at the Press Club? *Achha ji.* I'll give him the message. May I know your name, sir? Thank you . . . Goodbye.

[*She writes the name in a notebook. The phone rings again.*]

[*Taking the phone.*] Yes, this is Mr Jaisingh Jadhav's residence. May I know who's speaking? He hasn't come back yet. I can give him a message. To the office? I don't know whether he'll be going there. Your number? [*She writes it down.*] Yes, I'll tell him that. He will be coming—but, of course, if some new work turns up he may stay there longer. Yes, everything's fine, thank you.

[*She writes in the notebook. As she comes towards the dining table, the phone rings yet again.*]

KAKASAHEB. Why don't you make Kamalabai sit by the phone? I tell you three-quarters of the calls will be *phaltu*. As it is, Jaisingh's a journalist—and on top of that, this is Delhi. Just answer the ones that ask for you by name.

[*Sarita by the phone.*]

SARITA [*Into the phone*]. Hello. Jaisingh Jadhav's residence. No, he hasn't come back to Delhi. He's gone out of town somewhere. He may come back today—or perhaps tomorrow. Please call tomorrow. Oh, Surinder! I didn't recognize your voice! I'm sorry. *Kya* message *hai*? He's coming today? Now? Thanks, Surinder! Thanks for the message. How are things otherwise? Yes, do come, do come. Drop in sometime when he's here . . . Bye!
[*Puts down the phone. Hurriedly tidies away the newspapers on the coffee table. Comes towards the dining table.*] That was from his office. They got a message on the teleprinter. He'll be back any moment. He left Ujjain last night.

KAKASAHEB. So I will meet him, after all. I thought he would be missing the one rare occasion that I've come to Delhi.

SARITA [*Calls out*]. Kamalabai!

[*Enter Kamalabai. A harassed expression on her face.*]

Sahib is just coming. Make a curry from that cauliflower in the fridge. See if those mangoes in the basket Kakasaheb brought are ripe. If they are, put out six or seven. See if there's any beer. If there isn't, send Ramdev to get some. Is last night's biryani still good?

KAMALABAI. Sure it is.

SARITA. Did Ramdev get the clothes from the dhobi?

KAMALABAI. Yesterday. I've put them in Sahib's cupboard.

SARITA. Good. You can go.

KAMALABAI. I want to go back to Phaltan. Buy my ticket.

SARITA. To Phaltan? Why? What's the matter?

KAMALABAI. It's this weather. It's like an oven in the afternoon.

And then, these servants. Not one of them does any work. You'll be asking me, why isn't the work done?

SARITA. We'll see. But now, please hurry. Sahib will be coming.

[*Exit Kamalabai.*]

KAKASAHEB. The poor thing seems to have got fed up of Delhi.

SARITA. Nothing of the sort. She'll get used to it.

KAKASAHEB. But I ask you, in the first place, why do you need servants from your mother's house? Aren't there any servants in Delhi?

SARITA. It's a strange city, after all. It's just as well to have someone you can trust.

KAKASAHEB. Don't tell me that! You rattle off Hindi—and Punjabi, too. In four years you've become a regular Delhiwali. Why do you have to send for reliable people from Phaltan? You may be highly educated, Sarita, but you are still a girl from the old Mohite *wada*!

SARITA. Never mind. Ma-Saheb feels somewhat reassured if I have someone from there in my house. And what's wrong with that?

KAKASAHEB. Everything! Adapt! Adapt to the place you live in! Our houseboy became the Defence Minister, but he hasn't forgotten the customs of Karad. He's got one foot in Delhi and the other in Karad. And finally, he's neither one thing nor the other.

SARITA. Well, never mind. Every time he meets us at a play or a reception, he always asks about you. Without fail.

KAKASAHEB. I'm honoured. Who asks after me now? I'm a back number—a remnant of times past. A dead journalist—who's just about staying alive! Now it is the day of your husband's type of journalism. The High-Speed type! Something catches fire—and there he runs! There is a riot somewhere else—and off he flies. If there's an atrocity in the heavens or a ministry topples in the sky—why, there he is! Eye-witness report! Being on the spot—that's what's important! Never mind what you write.

SARITA. That's not so, Kakasaheb. He never writes anything without first-hand knowledge.

KAKASAHEB. That's why there's such a correspondence later. 'This is a mistake'—or 'That's a lie'—'It just didn't happen that way'—

SARITA. Of course, there will always be some people who say that kind of thing!

KAKASAHEB. Who's got the time to get first hand-knowledge? If you hesitate, you're lost. High-speed Journalism! Let's see who runs fastest—if it comes to that, write any old nonsense!

SARITA [*Mischievously*]. Just you wait. I'll tell my husband.

KAKASAHEB. Tell him. Go on, tell him! How will he find the time to reply to it? Even if he's here when you start telling him—by the time you finish he'll be in Biharsharif—or perched on Laldenga's roof—gathering eyewitness evidence! And what will he be observing? Murder, bloodshed, rape, atrocity, arson!

SARITA. If it's happening shouldn't he observe it?

KAKASAHEB. Why does he have to? My dear, it's not the facts of an occurrence that are important. But the topic is. Discuss that. Comment on it. Suggest a way to stop it—suggest that. After all any murder, rape or arson is like any other. What difference can there be? Why waste our country's time, and ours, writing accounts of them? What sort of journalism is it that smacks its lips as it writes blood-thirsty descriptions instead of commentary? Its business isn't news—it is bloodshed!

SARITA [*Trying to change the subject*]. Oh, thank goodness I remembered. A button came off that new bush-shirt of his. I'll just go and see if Kamalabai's put it on again. Do go ahead with your breakfast in the meantime.

[*Sarita goes upstairs. The phone begins to ring. Kakasaheb waits to see if anyone will answer it. Then is obliged to get up and do so himself.*]

KAKASAHEB [*Into the phone*]. Hello. Jaisingh Jadhav's residence. Who is speaking? He's not here. Not here, I said! What? Paper? Which paper? The twenty-third? A news item? What about? [*Listens*] . . . So? [*Listens—then, very loudly*] Who's speaking? Tell me your name. Tell me your name or I'll call the police—I'll send you to jail—who do you think you are—Hello!—Hello!

[*The phone has been disconnected. Enter Sarita from upstairs with the bush-shirt and the materials to sew on the button.*]

KAKASAHEB [*Banging the phone down angrily*].
Haraamkhor. What does he think . . .

SARITA. What's happened, Kakasaheb? Who phoned?

KAKASAHEB. Didn't bother to give his name. Just made threats . . . What did Jaisingh write in the paper on the twenty-third?

SARITA. That was yesterday. I remember . . . He wrote about an M.P. from Madhya Pradesh, who suspected his servant of theft. And locked him up and gave him a thrashing—all quite illegal.

KAKASAHEB. Well, that was a murder threat on the phone just now—about that very item. We'll drag you out of your house and kill you, he said—this is the last warning! Is it really necessary for Jaisingh to write all these things under his own name? Can't he write them 'From Our Correspondent'?

SARITA. He is absolutely determined to write everything under his own name. Once they forgot to print his name—and he nearly resigned.

KAKASAHEB. But this way, he gets these threats of murder.

SARITA. Oh, that's nothing unusual. We get those from time to time. Sometimes the phone rings in the middle of the night. If I pick it up, I have to hear some terrible things. Often, my husband isn't at home. And I wouldn't know where to look for him. I've got used to it.

KAKASAHEB. But is he armed? A gun or something?

SARITA. No.

KAKASAHEB. Do the police know, at least? About these threats?

SARITA. He says, half of them are *from* the police, anyway. So whom will you inform? I get upset sometimes. But he doesn't let it bother him.

KAKASAHEB. This isn't manliness. It's madness. If you're going to wake up the jungle, then carry a gun.

SARITA. Try telling that to him.

KAKASAHEB. Of course I will. This is something that concerns the whole life of one of our girls—your life. We didn't give you to him, to take you back as a widow.

SARITA. But you did give me away, didn't you? Then that's that. Do you think he's going to change—just because you tell him to? I tried that once—I got so fed up, I said I was going back to Phaltan. What was the result? He started booking my ticket.

[*The doorbell rings four or five times in an uneven pattern.*]

[*Loudly*] Wait a minute! [*She goes off to open the door. Enter Jaisingh, Sarita, and a village woman draped in a dirty white sari, her face hidden behind it. She carries a bundle in the crook of her arm. Jaisingh is travel-stained and tired.*]

JAISINGH. I missed the night train—then I chased it in a private taxi and caught it at Donpur—then it looked as if it would be late . . . [*noticing Kaka*] Well—well—well, Kakasaheb! What a rare pleasure! When did you come?

KAKASAHEB. Yesterday. I wondered whether I'd meet you at all.

JAISINGH. Why, are you going back right away? [*To Sarita*] Well,

Sarita, are we going to send him back straight away? No, no, it won't do—he must stay here now, for at least a week.

KAKASAHEB. *Nahi re baba*, I must return tomorrow.

JAISINGH. No, no, you just can't go. It's not as if you come to Delhi every day.

KAKASAHEB. Okay, leave me here—and go to Kerala or else to Nepal and conduct your—your murder investigations.

JAISINGH [*Laughing loudly*]. That's a good one. Murder investigations! [*To Sarita, who has brought the newspaper and handed it to him.*] I've seen it. I bought it at the station. Well, who were all the people who phoned me? [*Sarita hands him the notebook.*] Ask someone to heat up water for my bath. After a journey like this, I like to strip naked and have a boiling hot bath. What a pleasure!

[*Sarita is embarrassed because of Kakasaheb's presence.*]

[*Noticing this, and laughing.*] Oh, sorry. These are our Punjabi manners, Kakasaheb. We don't know when to hold our tongues. [*To Sarita*] Oh, and also bring some tea. And that suitcase has four days' worth of dirty clothes in it. Take them out and give them for the wash. But hold your nose while you do it. They must be stinking. Don't tell me I didn't warn you.

[*He is absorbed in reading the phone messages in the notebook.*]

KAKASAHEB. Oh, Jaisingh, one of the phone calls isn't written down. I took it.

JAISINGH [*Looking through the book*]. Oh? Who was it?

KAKASAHEB. It was anonymous.

JAISINGH [*At this word, glances at Kakasaheb, then casually, looking through the notebook*]. What was it about?

KAKASAHEB. He said, tell him we are going to drag you out of your house and hack you dead. Chop you to bits. We'll be damned if we don't do it. This is the last warning.

JAISINGH [*Looking at the notebook*]. I see. [*Looking at Kakasaheb.*] What was it about? Didn't he mention the date of the paper?

KAKASAHEB. The twenty-third.

JAISINGH [*Looking through the notebook again*]. I thought as much. [*Absorbed in reading the messages.*]

KAKASAHEB. Don't you feel anything?

JAISINGH [*Looking up*]. Huh? What about?

KAKASAHEB. You're being threatened with murder!

[*Jaisingh smiles slightly and goes to make a phone call.*]

What are you laughing at? They won't always stop at threats! One day, they'll . . . .

[*Jaisingh's number is engaged.*]

JAISINGH [*Slamming the phone down*]. These Delhi phones!

[*Kakasaheb is silenced.*]

[*To Kakasaheb*] Sorry! You were saying something.

[*Enter Sarita with his tea.*]

[*Seeing this*] Tea! That's wonderful! Put it down, I'll just make this phone call. Or better still, bring it here. [*Sipping at his tea, he dials his number once or twice. The receiver is held casually but firmly between his cheek and his shoulder.*]

[*Kakasaheb seeing this starts to drink his tea. He is upset.*]

JAISINGH. Hello Jaspalji, *main Jaisingh bol reyae.* I've just come back. Mission accomplished! Yes, brought her with me! [*Saying this, he glances at the countrified woman who has entered the room with him, and is standing in a corner, her face hidden by her pallu. He gestures to Sarita to give her some tea.*] What's she like? Why don't you come and see for yourself, yaar? *Ekdum Id-ka Chand!** [*He laughs loudly.*] What time have you fixed the Press Conference? . . . That's wonderful. Is everything else ready? Excellent! They can still prosecute me? Let them proceed. That'll make a nice front-page item. Even more publicity! We'll make them dance like monkeys this time! Oh no, not just me, it was the whole team. All of us. All because of your support. Thank you. Does Sethji know? *Nahi na?* Right, let it be a surprise for the old man. [*Laughs loudly.*] Let's see. Why not? Yes, he can sack me. I am not worried. Why should I worry, when you are with me, Jaspalsaab? That's really marvellous. *Achha* then! Bye for the time being. I still have to take my bath. Haven't had the good fortune to bathe for four days! Now that I'm here . . . [*He puts down the receiver.*]

[*Sarita has served tea to the village-woman. Sitting on her haunches by the wall, the latter is drinking it with modesty but with appreciation, blowing on it to cool it. Her face is still veiled. Jaisingh, carrying his cup of tea, now comes and sits by Kakasaheb. Sarita on the other side of the stage.*]

* *Ekdum Id-ka Chand*: just like the crescent moon (seen at the time of the Muslim festival of *Id*).

Sorry Kakasaheb, that's the way this business is. You were telling me something . . . something about a threatening phone call . . . .

KAKASAHEB. Is it any use to tell you?

JAISINGH [*Laughing*]. Try and see.

KAKASAHEB. Don't make a joke out of it. You may be caught in a terrible jam some time.

JAISINGH [*As if it has just occurred to him, casually*]. But tell me—how come you're in Delhi?

SARITA. He wrote to us. I told you about it.

JAISINGH. Oh—oh, yes. I remember. You had some work in Delhi.

SARITA. He had to get a quota of paper for his magazine.

JAISINGH. That's right. And did you get it?

KAKASAHEB. I got tired of sending them reminders. So I came here myself. I spent yesterday being posted from desk to desk. Finally, someone took pity on me. He has promised to do something.

JAISINGH. Sarita take the details from Kakasaheb. I'll phone the Secretary of the Department. Remind me.

KAKASAHEB. Don't do anything for me that goes against your principles, Jaisingh . . . . .

JAISINGH. The Secretary's a friend of mine. And I'm only going to ask him to do quickly whatever he's able to do. Kakasaheb, do stay on, now that you've come here. Finish your work, get your sanction, and *then* go. Eh, Sarita?

KAKASAHEB. Then I'll probably be here till my dying day! Don't tell me anything about Delhi! But tell me this, what are you planning to do about this girl?

JAISINGH [*Surprised*]. This girl? Why?

SARITA. I haven't said anything to him. He's been saying that since this morning.

KAKASAHEB. You go off anywhere—you come back any odd time—You don't even say where you're going—when I came here this time and asked her, she said, I don't know—all kinds of terrible threatening phone calls come here—you don't carry any kind of weapon with you—

JAISINGH [*Bored expression; shrugging his shoulders, trying to make a joke out of it*]. Oh, that. She seems to have told you quite a lot. [*He doesn't seem very pleased about it.*]

SARITA. It was he who asked me.

JAISINGH [*Rather sourly*]. Why don't you admit that you told him? Kakasaheb, you have been a journalist—fought many battles as a result of it—fought against the British Raj—went to jail for it—Did you have bodyguards—or wear armour when you travelled?

KAKASAHEB. Jaisingh—don't make a mistake. Those battles were very different ones. The enemy wasn't hidden in the dark, he was right there, out in the open—in front of us. The situation's different now. And your attacks are on different people every day—

JAISINGH. Not on people. On bad trends. I have no obligation—no concern with individuals.

KAKASAHEB. All the same, it is against individuals. Aren't you going to look at where all this is leading? What's going to be the outcome of it all? And on top of that—you're not prepared to take care to protect yourself.

JAISINGH. Kakasaheb, if one's going to die, one can die sitting at home. What does one do then—just a minute. [*His attention has wandered to the veiled village-woman sitting in a corner. He goes towards her.*]

[*Aware of his approach, she sits yet more modestly, pulling her veil further down over her face.*]

Kamala . . . .

KAMALA [*Indistinctly*]. Sir?

JAISINGH. How are you? All right?

[*She nods her head.*]

Want some more tea?

[*She shakes her head.*]

Something to eat?

[*She shakes her head.*]

Look, think of this as your own house. You are quite safe here.

[*She moves her head to show she has understood.*]

KAKASAHEB. Who's this woman?

JAISINGH [*A little embarrassed at the question—then says reticently*]. Oh, just someone. I've got to escort her to a certain place.

[*Kakasaheb is aware that he is being evasive.*]

[*Realizing this.*] I sometimes have to do chores like this when I travel around.

KAKASAHEB. And am I allowed to ask where you went this time?

JAISINGH [*Becoming even more reticent*]. Here and there—over in Bihar.

KAKASAHEB. Bihar's a very big state.

JAISINGH [*Changing the subject*]. I must get my bath over and done with. I feel so greasy—sweat layers deep on my skin. I'll just be back. Is the water ready?

SARITA [*She has grasped the situation. Rising*]. I'll have a look.

[*Sarita exits upstairs. Jaisingh follows her. Kakasaheb sits lost in thought. In one corner sits Kamala, behind her veil. She looks extremely out of place in this drawing-room, because of her ragged appearance. Kakasaheb gets up and goes towards the guest-room. Now Kamala slowly moves her veil aside, and with great daring looks all round the drawing-room. Just then, the phone begins to ring. She starts and veils herself again at once, and sits shrinking into herself once again. As if she's the last person who'd ever look around that drawing-room. Kamalabai hurries into the room and most unwillingly answers the phone.*]

KAMALABAI. Hello? [*The phone gets disconnected.*] If you don't want to speak, don't! Who's forcing you. Damn cheek! [*Puts down the phone. Notices Kamala. Goes towards her. Studies her.*] Hey! Who are you? Where did you come from?

[*Kamala doesn't say a word.*]

I'm asking you a question. Are you deaf? What's your name? Your name? Name!

KAMALA. Kamala.

KAMALABAI [*Displeased*]. Kamala? [*Angrily.*] Hmm! Where are you from? Where's your village? Village!

KAMALA. Karimsharif.

KAMALABAI [*Still more annoyed*]. Karimsharif? Where's that?

KAMALA. The other side of Luhardaga.

KAMALABAI [*Deciding that it's better not to reveal she hasn't understood*]. That so? I see. Daga. Hmm. Where are you going?

KAMALA [*after a pause*]. Nowhere.

KAMALABAI. Meaning? What do you mean, nowhere? Must be going *some*where.

[*Kamala shakes her head.*]

What, you mean you're staying here? *Here?*

[*Kamala nods.*]

KAMALA. I've been bought, haven't I?

KAMALABAI [*Thunderstruck*]. What?

KAMALA. HE—he bought me. In the bazaar.

KAMALABAI. *Bought* you? Who did?

KAMALA. He . . . the gentleman . . . .

[*Kamalabai can understand nothing of this. Enter Sarita from above stairs.*]

SARITA. Kamalabai? Who phoned?

KAMALABAI [*She still hasn't recovered herself*]. Phone? Oh. Yes. Who knows? They didn't speak.

SARITA. What are you doing here? Off with you—and do the cooking. I've left the mutton on the stove.

[*Throwing a baleful glance at Kamala, exit Kamalabai. Jaisingh comes back, his bath over, dressed in indoor clothes.*]

JAISINGH. This is why one should make a filthy journey now and then. How marvellous ordinary household things seem! A commode, for instance. [*Seeing Sarita's face.*] I'm not joking. It's a comfort fit for a king. [*His glance falls on Kamala.*] Why is she still here?

SARITA. You didn't say what was to be done with her.

JAISINGH. What do you think? She's going to stay here for the time being.

SARITA. For how long?

JAISINGH. Today, at least. [*Suddenly realizing it.*] But actually, I haven't told you anything at all about her—well, she's from the place I went to. You'll get an idea about the rest from the way she looks. She's just like that. [*Struck by a thought.*] Kamala, how do you like it here?

KAMALA [*Not emerging from the veil*]. It's nice. Such a big house! Like a royal palace.

JAISINGH [*Winking at Sarita*]. Would you like to stay here always, Kamala?

KAMALA [*Nodding her head delightedly*]. Yes!

JAISINGH. You won't have to do any work here. Just eat and relax.

KAMALA. As you say, master. But I'd like some little work or the other.

JAISINGH [*To Sarita.*]. Did you hear? She says, she'll do some little work or the other. These downtrodden people are happy at the slightest excuse. Toil and labour take getting used to. Luxury doesn't. [*To Kamala.*] Go inside, Kamala.

[*Kamala rises, pulls the veil further over her face, picks up her bundle and exits.*]

SARITA. She's an innocent, the poor thing.

JAISINGH. She looks one right now. But these people can be very smart, too. Give them half a chance. [*He hesitates—seems to want to say something more, then stops himself. Then uncontrollably.*] Do you know where I found her?

SARITA. Where?

JAISINGH [*Undecided whether or not to tell*].   Where do you think?

SARITA. I don't know.

JAISINGH. That's it. [*Falls silent, as if he's decided it's better not to tell.*]

SARITA. Where did you find her? Tell me.

JAISINGH. Will you keep it to yourself? It's important that no one should know about it today. No one.

SARITA. All right.

JAISINGH. I bought her—in the Luhardaga bazaar in Bihar.

SARITA. Huh? [*She can't understand.*] Bought her?

JAISINGH. Yes. For two hundred and fifty rupees. Even a bullock costs more than that.

[*Sarita is stunned.*]

[*Brightening as he notices her reaction.*] They sell human beings at this bazaar at Luhardaga beyond Ranchi. Human beings. They have an open auction for women of all sorts of ages. People come from long distances to make their bids.

SARITA. They auction—women?

JAISINGH. Yes, women. Can't believe it, can you? The men who want to bid—handle the women to inspect them. Whether they are firm or flabby. Young or old. Healthy or diseased. How they feel in the breast, in their waist, in their thighs and . . . . . .

SARITA. Enough.

JAISINGH. This upsets you, perhaps. This Kamala had no customers at all. She was sitting to one side with her head down. I said, *chalo*, let's buy her. I bought her dirt cheap.

SARITA [*Annoyed*]. What for? Why did you go there?

JAISINGH. To prove that such auctions are taking place—in this country now—at this very moment.

[*Sarita shudders at the thought.*]

[*Seeing this, and enjoying it.*] There are lots of people like you who don't even know this is going on. The police know it's true, but don't want to admit it. They say, we reporters are sensation-seekers and that's why we're digging into it. And the government—oh they're pure and lily-white. They say, *Shantam Papam* —perish the thought! These newspaperwalas have the bad habit of misusing the freedom of the press.

SARITA. I don't like it at all—what you've been doing.

JAISINGH. I don't like it either. But someone's got to do it.

SARITA. Why must it be you?

JAISINGH. Because when I first wrote about it, I didn't have any definite facts. But I could smell something wrong. The police, as usual, washed their hands of it. The Home Minister put his hands over his ears. They made the false charge that newspapermen tell lies. So it fell on me to put the noose round the right neck—with evidence. Who else would have done it?

SARITA. But for that, did you have to buy a woman?

JAISINGH. I needed evidence, didn't I? Do you know, I turned the world upside down to find this bazaar. I was the first journalist to reach it! [*His face, his voice, are happy.*] Today I'm going to throw the whole caboodle in the government's lap—along with the evidence. Just watch! Let them deny it this time. I've caught them properly—the bastards! [*Recollecting himself.*] But keep this absolutely secret for the time being. No one at all must find out. If there's even a slight leak, all my work is wasted.

SARITA [*Noticing his warning glance*]. Yes.

JAISINGH. I'm not sure about you. [*Realizing the distrust he is showing, he mends it with*] I don't mean you'll do anything on purpose . . . There's a press conference to be held by my paper this evening. Once I've announced everything in that, there's no problem. Then you can talk about it.

SARITA [*Emboldened*]. Suppose someone finds out. What'll happen?

JAISINGH. It'll be the end. Our entire plan will fall flat. My editor and I have put this thing together with great care. Even the proprietor of the paper has no idea. There is a way of doing these things. You have to build them up that way. What's so unusual about the Luhardaga flesh market? Women are sold in many places like that, all over the country. How do you think all the red-light districts could operate—without that? That's not the point. The point is how we project Luhardaga—the technique of it. The art lies in presenting the case—not in the case itself! Keep watching. See how we'll blast out this shameful affair. There'll be high drama at today's press conference. It'll create an uproar! [*He is pacing about excitedly.*]

[*Sarita seeing his state, walks out. Jaisingh lost in thought for a while. The doorbell rings. Jaisingh is startled out of his musing. His movements are now tense and careful. Enter Kamalabai who goes to open the door.*]

JAISINGH. Wait, Kamalabai. First ask who's there. Then come and tell me.

[*Kamalabai goes to the door. She comes back. Jaisingh is waiting, tense.*]

KAMALABAI. That Jain-saheb's here.

JAISINGH. He *would* turn up now. [*Thinking.*] Let him in. But while he's here, don't let that woman I brought set foot in here. Understand? What did I say?

[*Kamalabai repeats what he has said. She goes to the door, then comes back. Behind her is Jain. A thirty-fiveish man. Exit Kamalabai.*]

JAIN [*Coming forward*]. Have you set a watch on me, Jaisingh? What's this new fashion? Inspection at the door! Is the President or someone coming here today? I thought for a moment Kamalabai was going to interrogate me!

JAISINGH. *Arre*, we've had some unwelcome visitors, who made a nuisance of themselves. That's why I've told Kamalabai not to let in anyone without asking me first.

JAIN. I see! So this is your state of affairs too! [*Sighs.*] How was the trip?

JAISINGH. Which one—Oh, fine. But how come you're here all of a sudden?

JAIN. I thought you've just returned from a journey—you won't have come empty-handed. Let's see what you've brought.

JAISINGH. Brought? Nothing in particular.

JAIN. You wouldn't tell me, even if you had! To tell you the truth, I had come for drinks to Iyer of the PTI across the road. So I thought I'd drop in on my way back. I thought you probably wouldn't be here, but anyway, I could say hello to Bhabhiji before going home. How is she?

JAISINGH. She is all right. [*Still tense.*] What else?

JAIN. Iyer was saying, Jaisingh's going to Ranchi too often. There's something fishy.

JAISINGH [*His voice unnecessarily loud*]. In our profession, we think everything's fishy.

JAIN. We're hunters by habit, what else? But Padmanabhan from the *Times* had come to Iyer's. And he was talking of this evening's press conference.

JAISINGH [*Warily*]. What was he saying?

JAIN. Simply guesswork. It's his opinion, it must be something about your editor's contempt-of-court case.

JAISINGH. I see.

JAIN. But Iyer said, there must be something more to it. For example, the scandal about your proprietor's new hotel.

[*Jaisingh is silent.*]

Sālé, I said, only I know the truth.

[*Now he is silent, too, letting the suspense grow.*]

JAISINGH [*Tense, uncontrollably*]. What is it?

JAIN. Nothing, I was just bluffing. [*He gets up and starts to exit towards the kitchen.*]

JAISINGH [*Getting up in a hurry*]. Unh? Where are you going?

JAIN. Why?

JAISINGH. No—it's just—you got up so suddenly.

JAIN [*Going close to him, in a confidential tone*]. Look here. What did I have at Iyer's? Drinks? What's the usual effect of drinks? If you let them accumulate—what happens? Hmm. [*Starts to exit.*] That's what.

JAISINGH. That—that toilet's out of order. Use this one. [*He turns him towards the guest room.*]

JAIN. Gladly. As long as I find a toilet. [*After ushering Jain to the guest room, Jaisingh stands by. Enter Sarita.*]

SARITA. Jain's here, isn't he?

JAISINGH. Yes. Don't ask him to stay for lunch. He's leaving, anyway. Just let him go.

[*Sarita says nothing. She thinks this is very peculiar.*]

You're keeping an eye on her, aren't you? Don't let her come out here. She must stay inside.

[*Jain returns.*]

JAIN. Hi, Bhabhiji, I mean, an English 'hi' to him, and a Marathi 'hai'* to you. This warrior against exploitation in the country is exploiting you. He's made a drudge out of a horse-riding independent girl from a princely house. *Hai, hai!* [*Theatrically, to Jaisingh.*] Shame on you! Hero of anti-exploitation campaigns makes slave of wife! [*Glancing at the watch on his wrist.*] My, my! It's already two. [*To Jaisingh.*] Bye. [*To Sarita.*] Bye, lovely bonded labourer—[*recollecting, to Jaisingh*] See you in the evening, at the Press Conference.

[*Exit Jain. Jaisingh breathes a sigh of relief. He is still somewhat tense.*]

SARITA. Lunch was ready—he could have eaten before he left.

JAISINGH [*Bursts out*]. Are you a fool? [*Controlling himself.*] Sorry.

[*A peculiar silence.*]

* *Hai-hai!*: Alas!

[*With an effort.*] What's Kamala doing?

SARITA. We've put her in Kamalabai's room for the moment. I'll just give her some hot water for her bath.

JAISINGH [*Loudly*]. No!

[*Sarita is uneasy once more.*]

I mean, she can have her bath tonight or tomorrow morning. And people of her kind don't have a bath for days on end. It's a famine area. Where would they get the water? And you'll be surprised—she'll feel dirtier after her bath. Please don't do anything concerning her without asking me first. For God's sake!

SARITA [*Obediently, but looking astonished*]. All right, I won't.

JAISINGH. Just let this evening's Press Conference get over. It's very important.

SARITA [*Changing the subject*]. Shall I serve your dinner? Everything's ready.

JAISINGH. Oh, yes.

SARITA. Just call Kakasaheb.

JAISINGH. I've told him I've got to reach her to a certain place. Be sure you tell him the same thing.

[*Sarita is blank.*]

I'm talking about Kamala.

[*All this is jarring greatly on Sarita. But she says nothing. Jaisingh goes towards the guest room.*]

JAISINGH [*Knocking on the door of the guest room*]. Kakasaheb! Dinner's ready!

[*DARKNESS*]

[*The stage lightens. The scene is still the drawing-room. It is the afternoon. Jaisingh is strolling about lost in thought. Kakasaheb is sitting on the sofa watching him pace about. Suddenly Jaisingh goes to the phone.*]

JAISINGH [*Dialling, then into the phone*]. Is everything set up? Perfect? [*Hearing the reply he puts down the phone and is lost to the world once more.*]

[*Kakasaheb quietly goes into his room. Jaisingh absent-mindedly watches him go.*]

JAISINGH [*Looking at his watch*]. Sarita! *Hey*, Sarita!

[*Enter Sarita.*]

What's she doing?

SARITA. She's asleep. She isn't feeling well.

JAISINGH. Wake her up.

SARITA. She's only just gone off to sleep.

JAISINGH. Never mind. Wake her up and send her here. I want to talk to her.

[*Sarita stands where she is for a moment.*]

What did I just say? Can't you hear?

[*Sarita goes off-stage. The phone begins to ring. Jaisingh picks it up.*]

JAISINGH. Hello.

VOICE ON PHONE. Hello, is that Jaisingh? Harbans here. There is going to be a Press Conference this evening, isn't there? Is it definite?

JAISINGH. What do you mean, is it definite? Why shouldn't it be?

VOICE. *Arre yaar*, I was just asking.

JAISINGH. Who said there wasn't going to be one? Who said it?

VOICE. Who would say so, *yaar*? I just asked you.

JAISINGH. Tell me the truth, Harbans. Did anyone say that? Is there a rumour like that?

VOICE. No *yaar*, there isn't. I just asked casually. It definitely is on, isn't it, a hundred percent sure? *Achha bhai, thik hai*. We'll meet in the evening. Okay, bye, Jai . . . .

[*The line is disconnected. Jaisingh puts it down, rather upset. Enter Kamala; she stands modestly in a corner. Her veil is over her face. Jaisingh is unaware that she has entered.*]

JAISINGH [*Rubbing his hands nervously, mutters*]. Oh, the bloody rumour-mongers. What's that? Kamala! Come here, Kamala.

[*She slowly moves in his direction and stands waiting.*]

Sit down.

[*She is still on her feet.*]

I told you, sit down.

[*She sits down modestly.*]

JAISINGH. How do you like it here, Kamala?

KAMALA. Very much, Sahib.

JAISINGH. Kamala, this evening we're going out together.

KAMALA. Oh! I'll see Bombay! They say it's a very big city.

JAISINGH. There's going to be a big feast where we are going.

KAMALA. Why, is there a Krishna temple there?

JAISINGH. No.

KAMALA. Then a Rama temple?

JAISINGH. No, it's a place where these big feasts take place. Very important people will be coming. There will be food and drinks.

KAMALA. You go, master. What will *I* do there?

JAISINGH. Those people will want to meet you!

KAMALA. *Hai dayya!** And me in this mess. Look at my clothes! I won't go there.

JAISINGH. But it's all in honour of you.

KAMALA. Don't embarrass me. Go on your own. You are an important person.

JAISINGH. Kamala, we'll have to go together. If I go alone, they will all be angry. They'll ask me, where's Kamala?

KAMALA. Tell them, she's had a long journey. She's ill. Really, tell them that.

JAISINGH [*His expression and tone of voice hardening as he speaks*]. You will *have* to come, Kamala.

KAMALA. I'm your servant, master. But I won't come today. I'll come tomorrow or day after. As soon as I'm well.

JAISINGH. Then I won't go, either.

KAMALA. No, no. You *must* go. Don't do this because of Kamala, master.

JAISINGH. I've said that I'll bring you, Kamala. If you don't come, that will make me a liar. It's better if I don't go.

KAMALA [*After a pause*]. Then let's go another time. That's it.

   [*Jaisingh in a dilemma.*]

JAISINGH. Kamala, you won't obey me?

KAMALA. How can that be? You are Kamala's master.

JAISINGH. I order you to come there with me. Today.

   [*Kamala is silent.*]

KAMALA. What will there be over there that's so important?

JAISINGH. We will be given a grand reception. People will clap, they will congratulate us. There will be a special chair for you to sit on.

KAMALA. Chair? I'll sit on the ground like always.

JAISINGH. Then people will laugh at us. No one sits on the ground here.

KAMALA. You'll—stay with me—won't you? I'll be very scared.

JAISINGH. I'll stay with you. And people will talk with you.

* *Hai dayya: O devi! (devi: goddess).*

KAMALA. With me? But I don't know how to talk with people. I'm an ignorant woman. What will I say in front of all those men?

JAISINGH. You will just have to answer questions.

KAMALA. What sort of questions?

JAISINGH. They will ask things about you. What your village is like, what your family is like. What work you did there. What you ate.

KAMALA. I'll have to tell it all?

JAISINGH. Yes.

KAMALA. Do I have to tell everything? How we starved? How we had no clothes?

JAISINGH. If the right people ask you, you must give the right answers.

KAMALA. You will help me, won't you?

JAISINGH. Of course I will.

KAMALA. Then I'll go with you. But these clothes are so bad. So torn and dirty.

JAISINGH. Don't worry Kamala. Everything will be all right. Now go inside, and come when I call you.

KAMALA [*Getting up*]. Yes, Sir. [*She exits shyly.*]

[*Jaisingh is still excited. He paces about the room. Looks at his watch. Goes to the phone and dials a number. Kakasaheb enters from his guest room and stands watching all this.*]

JAISINGH [*Into the receiver*]. Jaisingh speaking. Is everything ready? Very good. Everything's fine here. *Arre baba*, all we have to do now is put the bride in the *mandap*. Didn't you get it? [*Laughs.*] At five o'clock exactly. On the dot. Keep the photographers ready. Okay? Bye. [*Puts down the receiver.*]

[*Enter Sarita. She hasn't seen Kakasaheb.*]

SARITA. Are you taking her out with you now?

JAISINGH. Why? What's happened? There's still a lot of time.

SARITA. She is asking me to lend her one of my saris.

JAISINGH [*Angrily*]. Who? Kamala? Don't do anything of the sort. Don't give her anything.

[*Sarita a little dampened by his anger.*]

I tell you, don't give her a thing without asking me.

SARITA. But I *am* asking you.

JAISINGH. That's exactly what I'm telling you. She will come to the Press Conference in the same clothes she's wearing now.

SARITA. She's a woman, after all. And her sari is torn.

JAISINGH [*His voice rising*]. I know, I know! You don't have to tell me, understand? I have a very good idea of all that. I want her to look just as she is at the Press Conference. It's very important.
SARITA. All right. [*Exit.*]
JAISINGH [*Calling*]. Sarita! Sarita!

[*She re-enters.*]

I'm sorry. I'm rather tense today. Just let this Press Conference be over.
SARITA. May I go?
JAISINGH. Yes. But just make some good strong tea. The kind you make—with ginger and all that.

[*Exit Sarita. Kakasaheb comes forward.*]

KAKASAHEB [*Calling out*]. Make some for me too, Sarita. [*To Jaisingh.*] How far has your conspiracy got?
JAISINGH. Conspiracy?
KAKASAHEB. Your bloodthirsty professional plot.
JAISINGH [*Laughing loudly but rather hollowly*]. Oh . . . Oh. Well, it's getting along.
KAKASAHEB. If I'm getting in the way, please tell me so.
JAISINGH. Oh, I will. Certainly I will.
KAKASAHEB. I was glancing through some old issues of your paper, in my room just now. And I had an idea. Shall I tell you what it was?
JAISINGH. Since when have you felt the need for my permission?
KAKASAHEB. You don't know anything about our district. How could you? There's never a big enough scandal there for you to visit it. But our district too has its own scandals. In the first place, it's a scarcity area. So there's plenty of greed there. To say nothing of *matka*, gambling, illicit liquor-making, red-light houses, bribery, and corruption. Rapes and murders too, from time to time. If someone big is involved there are cover-ups as well. There are Harijans there—so there are injustices and atrocities against them—whenever it can be managed. Princely intrigues, besides. What I'm saying is, suppose I decide to run my little rag of a newspaper in your fashion?
JAISINGH. You? In our fashion? Then what about your passion for evidence?
KAKASAHEB. Oh, that'll be discarded. In any case, what has it done for me all these thirty years? But, listen. I'm the proprietor. It may be a tuppenny-ha'penny paper—but I'm the owner. Now

I'm going to employ two smart young chaps like you. They may not be as outstanding as you—but for our district—they will do.

JAISINGH [*Enjoying this*]. I see.

KAKASAHEB. They'll use all those methods of running around, tapping secret sources and so on—and every day they will bring me some fresh *mal-masala* from every nook and corner of the district. I'll spice them up a bit and print them. Every day new movements, new exploitations, new intrigues, exposures, and counter-exposures. Higher circulation, more advertising, more income. Respectability and a packet of money—instead of standing in the doorway waiting patiently for something good to happen. I reckon that in four or five years I'll have built a bungalow.

JAISINGH [*Sarcastically*]. Is that all—is that the only aim?

KAKASAHEB. Yes, well, I'm not your employer—I won't be able to manage two or three newspapers and a skyscraper in every big city. My appetite is small. If I can save enough in ten years or so, my wife and children will never want for money.

[*Jaisingh is silent.*]

What do you think of it?

JAISINGH [*Sourly*]. You're trying to say that what we're doing is just another form of mercenary journalism.

KAKASAHEB. And if you can manage it—it's not a bad form. There may be danger in it—but there's profit too. For example, five years ago you were living in the shed outside a house in Karol Bagh. And today you're in a bungalow in Neeti Bagh—even if it is a small one. You have servants, you have a car. You travel by plane all over the country. You stay in five-star hotels. You get invitations from foreign embassies. You have access to ministers and Chief Ministers—or even to the Prime Minister! What's bad about that? The moral is: there's no harm in this game—if you know how to play it right.

JAISINGH. Game!

KAKASAHEB. Well, it's as difficult as riding a tiger. It's not an easy one.

JAISINGH. Kakasaheb—this is no game, and I'm not involved in it for the sake of the things you mention—

KAKASAHEB. Really? Then why are you taking such desperate risks?

JAISINGH [*Eagerly*]. There's a commitment behind it, there's a social purpose. So what if you don't recognize it? What I'm doing—what we are doing—there's a great need today for somebody to do just that. In the moral rot that's set in—in this country, someone's got to uphold moral principles, moral norms, moral values. Someone has got to hold back the uncontrolled licence of those who have the machinery of power in their hands. The weak and backward sections of society are under attack. We need someone to make a noise against it. The common man is living in a—a kind of unconscious haze today. He needs to be shocked into looking at the truth now and then. We need a force that will raise his consciousness, prepare him to struggle for social and political change.

KAKASAHEB. And you are doing all this. All of you?

JAISINGH. Yes, yes, we are.

KAKASAHEB. In English.

JAISINGH. What did you say?

KAKASAHEB. I said, in English. You're doing all this in English?

JAISINGH. So, what's wrong with that?

KAKASAHEB. Oh, nothing—nothing at all. But you're doing all this for the small percentage of the common people who have the good fortune of knowing English. And these fortunate people are going to effect a change in the government of this country. The rest of the population—the majority—poor things—are going to carry on in their haze. Because they don't know English. And can't read what you write.

JAISINGH. Kakasaheb, tell me plainly whatever you're trying to say.

KAKASAHEB. Shall I? This new journalism of yours—if money-making is not the object of it—then it's a *vandhya-sambhog*. In case you don't understand these difficult Marathi words, I'll explain. What I mean is—nothing will ever come of it. *Arre*, write the people's language first. Speak it. Then try and teach them.

[*Enter Sarita with tea. She notices Jaisingh's tension. Jaisingh drinks his tea, still tense.*]

SARITA. What's the matter? Have you had an argument?

KAKASAHEB [*With an innocent expression*]. No. No. What would I argue about with him? It's he who has been looking upset ever since this morning.

[*Jaisingh and Kakasaheb drink their tea. Jaisingh is still tense. Sarita sits and watches them.*]

KAKASAHEB. Eh, Jaisingh. Don't be so tense. Look, Sarita's worried about you.

[*No change in Jaisingh.*]

Shall I go? Will that make you feel better? I'm all ready.

[*Jaisingh sits as he is. Drinking his tea.*]

Arre baba. I apologize. Is that all right? Seeing I'm a journalist born and bred, I'll apologize, as often as you like—special apologies—without any reserve.

[*Jaisingh relaxes a little.*]

KAKASAHEB [*To Sarita*]. Now he's opened up a little, hasn't he? When I said special apologies—yes . . .

[*Enter Kamalabai.*]

SARITA [*Noticing her*]. What is it, Kamalabai?

KAMALABAI. Come here. Come aside a little.

SARITA [*Going over to her*]. What is it?

KAMALABAI. What's this you've brought into the house?

SARITA. What are you talking about?

KAMALABAI. Her. That creature. The one Sahib brought here this morning.

SARITA. What about her?

KAMALABAI. She asks me, were you bought or were you hired? And that wasn't all. She asks me, how much did they hire you for? What work do you have to do? Me, she's asking me. I said, what's it got to do with you? Do you know what she said? Servants shouldn't raise their head and answer back. They should be grateful for their daily bread. She said that to *me*! I tell you, if she's going to stay here, I'm going back to Phaltan! I won't stay here one day. Buy my ticket.

SARITA [*Hushing her*]. Shh, Kamalabai! I'll take care of it.

[*Exit Kamalabai.*]

KAKASAHEB. What's happened to Kamalabai? What's bothering her?

SARITA [*Modifying the matter because Jaisingh is present*]. Nothing. A trifling upset.

KAKASAHEB. I see. I see. More of your secrets. [*Rises and starts walking.*] I'll go to my room.

SARITA. I didn't mean that, Kakasaheb.

KAKASAHEB. What's the problem? Go on, talk freely, the two of you. [*Goes to the guest room.*]

JAISINGH. Tell Kamalabai that the woman won't be staying here tomorrow.

SARITA. What will you do with her?

JAISINGH. We have arranged for her to stay in a women's home. She'll go there tomorrow.

SARITA. A women's home?

JAISINGH. That's not simple, either. The police will definitely try to get her into their custody. But we won't let them. We've kept a lawyer ready.

SARITA. What have the police got to do with this?

JAISINGH. Don't talk like a fool. Just as it's a crime to sell people —according to the Indian Penal Code, it's a crime to buy them, too. I can be tried and sentenced for it.

SARITA. If that's the case, why did you have to do all this?

JAISINGH. If I hadn't, no one would have known the seriousness of this problem.

SARITA. Supposing you're sent to jail?

JAISINGH. I don't mind. My editor is going to fight this case right up to the Supreme Court. That'll give a lot of publicity to this problem. And I probably won't be sentenced—because we've safeguarded ourselves legally. We gave a lot of thought to the plan.

SARITA. Did you give any thought to her?

JAISINGH. To whom? To Kamala? She'll find the home a luxury after starving the way she used to. Two square meals a day and no work to do. A proper roof over her head. She'll be more than happy. There were some adivasi women once, who were sent to jail because of a riot. When I interviewed them in jail, they were thrilled to be there. They said, it's lovely here. Why don't you fix it so we can stay here for ever?

SARITA. I don't like the idea of sending her straight to a home.

JAISINGH. Look here, don't be sentimental about it. Look at it from her point of view. She won't feel a thing about it. She must go there tomorrow. Once today's Press Conference is over, she has no business here. It's all been arranged. [*Looking at his watch.*] Come on, I'm off. Send her here.

[*Sarita, deep in thought, goes off-stage. She returns with Kamala. Meanwhile, Jaisingh has got himself ready to go.*]

JAISINGH. *Chalo*, Kamala.

[*Kakasaheb has come out of his room and is watching. Kamala veils herself carefully from head to foot. She exits, walking behind Jaisingh. Sarita and Kakasaheb stand where they are. The phone begins to ring.*]

CURTAIN

ACT TWO

Night. The drawing-room. The door-bell rings. Sarita enters and goes and opens it. Enter Jaisingh and Jain, followed by Kamala. She goes off-stage inside the house. Re-enter Sarita, last of all. Jaisingh and Jain have had plenty to drink and are in a good mood. Jaisingh looks very pleased with himself.

JAIN. *Tu chup rah be! Sālé,* it was for this you wouldn't let me go inside to the toilet, eh? It was 'out of order' was it? Out of order! [*To Sarita.*] He's a first class rascal, I tell you, *bhabhiji. Sālā,* hiding secrets from your friends! Hiding them! But I salute this rascal. Because he's a *mahā* rascal, not an ordinary one. What a hit he made with that Press Conference! All our reporters sat there with their eyes falling out. No one had an inkling—and he produces Madam Kamala! Sensation! You rascal, I salute you!

JAISINGH. Oh, let it be. All's fair in love and—

JAIN. Sensational journalism! You're all right, but from tomorrow our editor's going to twist all our tails. Look what Jaisingh brought! You have to bring something more sensational, more explosive.

[*Enter Kakasaheb from his room.*]

JAISINGH [*Happily*]. Come, Kakasaheb, come. Sit down.

KAKASAHEB. I was asleep. I heard loud voices and came out to investigate. If it's private, I'll leave you alone.

JAISINGH. There's nothing private now. It's all over. It's all going to come in tomorrow's paper. Oh, sorry. *Arre* Jain, this is Sarita's uncle. [*To Sarita.*] Bring some water. [*To Jain.*] Shivajirao Mohite—Journalist. He has his own paper. Kakasaheb, this is Jain—

JAIN [*To Kakasaheb*]. Pleased to meet you, Kakasaheb. It's the second time we've been introduced—but never mind—

JAISINGH. Oh, sorry, have you met before? My memory's very bad.

JAIN. We met when Kakasaheb visited you in that outbuilding home of yours. Am I right, Kakasaheb? Kakasaheb, your son-in-law showed us a terrific *tamasha* today.

JAISINGH. Don't call it a *tamasha.* Call it a drama.

JAIN. Well, dramas performed at the Press Club are called *tamashas.*

[*Enter Sarita with a tray.*]

Bhabhiji, this fellow's heroine knocked Shabana and Smita right out of the game today. Where is she by the way? Seems to have gone inside. What a specimen you found! *Bhabhiji*, she swallowed half the Press Conference just by coming in and sitting down! The photographers were falling over each other to get the right angles. One of them asked her to move her veil and show her face. One even tried to get her to pose hand-in-hand with Jaisingh. Our fellows are like that, Kakasaheb. But this girl—facing it for the first time—I thought—she's going to run away from the Press Conference.

JAISINGH [*Preparing to drink*]. That's just what would have happened. I was right next to her and sunshining at her all the time. That's how she stayed on. [*To Kaka.*] Kakasaheb, will you have one? [*Kakasaheb says no. Then to Sarita.*] You? [*Sarita says no.*]

JAIN. [*Accepting the glass Jaisingh gives him.*] Cheers. The questions were a joke. Some of our journalists are such fools. It just doesn't get into their heads that you put different questions to a minister and an *adivasi*. One fellow stares at her through his glasses and asks her—asks her, what are the important social questions in your area?

JAISINGH. Not questions—problems—he's asking that woman—problems—[*Laughs heartily.*]

JAIN. Another asks—what are your opinions about the economic exploitation of the tribals?

[*They both burst out laughing. The drinking continues.*]

JAISINGH. And what about Guptaji's question?

JAIN. Which one, *re*?

JAISINGH. 'Above the poverty line and below the poverty line'—

JAIN. Ha, ha, ha, that one! Unbeatable! [*Laughing*] As if Kamala-devi's come straight from the Delhi School of Economics to hold a Press Conference! That was smashing, I must say.

[*They both laugh.*]

JAISINGH. Gupta's only happy if he dangles from the poverty line at least once a day.

JAIN. Someone said in the Press Club the other day—Guptaji's new address is:

> Poverty Line,
> Opp. Socialism,
> Ashok Vihar,
> New Delhi.

JAISINGH [*Drinking*]. That's a good one.

[*Sarita starts to exit.*]

JAIN. Where are you off to, *Bhabhiji*? Wait. The best bit is still to come, *kya re*?

[*Jaisingh, drinking, shakes his head.*]

Some of us are absolute donkeys. But some of us are brilliant. They are a match for ányòne who comes in front of them. There was one question—if there is free sex among you, what do you do with the illegitimate children?

JAISINGH. He thought all adivasis indulged in free sex day and night. What nonsense!

JAIN. With that, another one began to itch to ask a question. He asked, you must be having free sex too. How many men have you slept with?

SARITA [*She can't help it*]. Weren't they ashamed to ask such questions?

JAIN. If they had any shame, they would be.

JAISINGH [*Drinking*]. But listen—there's more.

[*Sarita has sprung to her feet. Kakasaheb makes her sit down again.*]

JAIN. Our Chand Vaswani got up, gesticulating. He said, threateningly—'Kamala—tell me where he—where Jaisingh Jadhav bought you. Tell me the truth. Was it in the bazaar? Or did he come home? Don't be afraid. Swear by God before you answer.' That Vaswani—he's a reporter—but when he asks questions he thinks he's cross-examining someone in Court.

JAISINGH. Third Class LL B. That's what he is.

JAIN. And Dubey tried to be funny, as usual. He asked—what was it, *yaar*?

JAISINGH. This new Sheth . . .

JAIN. Yes, that's it. [*Puts on a voice.*] 'You must have had some free sex with this new Sheth—tell us something about it—how did it compare?'

KAKASAHEB. This is your Press Conference!

JAIN [*Drinking*]. This was only today's Press Conference.

JAISINGH [*Drinking*]. Just a minute. Don't misunderstand, Kaka-saheb. We people ask serious and good questions too. If the subject is serious, sometimes they leave an intelligent politician speechless.

JAIN. Of course. But you need a serious situation for that.

KAKASAHEB. So today's case was funny, was it?

JAISINGH. It's not that—but after the first shock, everyone relaxed.

JAIN. They had some fun with it—once they saw it wasn't the usual political stuff.

KAKASAHEB. Fun! At that poor woman's expense!

JAISINGH. She couldn't understand a word.

SARITA. How do you know?

JAISINGH. I was next to her, wasn't I?

[*Turning to Kakasaheb.*] Please don't misunderstand—she laughed too, just because the others were laughing. She hadn't understood a thing. And I didn't expect her to. I just wanted to present her as evidence. And that was done.

JAIN. It was a very successful and convincing press conference. Really.

JAISINGH. It was I who talked. She just sat there. Ask Jain.

JAIN [*Sighing*]. Now my problem is—where to go and what to bring back with me. [*To Jaisingh.*] I will score over you, you'll see, you bastard! [*Remembering Kakasaheb, says.*] Sorry! I thought I was still at the Press Club.

JAISINGH [*To Sarita, drinking*]. We look at things too sentimentally. These people from the jungle are good and tough. They can take a lot. I tell you, Kakasaheb, I've seen adivasis clawed to the bone by bears—coming to the Mission Hospital on their own two feet. Those missionaries operate on them without anaesthetics—out there in the jungle—and no one makes a sound. They've got natural endurance.

KAKASAHEB. And you want to test the limit of their endurance?

JAISINGH. I don't mean that—

SARITA. So while they were asking her those terrible questions, and making fun of her—you just sat and watched, did you?

JAISINGH. Both of you have misunderstood things a little. Jain. you've painted a distorted picture as usual, *yaar*. [*To Sarita.*] Look here—there were also some sober and straightforward questions there today.

JAIN. Absolutely! Of course!

JAISINGH. And I am trying to say—some of the questions she was asked were just strange to her; she didn't see in them what you and I did.

KAKASAHEB. That doesn't change the fact that she was made a laughing stock.

JAISINGH. Kakasaheb, everyone who holds a Press Conference in

Delhi is made a laughing stock to some extent. It's all in the game.

JAIN. He's right there. Anyone who doesn't want to be laughed at shouldn't hold a Press Conference in Delhi.

SARITA. It wasn't she who held this one.

JAIN [*To Jaisingh*]. She has a point there! It was you.

JAISINGH [*Annoyed*]. Whose side are you on?

JAIN [*Shrugging*]. Must admit the truth, whoever's side it's on.

JAISINGH [*He is rather drunk*]. I didn't hold this Press Conference for my own benefit. It was to drag this criminal sale of human beings into the light of day.

KAKASAHEB. And you sold a woman to them to do so.

JAISINGH [*Glaring*]. What did you say?

KAKASAHEB. You sold a woman—that poor and illiterate woman— by doing so.

JAISINGH [*Getting up excitedly, shouts*]. Take that back—take it back—

[*Sarita alarmed. She gets up and comes between the two of them.*]

SARITA [*To Jaisingh*]. Sit down. Come on, do sit down. [*She seats him bodily.*]

JAISINGH [*Growling*]. He has to apologize for that.

SARITA [*To Kakasaheb*]. Don't pay any attention to him. He sometimes gets like this. [*To Jaisingh.*] Come on, have your dinner. [*To Jain.*] Will you eat with us?

JAIN [*Nervous*]. Uh—no, thank you. My wife must be waiting at home. I wasn't at home for lunch. At least tonight I should— [*nervous laugh*] must get there. Or I'll have to move out permanently. [*To Jaisingh.*] See you, rascal—[*To Sarita.*] He isn't able to take his drink these days. [*To Kakasaheb.*] Namaste.

[*Exit Jain. There is still tension in the air.*]

KAKASAHEB. I apologize. I ask your forgiveness, Jaisingh.

JAISINGH. I'm sorry. I lost my balance. [*Remembering.*] Have you eaten?

SARITA. I made him eat. He wanted to wait for you.

KAKASAHEB. Good night, Jaisingh. Good night, Sarita.

JAISINGH. Good night.

[*Kakasaheb goes into his room. Uneasy silence between Jaisingh and Sarita. Jaisingh has started drinking once more.*]

SARITA [*Removing the glass from his hand*]. Now that's enough.

JAISINGH [*Slowly coming alive because of this*]. I'm sorry. It's just the relief—after so many days of tension.

SARITA. Is that any reason to be rude to our elders?

JAISINGH. I said I was sorry. I said it to him; I'm saying it to you. [*Catches hold of her hand tightly.*]

SARITA [*Disengaging it*]. Come, get up. Have your dinner.

JAISINGH. I am not hungry.

SARITA. It's good to have food after you've been drinking.

JAISINGH [*Coming alive even more*]. Not today.

[*Sarita has noticed the change in him. She is ill at ease.*]

JAISINGH. Come upstairs.

SARITA [*Emphatically, without even realizing it*]. No.

JAISINGH. I'll have my dinner afterwards. We'll both eat together.

SARITA [*Without losing her self-control*]. Uh-hunh, let me go. I've got work to do.

JAISINGH [*Trying to embrace her*]. Work later. Come upstairs now.

SARITA [*Throwing him aside with a single shove*]. Move aside. What are you doing?

JAISINGH [*Hurt*]. What's the matter? What did I do? Why are you making a face like that? Why did you push me away? You've never done that before.

[*Sarita is in the grip of heartfelt aversion. She is in no state to reply.*]

JAISINGH. Tell me, come on. I'm your husband, after all. What was wrong about what I said?

[*Sarita is trying to control her aversion.*]

JAISINGH. You must tell me. I must know. Don't I have the right to have my wife when I feel like it? Don't I? I'm hungry for that too—I've been hungry for six days. Is it a crime to ask for it? Answer me!

[*Exit Sarita towards the kitchen.*]

JAISINGH. Sarita!

[*She has gone.*]

[*Slamming his fist into his hand.*] The bitch! [*Stands still for a while. Then swallows the rest of his drink at a gulp and goes off upstairs.*

For a moment, the drawing room is untenanted. Brightly lit. Then the light dims. It's hard to say how much time has passed. Gradually one notices Sarita sitting alone. The ticking of the clock suggests night-time.

Sarita is motionless. One can't see clearly whether she is awake or asleep. An outline peers into the room from off-stage. Then, thinking there is no one in the room, comes in slowly and gently. It is Kamala.]

SARITA. What is it, Kamala?

[*Kamala starts. She hurriedly turns to go back inside.*]

Wait.

[*Kamala stands still. Sarita puts on the big light. Kamala has veiled her face.*]

Do you want something?

[*Kamala stands as she is. Then slowly her head shakes in the negative.*]

Didn't you sleep?

[*Kamala is silent at first. Then shakes her head.*]

Why? Couldn't you?

[*Kamala shakes her head.*]

Why did you come here?

KAMALA [*After a pause*]. No reason.

SARITA [*Suspecting something*]. You don't want to run away, do you?

KAMALA. Where would I go?

SARITA [*Sitting*]. Sit down, Kamala.

[*After a pause, Kamala sits on the ground.*]

Sit up here. I said, sit up here.

KAMALA [*Still on the ground*]. I like it down here. It's a habit.

SARITA. Is Kamalabai asleep?

KAMALA. Yes, she's snoring loudly. Didn't you sleep? Why are you awake?

SARITA. No reason. I just couldn't sleep.

KAMALA. *Hai daiyya!* You couldn't sleep either?

SARITA. That's right.

KAMALA. Why not?

SARITA. Sometimes I can't.

KAMALA. Do you sleep here?

SARITA. No. Upstairs in the bedroom.

KAMALA. Are there rooms upstairs too?

SARITA. Yes.

KAMALA. My word! What a big house! [*Pause.*] And so beautiful. Even our raja's palace isn't as beautiful.

SARITA. Do you like this house, Kamala?

KAMALA. It's got everything. Just like a dream. Really. [*Pause.*] Where does *he* sleep?

SARITA. Who?

KAMALA. He—the one who bought me.

SARITA. In the room upstairs.

KAMALA. Then the room upstairs must be the finest of all . . . No little ones?

SARITA. What little ones?

KAMALA. Children.

SARITA. We don't have any. [*Kamala falls silent.*] Why? Why are you silent?

KAMALA. No reason. [*Pauses.*] God's ways are strange, such a big house . . . and . .

SARITA [*Theatrically, enjoying herself*]. Yes, Kamala. The house . . . it devours us. It's so empty. . . .

KAMALA. Did you take any treatment? . . .

SARITA. Yes. No effect.

KAMALA [*Pauses*]. The Sahib must be very upset.

SARITA. Of course!

[*Kamala silent again for a while.*]

KAMALA. Can I ask you something? You won't be angry?

SARITA. No. Go on.

KAMALA. How much did he buy you for?

[*Sarita is confused at first.*]

SARITA. What?

KAMALA. I said, how much did he buy you for?

SARITA [*Recovering*]. Me? Look here, Kamala. [*Changes her mind, and sits down beside her.*] For seven hundred.

KAMALA. My god! Seven hundred?

SARITA. Why? Was it too little?

KAMALA [*Pauses*]. It was an expensive bargain, memsahib. If you pay seven hundred, and there are no children . . .

[*Sarita assumes a sad expression.*]

Then he has to pay for clothes, and for food. He must be very unhappy. Really.

SARITA. How many children do you have, Kamala?

KAMALA. I'll have as many as you want. And work as hard as you want. I can work hard . . . from morning to evening. Does he have property of his own, memsahib?

SARITA. Who? [*Realizing who she means.*] My master? No, this is all.

KAMALA. A farm, then?

SARITA. No.

KAMALA. That's bad. If you have some fields, it rains gold. I can work in the fields, too. Can you?

SARITA. No.

KAMALA [*Thoughtfully*]. Huh. [*She is lost in thought.*]

SARITA. What are you thinking, Kamala?

KAMALA [*Still lost in thought*]. Nothing.

SARITA. You must be thinking of something. Tell me.

KAMALA. Unh-hunh.

SARITA [*Waits a little, and then*]. Come on, tell me.

KAMALA [*Prepares herself mentally. Then speaks very seriously*]. Memsahib, if you won't misunderstand, I'll tell you. The master bought you; he bought me, too. He spent a lot of money on the two of us. Didn't he? It isn't easy to earn money. A man has to labour like an ox to do it. So, memsahib, both of us must stay here together like sisters. We'll keep the master happy. We'll make him prosperous. The master will have children. I'll do the hard work, and I'll bring forth the children, I'll bring them up. You are an educated woman. You keep the accounts and run the house. Put on lovely clothes and make merry with the master. Go out with him on holidays and feast-days. Like today. I can't manage all that. And we must have land of our own. Don't worry about it, that's my responsibility. Fifteen days of the month, you sleep with the master; the other fifteen, I'll sleep with him. Agreed?

SARITA [*In a whirl at all this, and also very moved by it*]. Agreed.

KAMALA. You tell the master about it. Tell him Kamala agrees to all this.

SARITA. You tell him.

KAMALA. My god, I? I feel too shy to talk to the master. He's such a big man—and I'm a stupid peasant . . . I won't be able to.

SARITA [*Making a decision*]. All right, Kamala. I'll have to do it myself.

[*The stage darkens. When the light comes up again, it is morning. Jaisingh is seen sitting at the dining table reading the morning papers. Breakfast is just over. Jaisingh has his head buried in one of the papers. Enter Kakasaheb from his room.*]

JAISINGH [*From inside the paper*]. Good morning.

KAKASAHEB. Morning. [*He sits at the table, puts on his glasses and picks up a paper at which Jaisingh isn't looking.*] May I see this please?

JAISINGH. Oh, yes, go ahead.

[*Kakasaheb starts looking at the paper. Jaisingh is occupied with the same thing. Enter Sarita from upstairs. She starts going off-stage towards the kitchen. Kakasaheb notices her.*]

KAKASAHEB. Got up late, didn't you?

[*Sarita says 'yes' and goes off-stage.*]

JAISINGH [*Looking at the paper*]. Kamalabai, tea for Kakasaheb.

KAKASAHEB [*Glancing from his paper at Jaisingh*]. I'll have my tea with Sarita. Why trouble Kamalabai three times?

JAISINGH [*Looking at his paper*]. What trouble? It's no trouble. That's what Kamalabai is here for. We pay her for that.

[*Kakasaheb says nothing. He looks through the papers. Jaisingh now throws the paper in his hand onto the nearby table and lights a cigarette. He takes contented puffs at it.*]

KAKASAHEB. All the papers seem to have carried the news.

[*Jaisingh says nothing. He puffs away.*]

KAKASAHEB [*Trying to break the ice*]. Kamala looks very different in the photographs.

JAISINGH [*Forced to speak, though still wrapped in thought*]. Yes.

KAKASAHEB. How much exactly did you pay for her? This paper says two hundred and fifty. But this one says three-fifty.

JAISINGH. Two-fifty.

KAKASAHEB. Even in that, each paper has to print something different. Even if something is the exact truth, they don't all print the same thing. Each one's truth must be 'Exclusive'.

JAISINGH. Read our paper. That has the accurate version.

KAKASAHEB. Compared to what you were saying about the Press Conference last night, these papers have taken the news very seriously. At least while printing it, they have been very responsible.

JAISINGH. They are responsible people—generally they're not as frivolous as they look. [*The last part rather emphatically.*]

KAKASAHEB [*Noticing this*]. That's good.

[*The two of them sit silently. The phone rings. Jaisingh goes and picks it up.*]

JAISINGH [*Into the phone*]. Thank you. Thank you. So nice of you.

[*Puts down the receiver. The phone rings again.*]

KAKASAHEB. It's started.

[*Jaisingh brings the phone to the dining table.*]

JAISINGH [*Into the phone*]. So you read it? Someone had to do it. Is everything all right, otherwise? Thanks again. Bye.

[*Puts down the receiver. The phone rings again.*]

JAISINGH [*Casually*]. Damn! [*Picks up the receiver.*] Hello! Hello— Hello—Jaisingh here. Liked it. Did you? *Bahut achhe.* Thank you, dear. Dinner? Why not? Remind me on Wednesday morning. Bye.

[*Puts down the receiver. Sarita has entered and sat down with tea for herself and Kakasaheb. The phone starts ringing again, loudly. Jaisingh mutters, 'Oh, hell!' and picks up the receiver.*]

JAISINGH [*Into the receiver*]. So, Rambhau, did you read it . . . Quite true . . . It's terrible. Yes, yes. Eh? Yes, it is. Yes, I remember. No, I don't like making speeches. I'll come if it's questions and answers. Okay, okay, we'll see. Let's meet.

[*Puts down the phone. Now it does not ring again. Kakasaheb is relieved. Jaisingh seems to be anticipating the next call. But it does not come.*]

SARITA. Shall I take the calls?

JAISINGH [*In an irritable tone, for no particular reason*]. First drink your tea.

[*The phone starts ringing again. Kakasaheb and Sarita are watching. Jaisingh now unplugs the phone from the wall connection, and taking it and his cigarettes and ashtray, starts towards the stairs.*]

JAISINGH. I'll be upstairs. Send me some tea.

[*Exit up the stairs.*]

SARITA [*When he is no longer visible*]. Kamalabai! [*She starts pouring the tea. Enter Kamalabai, filling the cup, says to her.*] Take this tea upstairs to Sahib. [*Kamalabai takes the cup and starts going upstairs.*] And bring down the two saris I've left in the room.

[*Kamalabai saying 'yes' goes upstairs.*]

KAKASAHEB. You didn't sleep last night, did you?

SARITA [*As a formality*]. I slept. But my sleep was a little disturbed.

[*Kakasaheb glances at her with understanding. He puts the papers closer to her. She looks casually through each of them.*]

KAKASAHEB. What do you think?

SARITA. Would you like some more tea? There is some in the pot.

KAKASAHEB. No. Answer my question.

SARITA [*Getting up*]. There's a lot of work. I woke up very late.

[*She starts to exit.*]

KAKASAHEB. I'm leaving today.

SARITA [*Shocked*]. Huh?

KAKASAHEB. No use wasting time. Your aunt must be waiting for me there. These days she finds it hard to stay alone. She's started to have low blood pressure.

[*Sarita looks into his eyes. Their gazes meet. Sarita understands everything.*]

KAKASAHEB. Really.

[*Sarita is upset.*]

KAKASAHEB. When you have time, remind Jaisingh to phone that Secretary. About our quota of newsprint. Tell him, no hurry.

[*He notices Sarita's dejection.*]

Look, I'm not going because of you. Not because of Jaisingh. I really have a lot of work there.

[*He realizes that Sarita doesn't believe him. She is standing with her back to the audience.*]

KAKASAHEB. Now, how can I convince you? [*Seeing her face, softly.*] Oh, you silly girl! What's all this? Wipe your eyes.

SARITA. Stay for today at least.

KAKASAHEB. And why? Why this day specially? All right, all right. I will stay. There's no arguing with you.

SARITA. Kamalabai!

[*Enter Kamalabai from upstairs with the saris. Sarita gives her the breakfast things. Kamalabai begins to exit.*]

Is Kamala awake?

KAMALABAI [*With a displeased expression*]. She's having a bath.

SARITA. Take these two saris to her. Tell her to wear whichever one she likes.

KAMALABAI [*Annoyed*]. Your saris—for *her*?

SARITA. Yes. Why?

[*Kamalabai exits, showing her displeasure. Kakasaheb is listening to all this. He looks at Sarita as Kamalabai goes out. Their gazes meet.*]

SARITA. Sit down. I'll just be back. I must put out the clothes for the dhobi. Give me yours, if you have any.

[*Sarita exits upstairs. Kakasaheb deep in thought. Enter Jaisingh down the stairs, disconnected phone in hand, a towel on his shoulder. He reconnects the phone. He looks tense.*]

JAISINGH. Kamalabai!

[*Enter Kamalabai.*]

How often have I told you that once I've read the papers, you are to fold them and put them on that rack?

KAMALABAI [*Muttering*]. I was about to . . .

JAISINGH. When? Tomorrow? Pick them up—pick them up at once.

[*Kamalabai picks up the papers, folds them and puts them on the rack in the hall. Kakasaheb is watching all this too, and Jaisingh knows it.*]

Tell that Kamala to hurry up and get ready. We've got to leave.

[*Kamalabai goes off-stage towards the kitchen.*]

KAKASAHEB [*Softly—he can't help it*]. Where are you taking Kamala?

JAISINGH. To the Women's Home. The Orphanage here. I've made arrangements for her there.

[*The phone rings. Jaisingh takes it.*]

JAISINGH [*Into the phone*]. Hello. Yes.

[*His face becomes tense. The voice on the phone can be heard saying 'Hello . . . Hello . . .' Then silence. Jaisingh puts down the phone. He hastily strides to the kitchen door and shouts.*]

Kamalabai, how much longer? Hasn't she finished? Tell her to hurry!

[*The phone rings again. Jaisingh stands still. Kakasaheb hesitates, whether or not to take the phone. Then he takes it.*]

KAKASAHEB [*Into the phone*]. Yes, this is Jaisingh Jadhav's residence. Who's speaking? Inspector Madhosingh? Neeti Bagh Police Station? [*He looks at Jaisingh, who shakes his head. Kakasaheb has*

sized up the situation. He says into the phone.] He is having a bath.
[*Listens; then*] It's urgent? *Accha*, I'll give him a message. My name
is Shivajirao Mohite. That's all right.

[*He puts down the phone, very serious. Enter Sarita from upstairs with
the clothes for the dhobi.*]

KAKASAHEB. There was a phone call from Neeti Bagh Police Station.
SARITA [*Concerned*]. What?
KAKASAHEB. They have some urgent business with Jaisingh.
They've left him a message to ring up as soon as he finishes his
bath.

[*Sarita says nothing, but she is sobered by it.*]

SARITA. May I know what this is all about?
JAISINGH. It's the effect of yesterday's Press Conference.
SARITA. I don't understand.
JAISINGH. Don't be so dumb. My buying Kamala in an auction is a
criminal offence.
SARITA. But you did it in Bihar! What have the Neeti Bagh police
got to do with it?
JAISINGH. The Delhi Police must have started moving after they
got instructions from the Bihar Police. Can't you even under-
stand that?
KAKASAHEB. Do they want to arrest you?
JAISINGH. Not yet. Just now they want custody of Kamala.
SARITA. We're not going to hand her over to them.
JAISINGH. We'll see about that. For the moment at least we won't
let her fall into their hands.

[*The phone begins to ring. Jaisingh looks expectantly at Kakasaheb.
Kakasaheb shakes his head. Sarita goes to take it.*]

JAISINGH [*To Sarita*]. Wait, don't take it. It must be from him. [*Goes
and takes the receiver off the hook. Then changes his mind and with his
hand over the mouthpiece says to her.*] No, take it. And if it's the
Inspector, tell him I've gone out. You don't know where I've
gone. Yes, say that.

[*Sarita is stiff at first. Then goes and takes the receiver from him. She
tells the caller, who is the Inspector, what Jaisingh has asked her to say.
Then puts down the phone.*

*Jaisingh breathes a sigh of relief, and as he turns away, he sees
Kamala, who has come on stage from the kitchen side.*

Kamala is dressed in one of Sarita's saris, but in her style. She is

*wearing a blouse. They all look at her. A smile grows on Jaisingh's face.
Then he bursts out laughing.*]

SARITA [*Upset*]. What's the matter?

JAISINGH. How atrocious! Only you could have thought of it.

KAKASAHEB. But she's looking very nice. What a shabby state she
was in yesterday. [*To Kamala.*] Why, Kamala! How sweet you're
looking!

[*Kamala turns shy and veils her face to hide it.*]

JAISINGH. Come, Kamala. Bring your luggage. Hurry.

[*Kamala becomes still as a statue.*]

Where's your luggage? We have to go.

KAMALA [*In feeble tones*]. Won't we be coming back?

JAISINGH. No. You'll have to stay where we are going now.

[*Kamala is silent. A statue.*]

It's a nice place. Nicer than this.

SARITA. You're taking her to the orphanage, aren't you? How can
it be nicer than here?

JAISINGH. I'm telling her that so she will feel better.

SARITA. You're deceiving her!

JAISINGH. It's not so bad there. She will like it.

SARITA. How do you know?

JAISINGH. I don't have time to argue with you. Kamala, bring your
luggage at once.

[*Kamala is in a fix.*]

SARITA [*With greater determination*]. Kamala is not going to come
with you.

JAISINGH. That's enough of your jokes. *Chalo*, Kamala. [*To Sarita.*]
Bring her bundle from inside.

SARITA. Kamala is not going with you. She's going to stay here.

JAISINGH. Stay here? Don't be absurd!

SARITA. I'm telling you this very seriously. Kamala is going to stay
here.

JAISINGH [*Tense*]. Who said so?

SARITA. I did.

JAISINGH [*Sarcastically*]. Well, what's Kamala going to do, staying
here?

SARITA [*Pauses for a moment, then*]. She'll stay here like Kamalabai
does.

JAISINGH. Have you gone mad or something?

SARITA. I've given it a lot of thought. Kamala and I have already discussed it.

JAISINGH. Kamalabai! Just bring Kamala's clothes—quickly.

[*Enter Kamalabai from within with Kamala's bundle.*]

SARITA [*Rather determinedly*]. Kamalabai, take them back.

[*Jaisingh tenses up. Kamalabai in a fix.*]

JAISINGH. Give them to me, . . .

[*Kamalabai goes and gives it to him.*]

JAISINGH [*Handing the bundle to Kamala, says to Sarita*]. It's I who takes decisions in this house, and no one else. Do you understand? *Chalo*, Kamala. [*To Sarita.*] I'll be back tonight—if there are any phone calls, say I've gone straight to the office, and write them down.

[*He reaches the door. Kamala is still standing there, her head bent, her bundle in her hands.*]

Are you deaf, Kamala? *Chalo*—Come on.
[*Kamala goes to the door as if she is being dragged there. Recognizing Kakasaheb's existence, he says to him in a rather milder tone*] I can't keep Kamala at home. Or we'll lose the case against me for buying Kamala. I could even be sent to jail. That's why Kamala has to stay in the orphanage. The police are going to ask for custody of her. For that reason too, it's better she should be in the orphanage. It will fortify our arguments in Court. It's going to be a long drawn-out battle now.

[*Kakasaheb nods to show he has understood. But there is tension in the air.*]

JAISINGH [*Looking towards Sarita and then at Kakasaheb*]. Bye, I'll be back tonight.

[*He exits. Kamala, who is following him, turns once again and looks at the house. Her bundle in her hands. She goes out as if she is being pulled away. Sarita stands like a statue watching all this. She is stationary still, but looks quite forlorn.*]

KAMALABAI. Good thing she's gone. She was a bad sort.

[*Sarita gives her a sharp glance. Kamalabai goes off-stage. Sarita and*

Kakasaheb look at each other. Sarita avoids meeting his gaze. She is incredibly disturbed.]

KAKASAHEB. You know, the reasons he gave were completely shallow ones. You see, Kamala is just a pawn in his game of chess.

SARITA. Not just Kamala, Kakasaheb. [*Trying to control her misery.*] Not just Kamala, Kakasaheb. Me too . . . me too.

[*The lights fade out. Then—light. It is evening—lighting up time. The drawing-room is empty. Enter Kamalabai, and after her Jaisingh from the outside entrance.*]

JAISINGH. What's memsaheb doing?

KAMALABAI. She's lying down upstairs.

JAISINGH. [*Going to the telephone note book and seeing if any numbers have been written down*]. Lying down? Did you tell her what I told you on the phone this afternoon?

KAMALABAI. Of course! 'Sahib says, you're going to a party this evening. Be ready at seven.'

JAISINGH [*Going to the sideboard*]. Is she dressed for the party?

KAMALABAI. No. She's as she was in the morning. She hasn't come out of her room at all.

JAISINGH [*Taking out a bottle and a glass*]. She's feeling all right, isn't she?

KAMALABAI. Who knows? She didn't say.

JAISINGH. Where's Kakasaheb?

KAMALABAI. He went out this afternoon and hasn't come back.

[*Jaisingh pours a drink. Goes and starts the tape-deck. Comforting music. Jaisingh comes and sits on the sofa.*]

KAMALABAI. Would you like some tea or coffee?

JAISINGH. What's this you see in my hand? And why are you offering me tea or coffee? Go upstairs. Tell memsahib I'm back, and we have to leave soon. And on your way back bring my blue jacket. Ask her; she'll give it to you.
[*Kamalabai goes off upstairs. Muttering.*] Stupid!

[*Jaisingh relaxed. Sarita slowly enters from upstairs. She is in the same clothes as in the morning. And her face has a drawn look. In her hands is his coat. Kamalabai follows her downstairs and exits.*]

JAISINGH [*Noticing that she has come, but without turning and looking at her*]. Hi.

[*Sarita does not answer. She puts the coat on the back of the sofa.*]

[*Looking at her*] I said, hi!

[*Sarita still doesn't reply.*]

Aren't you well or something? Now get ready, quick—[*looks at his watch*]. We start at quarter past seven. Exactly twenty minutes to go. Put on that sari I brought you from Trivandrum. You haven't yet worn it to a party. And look happier. Today's crowd is a rather different one. You know, the Director of the National Mineral Corporation is going to be there. The big fish in that seventeen crore fraud case. I want to talk to him over drinks. Let us see if I get something. [*Finishes his peg and rises.*]

SARITA [*From where she is sitting*]. What happened about Kamala?

[*Jaisingh acts as if he hasn't heard her.*]

JAISINGH [*Growling*]. It's seven. Go, get dressed, quickly.

[*Sarita doesn't get up.*]

SARITA [*Emphatically*]. What happened about Kamala?

JAISINGH. Kamala? What do you think happened? She is in the Women's Home. The Police will put their case before the Court tomorrow. From now on, our lawyer will look after it. But first, get dressed, will you? We are already late.

[*Jaisingh has gone to the phone. He dials a number.*]

[*Into the receiver*] Press Club? Who is it—Chadda? It's Jaisingh. If my editor is there, please call him to the phone. Yes. I'll wait. [*To Sarita*] I'll probably have to go to Andhra tomorrow. There's been a police firing on an assembly of Gond tribesmen. They say they put a cordon round the assembly, and started shooting. They think nine or ten people were killed. And over a hundred wounded, they say. [*Into the receiver*] Yes, Chadda? He hasn't come? *Accha*, it doesn't matter. I'll contact him afterwards. No problem. Thank you, Chadda. [*Put down the receiver.*] A massacre. What else would you call it?

[*Sarita sitting as she was.*]

[*Turning and seeing her*] Don't you want to come to the party?

SARITA. No.

JAISINGH. You don't want to come? Why?

SARITA. That's my will.

JAISINGH [*Rather surprised*]. Your will?

SARITA. Aren't I allowed to have a will of my own?

JAISINGH [*Sarcastically*]. Never noticed any signs of it before. If you didn't want to come, you could at least have told me earlier. Then I wouldn't have accepted for both of us.

SARITA. Did you ask me?

JAISINGH. Of course! I left a message with Kamalabai.

SARITA. That isn't called asking.

JAISINGH. You could have phoned me back.

SARITA. You could have waited till I came on the phone.

JAISINGH. I was busy.

SARITA. I didn't feel like phoning you.

JAISINGH. What's special about your feelings today?

SARITA [*Pointedly*]. Do you want to hear?

JAISINGH. Let it be. But first decide, once and for all, whether you're coming with me.

SARITA. I decided that a long time ago.

JAISINGH. You don't want to come? Okay. Your choice. I have to go. Well, I'm off. I'll be late, don't wait up for me. I have the latch key. Bye.

[*Exit Jaisingh. The sound of a car starting and driving away. Sarita still sitting on the sofa. Enter Kakasaheb from outside. At first he doesn't see Sarita.*]

KAKASAHEB. These Delhi roads—[*Sees Sarita.*] Who? Sarita? What's the matter, why are you sitting doing nothing? It's the first time I've seen you like this! Aren't you well? [*Goes to her and feels her forehead.*] No, you haven't got a temperature. Is your head aching?

SARITA. If I had one, it would.

KAKASAHEB. You don't have a head? Then who does?

SARITA. The gentleman who just left.

KAKASAHEB. Gentleman? What gentleman? I didn't meet any one.

SARITA. I did.

KAKASAHEB. Don't talk in riddles. Say what you want to say—straight out.

SARITA. Never mind. [*After a pause.*] I'm planning something.

KAKASAHEB. What? A party?

SARITA. A Press Conference.

KAKASAHEB. A Press Conference? What, you've caught the infection too, have you?

SARITA. A Press Conference at the Press Club. Every last journalist in Delhi must come to it.

KAKASAHEB. And what will this Press Conference of yours be about?

SARITA. I am going to present a man who in the year 1982 still keeps a slave, right here in Delhi. Jaisingh Jadhav. I'm going to say: this man's a great advocate of freedom. And he brings home a slave and exploits her. He doesn't consider a slave a human being—just a useful object. One you can use and throw away. He gets people to call him a sworn enemy of tyranny. But he tyrannizes his own slave as much as he likes, and doesn't think anything of it—nothing at all. Listen to the story of how he bought the slave Kamala and made use of her. The other slave he got free—not just free—the slave's father shelled out the money—a big sum. Ask him what he did with it. [*An uncontrollable sob bursts from her. She controls it.*] Sorry.

KAKASAHEB [*Worried*]. Sarita, what's all this you're thinking?

SARITA. I said, I'm sorry.

KAKASAHEB. Do you really think this way about Jaisingh?

SARITA. This is very little, what you've heard so far. There is much more.

KAKASAHEB. Anyone would think Jaisingh is a slave-driver.

SARITA. Not just anyone. I do.

KAKASAHEB. What on earth happened between you two?

SARITA. Marriage.

KAKASAHEB. That's been going on for the last ten years. Why did you think of all this only today?

SARITA. Why did I, you ask? I was asleep. I was unconscious even when I was awake. Kamala woke me up. With a shock. Kamala showed me everything. Because of her, I suddenly saw things clearly. I saw that the man I thought my partner was the master of a slave. I have no rights at all in this house. Because I'm a slave. Slaves don't have rights, do they, Kakasaheb? They must only slave away. Dance to their master's whim. Laugh, when he says, laugh. Cry, when he says, cry. When he says pick up the phone, they must pick it up. When he says, come to a party, they must go. When he says, lie on the bed—they [*She is twisted in pain.*]

KAKASAHEB. Sarita, something's really gone wrong.

SARITA. And it will never get better, Kakasaheb. After this, I'll never think that this is my home.

KAKASAHEB. Look Sarita, Jaisingh is no different from other men. He's not unusual. You're wrong to think that he's a bad man. A man is always too proud of his achievements. It doesn't matter if his achievements are just silly little ones. By that standard,

Jaisingh is really a go-getter. He's made a name for himself in his field. Whatever he's got, he's earned with his own initiative.

SARITA. And therefore he's entitled to keep a slave. [*Tormented.*] But why? If a man becomes great, why doesn't he stay a great man? Why does he become a master?

KAKASAHEB. Sarita, the questions you are asking have only one answer. Because he's like that. That's why he's a man. And that's why there's manhood in the world. I too was just like this. Don't go by what I seem to be today. I gave your aunt a lot of trouble. As if it was my right. I didn't care what she felt at all. I just marched straight ahead looking in front of me. I was confident she would follow, even if she was limping. And she did follow, the poor thing.

SARITA. So, Sarita, go behind your master like that. It's your duty to do it—is that what you're saying?

KAKASAHEB. It may be unpleasant, but it's true. If the world is to go on, marriage must go on. And it will only go on like this.

SARITA. Why? Why can't men limp behind? Why aren't women ever the masters? Why can't a woman at least ask to live her life the same way as a man? Why must only a man have the right to be a man? Does he have one extra sense? A woman can do everything a man can.

KAKASAHEB. But that isn't manhood.

SARITA. What a man does is manhood. Even if he washes people's dishes, that's manhood.

KAKASAHEB. It is.

SARITA. This must be changed. Those who do manly things should be equal to men. Those who don't, are women. And there will be some among them who have beards and moustaches too. Isn't being Prime Minister of India a manly thing? And isn't it an effeminate thing to grovel at that Prime Minister's feet?

KAKASAHEB. You are very angry. Grown-up people don't act angrily, Sarita, they act with thought. You've got to have understanding.

SARITA. Only a woman must! Why must she alone have it?

KAKASAHEB. You're wrong. Sarita, my girl, doesn't a man make mistakes? When he does he has to endure it. If you put your hand in the ox's mouth, it's going to feel cold. That's a Marathi proverb. You'll feel cold whether you're a man or a woman.

[*The doorbell rings loudly. Then again.*]

SARITA. One second. I'll see who it is.

[*She goes to open the door and comes back with Jain. In the meantime, the phone rings, and then stops ringing.*]

JAIN [*Tense. Excited*]. There's a terrible mess, *bhabhiji*. I must get hold of Jaisingh at once. I rushed here as soon as I heard.

SARITA. Why? What's happened.

JAIN. He has been sacked.

SARITA [*Incredulously*]. What?

KAKASAHEB. What did you say?

JAIN. Jaisingh's boss has dismissed him from his job.

[*Sarita stands there.*]

KAKASAHEB. Just like that? With no warning?

JAIN. It was decided only this evening. He'll get the letter tomorrow. I ran here as soon as I got the news. I went to the Press Club on the way. I thought he would be there. The news had reached there already. They were discussing it.

KAKASAHEB. Why was he dismissed?

JAIN. There have been pressures on the proprietor. I learnt that some very big people are involved in this flesh racket.

KAKASAHEB. But a man who's doing such a wonderful job—his proprietor's paper has become famous and respected because of it.

JAIN. A big paper doesn't recognize respect and all that, Kakasaheb—it only knows about circulation and advertisements. And profit and loss.

KAKASAHEB. But there are laws about journalists' jobs. How can anyone be sacked slam bang—just like that? Is it Jaisingh's fault? What mistake did he make?

JAIN. His mistake was to cross the path of the wrong people. He jeopardized the wrong friendships.

KAKASAHEB. There can be an inquiry into it. Jaisingh must get the chance to explain everything. How can they sack him overnight?

JAIN. You're talking to me as if I'm the owner. Where am I disagreeing with you? But the owner has decided. *Bhabhiji*, where is the party, tell me. Is there a phone there? If there is, let's call him here. We must decide our plan of action right away.

[*Sarita goes to the phone. She hunts for the number in the notebook, then dials it. Someone comes on the phone at the other end. She tells him in Hindi to call Jaisingh. She is tense. Kakasaheb and Jain are excited. Slowly, the lights dim, and it is dark.*

Light. Some time has passed. Kakasaheb, Jain, and Sarita are waiting for Jaisingh. They are in new positions in the room. The doorbell rings. Sarita quickly goes to the door, and comes back with Jaisingh.]

JAISINGH. What's the matter? Why did you call me? What, Jain? How come you're here?

SARITA [*Seating him gently*]. Do sit down. What will you have, Jain? Gin, Whisky—[*to Jaisingh*] what would you like?

JAISINGH [*Not looking at her*]. Whisky and water. [*To Jain*] What is it?

[*Sarita is at the sideboard. She makes the drinks. Jain lights a pipe.*] What is it, Jain? Must be something special—you called me away from a party.

JAIN. It is special. You haven't heard anything?

JAISINGH. What about? Nothing about Kamala, is it?

JAIN. Oh, no.

JAISINGH. Then? What's it about?

JAIN. Wait, you'll soon find out. Settle down a little, *yaar*.

JAISINGH. I have. Now tell me, what's the game?

[*Sarita serves the drinks.*]

SARITA [*To Kakasaheb*]. Shall I give you plain lemonade or something?

KAKASAHEB. No, tnank you.

JAISINGH [*To everyone*]. Arre, say what it is, at least!

SARITA. It's about your job.

JAISINGH. My job?

SARITA [*In a semi-playful tone*]. Your owner is pleased with you and he's decided to relieve you from your job.

JAISINGH. Me? You're joking.

SARITA. It is a joke—but the owner is serious, says Jain.

[*Jaisingh looks at Jain.*]

JAIN. I heard it just a little while ago. When I went to the Press Club to look for you, the news had reached. Of course, it is supposed to be secret just now.

JAISINGH [*He still can't believe it, but seeing the seriousness around him*]. Are you telling the truth? Or is this a joke?

JAIN. There was a high-level meeting this evening, for your information. Your editor was present at the meeting. And a few others—I haven't found out who—it was decided to give you your letter tomorrow morning. The draft is ready too.

JAISINGH [*Suddenly leaping to his feet*]. It just cannot be. [*He pours all the whisky in his glass down his throat. Then turning to Jain.*] Who told you?

JAIN. Don't embarrass me. I won't tell you the name but I'll tell you that the news is 100% reliable, really.

JAISINGH [*Going to the telephone*] Let me ask my editor. [*He pauses, then to Jain.*] Or was it he who told you?

[*Jain is silent. Jaisingh starts dialling.*]

JAIN. He's not in Delhi. He's just taken the plane to Bombay.

[*Jaisingh stops dialling, and puts down the receiver. He paces about like a tiger.*]

JAISINGH [*Pacing, growls*]. No ... No ... [*He goes once again to the phone. Then decides not to and paces around again. Goes to the sideboard. Pours another peg and takes a big gulp of it.*]

SARITA [*Gently*]. Will you have some food? You can talk while you eat. [*She makes a sign to Jain.*]

JAIN [*Taking the hint*]. Oh yes. Let's sit at the dining table. Come on, *yaar.* [*Goes to the dining table himself and sits down.*] Come Jaisingh. [*Jaisingh is wrapped up in his own thoughts, his glass in his hand. Sarita, seeing this, goes inside to the kitchen.*]

JAISINGH [*Excited, tense*]. Rather interesting ... That's something ...

KAKASAHEB. I tell you, Jaisingh, there will be an uproar about this decision. The owner of your paper won't get away lightly with it.

[*Sarita comes from the kitchen carrying food. After her comes Kamalabai. They lay the table and arrange the food.*]

KAKASAHEB. Your employer is going to regret this.

SARITA [*Going to Jaisingh, softly*] Come on, talk while you eat. Eat just a little. Please. Jain hasn't eaten, either. [*She guides him to the dining table.*] Come on, sit down.

JAISINGH [*Suddenly flaring up and banging his fist on the table*]. The bastard! Do you hear me? He is a bastard. That Sheth Singhania! I'll teach him a lesson!

[*Everyone realizes he is rather drunk.*]

SARITA. All right. But sit down, at least. Eat just a little bit.

JAISINGH [*Gets up roaring*]. No! Shut up! Let me speak—you shut up. What does he imagine himself to be? What is he? A bloody capitalist. A swindler. A black marketeer. A bloody income-tax evader. A criminal. I'll hold a press conference tomorrow—I'll strip the cover off him! I'll expose all his dirty secrets! I'll strip him naked! I'll tear him to pieces—the dirty pig!

JAIN [*Going towards him*]. Look here, Jaisingh. It's no use getting wild. We must plan something carefully.

JAISINGH. Care be damned! I'm going to fuck that scoundrel tomorrow!

SARITA [*Placating him lovingly*]. First, just calm down. Come on, eat something. See, Kakasaheb's waiting for you.

[*Jaisingh somehow seats himself at the dining table. Sarita helps him to some food.*]

JAISINGH [*Suddenly, pushing her aside*]. No, I don't want to eat. Sack me, will he? Me. Jaisingh Jadhav. His father can't touch me. I'm going to hack that croaking ass to pieces . . . bloody bastard.

[*Little by little his voice is weakening. His control over his limbs gradually decreases, and he collapses onto the sofa.*]

SARITA. Thank you so much, Jain. For coming here. For waiting.

JAIN. Oh, that's nothing. He got drunk so soon! I thought we would at least make sensible plans of some kind.

SARITA. He must have drunk a lot already at the party, I think. And then this shock. He must never have dreamt that anyone would ever sack him.

JAIN. Yes, no one could have dreamt it. I was shocked.

KAKASAHEB. I tell you, the owner will have to change his decision in court.

JAIN. This much is true—that we must make an absolute hullaballoo about this. It's not what's happened. It's the principle that's shocking. Jaisingh will get any number of new jobs. That's not the point.

SARITA. Anyway, thanks again.

JAIN [*Leaving*]. Tell him to phone me as soon as he gets up tomorrow. I'll be waiting.

SARITA. Yes, yes.

[*Jain and, after him, Sarita go chatting to the door. Kakasaheb stands still. Jaisingh unconscious on the sofa. Sarita returns.*]

KAKASAHEB. This is the mistake men make. That manhood makes. Do you understand now?

[*Sarita nods to show comprehension.*]

SARITA. But that doesn't mean that what I said was wrong either.

KAKASAHEB. You mean, you still feel like that?

SARITA. I'll go on feeling it. But at present I'm going to lock all that up in a corner of my mind and forget about it. But a day will come, Kakasaheb, when I will stop being a slave. I'll no longer be an object to be used and thrown away. I'll do what I wish, and no one will rule over me. That day has to come. And I'll pay whatever price I have to pay for it.

[*Kakasaheb is fascinated and impressed by the quiet determination in her words.*]

KAKASAHEB [*Indicating Jaisingh*]. But first, tell me, how will you get him up to the bedroom?

SARITA [*Looking at Jaisingh's face*]. How innocent even the masters look when they're asleep, don't they? Let me stay here. I'll stay here with him.

KAKASAHEB. Good night.

SARITA. Good night.

[*Kakasaheb slowly goes to his room. Sarita turns off the lights in the drawing-room one by one, leaving just one light on. She comes close to Jaisingh and sits on the ground by the sofa, her head against it. Closes her eyes, exhausted. Opens them again. Her gaze is calm, steadily looking ahead at the future. Determination on her face.*]

CURTAIN

SILENCE!
THE COURT IS IN SESSION

(*Shantata! Court Chalu Ahe*)

Translated by
Priya Adarkar

CHARACTERS

SAMANT

BENARE

SUKHATME

SERVANT

BALU ROKDE

PONKSHE

KARNIK

MRS KASHIKAR

MR KASHIKAR

LOCAL RESIDENT

NOTE

I must express my thanks to Amol Palekar and Professor D. N. Govilkar for their help in checking respectively the language of the first and final drafts of the translation.

P.A.

ACT ONE

The lights go up on a completely empty hall. It has two doors. One to enter by, and one to go to an adjoining room. One side of the hall seems to go leftwards into the wings. Within the hall are a built-in platform, one or two old wooden chairs, an old box, a stool—and sundry other things lie jumbled together as if in a lumber-room. A clock, out of order, on the wall. Some worn-out portraits of national leaders. A wooden board with the names of donors. A picture of the god Ganesha, hung on the door. The door is closed.

There are footsteps outside. Someone unlocks the door. A man sidles in, and stands looking around as if seeing the hall for the first time. This is Samant. In his hands, a lock and key, a toy parrot made of green cloth, a book.

SAMANT [*looking around*]. This is it. Come in. This is the hall. They seem to have cleaned it up a bit this morning—because of the show. [*Miss Benare has entered after him, and is standing in the doorway. One fingertip is between her lips. She holds a basket of equipment, and a purse.*] What's the matter? Did you catch your finger in the bolt? These old bolts are all the same. They just won't slide straight. And if the bolt stays out just a little bit, and you don't pull it clean to one side, then what happens? Shut the door—and you've had it! Locked yourself in! Suck it a little. You'll feel better. This finger of my right hand once got caught in the lock. For five days it was so swollen, I couldn't tell the difference between my finger and my thumb. I had to do *everything* with four fingers!

BENARE. Goodness! [*to him*] It's nothing. Nothing at all. It's just a habit with me. But I *am* feeling marvellous. I got down at the station with all the others, and suddenly, after many days, I felt wonderful!

SAMANT. Why's that?

BENARE. Who knows? And I felt even more wonderful coming here with you. I'm so glad the others fell behind! We rushed ahead, didn't we?

SAMANT. Yes, indeed. I mean to say, I'm not in the habit of walking so fast. You do set a very lively pace, very lively.

BENARE. Not always. But today, how I walked! Let's leave everyone behind, I thought, and go somewhere far, far away— with you!

SAMANT [*in confusion*]. With me?

BENARE. Yes, I like you very much.

SAMANT [*terribly shy and embarrassed*]. Tut-tut. Ha ha! I'm hardly . . .

BENARE. You're very nice indeed. And shall I tell you something? You are a very pure and good person. I like you.

SAMANT [*incredulously*]. Me?

BENARE. Yes, and I like this hall very much, too. [*She walks round it.*]

SAMANT. The hall too? It's just an old one. Whenever there are functions in the village, they take place here. You could say this hall just exists for the sake of functions. Speeches, receptions, weddings . . . to say nothing of the women's *bhajan* group. They practise here in the afternoons. Tonight there's this programme, you see. So the *bhajan* practice must be off. They give *bhajans* a holiday when there's a show at night! How else would the women finish their chores by nightfall? Eh?

BENARE [*cautious but inquisitive*]. Your wife is in the *bhajan* group, I suppose?

SAMANT. Uh huh. Wrong. Not wife, sister-in-law. I don't have a wife at all.

BENARE [*pointing a finger at the green cloth parrot in his hand*]. Then who is *that* for?

SAMANT. This, you mean? For my nephew. A lovely child! Do you like this toy?

BENARE. Yes.

SAMANT. I'm not married yet. No particular reason. I earn enough to keep body and soul together. But I never got married. Do you know—there were magic shows here some time ago? Sleight of hand, hypnotism and all that . . .

BENARE. Did you see them?

SAMANT. What do you think! I'm here for every show.

BENARE. Is that so?

SAMANT. Yes. I don't miss a single one. What other amusement is there in the village?

BENARE. That's true. [*She goes very close to him, and says in confiding tones.*] Did you see the magic—from very near?

SAMANT. Yes. That is, I wasn't *very* close. But still, close enough. Why?

BENARE [*as close as ever*]. How do they do that—cutting a tongue, and putting it together again?

SAMANT [*backing away a little*]. A tongue? Tongue . . . well, it's hard to describe . . .

BENARE. But tell me?

SAMANT. Eh? But . . .

[*She comes as close as before. Embarrassed, he backs away once more.*]

It's like this . . . I'll try . . . I mean, I won't be able . . . look, this is my tongue . . .

[*He stretches the first joint of his finger towards her.*]

BENARE. Let me see.

[*She makes it an excuse to get even closer to him. For a moment or two, she is keenly aware of his nearness to her. But he is not.*]

SAMANT [*with concentration*]. This is my tongue. Look, it's cut! Now what? It'll bleed! But it doesn't? Why doesn't it bleed? There must be something for it in hypnotism—that is, some trick. That's why it doesn't bleed. Nothing happens, nothing at all . . . it doesn't even hurt—so . . .

[*Perhaps as a response to his complete innocence, she moves away from him.*]

BENARE. Why haven't they reached here yet? They always amble along. People should be brisk!

SAMANT. Yes. I was telling you about the tongue . . . hypnotism—

BENARE. In school, when the first bell rings, my foot's already on the threshold. I haven't heard a single reproach for not being on time these past eight years. Nor about my teaching. I'm *never* behindhand with my lessons! Exercises corrected on time, too! Not a bit of room for disapproval—I don't give an inch of it to any one!

SAMANT. You're a schoolmarm, it seems?

BENARE. No, a teacher! Do I seem the complete schoolmarm to you?

SAMANT. No, no . . . I didn't mean it like that . . .

BENARE. Say it if you like . . .

SAMANT. But I didn't say it at all! A schoolmarm just means . . . someone who—teaches—instructs!—children—that's what I meant to say . . .

BENARE. They're so much better than adults. At least they don't have that blind pride of thinking they know everything. There's no nonsense stuffed in their heads. They don't scratch you till you bleed, then run away like cowards. Please open that window. It's become too hot for me.

[*He opens the window eagerly. Benare takes a deep breath.*]

Ah! Now I feel better. No, no, I feel wonderful!

[*She starts walking freely round the hall once more.*]

SAMANT. Shall we finish that tongue trick now? The hypnotism? [*putting his finger out again.*] See that now. That's my tongue. Now it's cut.

BENARE. No! Not now.

SAMANT [*obediently*]. All right. [*He lowers his hand. Then suddenly comes forward, picking up a chair, and puts it down near her.*] Why are you wandering about? Do sit down. Your feet will hurt.

BENARE. I'm used to standing while teaching. In class, I never sit when teaching. That's how I keep my eye on the whole class. No one has a chance to play up. My class is scared stiff of me! And they adore me, too. My children will do anything for me. For I'd give the last drop of my blood to teach them. [*In a different tone.*] That's why people are jealous. Specially the other teachers and the management. But what can they do to me? What can they do? However hard they try, what *can* they do? They're holding an enquiry, if you please! But my teaching's perfect. I've put my whole life into it—I've worn myself to a shadow in this job! Just because of one bit of slander, what can they do to me? Throw me out? Let them! I haven't hurt anyone. Anyone at all! If I've hurt anybody, it's been myself. But is that any kind of reason for throwing me out? Who are these people to say what I can or can't do? My life is my own—I haven't sold it to anyone for a job! My will is my own. My wishes are my own. No one can kill those—no one! I'll do what I like with myself and my life! I'll decide . . .

[*Unconsciously, her hand is on her stomach. She suddenly stops. Seeing Samant, she falls silent. Gradually she regains her poise. Samant is embarrassed.*]

SAMANT [*awkwardly*]. Shall I go and see why the others haven't arrived yet?

BENARE [*hastily*]. No. [*then coming back slowly to normal.*] I feel scared when I am alone, you know.

SAMANT. Then I won't go. Are you not feeling well?

BENARE [*with a sudden access of energy*]. Nonsense! Nothing's the matter with me. I'm fine. Just fine! [*Clapping her hands she starts crooning an English song to herself.*]

> Oh, I've got a sweetheart
> Who carries all my books,
> He plays in my doll house,

And says he likes my looks.
I'll tell you a secret—
He wants to marry me.
But Mummy says, I'm too little
To have such thoughts as these.

[*She leaves off singing.*] Do you know what we are going to do today, Mr—er—

SAMANT. Samant.

BENARE. Just so.

SAMANT. Yes. There's a notice by the temple. The Sonar Moti Tenement (Bombay) Progressive Association's Mock Law . . . law . . . what was it? Yes, Lawcourt! At eight sharp tonight.

BENARE. But what does that mean, do you think?

SAMANT. That I don't know. Something to do with the court . . .

BENARE. Quite right. Not a real court; a fake one, a make-believe one!

SAMANT. In other words, some fun to do with a court.

BENARE. Exactly. Fun. But Samant, 'spreading enlightenment is also one of the Prime Objectives behind our programme'. So our chairman Kashikar will tell you. Kashikar can't take a step without a Prime Objective! Besides him, there's Mrs Hand-that-Rocks-the-Cradle. I mean Mrs Kashikar. What an excellent housewife the poor woman is! A real Hand-that-Rocks-the-Cradle type! But what's the use? Mr Prime Objective is tied up with uplifting the masses. And poor Hand-that-Rocks-the-Cradle has no cradle to rock!

SAMANT. You mean they have no—[*He rocks an imaginary baby in his arms.*]

BENARE. Right. You seem to be very bright, too! Mr Kashikar and the Hand-that-Rocks-the-Cradle, in order that nothing should happen to either of them in their bare, bare house—and that they shouldn't die of boredom!—gave shelter to a young boy. They educated him. Made him toil away. Made a slave out of him. His name's Balu—Balu Rokde. Who else? . . . Well, we have an Expert on the Law. He's such an authority on the subject, even a desperate client won't go anywhere near him! He just sits alone in the barristers' room at court, swatting flies with legal precedents! And in his tenement, he sits alone killing houseflies! But for today's mock trial, he's a very great barrister. You'll see the wonders he performs! And there's a 'Hmm!' with us! [*Puts an imaginary pipe in her mouth.*] Hmm! Sci-en-tist! Inter-failed!

SAMANT. Oh, it does sound good fun!

BENARE. And we have an Intellectual too. That means someone who prides himself on his booklearning. But when there's a real-life problem, away he runs! Hides his head. He's not here today. Won't be coming, either. He wouldn't dare!

SAMANT. But what's today's trial about?

BENARE. A case against President Johnson for producing atomic weapons.

SAMANT. Good heavens!

BENARE. Ssh! I think they're here. [*She has an idea.*] Come here. Come on, hide like this. I'll stay here, too. Hide properly. Now ask them to come in.

[*Samant and Benare hiding behind the door that leads outside. Their bodies touch. Voices are heard saying, 'Here it is!' 'Found it at last!' as lawyer Sukhatme, science student Ponkshe and Balu Rokde, the Mock Lawcourt's general factotum, carrying between them two or three suitcases, two bags, a battery-operated microphone set, and the like, come in through the door. A lighted beedi in Sukhatme's mouth. A pipe between Ponkshe's lips. After them, a servant carrying two wooden enclosures—the dock and the witness-box. As they come in, Benare and Samant leap out from behind the door. She shouts 'Boo' in a tremendous voice. They all start for just a moment. Then one by one they recover their poise. Benare laughs to her heart's content. Samant stands looking around at all this, eagerly and wonderingly.*]*

ROKDE [*going and setting down all his luggage at one spot*]. How loudly, Miss Benare! All this might have fallen down! I would have been scolded by Mrs Kashikar. And all for nothing. Whatever happens, it's me she blames. I got a free education off them, didn't I? So I'm paying for my sins!

[*The servant goes and puts the enclosures into the wings at left, and returns. Ponkshe pays him his porter's fees. Exit the servant.*]

PONKSHE [*weightily, removing his thick-framed spectacles*]. Oh, gosh! Where is it? . . . [*He goes muttering into the inner room, to hunt for the lavatory.*]

SUKHATME [*inhaling deeply, and blowing out smoke*]. There is a little lassie, deep in my heart. Miss Benare, whatever happens, you don't want to grow up, do you? Eh?

BENARE. Why, in the class room, I'm the soul of seriousness! But I don't see why one should go around all the time with a long face. Or a square face! Like that Ponkshe! We should laugh, we should play, we should sing! If we can and if they'll let us, we should dance too. Shouldn't have any false modesty or dignity. Or care for anyone! I mean it. When your life's over, do you think anyone will give you a bit of theirs? What do you say, Samant? Do you think they will?

SAMANT. You're quite right. The great sage Tukaram said . . . at least I *think* it was him—

BENARE. Forget about the sage Tukaram. I say it—I, Leela Benare, a living woman, I say it from my own experience. Life is not meant for anyone else. It's your own life. It must be. It's a very, very important thing. Every moment, every bit of it is precious—

SUKHATME [*clapping*]. Hear! Hear!

[*Ponkshe comes out.*]

BENARE. Not here. [*She points to Ponkshe.*] There! [*Tries hard to control her laughter, but can't.*]

PONKSHE [*puzzled*]. What's the matter?

BENARE. Ponkshe, tell the honest truth. Did you or did you not go in looking for the 'arrangements'? To deal with your usual nervousness before a show?

SUKHATME. Say what you will, Miss Benare. Our Ponkshe looks most impressive during the trial. The scientist in the witness-box! A pipe and all that! No one would believe he has just taken his Inter-Science for the *second* time. Or works as a clerk in the Central Telegraph Office!

[*Here Rokde, unable to control himself, laughs a little.*]

PONKSHE [*irritated*]. Don't you laugh, Rokde! I didn't get my education on Mrs Kashikar's charity! I may have failed my Inter-Science. But at least I did it on my own father's money. Nonsense!

BENARE. Nonsense! [*She catches his exact intonation, and laughs*]. Shall I tell you people something amusing? When I was small, I was very, very quiet. I just used to sit and make plans—all by myself. I wouldn't tell anyone. And at the slightest excuse, I used to cry loudly!

PONKSHE. In other words, the exact opposite of what you are now.

BENARE. Yes! Yes! Do you know, Samant—

SAMANT [*promptly*]. Yes! That is, perhaps I don't . . . probably not, in fact . . .

BENARE. On the first day of school, I used to put nice fresh covers on every book I had. On the first page I used to write, in beautiful tiny letters, with pictures of flowers and things:

> The grass is green,
> The rose is red.
> This book is mine
> Till I am dead!

Till I am dead! And do you know what happened?

SAMANT. What happened?

BENARE. Every single book got torn one by one and went I don't know where—but I am still here. I am not dead! Not dead! The grass is still green. the rose is still red, but I am not dead! [*She starts laughing once more.*]

ROKDE [*Quickly takes a notebook out of his bag and starts writing down the verse.*]

That's lovely! The grass is—green. The—rose—is—red . . . What was the rest of it, Miss Benare?

BENARE [*the smile off her face*]. Rokde, this is a bad habit! I always tell the girls in class, don't be in a hurry to write down what you've hardly heard! First listen . . . say it to yourself slowly . . . send it deep inside you. Then it'll stay with you. It must mingle with your blood. It'll only stay once it's in your blood. No one can take it from you then—or make you forget it!

SAMANT. Our dear teacher used to say the same thing. He taught us verses by heart in just this way. Only, he didn't say all that about blood . . .

SUKHATME. Go on, Miss Benare.

BENARE [*suddenly expansive*]. Shall I tell you a story? Children, be seated. There was once a wolf . . .

ROKDE [*suddenly sitting down cross-legged*]. Do tell it, miss. Sit down, Mr Sukhatme. Ponkshe, sit down.

[*Ponkshe goes out with a look of annoyance on his face.*]

BENARE. No. I'll recite a poem . . .

> Our feet tread on upon unknown
> And dangerous pathways evermore.
> Wave after blinded wave is shattered
> Stormily upon the shore.
> Light glows alive again. Again
> It mingles with the dark of night.
> Our earthen hands burn out, and then
> Again in flames they are alight.
> Everything is fully known,
> And everything is clear to see.

> And the wound that's born to bleed
> Bleeds on for ever, faithfully.
> There is a battle sometimes, where
> Defeat is destined as the end.
> Some experiences are meant
> To taste, then just to waste and spend . . .*

[*leaving the poem in the middle*]. No—I'll sing a song. 'An old man from Malad came up to the fireside . . . An old man from Malad, the old man's wife, the wife's little baby, the baby's nurse, the nurse's visitor . . .'

[*Sukhatme seated. Samant curious. As Benare sings, for a moment they all start beating the rhythm. Sukhatme claps hands as if at a religious ceremony. Enter the experimental theatre actor, Karnik. He is chewing pan.*]

KARNIK [*entering*]. Here we are. I thought I had lost my way. [*He notices the others.*] What's happened?

ROKDE. Oh no! That's spoilt everything!

SUKHATME. Benare was singing. [*In affected tones*]. Very nice. Very sweet, Miss Benare.

[*Benare sticks out her tongue at him to signify 'I know what you mean!' and goes on laughing. Karnik is gazing round the hall. Rokde stands up.*]

SUKHATME [*in a flamboyant lawyer's voice*]. One minute, Mr Karnik! shall I tell you what's going through your mind right now? This hall, you are thinking, is ideal for Intimate Theatre—in other words, for those plays of yours for a tiny audience. Which go over their heads in any case! Yes or not? Answer me.

KARNIK [*on purpose, calmly chewing his* pan]. No. I was saying to myself, this hall would put even a real court to shame.

BENARE. *Goodness!* That's wonderful! Our mock court tonight should go over well! Just like a real one!

ROKDE [*anxiously*]. But where's Mrs Kashikar got to?

KARNIK [*chewing his* pan]. She's on her way here. They stopped because Mr Kashikar wanted to buy a garland for her hair. So I

* From a Marathi poem by Mrs Shirish Pai.
Vijay Tendulkar, in the preface to the Marathi original of this play, writes, 'The central character of Miss Benare came to me through a poem. This beautiful poem by Mrs Shirish Pai has been put into the first Act, in the lips of Miss Benare herself.'

bought my *pan*, and came ahead. Rokde, I hope the mike's batteries are all right. Test them now if you like. Or else you'll make a mess of it tonight! We must avoid last-minute disasters. But somehow they always happen. Last month, right in the middle of our show, a fuse blew! I myself was on stage. So what if the role was a small one? Somehow or other I managed to carry it off.

ROKDE. It was just an ordinary amateur play for the Ganapati Puja.

KARNIK. But the *mood* was destroyed!

BENARE [*yawns; then mischievously*]. Oh, it's not at what you were saying, Karnik. You see, I have to get up so early every day. There's the Morning Session, then the Afternoon Session. And on top of that, private tuition in the evening! I say, who's noticed something about Mr and Mrs Kashikar?

ROKDE [*with instinctive, unconscious interest*]. What?

PONKSHE [*re-entering*]. Yes, what?

SUKHATME. I'll tell you. But no, I won't. You tell us yourself first, Miss Benare . . . eh? Let me see . . . come on—out with it—

BENARE. You haven't understood a thing, Sukhatme. Don't give yourself those meaningless legal airs! Well, although our Kashikar is a social worker and Mrs Kashikar is quite—er—quite uneducated and so on—of course, *I* don't think that education has any connection with a person's intelligence—well, although Mrs Kashikar is not so educated, they are both so full of life! I mean, Mr Kashikar buys garlands for Mrs Kashikar. Mrs Kashikar buys readymade bush-shirts for Mr Kashikar . . . It really makes one feel nice to see it!

[*Karnik opens a window backstage, spits* pan *juice through it, and comes downstage again.*]

KARNIK. When I for one see such public formalities between husband and wife, I suspect something quite different in private.

ROKDE [*rather angrily*]. That's the effect of modern theatre!

KARNIK. Don't meddle in what you don't understand, Rokde. You're still a child. Just stick to your college work. For my part, I never buy garlands for my wife. Even if I feel like it, I suppress the idea.

[*Benare tut-tuts audibly.*]

What's the matter?

BENARE. If I were in your place, I would buy one for her daily!

SUKHATME. Then hurry up and start buying bush-shirts for your husband, Miss Benare! I wonder what that most fortunate man will be like! If he's half as mischievous as you are, you've both had it!

BENARE. Never mind about that. [*suddenly looking around, to Samant*] Couldn't we please have some chairs here, Mr—What's-your-name—

SAMANT. Chairs? Oh, my name's Samant, I mean! [*Gets up and looks here and there*]. I'll have a look. How should I know . . . [*Exits, hunting.*]

PONKSHE. They're inside. Folding chairs. I could do with some tea.

SUKHATME. When we had some at the station, you said no. ['*So now do without,' says his tone.*]

PONKSHE. Gosh, I didn't want it then. I don't agree with the way you people plan everything in advance. Call that living? In this scientific age, it's fun to get everything at the last minute, without effort. [*Snaps his fingers.*] Like that!

[*Just then, Samant enters from the inner room, and stands in the doorway, both arms full of as many folding chairs as he can carry.*]

SAMANT [*putting them down in the hall*]. There are more if you want. Inside. [*All of them snappily open the chairs and sit down wherever they can. Conversation. Ponkshe still standing showing off his pipe*].

SAMANT [*to Ponkshe, awed by his sahib-like appearance*]. Do sit down, sahib.

PONKSHE [*pleased at the 'sahib'*]. No, thank you. I was sitting in the train. Er—what's your name?

SAMANT. Samant. I'm from this village, sir.

PONKSHE. Good! Can we have some tea here?

SAMANT. Tea? Yes, sir. But sugar will be the problem. You can't get sugar these days. If *gur* will do—

PONKSHE. No. You probably don't know, Mr Samant. *Gur* in tea is poisonous.

SAMANT. But at our house, that's what we grown-ups usually take. Normally the sugar ration isn't even enough for my brother's children. They just can't drink tea without sugar. So what can we do?

PONKSHE [*pipe in mouth, most scientist-like*]. Hmm!

BENARE [*unable to resist teasing him, mimics him from where she is sitting*]. Hmm. Once there was a Hmm! And he knew a girl called Erhmm!

PONKSHE. Stop it, Benare! Don't be childish. [*Samant still standing. Mr and Mrs Kashikar enter.*]

MRS KASHIKAR [*unconsciously stroking the garland in her hair*]. Look, here they all are, after all!

SUKHATME. Come in, Kashikar! How did the garland-buying go?

[*Benare is pointing them out to Samant with gestures.*]

ROKDE [*coming forward*]. Yes, how did it?

MRS KASHIKAR. Balu, have you brought all the luggage?

ROKDE. Absolutely.

KASHIKAR. Each time you say you've brought it all, Rokde, and each time you forget something. Have you got the usher's staff? Don't just nod your head. Show it if you have it. Let me see.

ROKDE [*producing it*]. Here it is. [*Pathetically*] I've got the uniform too. I only forget things sometimes. Not all the time.

KASHIKAR. I don't care if you always forget. At least today I hope everything's in order. Or you'll make a mess of things. My judge's wig? Did you bring it?

ROKDE. Yes. I brought that first. [*Rokde grows increasingly miserable and irritated.*]

KASHIKAR. You, Sukhatme? Did you bring your lawyer's gown?

SUKHATME [*bowing as if in court*]. Yes, milord! I don't forget that even in my dreams! What about you, Ponkshe?

PONKSHE. Well, I come fully dressed, so I won't forget a thing. I have this nervous temperament a bit, you know. If I don't have my pipe, I can't remember a thing in the witness-box.

MRS KASHIKAR. I'll rehearse your lines with you a little, before today's show.

PONKSHE. No need for that.

MRS KASHIKAR. I say, Benare—[*stroking the garland in her hair*] I did mean to buy a garland for you too—

BENARE [*in Ponkshe's tones*]. Hmm!

[*Ponkshe bites his lips angrily.*]

MRS KASHIKAR [*to Mr Kashikar*]. Didn't I, dear? But what happened was that—

BENARE [*laughing heartily*].—The garland flew away—pouf! Or did the dicky-bird take it? I never want garlands. If I did, couldn't I afford to buy them? I earn my own living, you know. That's why I never feel like buying garlands and things.

[*Benare hands out the snacks Mrs Kashikar has brought.*]

MRS KASHIKAR. Well, what does your school have to say for itself?

BENARE [*carefully*]. My school says nothing.

KASHIKAR. I wonder, should we have the judge's chair this side or that?

KARNIK. Here, of course. The entrance is over there. That room next door can be used for the judge. You can enter from there. President Johnson will stand over here like this—

SAMANT [*amazed*]. President Johnson!

KASHIKAR. No, no. Johnson's dock should be left over there. So when I speak as the judge—

KARNIK. I don't agree. If you look at it from the audience's point of view, it should be right here—

SUKHATME. Mr Karnik, I shall prosecute you for seeing things from the audience's point of view! And you a man of the modern theatre! [*A lawyer's laugh.*]

KARNIK. Yet again! Will someone please tell me what this Modern Theatre is supposed to be? People just play with words without knowing what they mean. I do what seems right to me. Whether it's modern or old-fashioned doesn't matter. [*They begin to argue.*]

SAMANT [*stopping Rokde*]. What's this business about President Johnson?

ROKDE [*Deep in his own thoughts, starts*]. Who?

SAMANT. They said 'President Johnson' or something just now.

ROKDE. Oh, that!

SAMANT. Do you mean President Johnson will really—probably he won't, however—I mean, what's it all about?

ROKDE. Not the real one! This fellow Karnik here plays him! [*He is getting his revenge on Karnik for putting him in his place earlier.*]

SAMANT. President Johnson!

ROKDE [*Suddenly remembering, comes and stops Mrs Kashikar*]. Madam, Professor Damle hasn't arrived yet!

[*Benare, who had been talking to Mrs Kashikar, suddenly falls silent and motionless. Then she goes by mistake to Ponkshe, and stands talking to him, with an artificial air. He is silent.*]

MRS KASHIKAR. Well, he'll come late as usual. He told me on the phone that he wouldn't be able to catch our train. He was doing a symposium—or something—in the university. I've told him about this twice. Benare, did you meet him?

BENARE [*who is talking to Ponkshe*]. Whom?

MRS KASHIKAR. Professor Damle.

BENARE. No, I didn't.

[*Starts talking to Ponkshe again. He is silent. No response at all.*]

ROKDE [*after consulting Samant, to Mrs Kashikar*]. But madam, Samant here says that the next train doesn't reach here till nine p.m. How will that do? It'll be too late!

PONKSHE [*in the gap in the conversation*]. What happened afterwards to that friend of yours, Miss Benare? That girl—the one in trouble—whom you found for me to marry . . .

[*Benare confused. In her confusion she goes to Samant.*]

MRS KASHIKAR. There was a train in between, wasn't there? [*to Kashikar*] Dear, Balu here says there's no train in between—

KASHIKAR [*interrupting his argument with Karnik*]. In between what?

ROKDE [*to him*]. Samant here says there's no train now before the show!

SUKHATME. There's one afterwards, isn't there? That's good enough!

KASHIKAR. But my dear Sukhatme, how will Professor Damle get here? He'll arrive late. If he comes at all! There's no train in between.

KARNIK. Then he won't come at all, I'm telling you. Professor Damle is quite calculating, that way. When you talk of being late, he just cancels the programme, and sits comfortably at home.

ROKDE [*tense*]. Madam, I did drop a postcard to him as usual—when I sent one to all the others—I mean, it's no fault of mine—I even wrote the address right—

KASHIKAR. Here's a hitch!

SUKHATME. What's so serious about it? Don't worry in the least!

KASHIKAR. How can I not worry? We owe something to the people, Sukhatme. A performance is no laughing matter.

PONKSHE [*coming up*]. What's happened?

MRS KASHIKAR [*to Sukhatme*]. But now who'll play the counsel for the accused?

SUKHATME. Don't you worry. For today, I'll do that role along with that of the prosecuting counsel. What's so serious about that? I'm a lawyer to the marrow! I tell you, Kashikar, just leave it to me.

KARNIK. Yes, I think that will be much more dramatic!

PONKSHE. Definitely! [*A pompous puff at his pipe.*]

BENARE. Definitely!

[*Ponkshe looks at her angrily.*]

ROKDE [*consulting a paper he is holding*]. And the fourth witness. Mr Sukhatme, he's missing, too. Rawte is sick with flu. We'd decided to take a local man. [*He catches sight of Mrs Kashikar, and corrects himself.*] That is, *you* had decided . . .

SUKHATME. True. A local man—that means . . .

ROKDE [*gathering up his courage*]. Can I please do that part today? It's just a small one—anyone can do mine—I know the fourth witness's lines off by heart . . .

KARNIK. I oppose it! Even if you're just an usher, your character isn't an easy one to play. So what if he has no lines? It can't be managed by putting up someone else at the last minute. Stick to your part, Rokde.

ROKDE. But how does it matter if just one day I play another role?

KASHIKAR. No.

MRS KASHIKAR. Balu, if he says no, then don't do it! [*Rokde falls back.*] But then, who will be the fourth witness?

SUKHATME [*starting at Samant*]. I—know! [*suddenly*] Here's your fourth witness—[*points to him*] Samant!

SAMANT [*starting*]. What's the matter?

PONKSHE [*puffing at his pipe*]. Not bad!

KASHIKAR [*to Samant*]. Have you ever acted in a play?

SAMANT. Good heavens, no! Never at all. What's the matter?

MRS KASHIKAR. Will you be the fourth witness? Look here, Benare. [*She comes over.*] What do you think of this gentleman as the fourth witness?

BENARE. This gentleman? Not bad—I think he's lovely!

[*Samant embarrassed. Benare smiling.*]

As a witness, I mean. The fourth witness.

SUKHATME. Mrs Kashikar, Karnik, Ponkshe, don't worry! I'll take the responsibility. Nothing to it! I'll prepare him. Mister—what's your name?—

SAMANT. Raghu Samant.

SUKHATME. Mr Samant, you have been called as fourth witness for today's Living Lawcourt.

SAMANT [*flabbergasted and trembling*]. But I honestly don't know anything about it!

MRS KASHIKAR. You've seen a court, haven't you?

SAMANT. Never in my life!

KARNIK. In a play, at least?

SAMANT. No. Not at all! No play like that has ever been seen here.

SUKHATME [*taunting Karnik*]. It's a good thing, he hasn't seen a courtroom in a play. At least he won't have all kinds of wrong notions about it!

KARNIK. Confine your remarks to *certain* plays!

SUKHATME. Mr Samant, I'll have you word-perfect before the show. After all, you don't have to teach a lawyer how to coach witnesses! [*He gives a lawyer's laugh.*]

SAMANT. But I'm not used to it at all! The very thought that it's a court will terrify me!

MRS KASHIKAR. I suggest we have a rehearsal with him. [*to Mr Kashikar*] What do you think, dear? [*He pays no attention, so*] What do you think, Benare?

BENARE. Yes. I've no objection at all. I was wondering what to do till the show. I forgot to bring a book to read.

SAMANT. Oh. Would you like the new novel by Suryakant Phatarphekar? I've just got it. [*Fishes it out and proffers·it.*] His novels are so thrilling! This is the 105th.

BENARE. Then I certainly don't want it!

SUKHATME. Well, we have the Bible and the Bhagavad-Geeta for the oath-taking—I mention it because you want something to read. By the way, Rokde, you did bring along the Bible and the Geeta, didn't you? Or have you forgotten?

ROKDE [*in an agonized voice*]. No, they're here. I'll show them to you if you want.

[*Goes towards the bags. But doesn't show the Geeta.*]

BENARE. Learned Counsel, I'm not yet so old as to be reading *those* books!

KASHIKAR. Then you must be reading *True Stories* or magazines like that. That's what my wife reads. Quite amusing, they are. Because of my social work, I can't manage to do more than look at the pictures.

MRS KASHIKAR [*protesting*]. Really!

KASHIKAR [*annoyed*]. What do you mean, 'Really'! Wasn't I speaking the truth?

[*Mrs Kashikar's face falls.*]

KARNIK. I think the idea of a rehearsal is excellent. If only someone would fetch four or five packets of cigarettes. That's all we need, so we won't have to go out in the middle.

PONKSHE. I don't mind. [*Puffing at his pipe.*]

SAMANT [*to Rokde*]. Then it doesn't matter. If I see it all once, there's no question about it. That'll reassure me. Eh?

[*Rokde doesn't answer.*]

BENARE. Shall I tell you something? We've done tonight's atomic weapons trial seven times in the past three months. Tonight's the eighth time. I've no objection to doing it once more before that. But I do think tonight's proper show will fall flat.

SUKHATME. I agree with Miss Benare. I have an idea. See if you like it. When we lawyers are at ease in the barristers' room, we sometimes play rummy. Or patience. Or a certain other game. Just to pass the time, that's all. You bring a new and imaginary case against someone. Eh? Shall we do that? Let's have an imaginary case. So Samant here will understand how a court works. And we'll pass the time more pleasantly. What do you say, Mr Kashikar? Do we have your sanction?

KASHIKAR. That's all right. It doesn't do for a man in public life to show too much hesitation. One must act according to the majority's wishes.

KARNIK [*excited*]. Three cheers for this new idea! In Drama Theory we call this a Visual Enactment. I heard of it at the Government Drama Camp last year.

SUKHATME. Why give such a hard name to a simple thing? This is just a game. Eh, Miss Benare?

BENARE. I'm even willing to play hopscotch, if you're talking of games. Games are very good for you. I often play quite happily with the children at school. It's fun.

PONKSHE. All right, we'll play. Mr Samant, could you please fetch some packets of cigarettes from the corner? Capstans for me. Here you are. [*Gives him money.*]

MRS KASHIKAR. Why are you paying, Ponkshe? Samant, give it back. What I say is, let's call it Performance Expenses—that'll be all right. In any case, we have to demonstrate our lawcourt to Samant because of the performance, don't we? That settles it. Samant, [*opening her purse, and taking out a banknote*] take this. Bring half a dozen packets of the kind everyone wants. And bring some *pan*, three or four. Sweet ones.

SAMANT. Yes. [*Goes out with the money. Coming back*] Don't start, will you? I'll be back in a minute. [*Exit.*]

BENARE. Poor thing! I'll be back.

[*Takes a face towel and a cake of soap out of her basket. Goes inside humming to herself.*]

MRS KASHIKAR. Balu, start arranging the court.

[*He sets to work.*]

KARNIK. **Ponkshe, come here a minute.** [*To Sukhatme and the others*] The same cast as tonight? In other words, the same judge, counsel etc.?

SUKHATME. Oh yes. By all means. Why change it? I'll play the lawyers.

MRS KASHIKAR. But what I say is, let the accused at least be different. What do you think, Karnik?

KARNIK. No. It's not necessary. [*Aside to Ponkshe, who has reached him*] Do you know something, Ponkshe?

PONKSHE. What?

KARNIK [*indicating the inner room*]. About her? About Miss Benare. Rokde told me.

PONKSHE. What?

KARNIK. Not now. Remind me tonight. After the show.

PONKSHE. I've got something to tell you, too. About Miss Benare. [*To the others*] If you ask me, it's a good idea. A different prisoner.

KASHIKAR. It'll add that bit of variety, I would say.

MRS KASHIKAR. Exactly.

KASHIKAR. What do you mean, exactly? Hold your tongue. Can't say a word! . . .

[*Mrs Kashikar is silenced.*]

SUKHATME. I don't mind. The accused—I feel—why not Rokde? [*Rokde is delighted.*]

ROKDE. Yes, indeed. I'm ready to—

PONKSHE. No! [*To Karnik*] I also have something to tell you— about her!

KARNIK. I'll be the accused.

KASHIKAR. I suggest that if we are going through with it, it should not be a frivolous, facetious affair! I'll be the accused, Sukhatme. Make me the accused.

KARNIK. What importance for him! He'll be the judge, he'll be the accused!

PONKSHE [*puffing at his pipe*]. Consider me, then! I'm not keen, as such, you know. But if I'll do, I'm game.

ROKDE [*to Mrs Kashikar*]. But what's wrong with me, madam?

MRS KASHIKAR. Shall I do it? I will if you like.

KASHIKAR. No!

[*Mrs Kashikar falls silent.*]

She can't get among a few people without wanting to show off! Shows off all the time!

MRS KASHIKAR [*quite put out*]. Enough. I won't do it! Satisfied? [*She is thoroughly disheartened.*]

SUKHATME. We don't need to take any of you. Kashikar, let's have a really different kind of accused. Eh? Let's have our Miss Benare! Eh, Ponkshe? What d'you think of my choice?

PONKSHE. It's good.

SUKHATME. Then where's the need for argument? Well, Mrs Kashikar?

MRS KASHIKAR. If you say so, it's all right. In any case, we'll be able to see what the trial of a woman is like. [*Out of sheer habit, to Mr Kashikar*] Isn't that so, dear? One should have that experience—

KASHIKAR [*sarcastically*]. Of course! I suppose they're just about to make you a judge of the Supreme Court!—

MRS KASHIKAR. That's not how I meant it . . .

SUKHATME. There's not much difference between one trial and another. But when there's a woman in the dock, the case does have a different complexion, that's true. That is my experience. Well, Mr Karnik?

KARNIK. It's all right. I won't stay outside the team. I believe in team spirit.

MRS KASHIKAR. Then it's settled. Our accused for now is Benare. But what's the charge?

KASHIKAR. It should be a charge with social significance.

PONKSHE. All right. [*Gets up.*] Sh! Shall we do something? Come to me, all of you. Come on. Come here.

[*Whispers some plan to them, gesticulating. Every now and then, he points to the room where Benare is.*]

KASHIKAR. Rokde, haven't you finished arranging the court yet?

ROKDE. I've finished. [*Bustles about, showing haste.*]

KARNIK. That's why I drew you a ground plan, Rokde. To show which properties go where.

ROKDE [*angrily*]. I don't understand your theatrical matters. I'm not used to them.

[*All of them arrange the furniture as in court, Ponkshe taking the lead. Kashikar supervises. On Ponkshe's instructions Rokde picks up Benare's purse from the luggage on the dais, and places it on a stool at left. The furniture arrangement is completed. Ponkshe and Kashikar go and stand by the door of the inner room. All the others go into the wings at the left.*]

KASHIKAR [*to the people going into the wings*]. I'll give you a signal.

[*Now Benare comes out singing, wiping her face on the towel. She looks very fresh.*]

BENARE [*singing while she puts away the napkin, soap etc. in the basket on the dais at right.*]

> The parrot to the sparrow said,
> 'Why, oh why are your eyes so red?'
> 'Oh, my dear friend, what shall I say?
> Someone has stolen my nest away.'
> Sparrow, sparrow, poor little sparrow!

PONKSHE [*coming from the doorway of the inner room and standing before Miss Benare on the dais*]. Miss Leela Benare, you have been arrested on suspicion of a crime of an extremely grave nature, and brought as a prisoner before the bar of this court.

[*She stiffens where she is. She looks around her numbly. He is gazing at her. She goes towards the wings at left, looking for her purse, to put the comb in her hands away. Picks up the purse from the stool. Meanwhile, Kashikar comes and seats himself on the judge's chair on the dais. He signals to the people in the wings. Karnik and Rokde silently bring the wooden dock and arrange it around Benare. Sukhatme comes from the wings putting on his black lawyer's gown, and sits in a chair next to the broken-down lawyer's table. The others go to their places. Samant enters and stands in the doorway.*]

KASHIKAR [*clearing his throat*]. Prisoner Miss Benare, under Section No. 302 of the Indian Penal Code you are accused of the crime of infanticide. Are you guilty or not guilty of the aforementioned crime?

[*Benare looks stunned. All are silent for the moment. The atmosphere is extraordinarily sombre.*]

CURTAIN

ACT TWO

The same hall. The situation is the same as at the end of Act One.

KASHIKAR [*sitting at the table with the dignity of a judge*]. Prisoner Miss Benare, under Section No. 302 of the Indian Penal Code, you have been accused of the crime of infanticide. Are you guilty or not guilty of the aforementioned crime?

[*The atmosphere is extraordinarily sombre. Miss Benare stands numbly with a chair for support.*]

SAMANT [*still standing in the doorway, says softly to Karnik.*] Here they are. *Masala pan* and cigarettes.

[*At this, the atmosphere at once lightens.*]

MRS KASHIKAR. A sweet one for me.

KARNIK. A packet of Wills for me.

PONKSHE. Samant, one special *pan* here.

SUKHATME. One *pan*, one packet of *beedis*. What about you, Kashikar?

KASHIKAR. A *masala pan*.

[*Rokde takes the* pan *from Samant and brings it over to Kashikar.*]

ROKDE [*with great politeness, to Kashikar*]. I've taken the astringent out of it.

SUKHATME [*offering a pan to Benare*]. Here, have one, Miss Benare.

BENARE [*who is sitting on the chair*]. What? Yes—I mean no. Thank you.

SUKHATME. Why are you so grave all of a sudden? After all, it's a game. Just a game, that's all. Why are you so serious?

BENARE [*trying to laugh*]. Who's serious? I'm absolutely—light-hearted. I just got a bit serious to create the right atmosphere. For the court, that's all. Why should I be afraid of a trial like this?

SAMANT [*lighting a cigarette Karnik has given him, to Karnik*]. It seems there was some joke just now?

KARNIK [*inhaling*]. What joke?

SAMANT. No, he made some accusation—Mr Kashikar . . . but I didn't quite catch it.

KARNIK. The charge? Infanticide.

SAMANT. That's right. But what's that? I just don't understand, that's why I ask . . . I'm just an ignorant person.

SUKHATME. The crime of killing a new-born child.

SAMANT. Good heavens! A terrible charge! That's exactly what happened in our village—it must be one or two years ago now—the poor woman was a widow.

SUKHATME. Is that so? Who was the lawyer on the case? Kashikar, you've really picked some charge! A first-class charge! There's no fun in a case unless there's a really thundering charge!

KASHIKAR. Did you notice, also, Sukhatme, that this charge is important from the social point of view? The question of infanticide is one of great social significance. That's why I deliberately picked it. We consider society's best interests in all we do. Come on, Miss Benare. Rokde, my gavel.

[*Rokde brings over the gavel fussily.*]

It wouldn't have mattered, if I didn't have it just now. I was checking whether you'd brought it. [*Banging the gavel*] Now to business. Come on, come on, Sukhatme. Make a start. *Adhikasya adhikam phalam.* 'Best efforts bring best results.' First my earpick . . . [*Searches for it in his pocket, and places it by him.*]

SUKHATME [*moving his lawyer's gown about with an important air, and chewing pan*]. Milord, in the interests of the smooth functioning of the matter before this court, I beseech the court for an adjournment of a quarter minute at the beginning, so that all present may spit out the *pan* in their mouths.

KASHIKAR [*spitting out bits of pan with all the dignity of a judge*]. Counsel for the accused should present his plea in the matter.

SUKHATME [*immediately rising,* and *becoming the counsel for the accused*]. Milord, I strictly oppose the suggestion of my learned friend, the counsel for the prosecution. Whereas ten seconds are enough to spit out *pan*, my learned friend is asking for a quarter minute. It is clear that my learned friend has an aim of wasting time, which is injurious and troublesome to my client. Therefore we move that an adjournment of ten seconds only be granted.

BENARE [*unable to restrain herself*]. Yes. Or else no—only nine-and-a-half seconds.

KASHIKAR. Miss Benare, the accused is not supposed to interrupt the court. It's one thing for Samant. But should I have to explain the court's etiquette to you afresh? [*Gravely summoning Karnik.*] Clerk of the court, please bring to the attention of this court the legal precedent concerning the matter which has been moved before us.

KARNIK [*removing the cigarette from his mouth, and blowing out a great deal of smoke*]. Considering that it has not been the normal practice in court to conduct a case while chewing *pan*, I do not think any precedent has been established in this matter. Moreover, this instance of a judge's chewing *pan* in court is the first one, and so somewhat unprecedented, Milord.

KASHIKAR. Counsel for the defence, are you able to establish before the court that it is possible to spit out *pan* in ten seconds?

SUKHATME. By all means. [*Goes outside, spits, and shutting the door*] Exactly ten seconds, Milord.

KASHIKAR. We must see for ourselves. [*Rising, goes inside to do just that.*]

BENARE [*sighing*]. Is this a court of law, Karnik, or a spitting contest?

[*Karnik pays no attention.*]

SAMANT [*after a moment, to Karnik*]. Sir, does a real court truly work like this? It's very interesting.

KARNIK [*blowing out cigarette smoke, with mock seriousness*]. Ssh. You'll commit contempt of court. Just listen. [*Winks at Ponkshe.*]

KASHIKAR [*coming back and sitting down*]. Clerk of the court, how long did that take?

KARNIK [*looking at his watch*]. Who knows?

MRS KASHIKAR. I'll tell you. It was fifteen seconds.

SUKHATME [*As the counsel for the prosecution, with a triumphant laugh*]. There! Not ten, but a full fifteen seconds—that is, a quarter minute. A quarter minute! Exactly the time I told you, Milord.

KASHIKAR [*maintaining his grave manner throughout*]. Yes. Now, seeing that more than half a minute of the court's time has been wasted in this research and experimentation on the subject of spitting *pan*, it is this court's serious decision that the matter before it should proceed without further delay. So long as it is done individually by you, and is inoffensive to the court, everyone may of course spit *pan*.

PONKSHE [*rising*]. Hear, hear!

KASHIKAR [*banging his gavel*]. Silence! Silence must be observed.

MRS KASHIKAR [*to Samant*]. Samant, all this about *pan* and so on is just in fun, you know. Just notice the practice in court. The important thing is, you need the court's permission for everything. Or you'll make a mistake tonight.

SAMANT [*excitedly*]. No. Of course, I'm watching. But—

KASHIKAR [*banging the gavel*]. Silence must be observed while the court is in session. Can't shut up at home, can't shut up here!

MRS KASHIKAR. But I was just telling Samant here—

SUKHATME. Let it pass, Mrs Kashikar. He's just joking.

MRS KASHIKAR. So what? Scolding me at every step!

BENARE [*a little worried, to Rokde, who is playing the usher*]. I say, Balu . . .

ROKDE [*angry but controlling his voice*]. Don't call me Balu!

KASHIKAR [*clearing his throat, and banging the gavel*]. Now, back to infanticide. Prisoner Miss Leela Benare, are you guilty or not guilty of the charge that has been brought against you?

BENARE. Would *you* admit yourself guilty of it?

KASHIKAR [*banging the gavel*]. Order, order! The dignity of the court must be preserved at all costs. Or Samant will not grasp how a court really works.

BENARE. Or how infanticide really works? Really, I don't like your word at all! Infanticide . . . infanticide! Why don't you accuse me instead of—um—snatching public property! That has a nice sound about it, don't you think? Sounds like 'snacking'!

MRS KASHIKAR. I don't think so at all. There's nothing wrong with the present charge.

BENARE [*banging her hand on the chair*]. Order, order! The dignity of the court must be preserved at all costs. Can't shut up at home, can't shut up here! [*Imitating a lawyer*] Milord, let the court's family be given a suitable reprimand. She has never committed the crime of infanticide. Or stolen any public property except for Milord himself!

MRS KASHIKAR. That's enough, Benare!

BENARE [*softly, to the usher Rokde*]. I say, Balu—[*He bites his lips angrily.*]

SAMANT [*enthusiastically, to Mrs Kashikar*]. Ha ha! Miss Benare is really amazing!

PONKSHE [*seriously*]. In many respects.

KASHIKAR. Prisoner Miss Benare, for abrogating the authority of counsel, and for obstructing the due process of the law, a reprimand is hereby issued to you.

BENARE [*getting up from her seat, and coming up to him, and offering him the pan nèar him*]. Thanks! For that, a *masala pan* is hereby issued to you.

KARNIK. This is it! This is what I meant! If nothing is going to be taken seriously at all, there's the end of the matter. Miss Benare, at least so that Samant can understand something, please obey the rules of the court. Be serious!

SUKHATME. Otherwise, this game becomes really childish. We need seriousness.

BENARE [*coming back to her place*]. Now, back to infanticide. I was wrong, Milord. But there's no reason for the prisoner to show such respect for the judge. I plead not guilty. I couldn't even kill a common cockroach. I'm scared to do it. How could I kill a newborn child? I know I got annoyed this morning in my class at school. And gave a naughty pupil a good whack! So what? What can one do? The brats won't listen to you.

KASHIKAR. Rokde, the book for the oath-taking?

[*Rokde hurriedly takes out a fat volume, places it on the stool nearby.*]

The witness-box?

[*Rokde goes to fetch it.*]

MRS KASHIKAR [*to Samant*]. After this, there's the prosecution's speech.

SUKHATME [*who is sitting with his feet stretched across another chair, and his hands clasped behind his head, gets up lazily. Mechanically, he says*] Milord, the nature of the charge brought against the accused [*lights up his* beedi *from Karnik's cigarette, and breathes out smoke*] is a most terrible one. Motherhood is a sacred thing—

BENARE. How do *you* know? [*seeing everyone's expressions*] Order, order!

[*Ponkshe, fed up, goes into the inner room.*]

KASHIKAR. Prisoner Miss Benare, for obstructing the work of the court, a second reprimand is hereby issued to you. Counsel for the prosecution, continue.

SUKHATME. Motherhood is pure. Moreover, there is a great—er —a great nobility in our concept of motherhood. We have acknowledged woman as the mother of mankind. Our culture enjoins us to perpetual worship of her. 'Be thy mother as a god' is what we teach our children from infancy. There is great responsibility devolving upon a mother. She weaves a magic circle with her whole existence in order to protect and preserve her little one—

KASHIKAR. You've forgotten one thing. There's a Sanskrit proverb, *Janani janmabhumishcha svargadapi gariyasi.*

> 'Mother and
> The Motherland,
> Both are even
> Higher than heaven.'

MRS KASHIKAR [*with enthusiasm*]. And of course, 'Great are thy favours, O mother' is quite famous.

BENARE. Order, order! This is all straight out of a school composition-book. [*Bites her tongue ironically.*] Prisoner Miss Benare, for abrogating the authority of the court, a reprimand is *once more* issued to you! [*Pretends to bang a gavel.*]

SUKHATME. I am deeply grateful, Milord, for your addition. In short, 'Woman is a wife for a moment, but a mother for ever.'

[*Samant claps.*]

MRS KASHIKAR. It's all right now, but you mustn't do that tonight, you know.

SAMANT. All right. I just couldn't help it. What a sentence, eh?

SUKHATME. It is true. Considering this, what would we respectable citizens say if any woman were to take the life of the delicate bundle of joy she has borne? We would say, there could be no baser or more devilish thing on earth. I intend to establish by means of evidence that the prisoner has done this same vile deed.

[*Rokde brings the witness-box.*]

BENARE [*softly and mischievously, to Rokde*]. I say, Balu—

[*He is thoroughly annoyed. Ponkshe comes out of the inner room.*]

SUKHATME. My first witness is the world-famous scientist, Mr Gopal Ponkshe. Well, Ponkshe? Are you happy? I've suddenly promoted you to world fame, eh?

KASHIKAR. Call the witness to the witness-box. [*He is picking his ear.*]

[*Ponkshe enters the witness-box. Rokde holds the big volume in front of him.*]

PONKSHE [*glancing at the first page of the volume, and placing his hand on it, says gravely*]. I, G. N. Ponkshe, placing my hand upon the Oxford English Dictionary, do hereby solemnly swear that I shall tell the truth, the whole truth, and nothing but the truth.

[*Benare laughs and laughs.*]

MRS KASHIKAR [*in intimidating tones*]. Balu, where is the Geeta?

ROKDE [*miserably*]. I forgot it. I brought the Dictionary by mistake. [*grumbling*] How much can I possibly remember?

BENARE. Poor Balu!

ROKDE. Don't pity me, I'm warning you!

KASHIKAR [*banging his gavel*]. Begin the examination!

MRS KASHIKAR [*to Samant, in a conspiratorial whisper*]. Just observe this examination. All right?

[*Samant nods his head.*]

SUKHATME [*approaching Ponkshe*]. Your name?

PONKSHE. G. N. Ponkshe. Go further on. We can have all the details tonight.

SUKHATME. Mr Ponkshe, are you acquainted with the accused?

BENARE [*suddenly, in Ponkshe's manner*]. Hmm!

PONKSHE [*looking carefully at Benare*]. Yes. Very well indeed.

SUKHATME. How would you describe her social status?

PONKSHE. A teacher. In other words, a schoolmarm.

BENARE [*sticking her tongue out at him*]. But I'm still quite young!

SUKHATME. Mr Ponkshe, is the accused married or unmarried?

PONKSHE. Why don't you ask the accused?

SUKHATME. But if you were asked, what would you say?

PONKSHE. To the public eye, she is unmarried.

BENARE [*interrupting*]. And to the private eye?

KASHIKAR. Order! Miss Benare, self-control. Don't forget the value of self-control. [*to Sukhatme*] You may continue. I'll just be back. [*Rises and goes to the inner room, where the toilet is.*]

MRS KASHIKAR. All this is all right for now, you know. It won't be like this at night. That'll have to be done properly.

SUKHATME [*to himself*]. The wrong things always seem to happen to Mr Kashikar at the wrong time . . . [*aloud*] Mr Ponkshe, how would you describe your view of the moral conduct of the accused? On the whole like that of a normal unmarried woman? You at least should take this trial seriously.

BENARE. But how should he know what the moral conduct of a normal unmarried woman is like?

PONKSHE [*paying no attention to her*]. It is different.

SUKHATME. For example?

PONKSHE. The accused is a bit too much.

SUKHATME. A bit too much—what does that mean?

PONKSHE. It means—it means that, on the whole, she runs after men too much.

BENARE [*provoking him*]. Tut! tut! tut! Poor man!

SUKHATME. Miss Benare, you are committing contempt of court.

BENARE. The court has gone into that room. So how can contempt of it be committed in this one? There's not much point in that remark, Sukhatme!

[*Samant laughs heartily.*]

SUKHATME [*to Benare*]. There's no point in coming to grips with you! Mr Ponkshe . . .

[*Ponkshe has slid out of the witness-box and is talking to Karnik.*]

Nobody at all is serioŭs!

[*Ponkshe returns to the witness-box.*]

Mr Ponkshe, can you tell me—does the accused have a particularly close relationship with any man—married or unmarried? [*Stressing the words*] Any married or unmarried man?

BENARE [*interrupting*]. Yes, with the counsel for the prosecution himself! And with the judge. To say nothing of Ponkshe, Balu here or Karnik.

ROKDE. Miss Benare, I'm warning you, there'll be trouble!

PONKSHE. In these circumstances, Sukhatme, is there any point in continuing this farce of a trial? Nobody is serious! Kashikar's gone inside. Benare's acting like this. No one lets me speak—

KARNIK. Even the rehearsals for our plays are more serious than this!

MRS KASHIKAR. Don't make trouble, Benare. It won't do if tonight's show's a flop because of you.

BENARE. I'm just helping the trial along.

KASHIKAR [*returning*]. What's happened? Sukhatme, continue. Where's my earpick?

BENARE. I think I'll go out for a stroll through the village. You can carry on your trial. Infanticide! Ha! At least I'll get some fresh air.

KARNIK. If that's so, let's call it a day.

MRS KASHIKAR. No. At least let's finish the trial. Let's at least complete the job in hand.

SAMANT [*courteously, to Mrs Kashikar*]. Does that mean it all ends here?

KASHIKAR [*finding his earpick*]. Found it! Come on now. The hearing is to continue. [*Gestures 'Patience!' to Benare*] Sukhatme, what are you waiting for?

SUKHATME. For your earpick to be located, milord. [*Then, striking the alert attitude of a barrister*] Mr Ponkshe—

[*Ponkshe, who has come out of the witness-box, once more enters it hurriedly.*]

Has anything ever struck you about the prisoner's behaviour?

PONKSHE. Yes, a lot.

SUKHATME. What? [*Breathes out smoke.*]

PONKSHE. The prisoner sometimes acts as if she were off her head. That is, there's sometimes no sense at all in her actions.

SUKHATME. For example?

PONKSHE. For example, once she tried to arrange a marriage for me, and—why go further? Right now she's sticking out her tongue like a lunatic! [*Benare hurriedly retracts her tongue.*]

SUKHATME [*as if he has discovered an important clue*]. Good! You can sit down now, Mr Ponkshe—the great scientist. Our next witness is Mr Karnik—the great actor.

[*Ponkshe comes out and, looking steadily at Benare, goes and leans against the wall at one side. Karnik enters the witness-box dramatically, and strikes an attitude.*]

KARNIK. Ask!

SUKHATME. Oath—name—occupation—all over? Now, Mr Karnik, you are an actor?

KARNIK [*like a witness in a melodrama*]. Yes, and I am proud of it.

SUKHATME. Be proud! But Mr Karnik, do you know this lady? [*Points to Benare.*]

KARNIK [*going through the stage motions of seeing her*]. Yes, sir, I—think—I—know—this—lady.

SUKHATME. What do you mean by 'think', Mr Karnik?

KARNIK. 'Think' means to consider or feel. There's a dictionary here if you want it.

SUKHATME [*who has moved unconsciously towards the dictionary, checks himself, and turns*]. I don't need that. Mr Karnik, please state definitely whether or not you know this lady.

KARNIK [*shrugging his shoulders*]. It's strange! Sometimes we feel we know someone. But in fact we don't. Truth is stranger than fiction.

SUKHATME. How did you get to know each other?

KARNIK. Through this group, you see. We do performances of the Living Lawcourt. She's a member. Yes, I remember it clearly. [*Theatrical throughout.*]

SUKHATME. What kind of performances are those, Mr Karnik?

KARNIK. Smash hits!

SUKHATME [*to Kashikar in a lawyer's tone*].   Milord, I submit that this important statement be noted in the official record.

KASHIKAR [*picking his ear*].   It shall be arranged. Proceed.

SUKHATME.   Mr Karnik, tell me truthfully. In the plays you perform, what is the description of a mother?

KARNIK.   The new plays don't mention them at all. They're all about the futility of life. On the whole, that's all man's life is.

KASHIKAR.   That's it! That's what I disagree with! Men should have some purpose in life. 'Endless is our zeal for striving' should be one's motto. A purpose in life, that's what one needs.

SUKHATME.   Let that pass. If you had to give a definition of a mother, how would you do it?

KARNIK [*after he has thought it over*].   A mother is one who gives birth.

SUKHATME.   Mr Karnik, who is the mother—the woman who protects the infant she has borne—or the one who cruelly strangles it to death? Which definition do you prefer?

KARNIK.   Both are mothers. Because both have given birth.

SUKHATME.   What would you call motherhood?

KARNIK.   Giving birth to a child.

SUKHATME.   But even a bitch gives birth to pups!

KARNIK.   Then she's a mother, of course. Who denied it? Who says only humans can be mothers, and not dogs?

BENARE [*stretching lazily*].   Bully for you, Karnik!

[*Karnik ignores her.*]

SUKHATME.   Karnik's in form today.

KASHIKAR.   Show us the form tonight, Karnik. Just now let's have straight answers.

SUKHATME.   Mr Karnik, think carefully before you answer my next question. What is your opinion of the prisoner's conduct?

KARNIK [*after striking two or three tremendous 'thinking' poses*].   Do you mean, in this mock trial, or in real life?

SUKHATME.   In real life, of course.

KASHIKAR [*picking his ear*].   I think it's better if these little questions refer to the trial, Sukhatme.

KARNIK.   That's right, is it? Then it doesn't matter. I don't know anything about the moral conduct of the accused.

SUKHATME.   Nothing? Are you sure?

KARNIK.   Nothing at all. Nothing where the trial is concerned.

[*Benare's expression is tense.*]

SUKHATME. Mr Karnik—[*with sudden fervour*] Have you, in any circumstances, on any occasion, seen the accused in a compromising situation? Answer yes or no. Yes, or no?

KARNIK. Not me. But Rokde has.

ROKDE [*confused*]. Me? I don't know a thing!

SUKHATME [*his chest swelling in great lawyerlike style*]. Mr Karnik, thank you very much. You may take your seat now.

[*Karnik leaves the witness-box.*]

Now, Mr Rokde, please enter the witness-box. Please enter it.

MRS KASHIKAR [*to Samant*]. You're grasping it all, aren't you?

SAMANT. Yes.

ROKDE [*staying where he is, in total confusion*]. Not me!

SUKHATME. Milord, the usher Rokde's evidence is extremely necessary to the trial. He should be summoned to the witness-box without delay.

ROKDE [*wretchedly*]. I won't come! You'll see! I'll go away—

[*Benare is laughing silently.*]

KASHIKAR. Rokde!—

[*Rokde obediently goes and stands in the witness-box. His body is trembling. He is visibly disturbed.*]

PONKSHE [*to Karnik*]. I say, what did he see?

KARNIK. Who says he did? I was just joking, that's all. You passed the buck to me, I passed it to him. The game's got to go on, hasn't it? Sukhatme's, I mean.

SUKHATME. Oath—name—occupation—to continue, Mr Rokde—

[*Rokde is close to tears.*]

Mr Rokde, you heard Mr Karnik refer to you while giving his evidence. Can you throw any further light on that subject?

MRS KASHIKAR. Balu, now give a marvellous, unbroken bit of evidence! If you can manage this, you'll get a chance later on in the show. You'll never get such a big chance again. Watch it all, Samant, watch it carefully.

[*Kashikar glares at her. Mrs Kashikar is silent.*]

SUKHATME. Speak on, Mr Rokde. What did you see?

[*Rokde is genuinely disturbed. He swallows convulsively.*]

Mr Rokde, take God as your witness, and tell me what you saw there.

[*Rokde is speechless.*]

[*Like a lawyer in a film*] Mr Rokde, what did you see in certain important circumstances, on a certain occasion? Answer me, please.

ROKDE [*with difficulty*]. I saw—hell!

[*This is what he is experiencing at the moment. He is all in a sweat. Benare is laughing unrestrainedly. Karnik winks at Ponkshe.*]

KASHIKAR [*picking his teeth*]. He's been a buffoon like this from the start.

MRS KASHIKAR. Balu, you won't have another chance. Answer him at once! How dare you be so scared! Shouldn't a man have *some* guts about speaking up in public? What do you think, Samant?

SAMANT. But it's difficult . . .

KASHIKAR. Speak quickly, Balu.

BENARE. Speak, Balu, speak. A—B—C—

ROKDE [*to Benare, furious in spite of his state*]. That's enough! [*Wipes away sweat repeatedly.*]

SUKHATME [*abandoning his legal voice*]. Mr Rokde—

ROKDE [*stopping him*]. No. Wait a minute. [*He summons up his courage and looks once or twice towards Benare, who is still laughing at him.*] I'll tell you. I went to his house some time ago—

SUKHATME [*in a lawyer's voice*]. Whose house? Mr Rokde, to whose house did you go?

ROKDE. Don't keep interrupting me! I went to—to Damle's house!

[*Benare tense.*]

PONKSHE. Our Professor Damle?

KARNIK. You must have been to his room in the college hostel, you mean?

ROKDE. Yes. I went there in the evening. As night was falling. And there—*she* was! Miss Benare.

ALL. Who?

ROKDE [*looking at Benare*]. Now laugh! Make fun of me! This lady was there. Damle and this—Miss Benare!

[*Benare has stiffened. Karnik signals to Ponkshe.*]

SAMANT [*to Mrs Kashikar*]. Is this true, or just for the trial?

SUKHATME [*with peculiar care*]. Mr Rokde, you went to Professor Damle's house, as night was falling. What did you see there? [*in a deep, cruel voice*] What did you see?

KASHIKAR [*although he is enjoying it all greatly*]. Sukhatme, I feel this is getting onto too personal a level—

SUKHATME. No, no, no, not at all, milord. It's just for the trial; so, Mr Rokde—

BENARE. I don't agree. I'm telling you! What's all this got to do with the trial?

MRS KASHIKAR. But why are you getting into such a state, Benare? [*to Kashikar*] Go on.

BENARE. There's no need at all to drag my private life into this. I can visit whom I like. Damle wasn't eating me up.

SUKHATME. What did you see there, Rokde? Yes, tell us. Tell us! Miss Benare, listen to me. Don't spoil the mood of the trial. This game's great fun. Just be patient. Now, Rokde, don't be shy—tell everything you saw.

ROKDE [*looking straight ahead, after a pause*]. They were sitting there.

SUKHATME. And?—

ROKDE. What do you mean—and? They were both sitting there— in that room.

SUKHATME. What else did you see?

ROKDE. That's all.

[*Sukhatme is disappointed.*]

But I got such a shock! Sitting there in Damle's room—the night falling . . .

BENARE. What a baby the poor thing is!

ROKDE. Then why did your face fall when you saw me? Just explain that! Damle got rid of me. Without letting me come in. Usually he always asks me in—into the room!

BENARE [*laughing*]. Damle alone knows why he got rid of you. And do you know why you imagine that my face fell? Because Damle snubbed you in front of me. Why should my face fall? It stayed right where it should be!

SUKHATME [*to Kashikar*]. Milord, I submit that what the witness Mr Rokde saw—and he alone knows why he stopped at that—I submit that what he saw be noted in record. Even to an impartial observer, it reveals that Miss Benare's behaviour is certainly suspicious.

BENARE. It reveals nothing of the sort! Tomorrow I may be seen in our Principal's office. Does that mean my behaviour is suspicious? Ha! Our principal is sixty-five!

SUKHATME. Milord, I request that this statement made by the accused may also be noted, as we wish to introduce it in evidence.

BENARE. If you like, I'll give you the names and addresses of twenty-five more people with whom I am alone at times. Holding a trial, are you? Suspicious, indeed. You don't even understand the meaning of simple words!

[*Karnik signals to Ponkshe.*]

SUKHATME. Milord, since I consider that statement, too, to be valuable, the prosecution requests that it be noted in evidence.

KASHIKAR [*picking his teeth*]. Which statement? 'You don't even understand the meaning of words'?

SUKHATME. No—'the names and addresses of 25 people'—with whom she sometimes—

BENARE. A little while ago, Mr . . . Mr . . . Samant and I were quite alone together. Go on, write his name down, too. Why don't you?

SAMANT [*rising suddenly, in confusion*]. No, no, this lady behaved in a most exemplary manner. We just talked of magic shows—hypnotism and the like—that's all—

SUKHATME. Milord, I request that the reference to hypnotism, being most important, should be noted in evidence.

KASHIKAR [*picking his teeth*]. But, Sukhatme, to what extent is all this within the jurisdiction of the court?

KARNIK. This is just a rehearsal, in any case. Just a rehearsal.

PONKSHE. This is just a game. A game, that's all! Which of us is serious about the trial? It's fun, Sukhatme! Do go on. [*To Karnik*] I say, this chap seems to be a good enough lawyer. How's it that his practice is so small?

SAMANT [*to Mrs Kashikar*]. But by hypnotism I only meant—that is—it was nothing—you know—only ordinary hypnotism—

PONKSHE [*making him sit*]. Do sit down! It's all just a joke.

KARNIK. Sukhatme, don't stop. Let the case go on. Well, Mrs Kashikar, what do you think, eh?

MRS KASHIKAR. The whole affair's warming up nicely. I wouldn't have imagined . . . Sukhatme, don't stop; carry on.

SUKHATME [*encouraged by all this*]. Mr Rokde, you may leave the witness-box.

[*Rokde heaves a sigh of relief at this and comes out of the witness-box, to go straight into the inner room.*]

Now, Mr Samant.

SAMANT [*standing up, distrustful and confused*]. Me? Did you say me?

SUKHATME. Come.

[*He indicates the witness-box. Samant comes and stands in it.*]

Don't be scared. You just have to answer—

SAMANT.—the questions I'm asked.

SUKHATME. How very clever you are!

MRS KASHIKAR. There are no odds and ends to remember. Besides, this is just a practice trial. The real one is tonight.

SAMANT. Yes, indeed. It's at night. I'm not at all scared. I just get a bit confused, that's all. [*To Sukhatme*] I'll take the oath, just for practice.

SUKHATME. All right. Usher Rokde!

[*Rokde is absent.*]

SAMANT. I think he's gone there, inside. I'll do it myself. [*At a bound, goes and fetches the dictionary. Placing his hand on it*] I, Raghunath Bhikaji Samant, do hereby swear to tell the truth, the whole truth, and nothing but the truth. True enough for the trial, I mean. Of course, what's true for the trial is quite false really. But I'm just taking the oath for practice. [*His hand is still on the dictionary.*] You see, I don't want the sin of falsehood. [*In apologetic tones*] I'm quite religious . . . The oath's over. Now. [*Enters the witness-box again.*] Go on. [*This is to Sukhatme; then, to Mrs Kashikar*] You see? I'm not frightened. I just get confused because I'm new to all this. [*To Sukhatme*] Well, you may go on.

SUKHATME. Name—occupation—that's all dealt with.

SAMANT. No. Do you want to ask all that? Then go ahead.

SUKHATME. No. Now, Mr—

SAMANT [*proudly*]. Samant. Sometimes people forget my surname. That's why I have to tell it.

SUKHATME. It's all right. Mr Samant, do you know the prisoner, Miss Benare?

SAMANT [*proudly*]. Of course! But not all that well. After all, how well can you get to know a person in two hours or so? But I am acquainted with her. She's a very nice lady.

SUKHATME. But your opinion, or the favourable impression you have formed of her, cannot be regarded as reliable in court, can it?

SAMANT. Yes—No, no, why not? Of course it can. My mother used to be able to sum up a person's worth in just one minute.

From his face! Now the poor thing can't see at all. She's grown too old.

[*Rokde enters and takes up his position. Benare is sitting in the dock, her eyes closed, her chin propped up in one hand.*]

She seems to have fallen asleep. Miss Benare, I mean.

BENARE [*her eyes shut*]. I'm awake. I can never, never sleep just when I want to. Never.

SAMANT. I don't have that problem. I can sleep any time I want. [*To Sukhatme*] What about you?

SUKHATME. My sleeping habits are quite different. When I am going to fall asleep it happens in a flash. Otherwise, I lie awake for hours at a stretch.

KASHIKAR [*still picking his teeth and ears*]. Put some corn oil on your head, Sukhatme, and rub it well in. That's what I do. Whatever important social problem there may be, corn oil gives me peaceful sleep. Basically, if your sleep's calm, your brain's bound to be so too. But if your brain's not calm, how on earth will social problems be solved? Most important things, your brain and your digestion. Both of them!

SAMANT. Yes. [*To Sukhatme*] Let's get those questions over with.

SUKHATME [*picking up the thread with fresh energy*]. Mr—

SAMANT. Samant.

SUKHATME. Mr Rokde saw the accused—Miss Benare—in Professor Damle's room in the evening when it was quite dark.

SAMANT. That's right . . .

SUKHATME. On that occasion, there was no third person there with Professor Damle and the accused.

SAMANT. Correct. But now, do ask me something.

SUKHATME. That's just what I am going to do. Half an hour after that, you reached there.

SAMANT. Where? No, no! Why, that room's in Bombay! And I was in this village. Hardly! It's silly—I don't know your Professor Damle from Adam. How could I get to his room? Isn't that right? What are you up to?

SUKHATME. You reached there.

SAMANT. You've got it all mixed up, counsel . . .

SUKHATME. Mr Samant, for the sake of the trial, we're taking some things for granted.

KARNIK. The crime itself is imaginary. What more do you want? It's all imaginary . . . that's what it is.

PONKSHE. Only the accused is real!

SAMANT [*to Mrs Kashikar*]. There! Now I'm in a mess! [*To Sukhatme*] All right. After half an hour, I reached Professor Damle's room. What next?

SUKHATME. You tell us that.

SAMANT. How can I tell you?

SUKHATME. Then who will?

SAMANT. That's true. I'll have to. But it's hard. The prisoner and Professor Damle. Room . . . evening . . .

PONKSHE. It was quite dark.

KARNIK. Half an hour after that. In other words, when it was very dark. Throughout the college grounds, complete silence . . .

SAMANT [*suddenly*]. Go on, ask me—so I reached there, eh? I reached there and—and what happened was—the door was locked!

SUKHATME. The door was locked!

SAMANT. Yes. The door was locked. Not from outside. From inside. And I banged on the door. No, that's wrong. I rang the bell. The door opened. An unknown man stood before me. Guess who it was. Professor Damle! I was seeing him for the first time. So he'd be unknown to me, wouldn't he?

PONKSHE. Bravo, Samant!

MRS KASHIKAR [*to Karnik*]. Oh, he's giving his evidence beautifully!

SAMANT [*gaining confidence*]. Damle was before me. When he saw me, he said with an annoyed expression, 'Yes? Whom do you want?'

PONKSHE [*to Karnik*]. He's describing Damle to the life!

SAMANT. I answered. 'Professor Damle.' He said, 'He's not at home.' And he slammed the door shut. For a second, I stood there stunned. I began to think, should I go home or press the bell once more. Because I had an important errand.

SUKHATME. What?

SAMANT. What?—Well, let's say—something. Let's suppose that I wanted to arrange a lecture by Professor Damle. He does lecture, doesn't he? I only ask, because he is a Professor—so he must lecture at times. So I stood there, wondering how I could go back without arranging the lecture. At that moment I heard a vague sound from the room. Of someone crying.

MRS KASHIKAR. Crying?

SAMANT. Yes. An indistinct sound of crying. It was a woman.

SUKHATME [*excitedly*]. Yes?

SAMANT. For a moment he stood where he was. 'He' means me. He—I mean I—couldn't understand who was crying. You will

ask me why I didn't think it was some female member of Professor Damle's family. Well, from the way the woman was crying,
she didn't seem to be a member of his family. Why? Because the
crying was soft. That is, it was secretive. Now, why would anyone
cry secretively in her own house? Thinking over all this, I stood
where I was. Just then, I heard some words.

MRS KASHIKAR. Some words?

KARNIK & PONKSHE. Who spoke?

SAMANT. Tut, tut, tut! You're not supposed to ask. This gentleman—the counsel—will ask me.

SUKHATME. Who spoke?

SAMANT. The woman, of course. The one inside.

MRS KASHIKAR. Good heavens! Tell us, do tell us, who was she?
[Looking unconsciously at Benare.]

SAMANT. No. He will ask me—the counsel will. Not you.

SUKHATME. I'm asking. Tell us, quick, Mr Samant. What were the
words you heard? Don't waste time. Tell us quick—Mr Samant—
be quick!

SAMANT. The words were—shall I tell it all?

SUKHATME. Whatever you can remember—but tell us!

SAMANT [hurriedly looking at a book in his hand]. 'If you abandon me
in this condition, where shall I go?'

[Benare is tense.]

MRS KASHIKAR. Is that really what she said?

SAMANT. 'How can I tell you?'

SUKHATME [snapping at him]. Then who else on earth can?

SAMANT. No, no! I'm telling you the Professor's answer. His
answer. Professor Damle's.

SUKHATME. Oh, I see.

SAMANT. 'Where you should go is entirely your problem. I feel
great sympathy for you. But I can do nothing. I must protect my
reputation.' At that, she said, 'That's all you can talk about, your
reputation? How heartless you are!' He replied, 'Nature is
heartless.'

KASHIKAR [picking his ear fast and furiously]. I see, I see.

SUKHATME [staggered]. Amazing—amazing!—

SAMANT. 'If you abandon me, I shall have no choice but to take my
life.' Then do that. I also have no choice. If you kill yourself, I
shall be in torment.'

SUKHATME. Simply thrilling!

SAMANT. 'But this threat will not make me budge an inch from my considered course of action,' he said. She replied, 'Bear it in mind that you will not escape the guilt of murdering two'—two?—I'm wrong—no, I'm right . . . 'Two living beings.' And then there came a terrifying laugh.

BENARE [*with sudden passion*]. That's enough!

KASHIKAR [*banging his gavel*]. Order, order!

BENARE. It's all a lie! A complete lie!

PONKSHE. Of course it is. So?

KARNIK. Even if it is a lie, it's an effective one!

MRS KASHIKAR. Do go on, Samant.

BENARE. No! Stop all this! Stop it!

SAMANT [*in confusion*]. But what's the matter?

BENARE. This has got to stop! Not a word of it is true!

SAMANT. Of course not.

BENARE. It's all made up! It's a lie!

SAMANT. That's quite right!

BENARE. You're telling barefaced lies!

SAMANT. What else? [*Brings out the book hidden behind him, and shows it.*] You see, everything I'm saying is out of this!

SUKHATME. Mr Samant, a terrifying laugh . . . What happened after that?

BENARE. If anyone says one word after this, I—I'll go away!

SUKHATME. Mr Samant . . .

BENARE. I'll smash up all this! I'll smash it all to bits—into little bits!

MRS KASHIKAR. But my dear Benare, as your conscience is clear, why are you flying into such a violent rage?

BENARE. You've all deliberately ganged up on me! You've plotted against me!

SAMANT. No, no, dear madam, really it's nothing like that!

SUKHATME. Mr Samant, answer. Professor Damle gave a terrifying laugh. Then what did the unknown woman inside the room say?

SAMANT [*hurriedly consulting his book*]. Wait, I'll find the page and let you know.

BENARE. Samant, if you say one word more—I'll—just you wait.

SUKHATME [*in the right soft and threatening tone*]. Mr Samant . . .

SAMANT. It's quite a problem. I just can't find the page—

SUKHATME [*to Kashikar*]. Milord, the occurrence as it has been related speaks so vividly for itself that there is hardly any need to add anything over and above it. This entire statement should be noted down as part of our evidence against the accused.

KASHIKAR. Request granted.

BENARE. Note it down. Note everything down! Just take down note after note! [*Her eyes are suddenly full of tears. Her voice is choked. She is agitated. Then, with tearful defiance*]. What can you do to me? Just try! [*Tears flow freely from her eyes. Exit into the wings.*]

[*Deeper silence. Except for Samant, everyone's expression changes. A peculiar and cautious excitement breaks out on each face.*]

SAMANT [*sympathetically*]. Dear, oh dear! Whatever's happened so suddenly to the lady?

KASHIKAR [*picking his ear*]. It's all become quite unexpectedly enjoyable—the whole fabric of society is being soiled these days, Sukhatme. Nothing is undefiled any more.

SUKHATME. That's why thoughtful people like us, Mr Kashikar, should consider these matters seriously and responsibly. This should not be taken lightly.

MRS KASHIKAR. You're absolutely right!

SUKHATME. And if thoughts alone are not enough, we must use deeds. Action! Eh, Karnik?

KARNIK. Yes. Action!

PONKSHE. Right!

SUKHATME. Here, feelings are not enough. We must all get together. We must act.

MRS KASHIKAR. But whatever's happened, really?

KASHIKAR. Keep quiet! What could have happened, Sukhatme? What's your guess?

SUKHATME [*as if he has a fair idea*]. That is the mystery!

[*Samant stands there, dismayed.*]

And I think we know the answer to this mystery!

KARNIK
PONKSHE
ROKDE   } —What?
KASHIKAR
MRS KASHIKAR

[*Benare comes out of the inner room and stands in the doorway.*]

SUKHATME [*unconscious of this*]. Well, children, the conclusion's obvious. There's some substance in what Mr Samant said. Even though it came from a book. It holds water!

MRS KASHIKAR. Do you mean that Miss Benare and Professor Da—

SUKHATME. Yes. Beyond a shadow of doubt! There's no question about it.

MRS KASHIKAR. Good gracious!

ROKDE [*now very daring*]. I knew it all along!

SUKHATME. Ssh!

[*Seeing Benare in the doorway, all fall silent. They all look at her. She comes in purposefully and picks up her bag and purse. She goes towards the other door, and unbolts it. All are watching. The door does not open. She pulls at it. It will not open. She starts tugging at it hard. It is locked from outside. She bangs on it with vehemence. And louder. But it is locked. A peculiar joy begins to show on everyone's face but Samant's.*]

SAMANT. There! It's happened! The bolt's slipped shut outside. That's always the trouble with this door. [*Gets up and goes forward. Struggles with the door.*] If you don't pull the bolt properly to one side when you come in, and then you close the door from inside, you've had it! The door's locked from outside. It's always the case. Try as you will, it just won't open. And what's more, the offices are closed. So there won't be anyone outside just now. [*He bangs on the door again and again.*] It's no use. [*To Miss Benare, who is by him.*] Madam, when you pulled the bolt you did it the wrong way. You should have pulled it back fully. [*He tries giving the door another thump. It's no use. Then coming and standing at one side.*] It's locked!

[*Benare is still standing by the door with her back to the others.*]

KASHIKAR [*cleaning his ears with concentration*]. I think that in the circumstances, Mr Sukhatme, the trial should continue.

SUKHATME [*bowing in legal fashion, with a completely perverse excitement*]. Yes, milord. [*His eyes gleaming.*] Milord, let the accused herself be summoned to the witness-box.

CURTAIN

ACT THREE

[*The same scene. Evening. The cast in the positions they were in at the end of the second act.*]

SUKHATME [*Bowing in the manner of a professional lawyer with a completely perverse excitement*]. Yes, milord, [*His eyes are gleaming.*] Milord, first let the accused herself be summoned to the witness-box.

KASHIKAR [*Picking his ear*]. Prisoner Miss Benare, enter the witness-box. Enter it, Miss Benare.

[*Benare stands where she is.*]

Incredible! Such insolence in court! Usher Rokde, conduct the accused to the witness-box.

ROKDE [*Frightened, trembling a little*]. Me?

[*Benare stands still.*]

MRS KASHIKAR. Wait, I'll take her. Why do you need him?

[*She starts pulling Benare along forcibly.*]

Come on, now, Benare.

[*She puts Benare into the witness-box. Benare's face reveals the terror of a trapped animal.*]

SUKHATME [*Looking at Benare as he puts on his gown ceremoniously*]. Milord, in consideration of the grave aspect which the case before us has assumed, it is my humble submission that if your lordship were to wear your gown henceforth, it would appear more decorous.

KASHIKAR. Exactly. Rokde, give me my gown.

[*He puts on the black gown that Rokde unpacks and hands to him. After that, his gravity and dignity increase.*]

SUKHATME. Mr Samant, Mrs Kashikar, Ponkshe, Karnik, seat yourselves there exactly as you should. [*He straightens up, closes his eyes, and meditates for a while. Then, slapping himself piously on the face, he raises his hands to his forehead in prayer twice or thrice.*] My father taught me the habit, Kashikar, of praying to our family god at the beginning of any new enterprise. How pure it makes one feel! The mind takes on new strength.

[*He takes one or two steps in the manner of a wrestler who has gained new strength.*] Good! Now to business. Let the accused take the oath.

[*Rokde comes and stands in front of Benare with the dictionary. Benare is silent. Like a statue.*]

KASHIKAR [*Adjusting his cap*]. Prisoner Miss Benare, take the oath!

[*Benare is silent.*]

SAMANT [*Softly*]. Why not get it over with, Miss Benare? It's all a game.

[*Benare is silent.*]

MRS KASHIKAR [*Coming forward*]. Give it to me, I'll make her take the oath; just wait. [*Taking the dictionary from Rokde.*] Benare, say, 'I hereby swear to tell the truth, the whole truth and nothing but the truth.'

[*Benare is silent.*]

KASHIKAR. This is the limit.

MRS KASHIKAR [*Giving the dictionary to Rokde*]. Let's say she's taken the oath. Her hand was on the dictionary. Go on, ask her what you want, Sukhatme.

KASHIKAR. Prisoner Benare, the court hereby warns you. Henceforth there must on no account be any conduct that constitutes contempt of court. Go ahead, Sukhatme!

KARNIK. Fire away!

SUKHATME [*Walking around in front of Benare a while, and suddenly, pointing a finger*]. Your name is Leela Damle.

SAMANT [*At once*]. No—no—Be-na-re. Damle is the Professor.

MRS KASHIKAR. Do listen, Samant. Let her answer.

SUKHATME. Miss Leela Benare—

[*She tries not to listen to or look at him.*]

SUKHATME. Please tell the court your age.

[*He has struck an attitude, confident that she will not tell it. Benare is silent.*]

KASHIKAR. Prisoner Benare, it is your responsibility to answer any questions put to you as a witness. [*Pausing a little*] Prisoner Benare, what are you waiting for? Answer the question!

MRS KASHIKAR. Why should *she* have to tell her age? I can guess it. Say . . . it's over thirty-two. A year or so more perhaps, but not less. Just look at her face!

SUKHATME. Thank you, Mrs Kashikar.

KASHIKAR. Wait. What do you mean, 'Thank you, Mrs Kashikar?' The accused has not yet told you her age. I was listening carefully. Prisoner Benare, your age!

MRS KASHIKAR. But I—

KASHIKAR. It is not the custom of any court to accept someone else's answer when the accused is questioned. Don't interrupt! Prisoner at the bar! Answer! Your answer please!

[*Benare is silent.*]

SAMANT. The fact is—it isn't thought—courteous—to ask a lady her age . . .

KASHIKAR. This is intolerable rudeness! No answer to any question! Is this a court of law, or what is it? [*Bangs the table for effect.*]

PONKSHE. Exactly. This is contempt of court!

KASHIKAR. We will have to take steps to deal with the prisoner's refusal to answer. This is a matter of the court's dignity. The accused will be granted ten seconds to answer. [*Holding his watch in front of him.*] No nonsense, please.

SUKHATME [*In a melodramatic manner, at the end of the tenth second*]. Milord, I withdraw the question. The accused, by her silence, has as good as answered me.

KASHIKAR. All right. She's not less than thirty-four. I'll give it to you in writing! What I say is, our society should revive the old custom of child marriage. Marry off the girls before puberty. All this promiscuity will come to a full stop. If anyone has ruined our society it's Agarkar and Dhondo Keshav Karve. That's my frank opinion, Sukhatme, my frank opinion.

SUKHATME [*With a lawyerlike bow*]. Yes, milord.

[*Rokde has meanwhile hastily written down Kashikar's sentence in his notebook. Benare is silent in the witness-box.*]

[*Going behind Benare, suddenly*]. Miss Benare.

[*She starts, jerking away from him.*]

Can you tell the court how you came to stay unmarried to such a mature—such an advanced—age? [*Waits; then*] Let me frame my question somewhat differently. How many chances of marriage have you had so far in your life? And how did you miss them? Tell the court.

KASHIKAR. Answer him! [*Takes out his watch and holds it in front of him. She is silent.*] This is really too much!

MRS KASHIKAR. It seems she's decided not to behave herself and answer properly!

[*Benare is silent.*]

SUKHATME. Milord, I close the examination of the accused for the time being. It could be resumed at the appropriate time.

[*Benare leaves the witness-box and goes to the door. It is locked. Ponkshe blocks the way, so she turns aside. By then, Mrs Kashikar has caught hold of her, and leads her to the dock.*]

KASHIKAR. Next witness.

SUKHATME. Mrs Kashikar.

[*At once, Mrs Kashikar eagerly enters the witness-box, tucking her sari round her fussily as she goes.*]

KASHIKAR [*To Sukhatme*]. Look. That's eagerness for you! You've hardly called her, and there she is!

MRS KASHIKAR. You needn't be like *that*! [*Then, talking like a stage witness*] I have already taken the oath. Benare and I—let's say we took it together. And of course I'll tell the truth. Who's scared?

SUKHATME. Very well. Mrs Kashikar, can you give me some information, please? How did Miss Benare remain unmarried till such a late age?

MRS KASHIKAR. That's easy! Because she didn't get married, of course.

SUKHATME. That's it. But, Mrs Kashikar, at the age of thirty-two—

KASHIKAR [*Interrupting*]. Thirty-four—count it as thirty-four!

SUKHATME. How is it that, till the age of thirty-four, an educated, well-brought-up girl—

MRS KASHIKAR. Girl? You mean 'woman'! If you call her a girl—you'd better call me young lady.

SUKHATME. All right. Let's call her a woman then. But, why isn't she married? Can you explain that?

MRS KASHIKAR. Damn the explanation! Anyone who really wants to can get married in a flash!

SUKHATME. You mean that Miss Benare didn't want to—

MRS KASHIKAR. What else? That's what happens these days when you get everything without marrying. They just want comfort. They couldn't care less about responsibility! Let me tell you—in my time, even if a girl was snub-nosed, sallow, hunchbacked, or anything whatever, she—could—still—get—married! It's the sly new fashion of women earning that makes everything go wrong. That's how promiscuity has spread throughout our society. [*Rokde is jotting it down. To Rokde.*] Finished writing? [*To Sukhatme.*] Go on. Ask me more.

SUKHATME. You said that this is what happens if you get everything without marrying.

MRS KASHIKAR. Yes, I did.

SUKHATME. What do you mean by 'everything'? Give me an instance.

MRS KASHIKAR. Well, really! [*She looks embarrassed.*]

KASHIKAR [*Picking his ear*]. Come on, don't pretend to be shy, at your age. Just answer his question. You've grown old, but you haven't grown any wiser!

MRS KASHIKAR. My age has nothing to do with it!

KASHIKAR. Answer him!

MRS KASHIKAR. 'Everything' means—everything in this life.

SUKHATME. Don't you feel that to say this about the accused might be unjust?

MRS KASHIKAR. I don't think so. We see too many such examples.

SUKHATME. Forget about the others. Have you any proof where Miss Benare is concerned? Any proof? Tell me if you have.

MRS KASHIKAR. What better proof? Just look at the way she behaves. I don't like to say anything since she's one of us. Should there be no limit to how freely a woman can behave with a man? An unmarried woman? No matter how well she knows him? Look how loudly she laughs! How she sings, dances, cracks jokes! And wandering alone with how many men, day in and day out!

SUKHATME [*Disappointed at the 'proof'*]. Mrs Kashikar, at the most one can say all this shows how free she is.

MRS KASHIKAR. Free! Free! She's free allright—in everything! I shouldn't say it. But since it's come up in court, I will. Just hold this a minute. [*She puts her knitting into Sukhatme's hands.*] Why must she have Professor Damle, and Damle alone, to see her home after a performance? Tell me that!

[*Benare is deliberately silent.*]

SUKHATME [*Brightening up*]. I see—so Miss Benare needs Professor Damle to see her home after a performance?

[*Ponkshe and Karnik are signalling to each other.*]

MRS KASHIKAR. What else? Once we—my husband and I—it was just last September—September, wasn't it dear?

KASHIKAR. No prompting the witness! You say what you want!

MRS KASHIKAR. Yes, it was September. We both said, 'Come, we'll drop you,' since she was to go home alone. But she very slyly went off with Damle. We looked for her, but she'd vanished!

SUKHATME [*In a lawyer's voice, sounding pleased*]. Peculiar!

MRS KASHIKAR. Just a while back, she was protesting, 'It's a lie! It's persecution!' Now how's she struck dumb? That shows you can't suppress the truth. Give me that wool.

SUKHATME [*Handing over the wool and needles to Mrs Kashikar*]. Mrs Kashikar, Professor Damle is a family man.

MRS KASHIKAR. Yes. He has five children.

SUKHATME. Then how do you know Miss Benare doesn't seek his company innocently, as a responsible elder person?

MRS KASHIKAR. Then do you mean to say that we—my husband and I—are just vagabonds? And Damle may be an older man—but what about Balu?

[*Rokde gives a great start.*]

SUKHATME [*Growing alert*]. What about him, Mrs Kashikar? What about Rokde?

[*Benare's expression is tense.*]

MRS KASHIKAR. That's what I'm telling you. After another performance, Benare made overtures to him, too. In the dark. It was he who told me. Didn't you, Balu?

[*Karnik excepted, commotion all round. Sukhatme is radiant.*]

ROKDE [*Weakly*]. Yes . . . no . . .

SAMANT [*To Karnik*]. No, no, she was alone with me a little while ago, and, . . .

[*Karnik silences him.*]

SUKHATME. Mrs Kashikar, you may step down. Your evidence is complete. Milord, I submit that Rokde be called once more to give evidence.
[*Rokde cringes where he is. Sukhatme strolls over to stand near Benare. In confidential tones.*] Miss Benare, the game's really warmed up, hasn't it?

KASHIKAR. Rokde, come and give evidence.

[*Rokde hesitantly goes to the witness-box without looking at Benare.*]

MRS KASHIKAR [*As he passes*]. Balu, speak the truth! Don't be afraid.

SUKHATME [*Going towards the witness-box*]. Mr Rokde—you've already taken the oath. Well, Mr Rokde, in the course of her evidence, Mrs Kashikar has made a most disturbing statement about you and the accused.

[*Rokde begins to shake his head.*]

MRS KASHIKAR. Balu! Didn't you tell me so?

SUKHATME. Mr Rokde, whatever happened after the performance that night, good or bad, pleasant or unpleasant, tell it all to the court. That is your duty. The performance ended. What happened then?

ROKDE [*Feebly*]. I—I—

SUKHATME. After the performance all of us left the hall. Then—?

KARNIK. And only these two remained behind.

MRS KASHIKAR. Then it seems, she took his hand—Balu's, I mean.

PONKSHE. Gosh!

SUKHATME. And then? What did she do then, Rokde? What more did she do? What next?

MRS KASHIKAR. I'll tell you!

KASHIKAR. No, you won't. Let him tell it. Don't interrupt all the time!

SUKHATME. Yes, Mr Rokde—tell it bravely—don't be afraid.

KASHIKAR. Afraid? Why should he be? There's some law and order here, isn't there?

[*Rokde takes stock of the situation. Then, realizing he has enough protection against Benare, he plucks up courage.*]

ROKDE [*Bravely*]. She held my—my hand.

SUKHATME. Yes?

ROKDE. So, then—So then I said—'This isn't proper. It's not proper!—I—I don't like this at all—it doesn't become you'— That's—that's what I said!

SUKHATME. And then?

ROKDE. I freed my hand. She moved away. She said, 'Don't tell anyone what happened.'

BENARE. That's a lie!

KASHIKAR [*Banging the gavel*]. Order! The accused is sternly reprimanded for disturbing the proceedings of the court. Continue, Rokde, continue.

ROKDE. 'If you tell anyone, I'll do something to you.' That's what she said to me, Anna.

SUKHATME. When did this happen, Mr Rokde?

ROKDE. Eight days ago, when we had our show at Dombivli.

SUKHATME. Milord, this means that the accused committed an outrage in a lonely spot, on a boy like Rokde, much younger than her—almost like her younger brother. Not only that, but she threatened him with consequences if the matter came to light. She tried to cover up her sinful deed!

MRS KASHIKAR. But the truth will out.

SUKHATME. So, Rokde, the accused threatened to harm you somehow. What next? What happened then?

ROKDE [*Unconsciously raising one hand to his cheek*]. I—I slapped her!

PONKSHE. What?

KARNIK. How melodramatic!

ROKDE. Yes—I said, 'What do you take me for? Do whatever you like! I won't stay quiet about this.' That's why I told Mrs Kashikar. Yes, that's why.

KASHIKAR. Go on, tell her everything, Rokde; don't tell anything to *me*!

ROKDE [*Indistinctly*]. I'm sorry, Anna. I was wrong. I thought—I thought, in any case you'd find out—from Mrs Kashikar here, I mean—so I—

SUKHATME. What happened next, Rokde? What next?

ROKDE. Then?—then nothing. That's all. Can I go?

SUKHATME. Yes, Mr Rokde.

[*Takes a scrap of paper out of his pocket, and writes on it, muttering loudly, 'Eight days ago, the performance at Dombivli.' Rokde hastily leaves the witness-box, and stands at a distance, wiping the sweat from his face. His expression is calm and satisfied.*]

MRS KASHIKAR. But you hadn't told me this last bit, Balu—about slapping her!

SAMANT [*To Ponkshe*]. Impossible! I can't believe it!

[*A pronounced excitement is in the air.*]

PONKSHE [*From his seat, puffing hard at his pipe*]. Sukhatme, my evidence now—call me as a witness! Call me now!

[*His gaze is on the hapless Benare. . . . His tone is impatient.*]

Just call me!

KASHIKAR. Sukhatme, call Ponkshe. Let's hear him . . . call him now. Let's hear him once and for all!

SUKHATME. Mr Ponkshe be called to the witness-box!

ROKDE. Next witness, Mr Ponkshe!

[*Ponkshe enters the witness-box.*]

PONKSHE. Shall I take the oath again? I hereby place my hand upon the Oxford English Dictionary, and swear that I—

KASHIKAR. It's understood. Sukhatme, proceed.

SUKHATME. Mr Ponkshe, the accused, Miss Benare—

PONKSHE [*Gazing at Benare*].—is what I have something important to tell you about.

[*Benare stiffens where she is.*]

Just ask her this. Why does she keep a bottle of TIK-20 in her purse?

[*Benare flinches.*]

MRS KASHIKAR. What more now!

PONKSHE. That is a powerful bedbug poison. It's famous.

SAMANT [*To Karnik*]. Perhaps she was taking it home—

SUKHATME. Can you tell us, Mr Ponkshe, how and when you first found out that the accused was carrying such a terrible poison as TIK-20 in her purse?

[*Benare is stiff and tense.*]

PONKSHE. Yes. One of her little pupils stays in my tenement. About ten days ago, she came to me and said, our teacher's sent you this.

KASHIKAR. TIK-20?

PONKSHE. No, a note in a sealed envelope. I opened it. Inside there was another envelope. That, too, was sealed. There was a slip of paper in it, which said, 'Will you meet me, please? I have something to discuss with you. Come at a quarter past one. Wait in the Udipi restaurant just beyond the school.' Of course, I didn't like it at all. But I said to myself, let's see what her game is. So I went along. Just for the heck of it.

Five minutes later, Miss Benare came there hurriedly, looking quite guilty.

[*Benare has become even more tense.*]

SUKHATME. I see—

KASHIKAR. Then? What happened then, Ponkshe?

PONKSHE. She said, 'Not here—in public—someone'll see us—let's go into a family room.'

MRS KASHIKAR [*Sarcastically*]. Magnificent!

PONKSHE. So we sat in a 'family room.' We ordered tea. When Miss Benare's problem had been discussed, she opened her purse to take out her handkerchief. And out of it there rolled a small bottle—

[*For a moment, there is silence.*]

SUKHATME. A bottle of TIK-20! Good! But Mr Ponkshe, what had happened between you and Miss Benare before that? I mean, what was the thing she wanted to discuss with you? You haven't told us that.

[*Benare is shaking her head with silent vehemence, telling him not to do so.*]

PONKSHE. She made known her desire to marry me.

KARNIK. What?

KASHIKAR. What?

[*Rokde and the others are astounded.*]

KASHIKAR. This appears terribly interesting, Sukhatme.

SUKHATME. True, milord, it is and it will be. [*His famished lawyer's gaze is on Benare.*] Did she tell you she was in love with you, etc.?

PONKSHE. No. But she told me she was pregnant.

[*Sensation. Benare is sitting like a block of stone, drained of colour and totally desolate.*]

KARNIK. Are you telling the truth, Ponkshe?

PONKSHE. What do you think? That I'm lying?

KASHIKAR. Who was the father—continue, Ponkshe, continue—don't stop there!

SUKHATME. Mr Ponkshe—

PONKSHE. Miss Benare made me promise never to tell anyone the name of the man who—so she said—had made her pregnant. So far I've kept my word.

MRS KASHIKAR. But who *was* it?

KASHIKAR. What'll you take to shut up? The cat'll be out of the bag soon, anyway. Don't be so impatient! But what I don't understand, Ponkshe, is why, if Miss Benare was pregnant by one man, she expressed a desire to marry another—I mean, to marry you!

PONKSHE. Exactly.

SUKHATME. What was your answer, Mr Ponkshe? Were you prepared to take a broad view of things for the sake of humanity, and accept the child along with the mother?

PONKSHE. The answer is quite clear.

SUKHATME. You weren't prepared, of course.

PONKSHE. No, I wasn't.

SUKHATME. And it was after this, Mr Ponkshe, that the bottle of TIK-20 rolled out of Miss Benare's purse!

PONKSHE. Of course! I myself picked it up and returned it to her. Shall I give you the whole conversation? If you want I'll tell that too.

BENARE [*Shooting up on to her feet*]. No! No!

KASHIKAR [*Banging his gavel*]. Silence! Mr Ponkshe, give us the conversation. [*To Sukhatme.*] Now we'll hear the name—

BENARE. No! You promised, Ponkshe!

SUKHATME. Mr Ponkshe, what indeed could the conversation have been, for Miss Benare to be so agonized?

KASHIKAR. Tell us, Ponkshe—don't wait—tell it quick—this is a matter of social importance.

PONKSHE. But she won't like it.

KASHIKAR [*Banging the gavel*]. Who is the judge here, Ponkshe? Since when has the question of the accused's likes and dislikes been admitted in court? When? I say to you—continue!

BENARE [*Coming in front of Ponkshe*]. Ponkshe—

KASHIKAR [*Banging the gavel*]. Order! The accused to the dock! To the dock! Rokde, conduct the accused to the dock!

[*Rokde moves forward a little and halts.*]

BENARE. Just you tell it and you'll see, Ponkshe—

KASHIKAR. Prisoner at the bar, go to the dock—Rokde, take her to the dock . . .

MRS KASHIKAR [*Coming forward and grasping Benare's hand*]. First stand over there. Come on, Rokde, hold her hand.

[*Rokde lingers behind them.*]

Come, Benare; come on.

[*She drags her to the dock. Mrs Kashikar and Rokde stand guard.*]

Discipline means discipline.

KASHIKAR. Speak, Mr Ponkshe, What was your conversation about? Where's my earpick? [*He finds it.*] Go on. Mr Ponkshe, what was it about?

PONKSHE. First, we chatted aimlessly. 'Sukhatme's a good man, but he's smothered by ill luck, poor chap. His practice is poor;—he just sits in the barristers' room playing patience—they say it's well known that if you take your case to him, it's jail for certain!—he just goes dumb before the judge . . .'

SUKHATME [*Swallowing his rage and sense of insult*]. I see . . . yes, go on—

PONKSHE. ' . . . Kashikar torments poor Rokde. Because he constantly suspects an entanglement between him and his wife. Because they have no children, you see . . .'

MRS KASHIKAR. Is that what she said?

[*Highly offended, she looks daggers at Benare.*]

MR KASHIKAR [*Picking his ear vigorously*]. Go on, tell us more, Ponkshe—

PONKSHE. After some talk of this nature, we came to the real issue.

KARNIK. Wait. What did she say about me, Ponkshe?

PONKSHE. Nothing.

KARNIK. She must have said something—that I'm a rotten actor, or something. I know what she thinks of me. I know it well.

PONKSHE. She asked jokingly; 'Well, are you fixed up somewhere?' So I said, 'Unless I find someone just to my taste, I'm not interested in marrying.' So she asked, 'What exactly do you mean by "to your taste"? What do you look for?' I replied, 'On the whole, girls are silly and frivolous—that's my opinion. I want a mature partner.' Then she asked, 'Don't you think that maturity—that is, a fully developed understanding—comes to a person only with experience?' 'I don't know,' I replied. She then said, 'And experience comes with age, with a slightly unusual way of life. And this sort of experience is never happy or pleasing. It gives pain to the person who gains it. And it's usually intolerable to others. But will you bear with it? I mean, supposing it is a really mature person. Older than you and more educated?' 'I haven't yet thought seriously about it.' 'Then you should,' she replied. So I asked whether she had some promising bride in mind. She said, 'Yes. I feel she's the kind you want. You just have to understand her unusualness.' I couldn't see why she was making this great effort to get me married. I asked casually, 'What sort of unusualness do you mean?' She replied, 'The girl's just gone through a shattering heartbreak, and'—wait, I'll think of the exact words—yes—'the fruit of that love'—here she stumbled a little—'is in her womb. Actually it is no fault of hers.

But her situation's very serious indeed. She wants to bring up the child. In fact it's only for the child she wants to go on living and get married.' She spoke some more in the same vein. I grew suspicious. So in order to get the truth out of her, I said, 'Oh! poor girl! Her luck seems really bad. Who is the scoundrel responsible?'

SUKHATME. Thereupon she said it was Professor Damle!

PONKSHE. No. First she said, 'Please don't call him a scoundrel. He may be a good man. He may be very great and wise. She may have fallen short. She may not have been able to convince him how deeply she feels for him. The woman is not the crucial factor. It's the baby that comes first.'

SUKHATME. And then?

PONKSHE. Then she said, 'She worshipped that man's intellect. But all he understood was her body.' She added other things. On the same lines. How she couldn't find a place in Damle's life. His—

SAMANT. ⎫
KARNIK. ⎬ Damle's?
SUKHATME. ⎭

KASHIKAR [Banging on the table]. The cat's out of the bag!

PONKSHE. To tell you the truth; I was bound by oath not to tell the name, but—

SUKHATME. Doesn't matter, Mr Ponkshe, it doesn't matter at all. It's no sin to break your oath inadvertently—at least, not in court. So the child she's carrying is Professor Damle's? Go on, go on—

PONKSHE. Then she fell at my feet.

KASHIKAR. I see—I see—

PONKSHE. Yes, she fell at my feet. And I said, 'This doesn't become you, Miss Benare. It's an insult to have asked me this at all. Do you think I'm so worthless?' When she saw my face, she got up at once, and said, laughing, 'Did you really think I was telling the truth? It was just a joke! That's all!' Then she burst out laughing.

MRS KASHIKAR. A joke, did she say!

PONKSHE. But she had tears in her eyes. That made everything quite clear. Then she went off in a hurry saying she was late.

SUKHATME. Thank you, Mr Ponkshe, for your valuable evidence.

[Ponkshe comes out of the witness-box. Sukhatme takes out the piece of paper, and muttering loudly, notes down, 'Ten days before the incident of holding Rokde's hand.']

That's fine. Milord, this evidence needs no comment. It's so
clear—and, I may add, so self-evident. The accused first
accosted Mr Ponkshe. When she realized there was nothing
doing in that quarter, she committed the outrage on Rokde. The
next witness will be the accused, milord.

[*He points to Benare. She looks half-dead.*]

KARNIK [*Raising his hand in a stagey gesture*]. Wait! Wait! I have
something important to disclose regarding the case.
SUKHATME. Mr Karnik, into the box.

[*He walks theatrically into it. Mr Kashikar is picking his ear
vigorously.*]

SUKHATME. Speak, Mr Karnik. What do you wish to tell the court?
KARNIK [*Stagily*]. The evidence given to the court by Rokde
concerning the accused, Miss Benare, and himself, is incorrect.
ROKDE [*In a whining tone*]. What business is it of yours?
KARNIK [*Stagily*]. Because, by chance, I happened to be a witness
of what was said and done on that occasion.
KASHIKAR [*Cleaning his earpick*]. Which one? Tell us what you have
to, without complicating the issue . . .
KARNIK [*Dramatically*]. Life itself is a complication these days. The
Western playwright Ionesco—
KASHIKAR [*Banging his gavel*]. To the point! Don't digress! Stick to
the point!
KARNIK. I only mentioned him because the subject of complications cropped up—
SUKHATME. What amendment would you suggest, Mr Karnik, to
what has been stated before the court, regarding the accused
and Rokde?
KARNIK. As God is my witness, I must state that Rokde did not slap
the accused.
ROKDE [*Whining*]. It's a lie!
KARNIK. What happened was roughly like this. The accused
accosted Rokde. I saw that. So I stood aside in the darkness to see
how it would develop. The accused asked, 'Then what have you
decided?' Rokde's answer came over, 'I can't do anything
without Mrs Kashikar's permission. Don't press me.' The
accused then said, 'How much more of your life will you spend
under Mrs Kashikar's thumb?' Rokde replied, 'I can't help it.
That's one's luck. I can't think of marriage.' The accused said to
him, 'Think again. I'll support you. You won't lack for anything

then. You won't have to fear Mr and Mrs Kashikar. You'll be independent.' Rokde replied, 'I'm scared. And if I marry you when you're in this condition, the whole world'll sling mud at me. No one in my family's done a thing like that. Don't depend on me. Or else I'll have to tell Mrs Kashikar.' Upon this, the accused, in a rage—

ROKDE. It's a lie!

KARNIK.—struck Rokde in the face.

[Rokde's hand has unconsciously gone to his cheek.]

ROKDE. It's a lie—a barefaced lie!

[Mrs Kashikar is glaring at him.]

SUKHATME. Thank you, Mr Karnik. This means that it is true the accused was pressing Rokde to marry her. The only difference in what you say is about who slapped whom.

KARNIK. Not just what I say—but what I saw.

SUKHATME. That's so, Mr Karnik [Showing him the way out of the witness-box]—

KARNIK. I have something more to say.

KASHIKAR. If it isn't anything useless and irrelevant, let's hear it. No complications.

KARNIK. Milord—

KASHIKAR [Banging the gavel]. Order! what do you think you are? A lawyer? Just say 'Your lordship' like any other witness!

KARNIK. Your lordship—

KASHIKAR. That's it. That's the way. Speak. But no complications! We want everything straight and simple.

ROKDE [Piteously, to Mrs Kashikar, in a soft voice]. Mrs Kashikar—

MRS KASHIKAR. Don't speak to me at all!

ROKDE. But Mrs Kashikar! . . .

[She turns her head away. Rokde is still more miserable.]

KARNIK. Your lordship, I happen to know a cousin of the accused's. I mean, I just got to know him by chance, at a cricket match at the Dadar Gymkhana. A common friend of ours was playing in the Bachelors' Eleven. My friend's friend turned out to be the cousin of the accused—so my friend told me. My friend knows the accused. I mean, not personally, but a lot of people know the accused, and like them, so did he. I mean, he knew about the accused.

KASHIKAR. I see. And with whom are you chatting like this? Show respect to the court.

KARNIK [*Striking the attitude of respecting the court*]. Yes. Well then, the cousin of the accused and I—we had just met—the subject casually came up. He gave me some important information.

SUKHATME. For instance?

KARNIK. For instance, the accused had attempted suicide once before.

SUKHATME [*Radiant*]. That's the point! There is a precedent for the bottle of TIK-20.

KARNIK. I can't say that exactly. I can only tell you what happened. My information is that the accused attempted suicide because of a disappointment in love. She fell in love at the age of fifteen, with her own maternal uncle! That's what ended in disappointment.

MRS KASHIKAR [*Totally floored*]. Her uncle!

SUKHATME. Milord—her maternal uncle—her mother's brother. What an immoral relationship!

KASHIKAR. In other words, just one step away from total depravity. Fine, Sukhatme, very fine!

SUKHATME. Milord, why do you say 'fine'? The present conduct of the accused is totally licentious. We know that. But it now seems that her past, too, is smeared in sin. This shows it as clear as daylight.

[*Benare struggles to her feet and tries to reach the door. Mrs Kashikar grasps her and forces her back to the dock.*]

MRS KASHIKAR. Where d'you think you're going? The door's locked! Sit down!

KARNIK. I've finished.

[*Bowing dramatically to Kashikar, he leaves the witness-box and returns to his place.*]

KASHIKAR [*Banging his hand suddenly on the table as if he has all of a sudden remembered something*]. There's no doubt at all, Sukhatme! No doubt.

SUKHATME. About what, milord?

KASHIKAR. I'll tell you! Sukhatme, I wish to set aside the tradition of the court, and give an important piece of evidence.

SUKHATME. Milord?

KASHIKAR. This case has great social significance, Sukhatme. No joking! I must put aside the practice of court, and give evidence. Sukhatme, ask my permission. Ask me. Ask!

SUKHATME. Milord, considering the importance of the case, I

humbly submit that tradition should be broken, to allow the judge's worshipful self to enter the witness-box.

KASHIKAR. Permission granted. [*He comes and stands in the witness-box.*] Examine me. Come on. [*He is bursting to speak. His eyes are on Benare.*] Not a doubt of it!

SUKHATME [*Striking a lawyer's attitude*]. Mr Kashikar, your occupation?

KASHIKAR. Social worker.

SUKHATME. Do you know the accused?

KASHIKAR. Only too well! A sinful canker on the body of society—that's my honest opinion of these grown-up unmarried girls.

SUKHATME [*Taking an even more typical lawyer's pose*]. Do not give your opinion unless you are asked, Mr Kashikar!

KASHIKAR. An opinion's an opinion. I don't wait for anyone's permission to give it.

PONKSHE. Bravo!

SUKHATME. Don't wait for it, then. Mr Kashikar, can you place before the court any important evidence about the charge that has been made here against the accused?

KASHIKAR. Well, that's why I'm standing here!

SUKHATME. Then speak.

KASHIKAR [*Looking at Benare*]. I often have cause to visit the famous leader Nanasaheb Shinde of Bombay. Of course, the bond between us is that of a common love for social work. Besides, he is the Chairman of the Education Society. Well, his greatness is different from mine. That's not the question here. But recently at his house, say at about nine o'clock at night—when I was waiting there to discuss some work, I heard conversation in the next room. [*Benare starts.*] One of the voices was Nanasaheb's. But the other voice, too, seemed familiar.

MRS KASHIKAR. Whose was it?

KASHIKAR. Sukhatme, give her a reprimand, go on. You mustn't interrupt a witness! Before I could tell whose the other voice was, the conversation was over. In a little while Nanasaheb came out. In the course of our conversation I asked about it. He replied, 'A school-mistress from our Education Society's High School had come here. She comes here continually. She wants us to drop an enquiry against her. She's a young woman. So I couldn't say no straight away. I have called her again, for a quiet talk.' Of course, I was still curious who this woman could be. Though Nanasaheb did not tell me, I have just realized that the woman, far from being some stranger, was this one—I mean, she was Miss Benare! I am 101 per cent certain! The same voice exactly. Not a doubt of it!

MRS KASHIKAR. Good gracious!

MR KASHIKAR. Ask me, Sukhatme, how I'm so certain. This very morning I took over a garland of flowers to Nanasaheb's house, as it's his birthday. There Nanasaheb was talking angrily to someone on the phone, 'It is a sin to be pregnant before marriage. It would be still more immoral to let such a woman teach, in such a condition! There is no alternative—this woman must be dismissed,' he was saying. Finally, he instructed, 'Send the order for my signature this very day!'

[*A shock for Benare.*]

Now who else comes to your mind? Tell me! I *say* it was Miss Benare!

SAMANT. Dear, oh dear! Is she going to lose her job?

SUKHATME. It can't be helped. Tit for tat! As you sow, so shall you reap . . . that's the rule of life. [*Rokde opens his notebook and writes it down.*] But Mr Kashikar, what made you think *that* woman was this one—was positively our Miss Benare?

KASHIKAR. My dear man, do you take me for a child, that I shouldn't understand such a simple thing? I've been studying society for the last forty years, I'll have you know! A word to the wise is enough! There is not the slightest doubt in my mind that I've guessed right. It was definitely Miss Benare. Just see whether or not she gets that order tomorrow, that's all! Order for dismissal! That's all I wanted to record here. [*He leaves the witness-box and seats himself on the judge's chair.*] The prosecution may continue.

[*A small bottle is in Benare's hand. Just as she is about to put it to her mouth, Karnik dashes forward and strikes it away. The bottle rolls towards Ponkshe's feet.*]

PONKSHE [*Picking it up and looking at it, then putting it on the judge's table*]. TIK-20.

[*Samant is shocked. Kashikar looks at the bottle and takes charge of it.*]

KASHIKAR. The prosecution may continue.

SUKHATME. With this last and most important piece of evidence, the testimony for the prosecution is complete. Milord, the case for the prosecution rests. [*He goes and sits down in his chair, as if exhausted.*]

KASHIKAR [*With all the gravity of a judge*]. Counsel for the accused!

[*Sukhatme goes and sits with lowered head on the stool reserved for the counsel for the accused.*]

Call the witnesses for your side!

SUKHATME [*Getting up with the gesture of a tired man, makes a lawyer-like bow and in equally exhausted tones, says*]. Yes, milord. Our first witness is Professor Damle.

ROKDE [*Acting the usher*]. Damle! Professor Damle! [*To Kashikar*] Professor Damle is absent.

KASHIKAR [*To Sukhatme*]. Next witness, please.

SUKHATME. Our next witness is Nanasaheb Shinde.

KASHIKAR [*Picking his teeth*] Absent! How could *he* come here? Next—

SUKHATME. The other member of this group, Mr Rawte—

KASHIKAR. He is absent, too. Are those all the witnesses for the defence?

SUKHATME. I wish to cross-examine the witness for the prosecution, milord.

KASHIKAR. Permission refused. Take your seat.

SUKHATME [*Sighing*]. The case for the accused rests. [*Goes and seats himself on the stool kept for the counsel for the accused.*]

KASHIKAR [*Spitting out something*]. Good! Now counsel for the prosecution, plead your case. Don't waste time, now.

[*Sukhatme changes his place. Sits down energetically on his previous chair. Then springs to his feet like a wrestler and comes forward.*]

KASHIKAR. Be brief.

SUKHATME [*Now the counsel for the prosecution*]. Milord, the nature of the charge against the accused, Miss Leela Benare, is truly dreadful. The woman who is an accused has made a heinous blot on the sacred brow of motherhood—which is purer than heaven itself. For that, any punishment, however great, that the law may give her, will be too mild by far. The character of the accused is appalling. It is bankrupt of morality. Not only that. Her conduct has blackened all social and moral values. The accused is public enemy number one. If such socially destructive tendencies are encouraged to flourish, this country and its culture will be totally destroyed. Therefore, I say the court must take a very stern, inexorable view of the prisoner's crime, without being trapped in any sentiment. The charge against the accused is one of infanticide. But the accused has committed a far more serious crime. I mean unmarried motherhood. Motherhood without marriage has always been considered a very great sin by our religion and our traditions. Moreover, if the accused's intention of bringing up the offspring of this unlawful maternity is carried to completion, I have a dreadful fear that the very existence of society will be in danger. There will be no such thing as moral values left. Milord, infanticide is a dreadful act. But bringing up the child of an illegal union is certainly more horrifying. If it is encouraged, there will be no such thing as the institution of marriage left. Immorality will flourish. Before our eyes, our beautiful dream of a society governed by tradition will crumble into dust. The accused has plotted to dynamite the very roots of our tradition, our pride in ourselves, our culture and our religion. It is the sacred and imperative duty of your Lordship and every wise and thoughtful citizen amongst us to destroy that plot at once. No allowance must be made because the accused is a woman. Woman bears the grave responsibility of building up the high values of society. *'Na stri swatantryamarhati.'* 'Woman is not fit for independence.'. . . That is the rule laid down for us by tradition. Abiding by this rule, I make a powerful plea. *'Na Miss Benare swatantryamarhati.'* 'Miss Benare is not fit for independence.' With the urgent plea that the court should show no mercy to the accused, but give her the greatest and severest punishment for her terrible crime, I close the argument for the prosecution.

KASHIKAR. Good! Counsel for the accused! The accused's lawyer!

[*Sukhatme assumes that character and changes his place, rising once more with a downcast face.*]

SUKHATME [*Walking forward with heavy steps, and in a tone full of false emotion*]. Milord, that the crime is very serious, I do not dispute. But consider this. Man is, in the last analysis, prone to error. Youth leads a person astray. Let the terrible crime that the accused has committed and is committing, be regarded with mercy. Mercy, milord—for humanity's sake, mercy.

[*He has come to the judge's table. Benare is motionless.*]

KASHIKAR. Good. Now, prisoner Benare—

[*She is quite still.*]

Prisoner Benare, before the sentence is pronounced, have you anything to say about the charge that has been made against you? [*Putting forward his watch*] The accused will be given ten seconds.

[*She is as motionless as before. From somewhere in the background, music can be heard. The light changes. The whole court 'freezes' in the positions they are in at the moment. And the motionless Benare stands up erect.*]

BENARE. Yes, I have a lot to say. [*Stretches to loosen her arms.*] For so many years, I haven't said a word. Chances came, and chances went. Storms raged one after another about my throat. And there was a wail like death in my heart. But each time I shut my lips tight. I thought, no one will understand. No one *can* understand! When great waves of words came and beat against my lips, how stupid everyone around me, how childish, how silly they all seemed. Even the man I call my own. I thought, I should just laugh and laugh till I burst. At all of them . . . that's all—just laugh and laugh! And I used to cry my guts out. I used to wish my heart would break! My life was a burden to me. [*Heaving a great sigh*] But when you can't lose it, you realize the value of it. You realize the value of living. You see what happiness means. How new, how wonderful every moment is! Even *you* seem new to yourself. The sky, birds, clouds, the branch of a dried-up tree that gently bends in, the curtain moving at the window, the silence all around—all sorts of distant, little noises, even the strong smell of medicines in a hospital, even that seems full to bursting with life. Life seems to sing for you! There's great joy in a suicide that's failed. It's greater even than the pain of living. [*Heaves a deep sigh.*] Throw your life away—and you realize the luck of having it. Guard it dearer than life—and it only seems fit to throw away. Funny, isn't it? Look after it. And you feel like throwing it away. Throw it away—and you're blissfully happy it's saved! Nothing satisfies. The same thing, again and again. [*In a classroom manner.*] Life is like this. Life is so and so. Life is such and such. Life is a book that goes ripping into pieces. Life is a poisonous snake that bites itself. Life is a betrayal. Life is a fraud. Life is a drug. Life is drudgery. Life is a something that's nothing—or a nothing that's something. [*Suddenly striking a courtroom attitude.*] Milord, life is a very dreadful thing. Life must be hanged. *Na jeevan jeevanamarhati.* 'Life is not worthy of life'. Hold an enquiry against life. Sack it from its job! But why? Why? Was I slack in my work? I just put my whole life into working with the children . . . I loved it! I taught them well! I knew that

life is no straightforward thing. People can be so cruel. Even your own flesh and blood don't want to understand you. Only one thing in life is all-important— the body! You may deny it, but it is true. Emotion is something people talk about with sentiment. It was obvious to me. I was living through it. It was burning through me. But—do you know?—I did not teach any of this to those tender, young souls. I swallowed that poison, but didn't even let a drop of it touch them! I taught them beauty. I taught them purity. I cried inside, and I made them laugh. I was cracking up with despair, and I taught them hope. For what sin are they robbing me of my job, my only comfort? My private life is my own business. I'll decide what to do with myself; everyone should be able to! That can't be anyone else's business; understand? Everyone has a bent, a manner, an aim in life. What's anyone else to do with these? [*At once, in the light, playful mood she has at school.*] Hush! Quiet there! Silence! What a noise! [*Comes out of the witness-box and wanders as if in class.*] Sit still as statues! [*She is looking at each figure frozen still.*] Poor things! Children, who are all these? [*Light illuminates each face one by one. They all look fearsome, silent, ghostlike.*] These are the mortal remains of some cultured men of the twentieth century. See their faces—how ferocious they look! Their lips are full of lovely worn-out phrases! And their bellies are full of unsatisfied desires.
[*Sound of the hourly bell at school. A distant noise of children chattering. For a moment, she is silent and concentrates on the sound. She loses herself in it. The sound then recedes and is heard no more. Silence. Looking around her as if she is walking up, she is suddenly terrified of the silence.*] No, no! Don't leave me alone! I'm scared of them. [*Terrified, she hides her face and trembles.*] It's true, I did commit a sin. I was in love with my mother's brother. But in our strict house, in the prime of my unfolding youth, he was the one who came close to me. He praised my bloom every day. He gave me love. . . . How was I to know that if you felt like breaking yourself into bits and melting into one with someone—if you felt that just being with him gave a whole meaning to life—and if he was your uncle, it was a sin! Why, I was hardly fourteen! I didn't even know what sin was—I swear by my mother, I didn't! [*She sobs loudly like a little girl.*] I insisted on marriage. So I could live my beautiful lovely dream openly. Like everyone else! But all of them—my mother too—were against it. And my brave man turned tail and ran. Such a rage—I felt such a rage against him then—I felt like smashing his face in public and spitting on it!

But I was ignorant. Instead, I threw myself off a parapet of our house—to embrace death. But I didn't die. My body didn't die! I felt as if feelings were dead—but they hadn't died either then. Again, I fell in love. As a grown woman. I threw all my heart into it; I thought, this will be different. This love is intelligent. It is love for an unusual intellect. It isn't love at all—it's worship! But it was the same mistake. I offered up my body on the altar of my worship. And my intellectual god took the offering—and went his way. He didn't want my mind, or my devotion—he didn't care about them! [*Feebly.*] He wasn't a god. He was a man. For whom everything was of the body, for the body! That's all! Again, the body! [*Screaming.*] This body is a traitor! [*She is writhing with pain.*] I despise this body—and I love it! I hate it—but—it's all you have, in the end, isn't it? It will be there. It will be yours. Where will it go without you? And where will you go if you reject it? Don't be ungrateful. It was your body that once burnt and gave you a moment so beautiful, so blissful, so near to heaven! Have you forgotten? It took you high, high, high above yourself into a place like paradise. Will you deny it? And now it carries within it the witness of that time—a tender little bud—of what will be a lisping, laughing, dancing little life—my son—my whole existence! I want my body now for him—for him alone. [*Shuts her eyes and mutters in mortal pain.*] He must have a mother . . . a father to call his own—a house—to be looked after—he must have a good name!

[*Darkness. Then light. The loud ticking of a watch. Benare is motionless in the dock as before. The others are all in their places.*]

KASHIKAR [*Lowering the hand which holds the watch in front of him*]. The time is up. The accused has no statement to make. In any case, it would be of no use. The cup of her crime is now full. Now—the judgement. Rokde, my wig, please.

[*Rokde hurriedly unpacks it and hands it to him. Kashikar puts it on and with all the grandeur of a solemn ritual, says*]

Prisoner Miss Benare, pay the closest attention. The crimes you have committed are most terrible. There is no forgiveness for them. Your sin must be expiated. Irresponsibility must be chained down. Social customs, after all, are of supreme importance. Marriage is the very foundation of our society's stability. Motherhood must be sacred and pure. This court takes a serious view of your attempt to dynamite all this. It is the firm opinion of this court that your behaviour puts you beyond mercy. And, what is more, the arrogance with which you conducted yourself in society, having done all these things, that arrogance is the most unforgivable thing of all. Criminals and sinners should know their place. You have conducted yourself above your station. The court expresses its indignation at your presumptuousness. Moreover, the future of posterity was entrusted to you. This is a very dreadful thing. The morality which you have shown through your conduct was the morality you were planning to impart to the youth of tomorrow. This court has not an iota of doubt about it. Hence not only today's, but tomorrow's society would have been endangered by your misconduct. It must be said that the school officials have done a work of merit in deciding to remove you from your job. By the grace of God, it has all been stopped in time. Neither you nor anyone else should ever do anything like this again. No memento of your sin should remain for future generations. Therefore this court hereby sentences that you shall live. But the child in your womb shall be destroyed.

BENARE [*Writhing*]. No! No! No!—I won't let you do it—I won't let it happen—I won't let it happen!

[*All are as still as statues. Benare comes sobbing to the stool for the defence counsel. There she sits down, half fainting. Then in paroxysms of torment, she collapses with her head on the table, motionless. Stifled sobs come from her.*

Silence. By now it is quite dark in the hall. There is a noise of someone opening the door. All start and look towards it. The door quietly opens little by little. A line of light comes in through it. Two or three faces look round.]

FIRST FACE [*Looking curiously at everyone in the hall*]. Has the show begun? The Living Courtroom?

[*Everyone is startled to the realization. Consciousness dawns afresh. Samant puts on the lights. Everyone quickly returns to normal.*]

SAMANT [*Getting up and going forward*]. Oh? No, no, not now—but it will, soon. But please wait outside. Come on—five minutes—come on. [*He takes them out somehow.*]

KARNIK. Well! It's really late, you know.

MRS KASHIKAR. Goodness, I just didn't realize the time!

PONKSHE. What's the time? It's quite dark.

KASHIKAR. Rokde, it's your job to look after the timing of the show. What were you doing all this time? Useless fellow!

SUKHATME. Let him be, Kashikar. We had some good fun! Felt just like fighting a real case!

KASHIKAR. Come on. Get ready quickly, everyone ... come on ...

PONKSHE. I am always ready—

[*He points to Benare. They are all arrested. Silent, serious. They gather round the motionless Benare.*]

MRS KASHIKAR [*Stroking the garland in her hair*]. She's taken it really to heart. How sensitive the child is!

KASHIKAR. You're telling me. She's taking it much too much to heart. After all it was—

SUKHATME. Just a game! What else? A game! That's all!

PONKSHE. A mere game!

KARNIK. Benare, come on, get up. It's time for the show. The show must go on.

MRS KASHIKAR [*Shaking her*]. Do get up, Benare. The show must start on time. Come on now. Look, it was all untrue. It would hardly be true, would it?

[*Samant has entered.*]

PONKSHE. Samant, please arrange for some tea. The lady needs some tea.

SAMANT. Yes.

KASHIKAR [*Taking off his wig as he gets up. He notices the bottle of* TIK-20 *in front of him on the table. For a moment, he stays looking at it with staring eyes. Then, removing his gaze, to the others*]. Come on ... Come on—come and wash and dress up—enough playing about! Now to business! Come on.

[*All withdraw with silent steps into the next room, in a herd behind him. Benare on the stage, motionless. Samant by the door watching her. Embarrassed, he comes diffidently in from one side and quietly picks up the bright green cloth parrot that he had put there earlier, from the luggage on the dais. He starts going back towards the door. Then, unable to restrain himself, he stops some distance from Benare. Looking at her, he is overcome by feeling. He can't think what to do. He calls out indistinctly, 'Miss . . .' but she does not hear. He is even more embarrassed. Since there is nothing else he can do, gently, affectionately, and with great respect he puts the green cloth parrot in front of her, from a distance. Exit. Benare feebly stirs a little. Then gives up the effort. The bright green cloth parrot is near her. From somewhere unseen, her own voice is heard singing softly.*]

The parrot to the sparrow said,
'Why, oh why, are your eyes so red?'
'Oh, my dear friend, what shall I say?
Someone has stolen my nest away.'
Sparrow, sparrow, poor little sparrow . . .
'Oh, brother crow, oh, brother crow,
Were you there? Did you see it go?'
'No, I don't know. I didn't see.
What are your troubles to do with me?'
O sparrow, sparrow, poor little sparrow . . .

[*Light on Benare only. The rest of the stage in darkness.*]

CURTAIN

SAKHARAM BINDER

Translated by
Kumud Mehta and Shanta Gokhale

CHARACTERS

SAKHARAM BINDER

LAKSHMI

DAWOOD MIYAN

CHAMPA

FOUZDAR SHINDE

SCENE

The action takes place in Sakharam Binder's house.

ACT ONE

SCENE I

It is evening. An old red-tiled house, the sort one finds in the alleys of small district towns. There are two rooms—an outer room and a kitchen with a window at the back. Both are visible to the audience. The shouts of children can be heard.

SAKHARAM [*offstage, roars at the children*]. Hey, you! What the hell's happening here? What're you gaping at? You think we're dancing naked round here? Move on, get the hell out of here! I'll shine your bottoms for you, I'm warning you, the whole lot of you! Now, get out!

[*Enters with a woman, after he has opened the door up left. He is middle-aged. A coarse but impressive personality. Moustaches; a salt-and-pepper stubble on the chin. He is wearing a* dhoti, *a grimy shirt and a jacket. The cap on his head is slightly askew. He is wearing* chappals.
The woman appears terrified. She clutches at the bundle held close to her bosom and cowers near the wall, trembling with fright.]

SAKHARAM. Come in. Have a good look around. You're going to live here now. This house is like me. I won't have you complaining later on. [*She casts a nervous glance across the room.*] Yes, look carefully around the place. If you think it's all right, put down your bundle and stay. Otherwise you can clear out. This is not a royal palace. It's Sakharam Binder's house. And Sakharam Binder is not like your previous man. You'll find out what he's like. No free and easy ways here, see? I'm hot-headed. When I lose my temper, I beat the life out of people. I've a foul mouth. There's always a *bidi* or an oath on my lips—that's what the whole town says about me. I'm not rich but I pull on. You'll get two square meals. Two *saris* to start with and then one every year. And not a fancy one at that. I won't hear any complaints later. I like everything in order here. Won't put up with slipshod ways. If you're careless, I'll show you the door. Don't ask for any pity then. And don't blame me either. I'm the master here. I don't care if they treat me like dirt outside. But a house must be a home, you understand?

[*She somehow manages a nod.*]

There's a well at the back of the house. The lavatory is further down. The well dries up in summer. Then you'll have to fetch water from the river. That's a mile from here. When it rains, we have scorpions moving around. And look, I won't have you leaving the house unless there's work to be done, you understand? If someone calls, you're not supposed to look up and talk. If it's a stranger, you'll have to cover your head and answer him briefly. That's all. And if I'm not around, don't admit anyone into the house. Maybe I'm a rascal, a womanizer, a pauper. Why maybe? I *am* all that. And I drink. But I must be respected in my own house. I am the master here. You agree to all this? Or have you something to say? If you have, you can clear out right away. In this house, what I say, goes. Understand? The others must obey, that's all. No questions to be asked. And one last thing . . . you'll have to be a wife to me. Anyone with a little sense will know what to make of that.

[*She is looking at the house.*]

You agree to the deal? Right, then, go in and make some tea. There's milk and sugar by the stove.

[*She hurriedly slips into the kitchen, puts her bundle on one side and goes to the stove.*]

If you live here, you don't need to fear anyone. This Sakharam Binder—he's a terror. . . . He's not scared of God or of God's father!

[*She starts. Then she stiffens.*]

Yeah . . . I've done every kind of thing. But never a dishonest act in my whole life. I told you. I womanize. I'm a drunkard and I'm ready to announce that to the whole world. Sure . . . with my hand on my heart. All the women I've been to, the number of times I've visited them. If a chap wants to come and see for himself, I'm quite ready to take him there. I haven't been going there lately, though. . . . In this bloody place the men are all the same. They slink out at night, on the sly. And they put on an act all the time. They'd like us to believe that they're an innocent lot! 'You hold your tongue and I'll hold mine!' Damn them all! Don't have the guts to do a thing openly! I ask you what's wrong with it? Damn it all, the body has its appetites! Who made it? God. You think He doesn't know? And He's supposed to be our Father.

[*Lights a* bidi *and sits on a stool.*]

We're not saints. We're men. I tell you, worship and prayer can't satisfy the itch. If you want a thing, well, you've got to have it! What's there to hide? And from whom? From our Father?

[*She is squatting by the stove, with the tea things. She is looking for something. Finally she gets up and comes to the kitchen door. Clears her throat softly to attract his attention.*]

[*Slightly more amiable now*] Go on, speak up. I know I'm foul-mouthed. Bothers you, doesn't it, even to hear me talk? I've been like this right from birth. Born naked, I was. My mother used to say, the brat's shameless. He's a *Mahar* born in a *Brahmin* home. And if I was, who's to blame? It wasn't my doing. . . .

[*She appears terribly embarrassed.*]

You look upset . . . so you must be a *Brahmin* then. . . .

[*She shakes her head. Wants to say something.*]

There you are! Not born a *Brahmin* and yet you've a *Brahmin*'s ways! And me! Born in a *Brahmin* family, but I'm a *Mahar*, a dirty scavenger. I call that a bloody joke! I ran away from home when I was eleven. Got fed up with my father's beatings. Nothing I did ever seemed right. You'd think I was his enemy or something. The way he'd thrash me! You, looking for something?

SHE [*her head bent*]. A matchbox.

SAKHARAM [*throws at her his own*]. There you are. Take this one. And you mustn't be shy. You must always ask for what you want. But if you don't get it, don't complain. Remember, this is not a king's, but Sakharam Binder's palace.

[*She turns to go, then halts.*]

Now what? You'll find the tea leaves in a tin. Or is it all finished? The one before you, she must have finished most of it. She used to drink a lot of tea. She left last Friday.

SHE [*shakes her head*]. Where are the gods?

SAKHARAM. I see . . . the gods? Must be around somewhere. . . . The one before her . . . she went in for that sort of thing. I think there were a couple of pictures. Don't know if she took the lot with her. The one who came after her, she wasn't interested. She used to worship her husband's shirt. The man was out to kill her, but, as far as she was concerned, he was God! The fellow who's out to kill them—he's a god! The chap who saves them—he's just

a man! She worshipped his shirt for two full years. She had T.B.
I took her to the hospital at Miraj. Last Friday that was. She died
there, hugging his shirt to herself. Look, I like a lot of sugar in
my tea and I like it strong and red. Go on, get it, quick!

[*She goes in. As she squats by the stove, she notices an old* sari *on the
clothes line. She gazes at it for a minute. Then she lights the stove and
puts the water on to boil. She is lost in thought. In the outer room,
Sakharam takes off his jacket and hangs it on a peg. He sees something
through the window.*]

Hey, you son of a bitch, you! Are you blind? Can't you see?

[*She shuts her eyes tight, unable to bear this.*]

Your cow's breaking my fence. Be careful! That fence costs
money.

[*Sakharam brings down his* mridanga *from a peg. He removes the
cover, handles the instrument with care. Then he begins to play it softly,
responding to its rhythms.*]

Fine! That's right!

[*She brings him his tea. Clears her throat to draw his attention.*]

Here, give me the cup.

[*She gives it to him. He pours it into the saucer, takes a draught and
roars.*]

Hah . . . hah . . . hah. . . .

[*She is scared.*]

Excellent!

[*She looks relieved. He finishes his tea and puts down the cup and
saucer. She picks it up and is about to go in.*]

Have some yourself. You must take what you want. Mustn't wait
to be told. No such pampering here!

[*She goes in. Squats by the stove. Is about to pour some tea for herself
and drink it when she hears a voice calling off.*]

VOICE. You there, Sakharam?
SAKHARAM [*shouting*]. Who's that? Dawood Miyan? Come, come
along. Come in.

[*Dawood enters.*]

DAWOOD. *Salaam Walekum!*

SAKHARAM [*loudly*]. More tea out here! [*To Dawood*] *Walekum Salaam!* Come, sit down!

DAWOOD. They say you've caught a new bird?

SAKHARAM. Yes. Just now. About an hour ago. How're you getting along?

DAWOOD. So-so. [*Peering inside*] Where did you get her from?

SAKHARAM. From Sonavane. I'd heard some rumour. So I went there this morning. I found her in a *dharmshala*.

DAWOOD [*peering inside*]. Let's have a look!

SAKHARAM. Nothing much to look at this time. Must have been all right once upon a time. But there's no spark left in her now. Her lord and master must have seen to that!

[*She is standing at the door with the tea.*]

I tell you, Miyan, those fellows—they can't father a brat and they take it all out on their wives. Beat her, kick her every single minute of the day. They're an impotent lot! For them the woman's just dirt, that's all.

[*Dawood motions to Sakharam to stop. She is at the door.*]

SAKHARAM [*walks to the door, takes the cup and comes back again*]. I've yet to meet a more gutless breed than these husbands. We're a whole lot better than those swine!

[*Dawood takes the cup. He has a sympathetic expression on his face.*]

Not that I don't give a blow now and then. I know I do. But that's not because I don't have any guts myself. I'm like this *mridanga* here. It plays better when it is warmed up. I'm like that.

[*She is looking for something inside the kitchen.*]

It's good thing I'm not a husband. Things are fine the way they are. You get everything you want and yet you're not tied down. If you've had enough, if she's had enough, you can always part. The game is over. Nothing to bother you after that. While it lasts, she has a roof over her head, and you get home-cooked food. That's a cheap way of fixing all your appetites. No need for you to go begging to another's house! And on top of it, the woman stays docile. She works well, she behaves herself. She knows that one wrong move and out she goes. Come to think of it—women— they're a clever lot. It's only when a woman gets married that she goes wrong. She begins to feel, 'Now I've got my man!' But the husband—he's a proper swine! He ties her down; he doesn't get tied down himself! He flits around again—a free bird! Now look! I'm being quite frank. As far as I'm concerned, I don't believe in double-talk. What have I to gain from that? I don't give a damn. . . .

[*He moves close to the* mridanga *and places it on his lap.*]

See this? Just now it's here on my lap. But I'm quite capable of throwing it away in a garbage can. I'll hardly feel the loss. I won't even look at it twice.

[*He beats the surface of the* mridanga *with his palm.*]

Everything comes to an end. So where's the point in getting involved? And involved with what? As long as one manages to be happy, without doing anyone any harm, that's about all. But—no dishonesty allowed. If you sin—you must be ready to slap your face and say, 'Yes, I sinned.' You must be ready to take the rap. You think one can play hide-and-seek up there? We'll have to face Him naked, won't we? We can do anything we like, but nothing that we might feel ashamed of. To feel ashamed— that's bad—very bad!

DAWOOD.   Yes, yes, Sakharam. [*In an embarrassed tone*] But . . . why not get the stuff out . . .?

SAKHARAM.   Stuff? What stuff? Oh, *chilum?*

[*Dawood motions him to be quiet.*]

Damn you! Why don't you call it by its name?

[*He goes to a niche in the wall and fetches the* chilum *paraphernalia.*]

Ganja. You think it is like a kept woman or what? Everything hush-hush and all that. *Ganja* is like a whore. There's nothing there to hide. Anyone can have a puff and push off. I tell you a whore can get to God much faster than all of us. All of us, mind you! Because she has really nothing to hide. She'll go up to God with her head held high. She'll say to Him, 'I had a living to make. I had to eat. But I didn't cheat anybody. I didn't bother a soul. I didn't get anyone tied down to me and torment him later. If I gave anything at all, I gave men joy. They're born with an itch. I satisfied them. Big and small, rich and poor, the healthy and the diseased—I treated them all alike. As equals! O Lord! If anyone has sinned at all, it's the others. Not me!'

[*In the meanwhile, she has ferreted out two or three pictures of the gods. She has wiped off the dust from the frames and arranged them in order.*]

Wait, I'll get the coals.

[*Sakharam enters the kitchen. He looks at her, sitting before the pictures of the gods.*]

I want some live coals.

[*She gets up with a start. She goes to the stove.*]

My meal has to be ready by seven o'clock. Four *bhakris* of *jowar*, and green chillis to go with them. You'll find some garlic *chutney* in a tin somewhere. The chillis are in that basket. The flour in that large bin there.

[*She gives him live coals on a metal plate.*]

This is no way to hand over coals for *chilum*.

[*He brings out an old incense-burner from the corner.*]

Give them in this.

[*She gives the coals to him.*]

If you're used to rice, look around—you'll find some in the house. The one before you, she liked rice. There must be some *dal* too. I don't eat rice.

[*She listens. He looks at her for a second and comes into the outer room with the coals. She begins to cook his dinner. She finds a small oil lamp and places it in front of the gods. A bell chimes in the distance. She folds her hands in prayer, turning in that direction. In the outer room Sakharam and Dawood are engrossed in their ganja. They are puffing away.*]

Bam-Bhole, Bam-Bhole. Pull, Dawood Miyan. Pull. This is real good.

[*The lights fade. The* mridanga *resounds.*]

SCENE II

The mridanga *continues. When the lights come on, she is in the kitchen. She is spreading out a few rags. Sakharam is playing the* mridanga *in the outer room. She folds her hands in prayer before the gods, then lies down on*

the rags, curled up, with her hands under her head. Sakharam pushes the
mridanga away.

SAKHARAM. *Bam-Bhole.*

[*He stops playing the* mridanga *and yawns loudly. He gets up, opens*
the door and steps out. Footsteps are heard fading out. She becomes
aware of this and sits up. She comes out and looks around her. Far
away, the sounds of a bhajan. *She picks up the* chilum *and puts it*
away. She begins to sweep the floor. Sakharam comes in. She starts and
cowers in fear.]

Carry on, sweep the room.

[*He hangs his shirt on the peg. He's bare-chested. He goes into the*
kitchen and splashes water on his face. He notices the rags on the floor.
Comes out. She is spreading out his mattress for him.]

Not here. There!

[*She hastily shifts the mattress. He is watching her with drugged eyes.*
She sits on the mattress to straighten out the sheet. Then she begins to get
up.]

Don't get up. Sit down.

[*She moves away and, head bent, begins to get up.*]

I said, don't get up!

[*She remains still.*]

Sleep here tonight.

[*She stands frozen. Then, somehow, she manages to get up and begins*
to go in.]

You heard me? The custom here is—to have my legs pressed
before I go to sleep. They came and they went, but the custom
hasn't changed. And it *won't* change, either!

[*She sits down on the mattress.*]

Bam-Bhole. My legs. Is Urdu being spoken here or what? I said
my legs.

[*She hastily comes forward and sits by his feet. He speaks a trifle softer*
now.]

Now press my legs.

[*She begins to press his legs, half-heartedly.*]

All the way up!

[*She presses them up all the way, but in a scared sort of way.*]

Do it properly. Those legs aren't going to bite you! I'm tired today. I set out for Sonavane early this morning and the return trip
was quite a walk. Too much for the legs.

[*She is quietly pressing his legs.*]

Now let's hear your name.

SHE. Laxmi.

SAKHARAM. Laxmi? [*Gazing at her*] Nice name that. And your
husband's name?

[*Laxmi silent. Presses his legs.*]

SAKHARAM. Your husband's name?

[*She continues to press his legs in silence.*]

Why, of course! A good wife is not supposed to utter his name?
I'm not used to all this!

[*She sobs and puts a corner of her* sari *to her eyes.*]

What's wrong? Oh, all right. I won't ask you. The whole lot of
you! All alike where this one thing's concerned. Mention your
husband's name and your eyes begin to brim over with tears. He
kicks you out of the house; he is out to squeeze the life out of you.
But he's your God. You ought to worship a god like that with
shoes and slippers! He should be whipped in public. Gods, eh?

[*She is pressing his legs.*]

You women, you're all the same. Suckled by dead mothers!
Corpses! That's what you are. You get kicked by your husbands
and you go and fall at their feet!

[*She is silent.*]

Did you eat?

[*She continues to press his feet.*]

I asked you something. I can't stand people not answering my
questions. Have you eaten?

[*She shakes her head.*]

Why not?

[*She is still pressing his feet.*]

What did I ask you?

[*He thrusts aside the blanket.*]

LAXMI [*slightly scared*]. It is *Chaturthi* today. And in any case I wasn't hungry.

SAKHARAM [*not expecting this kind of reply*]. So you fast?

[*Laxmi nods.*]

You couldn't have eaten in the morning either. What about yesterday?

[*Laxmi shakes her head.*]

SAKHARAM. Do you want to kill yourself, fasting like this?

LAXMI. I am used to it.

SAKHARAM. Used to it! It won't do in this house. Here you must eat well. Twice a day. You'll need all your strength, if you are going to serve me. All these fasts must end. I'm warning you!

[*Laxmi does not answer him.*]

Go. Go and sleep.

LAXMI [*hesitating*]. There's something I want to ask you. May I?

SAKHARAM. Yes, what is it?

LAXMI [*fumbling*]. Where do you keep the cotton? I'd like some to light the oil-lamp in front of the gods.

SAKHARAM. I've no idea where the one before you kept it. I never give any thought to such things. Ask me where the *chilum* is, or the *mridanga*. I can tell you that. That's my sphere. If there is no cotton in the house, I'll get some tomorrow. What else?

LAXMI [*unable to resist the impulse*]. What was she like—the one before me?

SAKHARAM. The one before? Now there is always this question to answer. The one who follows *must* ask about the one who came before. There have been six of them. And always the same question. What was she like—the previous one? Well, she wasn't much in bed. She just seemed to dry up. She wasted away. No flesh, just bones she was. But very devoted. She never raised her eyes, not once. Let alone answering back. She died in the hospital at Miraj. It's a week now.

LAXMI. Any children?

SAKHARAM. Two. The husband kept them. That's why she pined
away. Those last moments she was gasping for breath, but she
kept on repeating her husband's name. She remembered the
children. I gave her her last sip of water, but the name on her lips
was her husband's.

[*Laxmi sighs.*]

What's the matter? I did everything good and proper. I lit the
funeral pyre. The crow wouldn't touch the rice. So I swore at
that soul of hers lodged in him. I said, 'It was that bloody
husband of yours who cast you off. What do you go on pestering
me for? I owe you nothing. I gave you a roof over your head.
Was that a wrong thing to do? Now let me go, without any more
fuss.' I yelled and the crow came down at once and pecked at the
rice. I had my bath and that was that! Once a person crosses this
threshold, she belongs here. When she leaves this house, it's all
over between us. After that I can't be bothered. But even when I
send her away, I do it good and proper. I give her a *sari*, a *choli*
and fifty rupees. Plus a ticket to where she wants to go. I'm glad I
remembered—I'd forgotten to tell you that. And you're free to
take all that you've been given here. I mean clothes, *chappals*,
bangles. Oh, yes. Everything good and proper, where Sakharam
Binder is concerned. He's no husband to forget common
decency. Go, go and sleep. Don't stand there nodding. There's
no strength left in you with all that fasting. But I'm warning you,
you won't last long in this house if you go around looking like a
corpse. Mine is no ordinary appetite. And I won't hear any
complaints later. I have to get to the Press at seven every
morning. I come home at noon. Then back to the Press at two
and home at six. When we have an urgent job on hand, I've to
work overtime. Then you must have those two *bhakris* ready for
me by six-thirty in the morning. One whole day gone today,
going to Sonavane! I'll have to work overtime tomorrow.

[*He turns on his side to go to sleep. She goes in into the kitchen. Far
away, the* bhajan *continues. The lights fade out.*]

SCENE III

*When the lights come on, the night is far advanced. Sakharam is snoring
away. Outside, a deep silence. Laxmi is by his feet; she is sitting with her*

*head on her knees. She closes her eyes for a while, then she opens them.
Gradually the lights fade out.*

SCENE IV

*When the lights come on again, Laxmi is seen sitting in the kitchen. She
looks less drawn and haggard now and shows more signs of life. The outer
room is empty.*

LAXMI [*bending down and laughing loudly*]. You little rascal, you're
trying to trick me, are you? I put you out, and you steal in again.
You want me to feed you all the time? You're getting spoilt,
aren't you? No you won't get anything now. I told you, didn't I?
No. Nothing. Don't look at me like that. Get away from here. Get
away. Didn't I tell you to move off? Pawing me all the time. Go
on. Don't come anywhere near me. Can't you hear? [*Laughs as if
tickled*] Oh, don't! Now watch out! I'll really hit you if you get into
my lap. Go away. Get away, you, you leech! I'm not going to give
you anything today. You've become a regular pest. Get off me
first. [*She giggles*] Get off me, you hear? Oh, dear—why're you
after my blood, you?

[*Sakharam, back from work, stands at the doorway, listening.*]

Get off me, please! Rightaway.

[*Sakharam is about to explode. He strides into the kitchen. Laxmi is
giggling away, all alone. She becomes silent the minute she sees him.
Repressing her giggles, she gets up and stands modestly.*]

SAKHARAM [*looking suspiciously all over*]. What was going on here?

[*Laxmi shakes her head, meaning, 'Nothing.'*]

Then what made you laugh so much? [*He looks at her suspiciously.*]
Who were you talking to?

[*Laxmi represses a laugh.*]

[*Grumbling*] You must be crazy, talking to yourself like this!

[*He's still looking round the room searchingly. Laxmi stands silent.*]

Who were you talking to?

[*Laxmi shakes her head. Sakharam comes to the outer room, taking off
his jacket.*]

She talks to herself!

[*Grunts and glances suspiciously in the direction of the kitchen. As soon as he is out, Laxmi looks hurriedly for something very near the spot where she has been sitting.*]

I don't want to hear this sort of thing again, I'm warning you. Laughing all by yourself!

[*Laxmi takes the tea off the fire. Then she fills a jar of water from a bucket and carries it out, beyond the front door where Sakharam is waiting for her. She pours the water out for him and he scrubs his hands, feet and face very vigorously. He wipes himself with the towel she gives him. Both come in. Sakharam in front, Laxmi behind him. Sakharam relaxes on a mattress on the floor. Very quietly Laxmi begins to press his legs. He's watching her with a trace of wonder on his face. Their eyes meet. She looks down.*]

SAKHARAM [*taking her hand in his*]. Why were you laughing?
LAXMI [*taking her hand away*]. Somebody might see us . . . .
SAKHARAM. You think I'm afraid of anyone?
LAXMI. I'll get the tea.
SAKHARAM [*still retaining her hand in his, thinks for a second, and then, letting go her hand*]. Come soon.

[*Laxmi goes in, gets the tea, and gives it to him.*]

SAKHARAM [*takes the tea, beckons to her to sit beside him*]. Sit down!

[*She continues to stand.*]

I said sit here.

[*She sits down reluctantly, keeping her distance.*]

Not like a wife! Closer!

[*He pulls her close. He offers her some tea.*]

Have some. . . .
LAXMI. I've left mine inside.
SAKHARAM. I'll knock out your teeth if I hear that again! I'm offering you tea from my cup and you tell me yours is in the kitchen. Here.

[*She takes a sip and holds up her hand, meaning, 'Enough.' He forces her to have more. Then he has some. She gets up to go in with his cup and saucer, but he stops her.*]

Who were you laughing with just now?

LAXMI. Nobody!

SAKHARAM. You mean I imagined it all?

LAXMI. No. Not that. . . .

SAKHARAM. Then . . .?

LAXMI. It was just something.

SAKHARAM. Just something?

LAXMI [*fumbles*]. To do with a black ant.

SAKHARAM. What?

[*Laxmi nods, as if to say, 'That's right.'*]

SAKHARAM. You were talking to a black ant?

LAXMI. Yes, I was.

SAKHARAM. Wasn't he talking to you, too?

LAXMI. Yes. I mean, no.

[*Sakharam is left gaping.*]

I mean, I was speaking for him, too.

SAKHARAM. You were talking to a black ant? What next?

[*Laxmi is silent.*]

SAKHARAM. You must have gone off your mind. Talking to an ant? You probably know the ant?

LAXMI. Oh, yes. Once you start talking, you get to know each other. I give him sugar, so he comes to me.

SAKHARAM. As if there's just that one black ant here! There must be heaps of them in the house. Any one of them might come and. . . .

LAXMI. But I can recognize him now.

SAKHARAM. How?

LAXMI. I can't say how. I know when he comes.

SAKHARAM. You know! And how?

LAXMI. From the way he walks.

SAKHARAM. The way the ant walks?

LAXMI. Yes, I swear to you. He doesn't come to me running. But he walks very slowly, and he goes round the grain of sugar before putting his mouth to it.

SAKHARAM. Who? The ant? What else does he do?

LAXMI. Well, once he's touched the sugar, he wipes his mouth with his foot.

SAKHARAM. He wipes his mouth. Really! And what else does this ant of yours do?

LAXMI. He picks up the grain of sugar and goes near the wall.

SAKHARAM. Then?

LAXMI. He's grown very bold these last two days. He leaves the sugar alone, and comes after me instead.

SAKHARAM. Oh really! Wonderful! And what else?

LAXMI. He climbs on me.

SAKHARAM. Very good. He climbs on you, does he? And then?

LAXMI. Then he refuses to get off. . . . Do what I may . . . he just will not get off. [*Gets up.*] Shall I bring him to you?

SAKHARAM. Who? The ant? Look here, I'm in my right senses still. The ant talks to you, you tell me! Listen, I won't stand such crazy nonsense! You'll have to behave more sensibly, if you want to stay. Understand? Remember that. Now go in. Go.

[*She takes the cup and saucer with her. He looks after her. He's humming the first line of a* lavani *in a discordant and masculine voice.*]

SAKHARAM. Now here we have something else again. The other one used to hug her husband's shirt. This one talks to ants. Just think what these damned husbands do to their wives!

[*She goes into the kitchen and washes the cup and saucer. Bends down, searching for something. Then sits down. Sakharam begins to bring out the* chilum *and its paraphernalia from the usual niche. He is muttering to himself.*]

Dawood hasn't turned up yet.

LAXMI [*softly but audibly*]. I had to face the music and all on account of you! That's right. You eat the sugar and I get the scolding. Nobody believes me. Ants, sparrows, crows—they all talk to me. Why do you talk to me? Eh? Why must you talkee-talkee to me? Go on . . . tell me. . . . You naughty little fellow. . . . Tell me. . . .

[*Sakharam comes in to fetch coals; he stands for a minute in the doorway, listening to her. He loses his temper.*]

SAKHARAM [*shouting*]. What the hell's going on here? Is this a house or a loony-bin?

[*She stands up, startled.*]

Remember what I told you. Don't you dare repeat this sort of thing! All this madness must stop at once.

[*She is trembling with fear.*]

I'll knock your brains out, I will. I want coals.

[*She quietly picks up the incense-burner, puts coals in it, and holds it out to him.*]

Stop whining! Is someone dead around here? And even if he is, no weeping in this house, I tell you!

[*She tries very hastily to wipe her tears with the end of her sari and as she does so, the incense-burner tilts and the coals fall on her foot. She sits down, clutching the burning flesh, holding her foot. She's in terrible pain. Sakharam quickly kicks the coals away.*]

SAKHARAM.　Good! I hope these coals roast your feet—roast them, nice and brown. I don't feel a bit sorry.

[*She is in agony. She gets up despite the pain, picks up the incense-burner and begins to put the coals back into it.*]

Must pay the price for being careless so that you don't repeat the mistake. Can't you hold a thing straight? Impossible creatures! You have to kick them and clout them. That's the only way they can keep their minds on their work. Give me those coals. And go in and put something on that foot of yours. Or else go to hell!

[*He carries the coals to the* chilum. *She goes in, sits by the stove, caressing her foot in an attempt to relieve the pain. Sakharam gets the* chilum *ready.*]

Dawood hasn't turned up yet. God knows where he's got to!

[*She is sitting by the stove, blowing her breath again and again on her foot. Outside Sakharam is blowing on the coals to bring them alive. Takes a puff.*]

Bam-Bhole. That's it!

LAXMI [*caressing her foot, eyes turned down, and in a despairing tone*].　Why do you look at me like that? What am I worth round here? After all, I'm just a cast-off wife. Who cares if my foot burns black? What are you staring at? Aren't you ashamed of yourself? Go away. Don't dare show me your black face again. Go on, get out. Oooh. . . . Go on, go, or else I'll hit you . . . you. . . .

[*The stage gets darker.*]

SCENE V

A very dim light in the kitchen, like a wick burning. The outer room is in complete darkness. Only the voices are audible.

SAKHARAM. Hey! there, get up. Come on, get up. Are you going to get up or . . .? I'll hit you now if you don't get up. Get up, I said!

LAXMI [*in a sleepy tone*]. What is it? I'll get up later.

SAKHARAM. No. Now!

LAXMI. Oh, God! What is it? It's night yet.

SAKHARAM. That's why I'm waking you up.

LAXMI. What?

SAKHARAM. Laugh. . . . Laugh like you did. . . .

LAXMI. What? [*Drowsily*] . . . It's night yet. . . .

SAKHARAM. First laugh. . . . Laugh like you did. . . .

LAXMI. What do you mean? Like what? God, I'm so sleepy! Haven't slept at all two whole nights.

SAKHARAM. Sleep later. Laugh first. Laugh . . . the way you laughed when the ant was crawling on you.

[*A pause.*]

Laugh. . . . Come on.

LAXMI. Later on, please! Oh, God, my foot! Oh!

SAKHARAM. Then why don't you laugh? Go on, laugh. Laugh.

LAXMI. I can't!

SAKHARAM. You laugh for the ant. But you won't laugh when I ask you to. I'll twist that foot of yours, you get me? Now sit up. You're not to sleep. Wake up.

LAXMI. Honestly, I can't. Let me sleep.

SAKHARAM. No, you can sleep later. Get up and laugh. Laugh or I'll choke the life out of you. Laugh! Laugh! Go on, laugh!

[*At first Laxmi forces herself to laugh. Then she laughs spontaneously, as she did in the evening. Then Sakharam's laughter is heard. Both continue to laugh together. Then the laughter stops. Silence.*]

LAXMI. Oh, God. I'm so tired. I can't laugh any more. Please let me sleep. My foot is throbbing.

SAKHARAM. Where? Let me see. Look, I'm warning you. If you're clumsy again, I'll break that leg of yours. All you women, you're a worthless lot!

[*Complete darkness.*]

SCENE VI

The lights come on. Laxmi is busy getting things ready in the kitchen. Outside, a shout: 'Mangalmurti Morya. . . . Shout, come on. Hey, you *kids, shout!* Mangalmurti. . . .' *This is Sakharam's voice. The children shout in unison:* 'Morya!' *Sakharam brings in an image of Ganpati; he is followed by Dawood, who is playing the cymbals. Both are in high spirits.*

SAKHARAM [*at the door*]. *Mangalmurti.* . . .

DAWOOD. *Morya!*

[*Laxmi hurries out to usher them in with the whole paraphernalia of* Puja. *The* Puja *is over. Sakharam places the image at centre of the usual kind of setting.*]

SAKHARAM. Be seated, *Mangalmurti.* I don't know about my ancestors, but this is the first time you have found your way into my house. Relax. Eat, drink and be merry. You have your mouse with you for company, all ready to pounce on. . . .

LAXMI. You shouldn't talk like that!

SAKHARAM. Why not? Dawood, did I say anything wrong? You tell me. Did I refer to his paunch? Or make fun of his tusks? Did I even mention his trunk? Tell me.

LAXMI. Please, that's enough.

SAKHARAM. No, first tell me if I said anything wrong, Dawood!

DAWOOD. Forget it. Don't say such things, if you're not supposed to. *Mangalmurti* is a god. He'll understand.

SAKHARAM. No, but why must she start ragging me the minute I step into the house? I go and do something I've never done before. I go and bring *Ganpati* home. . . .

DAWOOD. Forget it, Sakharam. Let's talk about the *prasad.* I've to go to work.

LAXMI. Nobody's to leave before the *aarti.* I'll just go and get the things.

[*Goes in.*]

DAWOOD. I'll wait. Might as well stay on the right side of all the gods. There's no telling which of them will get annoyed with you and start doing you harm.

SAKHARAM. If you're clean and straight, Dawood, there's not a god in this world who can do you any harm.

DAWOOD. But, Sakharam, I am not clean and straight. When you're alive and kicking it's so damned hard to remember that last reckoning with God. You pile up new sins every day.

SAKHARAM. That's here in the lower court—among men. Dawood, they recognize only one sin in God's court. That's falsehood. It is the worst possible sin. And the sentence for falsehood is a noose round your neck. Who put bones and flesh together in this body? And who sent it here? God. You think he doesn't know about the body and its itch? Remember, what happened every time God came to earth in human form? Just think of Krishna, Dawood Miyan.

[*Laxmi comes out with the* aarti.]

LAXMI [*to Sakharam*]. Here. Take this.

[*Sakharam takes the* aarti *things from her. She lights the lamp. Dawood helps.*]

Please move away, Dawood Miyan.

[*Dawood Miyan moves away.*]

[*To Sakharam*] All right. You can start now.

SAKHARAM. Dawood, come on, sing with me. *Sukhakarta Dukhaharta varta vighnachi—*

[*Dawood begins to accompany him on the cymbals. Both begin to chant the* aarti *in loud voices. Laxmi moves away in disapproval.*]

LAXMI [*signalling to Dawood*]. Not you!

[*He is silent.*]

SAKHARAM [*stopping in mid-chant*]. What's happened? Come on, Dawood . . . *varta vighnachi, nurvi purvi prem kripa jayachi—*

[*Dawood is silent.*]

SAKHARAM. Come on, Dawood, open your mouth. Sing! Why did you stop? *Sarvangi sundara—*

[*Dawood's eyes are fixed on Laxmi.*]

What's happened? Why aren't you singing *aarti*?

[*Dawood is silent.*]

Tell me, why not?

[*Dawood looks furtively at Laxmi.*]

Were you told not to?

[*Dawood is silent.*]

Who told you?

[*Turns to Laxmi.*]

I see. Why shouldn't Dawood sing *aarti?*

LAXMI. Because—he's a Muslim, isn't he?

[*Sakharam suddenly flings the* aarti *things down. Dawood and Laxmi both look scared.*]

SAKHARAM. Who dares stop Dawood singing the *aarti?*

DAWOOD. Never mind, Sakharam.

SAKHARAM. You shut up. [*To Laxmi*] Why shouldn't he sing it?

LAXMI. He's a Muslim—and we—we're Hindus.

[*Sakharam slaps her hard. She lifts her hand to her face in pain.*]

SAKHARAM. Say it again!

LAXMI. What's wrong with what I said? How can a Muslim join in a prayer to *Ganpati?*

SAKHARAM. Why not? If I can join in, why can't he?

[*Sakharam hits her again and again.*]

DAWOOD. Sakharam, let her go.

[*Sakharam takes a belt off the peg.*]

SAKHARAM [*to Laxmi*]. Say it again. Just say it again!

[*Straightens up, her body convulsed with pain.*]

LAXMI. I'm only speaking the truth. A Muslim singing an *aarti* to *Ganpati* and in my house—

[*Sakharam lashes at her with the belt.*]

DAWOOD. Sakharam!

LAXMI [*straightens up, her body is still twisted in pain*]. If you want to beat me, beat me inside. Not in front of God! He's only come to the house today.

DAWOOD. Sakharam, listen to me!

SAKHARAM [*considers Laxmi's upright and quivering stance a challenge*]. All right. Come in. I'll fix you.

[*She turns and goes in. Sakharam follows with the belt. Dawood remains where he is. From within the dark kitchen the sound of blow upon blow. Laxmi's agonized moans, but no whining. Dawood, unable to bear it, goes out. The beating continues. The lights fade out.*]

SCENE VII

When the lights begin to come on, there is no sign of Sakharam. Laxmi's moans are heard in the kitchen. Somehow she manages to get up. Still moaning, she limps towards the God. She picks up the aarti *things lying on the floor. She lights the wick, and sits in front of the image. Then she gets up and manages to drag herself back. She lies down for a while.*

SAKHARAM [*outside*]. Says a Muslim can't join in an *aarti*. He won't do! Dawood, you're a real friend. All right, you can go now. Come for the *aarti* tomorrow. I'll see how that bloody woman stops you!

[*Stumbles in. He's drunk. Muttering to himself, he goes to the peg and hangs his jacket and shirt on it. Notices the belt there. Then looks at the image of* Ganpati.]

SAKHARAM. No. You're not to blame. Not to blame at all.

[*Approaches the God. Looks for the* aarti *things. Finds a matchstick and lights the* aarti *lamp, using a wick from the larger oil-lamp. Somehow he manages to balance it all in his hand.*]

Forgive me. I'm drunk today.

[*Begins to sing the* aarti *in a dissonant voice. His face is bloated.*]

[*The stage darkens.*]

SCENE VIII

The light of the oil-lamp in the outer room. The kitchen is dark. A conversation can be heard.

SAKHARAM. Now laugh. Are you going to laugh or not?
LAXMI [*moaning*]. No.
SAKHARAM. Are you or aren't you?
LAXMI. My whole body is throbbing with pain. Such gnawing pain. [*Moans*] You'd think my flesh was on fire.
SAKHARAM. So what? You have to laugh. You hear me? My orders must be obeyed in this house. What I say, goes. Are you going to laugh or shall I throw you out? Shall I? Come on, get up.
LAXMI. Let me go. Oh, God! Oh, my God!
SAKHARAM. I won't let you go till you laugh.
LAXMI. I'll die!
SAKHARAM. Laugh, and then die!

[*Laxmi continues to moan.*]

SAKHARAM. Laugh! Laugh this minute. Or I'll twist your arm. I will. I'll get the belt. Laugh.

[*Laughs.*]

Laugh like that. Now. This very minute. You hear me?

[*Laxmi tries to laugh. Her laughter is punctuated with agonized moans. The laughter becomes louder. It continues. One might think she was being tickled, and rather violently. And to add to it, there is Sakharam's intoxicated laughter. The oil-lamp in the outer room dies down. Darkness. The* mridanga *beats begin.*]

SCENE IX

The mridanga *continues for some time. The lights come on. Sakharam is beating the drum in a trance. Laxmi comes in with the water-pots, and carries them with a lot of effort to the kitchen. Supporting herself against something, she tries to catch her breath.*

SAKHARAM [*shouts*]. Make a cup of tea. Quick!

[*Laxmi is still out of breath in the kitchen.*]

[*Shouts*] Can't you say yes? Something sticking in your throat? I want my tea at once!

[*Laxmi goes to the stove.*]

LAXMI [*grumbling*]. I'm getting it. Wait. I almost died bringing the water in. You think I'm made of stone? When I'm dead, you'll be free of me.

SAKHARAM [*gets up and comes to the kitchen*]. What did you say?

LAXMI. I've put the water on to boil.

SAKHARAM. First repeat to me what you said just now.

[*Laxmi watches the water boiling.*]

Why don't you repeat what you said? Go on!

LAXMI [*suddenly bursts out*]. You think I am afraid to tell you? How much more can a person bear? It's a year now since I entered this house. I haven't had a single day's rest. Whether I'm sick or whether it's a festal day. Nothing but work, work; work all the time. You torture me the whole day, you torture me at night. I'll drop dead one of these days and that will be the end.

SAKHARAM. What if you do? I'll perform your last rites. Who came to help you when your husband threw you out? I brought you here. Gave you food, clothes and a roof over your head. Mind you, I don't have money to throw away.

LAXMI. I'd have gone where my feet took me. Or else I'd have jumped into the river. Did I come to your door begging you to take me in? If I'd drowned myself in the river, that at least would have been the end of all my troubles.

SAKHARAM. You can still go there and drown yourself for all I care. You've just come from the river. You go there every day, don't you? What's there to stop you?

LAXMI. My life's not that worthless. You think my mother carried me in her womb for nine whole months just to have me kill myself in a breath? Maybe I'm homeless now, but I come from a good family. My father used to be a *Munsif*.

SAKHARAM. *Munsif* be damned! Once a woman is thrown over, nobody calls her respectable. Remember that. I at least took you in.

LAXMI. I, at least, stayed on. Another woman would have walked out.

SAKHARAM. There were six who stayed. Six in all. You're the seventh.

LAXMI. But if just one of them had lived here in comfort, why would you have brought me?

SAKHARAM. You mean to say I needed you?

LAXMI. You think you were doing me a favour?

SAKHARAM. Leave that tea and just get the hell out of here!

[*Laxmi pours the tea in a cup.*]

Get out, this very minute, out.

LAXMI. I will. Drink your tea.

[*Pushes the tea forward.*]

SAKHARAM. So, a year's stay has gone to your head, eh?

[*Sits cross-legged to drink his tea.*]

Go. Get out of here. Don't show me your face again.

LAXMI. I won't, you'll see. I've got a nephew in Amalner. I'll go there.

SAKHARAM. Just make yourself scarce.

LAXMI [*absorbed in her work*]. I will when I want to.

SAKHARAM. What the bloody hell! Such damned airs!

LAXMI. A dead hen doesn't fear the fire! Nothing more terrible can happen to me now. I've been through everything in this house. The whole world knows what goes on here. Even the children talk.

SAKHARAM [*finishing his tea*]. What do they say?

LAXMI. Why don't you listen if you're so interested?

SAKHARAM. I don't pay any heed to brats and what they say. But what do they say?

LAXMI. Why should I go and foul my mouth? Just to get beaten in the end?

SAKHARAM. You don't get beaten for nothing. You should admit your mistakes.

LAXMI. I do. My coming here was itself a mistake.

SAKHARAM. You just be careful about what you say or else. . . .

LAXMI. More beatings in store for me! Isn't that so? In any case my body is one big sore—with all that beating I get from you. What else do I get here?

SAKHARAM. Laxmi, I'm warning you. Don't provoke me.

LAXMI. I've never heard a kind word here. Always barking orders. Curses. Oaths. Threatening to throw me out. Kicks and blows. [*Wipes her eyes with the end of the* sari.] There I was in agony after I'd been belted, and all you wanted me to do was laugh. Laugh and laugh again. Here I am on the point of death and I'm supposed to laugh. Hell must be a better place than this. [*Whimpers*] If I die, I'll be free of this once and for all.

SAKHARAM. Right at the start I'd warned you. I'd told you what I was like. I never hide anything. I told you quite plainly, again and again. 'Stay if you're ready to put up with all this, or else go your way.' Were you deaf then? You had feet. You could have walked away. Haven't I been drinking less this year? Eh? Not that I don't drink now and then but isn't it much less? Tell me. Last month I had *ganja* just twice. And don't I do my *puja* properly? Go on, tell me. I bathe every morning, and then I sit here for my *puja*. Don't I? Answer me or I'll break your jaw. Tell me. Don't I wear clean clothes nowadays? Why don't you answer me? What are these ears for?

LAXMI [*sarcastically*]. I'm much obliged!

SAKHARAM. I had six before you. I disowned my own father. I wouldn't let anyone boss over me. But I did listen to you, didn't I? Didn't I?

LAXMI. And you beat me in return. And cursed me and tortured me.

SAKHARAM. Then what did you expect me to do? Be your slave and lick your feet?

LAXMI. You'll know that once I'm gone.

SAKHARAM. Then why don't you go? When you're forced to lead a dog's life, you'll come to your senses.

LAXMI. Is my life any different now?

SAKHARAM. From a dog's? You mean you don't feel the difference in this house? Then get out. Clear out at once. Come on.

[*Pulls her up from near the stove, drags her to the door, pushes her out, and comes in as if he has washed his hands of her.*]

Don't you dare step into this house again or I'll kill you. I don't mind going to the gallows for killing an ungrateful wretch like you.

[*Shuts the front door.*]

Go! Good riddance!

[*Sits down, smouldering. No movement outside.*]

Don't you ever come in again. Just go your way. Go, find someone who'll feed you and put up with all your queenly airs. Go and live with him. Where you are concerned, I am dead. Damn you, you wretch! And I'm supposed to be the villain. That's the reward I get for giving you a roof over your head. I call that a bloody joke!

[*Paces up and down. Knocking at the door.*]

Go! As far as I'm concerned, you're dead and gone. I won't take you back. Get out!

DAWOOD. Sakharam. Hey, Sakharam!

SAKHARAM. Dawood? Is that you?

[*Goes to the door, is about to open it, then stops.*]

Dawood, you're alone out there, aren't you?

DAWOOD. Of course I'm alone.

SAKHARAM. That ungrateful bitch has gone, I hope?

DAWOOD. Will you open the door first?

[*Sakharam opens the door. Dawood enters.*]

What sort of *tamasha* is this?

[*Laxmi comes in from behind him and starts walking towards the kitchen.*]

SAKHARAM [*shouts*]. You dare come back here again, you?

DAWOOD. Why don't you let her be?

SAKHARAM. Now why have you come back? Who wants you here?

[*Laxmi goes to the kitchen and sets about her chores.*]

I don't need anybody. I'll live alone. And if you have it in you, you can always bring in women by the dozen. It's not as if she's got a special one made of gold while every other woman's is just a brass one. . . . I'll knock her teeth in, every single one of them.

DAWOOD. Why do you get so worked up every now and then? Take it easy. It's always like this between a man and a woman.

SAKHARAM. I've never put up with even a word from anybody and here's this niggling bit of cast-off woman trying to lord over me. Forget it! I'll beat the life out of her. Sit down. I'll go and get the coals.

[*Goes in with the incense-burner.*]

I want coals.

LAXMI. Help yourself.

SAKHARAM. I said I want burning coals.

LAXMI. I thought you said you don't need anybody! Then why don't you help yourself?

SAKHARAM [*between clenched teeth*]. Coals!

LAXMI. Am I a slut? A bitch? A niggling bit of a cast-off woman? Then beat me? Why're you waiting! Go ahead and beat the life out of me. Burn me alive. There's nobody I can call my own. So my life is worth nothing. . . .

[*Sakharam controls himself with great effort. Somehow he manages to help himself to the coals, and joins Dawood. Silently he prepares the* chilum. *Laxmi goes on cooking. She wipes her eyes every now and again. Darkness. The* mridanga *beats begin.*]

SCENE X

The mridanga *is being played at a faster tempo. A dim light in both the rooms. Laxmi is lying on her rags in the kitchen. Sakharam sits in the outer room beating the* mridanga *furiously. He is like some wild spirit of the night.*

VOICE [*off, annoyed*]. Hey you! Stop that noise, will you? What an hour to choose for this racket!

ANOTHER [*off*]. Hey!

[*Sakharam goes on playing the* mridanga *numbly. Then suddenly he stops, gets up and goes in. Comes to a halt by the sleeping Laxmi.*]

SAKHARAM. You awake?

[*No answer.*]

Are you awake or are you sleeping?

[*No answer.*]

The bitch, she won't answer me, eh? Get up. Listen to me! [*Pulls the rags from under her and makes her sit.*] Now listen! I was wrong. I'm short-tempered. But you always rub me the wrong way with all the things you say and do. Isn't that right? Tell me. I haven't been drinking so much this last year. I do my *puja* regularly, don't I? You mean to say all this is nothing?

[*She is sitting there with her* sari *covering her face.*]

I had six before you, but I refused to put up with any nonsense from them. I kept them. They worked for me. I told them to go—they went. You are different. Still waters run deep, they say. Not just deep. They're damned dangerous. Am I wrong? Tell me. You daren't say I'm wrong. Pretending to be asleep, are you? You've had enough sleep. Now listen. Are you listening? Say yes; say yes this very minute; say it.

LAXMI [*in a sleepy voice*]. Yes.

SAKHARAM. You've been a lot of trouble to me, this whole year. I tormented you, too. But I'm fed up now. And you've had enough. Isn't that right? Say, yes.

LAXMI [*in the same tone*]. Yes.

SAKHARAM. You can't really cope with me any more. And I can't cope with your sort of nature. The blood goes to my head. I feel it bursting.

LAXMI [*sleepily*]. Yes.

SAKHARAM. What do you mean, 'yes'? I sometimes feel I'll go mad with your. . . .

LAXMI. Yes.

SAKHARAM. Stop your yessing. Enough is enough. We're not married. There's nothing to bind us. We don't need to remain tied to each other. You can go your way. I can go mine. You don't owe me anything. I owe you nothing either. Let's be free of each other. Didn't you say you had a nephew in Amalner? Go to him tomorrow. I'll buy your ticket. I'll give you a *sari* and a *choli*. All good and proper. You can take away everything you brought with you. And also what you're wearing now and some money that I'm going to give you. Don't want you to say later that I didn't treat you well. Go in peace. I don't blame you for anything

that's happened. But it's best to break it up now. You understand? Don't you?

LAXMI [*faintly*]. Yes.

[*Darkness.*]

SCENE XI

*The lights come up. There's a bundle near the door. Near it a small trunk.
A tired, swollen-eyed Laxmi is putting things in order in the kitchen.
Sakharam is at the door.*

SAKHARAM. Have you finished? Time we left.

LAXMI. I'll just say my prayers and come.

[*She lights the little oil-lamp before the gods. Folds her hands in prayer
and is about to leave. Suddenly remembers something and goes back.*]

SAKHARAM. Hurry up!

[*Laxmi comes out. Sakharam picks up the small trunk and the bundle.*]

LAXMI. I'll just tell the neighbours. Won't look right if I leave
without. . . .

[*Goes out. Sakharam has put the trunk down and is waiting. Laxmi
comes back.*]

SAKHARAM. Is that all?

LAXMI. You must never sweep the house soon after someone
leaves it. It brings you bad luck, they say. And ruin to the family.
I'll just sweep the place and then we can start.

SAKHARAM. But the train will leave!

[*Laxmi hurriedly sweeps the rooms.*]

Now hurry up!

LAXMI. Come. [*Suddenly*] Oh, I forgot one thing.

[*Goes in. Sakharam stands there helpless. Laxmi comes out.*]

SAKHARAM. What was that?

LAXMI. I'd forgotten to put out sugar for the ants. I'm glad I
remembered.

[*Goes to the window. A crow is cawing outside.*]

I'm off, Crowie dear. He used to come here every day. And he'd
eat only when I fed him. Who'll feed him now?

SAKHARAM. I'll feed him but please hurry.

LAXMI. My feet won't stir.

SAKHARAM. That's quite obvious.

LAXMI [*looking at the house*]. I stayed here for a whole year. This house became my home. And now again [*Lifts a corner of the* sari *to her mouth*.]—It's a bad thing to be so attached.

SAKHARAM [*impatiently*]. Then don't be. Come along now.

[*Laxmi bends down to touch his feet. He quickly withdraws them.*]

What's this? Why're you doing that?

LAXMI. I won't be seeing you again. The gods and the *Brahmins* had meant him for me. But he didn't come to my lot. He couldn't stand the sight of me. I came to this place. I made it my own. I gave it all I had. I kept nothing back.

SAKHARAM. All right. All right. But let's get going.

[*He herds the whimpering Laxmi out before him. He shuts the door and locks it. Both go away. The scene does not change for a few seconds. Then darkness descends.*]

SCENE XII

The lights come up gradually. Dawood and Sakharam are high. They've had their ganja.

SAKHARAM. There have been many women here, but this one left a mark before she went away.

DAWOOD [*muttering*]. Yes, that happens.

SAKHARAM. But there was no point in continuing. Just a lot of trouble for both of us. And a strain—especially for her. In any case she was tired out after all that hell her husband had given her. She was getting on in years, too. And you know what I am like. Everything said and done, there's the body, the home of all our appetites. Try keeping them down—you can't. Impossible. So I decided, once and for all. No point in troubling her any further. She'll stay with her nephew for the rest of her life and worship those gods of hers.

DAWOOD [*in a trance*]. Good thing you did that!

SAKHARAM. You agree, don't you?

DAWOOD. Yes, yes. Of late I've been thinking on the same lines and. . . .

SAKHARAM. What?

DAWOOD. Time now for you to finish off this affair. . . .

SAKHARAM. Don't call it an affair!

DAWOOD. All right then. . . .

[*They pull at the* chilum *in turn. They are in a trance.*]

[*A little later.*]

DAWOOD. Sakharam, what next?

SAKHARAM. Next? What do you mean?

DAWOOD. I mean a new one.

SAKHARAM. A new one?

DAWOOD. I mean, when are you going to get a new bird?

SAKHARAM [*thinking*]. Eh? Oh yes, of course. Actually I did hear something two days ago. A police *fouzdar* in Chimkhada has just been sacked. My guess is that his wife will leave him in another week or so. Nobody she can call her own. There's just a stepmother. For all you know, something might happen in a day or two.

DAWOOD. Good!

SAKHARAM. I'll be on the track from tomorrow.

DAWOOD. Quite right. Here. Take a puff!

[*Both sit still. Gradually the stage darkens.*]

CURTAIN

ACT TWO

SCENE I

The same outer room and kitchen. A few days later. Evening.

SAKHARAM [*off*]. Damn you. What do you want? Bloody brats! You hear me? How many times have I told you? Get out, you hear! You think this is some kind of *tamasha*? I'll skin your backs if you don't move on.

[*The door opens from outside. Sakharam enters, carrying a leather bag. He is followed by a woman. This is Champa. She is younger than Laxmi, slightly more plump and better built. Sakharam goes through the ritual of repeating for her benefit what he has said before to Laxmi. But there is a difference.*]

Come in. Have a good look around you. You're going to live here now. Right? [*Their eyes meet.*] This house is like me. I won't have you complaining later on. Yes, look carefully round the place. If you think it's all right, put down your bundle. No . . . not your bundle . . . it's a bag. This is not a king's palace. It's Sakharam Binder's house. And Sakharam Binder is not like your previous man. You'll have to find out what he's like. No free and easy ways here, see?

[*She is looking around the house. At this point looks into his eyes. He is rendered speechless.*]

[*Coming back to his senses*] Everything different here. I'm hot-headed. When I lose my temper, I beat the life out of people. I've a foul mouth. There's always a *bidi* or an oath on my lips. I'm not rich but I manage. You'll get two square meals. Two *saris* to start with, then one, every year. [*Looking at her, he hesitates a little.*] And not a fancy one at that. I like everything in order here. Won't put up with slipshod ways. If you're careless, I'll show you the door. Don't blame me then, you understand? I'm the master here. I don't care if outside they treat me like dirt. But a house must be like a home, you understand?

[*She is still looking around. The minute he addresses this query to her, she looks in his direction and nods. Smiles a little without cause. He is enraptured. Controls himself.*]

CHAMPA. The house must be like dirt. . . . No, no, like a home.

[*As she says this, she smiles more distinctly. He smiles. She smiles. He smiles again. Once again he collects himself.*]

SAKHARAM. The well is there behind the house; the lavatory is further down . . . there.

[*She wriggles a little.*]

What's the matter? The well dries up in summer. You'll have to fetch water from the river. That's a mile away. When it rains, we have scorpions moving around. I won't have you leaving the house except on work. If someone comes. . . .

[*She turns to look at the door.*]

No one has come. But if someone does come, you mustn't look up and talk. If it's a stranger, you'll have to cover your head and answer him. If I'm not at home, don't admit anyone.

CHAMPA. The scorpion?

SAKHARAM. Eh? [*Regaining control, and in a stern voice.*] No, not him either. He bites.

CHAMPA. Sharp! Very sharp!

SAKHARAM. I may be a rascal, a womanizer. . . .

[*She is watching him, her little finger on her chin.*]

Not any more. But I may be a pauper. May be anything. I drink . . . but I must be respected in the house.

[*Dawood is standing in the doorway.*]

DAWOOD [*involuntarily*]. Wow!

[*Sakharam and Champa look confused.*]

[*Sheepishly*] Excuse me, I. . . .

SAKHARAM. Oh, it's all right!

DAWOOD. I've never seen anything like this before. That's why.

SAKHARAM. What do you mean anything like this? Like what?

DAWOOD. Now don't be embarrassed. But, Sakharam. . . .

[*Winks and makes an appreciative gesture with his thumb and forefinger. He whispers in his ear.*]

You are a lucky chap, aren't you? She belonged to another and she just walked into your arms. I'm off. I'll come later.

[*Looks once again at Champa and hurries away. Sakharam and*

Champa look at one another and laugh. Sakharam is infatuated with her body.]

SAKHARAM [*making a feeble attempt to regain control*]. You like the house?

CHAMPA. No. Our house was much bigger. Besides it was new.

SAKHARAM. Well, this is not. So. . . .

CHAMPA. Looks too old to me.

SAKHARAM [*now in control*]. If you don't like it, you can go out.

CHAMPA. Why? Is there another house outside?

SAKHARAM. No. This is all there is. And it's not a king's palace. It's Sakharam Binder's house.

CHAMPA. Sakharam Binder? Who's he?

SAKHARAM [*slightly confused*]. Me!

CHAMPA. Oh, I see! I thought it was someone else. Really I did!

SAKHARAM [*again tries hard to free himself of the lure of her body*]. If you want to go . . . I mean stay . . . you can go into the kitchen and see about the tea, you'll find the milk near the stove. And one last thing, you're going to be a wife to me.

CHAMPA. I'm famished. Is there anything to eat?

SAKHARAM. You'll find something in the kitchen.

CHAMPA [*sits down*]. Then why don't you go and have a look?

SAKHARAM [*confused*]. In this house, the woman must behave properly. She must treat me with due respect.

CHAMPA. Yes. Go and see if there's anything to eat. There's been nothing in this belly since yesterday. Just that guava I picked up as I left the house. That's all.

SAKHARAM [*forcing himself to take his eyes off her body*]. While you're staying with me, you don't need to be scared of anybody. Sakharam Binder is here to deal. . . .

CHAMPA. Scared? Who, me? And scared of whom? My husband? [*Spits*] What can he do to me? If I'd stayed with him longer, I'd have shown that corpse what I can do! But I got fed up living with him. All he does is to drink and then he keeps on threatening to kill himself. You think he'd have the guts to do it, that ninny? Why don't you give me something to eat?

SAKHARAM [*hesitates and then goes in*]. Yes.

[*Begins to look around in the kitchen. Champa fiddles with the* mridanga.]

CHAMPA. Looks like you play the *dholki*.

SAKHARAM [*from the kitchen*]. Not the *dholki*! I play the *mridanga*.

CHAMPA. Same thing. They both look the same, anyway. But let me tell you about that clownface husband of mine. He was a *fouzdar*, but even a thief wouldn't have pissed on his face. They sacked him because a pistol was stolen from the station. That stupid clod, he didn't even notice it had gone till the next morning. The way he drinks!

[*Sakharam, who is coming out with something to eat on a metal plate, is shocked by this.*]

SAKHARAM. In this house the woman must always speak with restraint. I won't put up with bad language.

CHAMPA. Right. [*Begins to eat.*] Just thinking about it makes my blood boil. He thought he could earn off me! His mother will have to drop a litter before he can make me do such things! [*Finishes eating and licks her fingers.*] What does he take me for? That sort of a woman? Now make me a nice cup of tea, will you?

SAKHARAM. What? That's a woman's job.

CHAMPA. Then call her.

SAKHARAM. I don't mean a servant. I mean the woman of the house.

CHAMPA. You mean me? But I've never made tea in all my life.

SAKHARAM. Never?

CHAMPA. That's right. In my husband's house my mother-in-law used to make it and, at home, my old man used to make the tea and cook the food. And mother used to sit in the tobacco shop. We did good business. Oh, yes! And we used to sell liquor too. That's where I met this dead duck, my husband. He came to raid the place and he raided something else instead. Then he kept dropping in. He kept on saying, 'Marry me, marry me.' So I did. How was I to know that he was such a son of a bitch! Sorry! I won't talk like that. I'll remember not to. But do something about the tea, will you? I *have* to have tea when I'm eating.

[*Sakharam doesn't know what to do. His eyes rove over her body. Just then Dawood peeps in.*]

SAKHARAM. Dawood, come here. [*Takes him aside.*] You think you could make tea?

DAWOOD. Of course, why not? For a peach like this, anything.... Oh, sorry!

[*He runs into the kitchen. Fishes out the tea-pot and puts it on the fire. His eyes dart in the direction of the other room.*]

SAKHARAM [*remembering something*]. The one who was here before you, the seventh, only a few days back she. . . .

CHAMPA. Poor thing, how?

SAKHARAM. I don't mean she died! I packed her off. I only keep a woman here as long as I need her. She has to carry out all the duties of a wife. When one of the two or both feel, 'Now, we've had enough of this,' we part. I buy her her ticket and I give her a *sari* and a *choli*. She can take away the things that she may have been given here.

CHAMPA. I don't want to leave just yet.

SAKHARAM [*cannot control himself*]. And I don't want to send you away either.

[*Both of them look foolishly at each other and then laugh, first she and then Sakharam.*]

[*Controlling himself with some effort*] But you've got to live according to the rules here.

CHAMPA [*calling*]. Dawood!

[*Dawood comes running out.*]

[*To Dawood*] Be a pet and go get me a nice *pan*. With tobacco, if you don't mind.

DAWOOD [*drooling*]. Eh? Yes. . . . Oh yes . . . . I'll fetch it. I'll get it. I'll come. . . .

[*Tears out of the room.*]

SAKHARAM. Hey!

[*Dawood reluctantly stops.*]

Don't run around like a nitwit. Here. Take this money and get two *pans*. And what have you done about the tea?

DAWOOD. It's almost ready. I'll be back. . . .

[*Glances at Champa and runs off.*]

CHAMPA. He's nice!

[*Sakharam feels a twinge of jealousy. He has followed Dawood to the door. Now, he casually shuts the door. Champa and Sakharam smile at each other without cause. Sakharam is slowly beginning to lose control of himself.*]

SAKHARAM [*coming near Champa*]. Of course he's nice.

[*They are now very close to each other. Sakharam puts his hand on her shoulder. A knock at the door. Dawood's voice is heard. 'Sakharam* bhaiya, *open the door.' Sakharam comes to his senses and hastily opens the door.*]

DAWOOD [*coming in*]. Door already shut, eh?

[*Gives a* pan *to Champa. She smiles bewitchingly at him. Dawood runs into the kitchen and begins to pour out tea.*]

CHAMPA [*following Dawood with her eyes*]. He's nice!

SAKHARAM. Yes. But in this house, I won't allow too much talking to strangers. I said so at the start. It's a very important point.

CHAMPA. Right, right. [*Opening her suitcase*] I must change my clothes.

[*She begins to take out her* sari *and is about to change.*]

SAKHARAM. Not here. Do all that in the kitchen when Dawood comes out.

CHAMPA. What's there to be so shy about, if I'm going to stay here?

[*Moves away a bit and starts changing her* sari. *Dawood comes out with two cups of tea. He sees Champa, bites his tongue and pretends he hasn't seen her.*]

DAWOOD. Sakharam, I've brought the tea.

[*Sakharam recovers a little. Again and again Dawood keeps glancing at her and pretending not to notice. She is totally unmindful of all this.*]

SAKHARAM. Dawood, from now on I'll come to your shop. We'll meet there. That'll be better. What?

DAWOOD [*punctuating Sakharam's remarks with the following words while he himself is absorbed in watching Champa*]. Oh yes. . . . Quite. . . . Absolutely. . . . [*And then, involuntarily*] Wow!

SAKHARAM [*now even more self-conscious*]. What's the matter?

DAWOOD. Terr-i-fic! [*Then, recollecting himself*] Sakharam, I'm off. [*Hesitates*] I'll . . . I'll come back later.

SAKHARAM. No, no, I'll come to see you.

DAWOOD. Oh, all right. [*To her*] Er . . . ah . . . now . . . I'm off. Your tea's there.

[*Hurries away.*]

CHAMPA [*looking at his departing figure*]. He's nice!

SAKHARAM [*unable to control himself*]. All right, all right. You've said that before. Now drink your tea.

[*They both drink tea.*]

CHAMPA [*sipping her tea*]. Very sweet!

SAKHARAM [*losing his temper*]. There you go again. Very nice! Very sweet!

CHAMPA. Isn't the tea sweet?

SAKHARAM [*grasping the point now*]. Oh, you meant the tea! I thought you. . . .

CHAMPA [*stuffs the* pan *into her mouth*]. First-class! Eat yours.

SAKHARAM. I'd like you to give it to me.

CHAMPA [*easily*]. All right. [*Stuffs* pan *into his mouth.*] Eat. God, am I sleepy! That mug face, he didn't let me sleep for four days and four nights. 'I'll kill myself! I'll kill myself!' That's what he says all the time. [*Yawns.*] I'll sleep for an hour or so.

SAKHARAM. But it's still day!

CHAMPA. So what? Just remember to wake me when the food's ready. Isn't there a cot here? Or a mattress?

SAKHARAM. No.

CHAMPA. What kind of a home is this?

SAKHARAM. And you'll have to make the food yourself. That's a woman's job, and women must do their own jobs. That is the rule around here.

CHAMPA. Rule! Is this a school or a court or something?

SAKHARAM. A rule is a rule. If you don't like it, out you go.

CHAMPA [*loud yawn*]. I'm so sleepy.

[*Picks up some rags from a corner of the room and begins to spread them out on the floor.*]

SAKHARAM. Not here. Go in. Suppose somebody drops in? What'll he say?

CHAMPA [*taking the rags indoors*]. He'll say, 'She's sleeping.' Sleep is not his father's property!

[*Spreads out her rags on the floor in the kitchen. Curls up on them, with her hands under her head. Within a few seconds she's asleep. Sakharam comes to the kitchen door and sees her. He paces about. Looks again and again at her sleeping form. He is fully roused again.*

A crow begins to caw outside.]

SAKHARAM [*shoos off the crow with annoyance*]. Hoosh—

[*The crow continues to caw. Sakharam is really restless now. He shuts the front door. Comes to where she is. Flings his jacket away. Sits down.*]

[*Huskily*] What are you sleeping for? Get up. Hey—come on, wake up. Why're you sleeping?

[*Outside the crow is making a bigger racket. Sakharam considers this an interruption; he shoos the crow away.*]

You son of a bitch you—

[*Glances at her again. Suddenly, unable to control himself, he lays his hand on her. She sits up with a loud and weird shout. Sakharam has moved away slightly.*]

CHAMPA.   What's it? What's going on? Eh? [*sees him.*] Oh, it's you. I thought it was that corpse, my husband. What's the matter? Is the food ready? Why did you wake me?

[*Sakharam feels repulsed. Doesn't answer.*]

Oh yeah? I see. So that's what's on your mind. I'm glad I woke up. Now look here, I may have walked out on my husband, but I'm not that sort of woman. See? I left him because I had my honour to save. The swine wanted to make a whore of me. Now you just behave yourself. Don't go around like a dog behind a bitch. You've come and ruined my sleep as it is. Now run along and fix some dinner for us, will you?

[*Yawns loudly. Sakharam, deeply mortified, hastily puts on his jacket and goes out. She sits alone drowsily. Pulls out a small box from under the rags. Takes some tobacco out, rubs it well on her palm and stuffs it in her mouth. The stage darkens.*]

SCENE II

It is daylight. Sunlight is streaming in. Sakharam is lying on his back on the mattress. He sprawls on it, fast asleep. The door is open. There's nobody else in the house. A stranger, dressed in khaki, comes to the door. He is wearing a police cap, slightly askew. He is unshaven and looks dissipated. But sober at this moment. Tucked in the crook of his arm is a cloth bag stuffed to the seams. He looks around once. Then finds courage to step in. Removes his chappals. Lowers the cloth bag softly to the floor. Walks once round the sleeping Sakharam. Lets out an acidic belch. Then sits down quietly in a corner. Continues like this for some time. Then gets up and peeps into the kitchen. Goes in and washes his hands and face. Peeps into the pans, comes out and takes a swig from a bottle in the cloth bag. Puts the bottle away and continues sitting silently. Sakharam stirs once. And then again. He is waking up.

SAKHARAM. Hey. . . . [*Again after a pause.*] Hey, where's all this glare coming from? [*Pause.*] Damn it, not again!

[*Tries to draw the bed cover over his face, but can't manage it. The man in the corner is watching all this with great interest.*]

[*Again*] Can't you hear me?

[*No answer. He is awake now, though his eyes are still closed.*]

Are you a wall or something? Can't you hear me? Shut the window, will you?

[*Sits up. He still cannot open his eyes.*]

Where is she? Where the hell has she gone to and so early?

[*Somehow opens his eyes. In front of him is the calm yet interested khaki-clad stranger.*]

[*Screwing up his eyes*] Who? Who's that?

[*The stranger just about gives a nervous smile.*]

Who are you? How dare you walk in just like that? Where the hell is that woman? Why is the door open?
[*Hastily staggers up*] The sun's come up quite high. Champa! But who are you anyway? How come you walked straight in? [*No answer.*] What d'you want? You think this is some *dharmshala* or what? [*Now he is fully awake.*] Stand up. This very minute. Who're you looking for? Out with it!

[*The stranger helplessly stands up. He shakes his head meaning 'Nobody' and smiles in an affectionate way.*]

Then why have you sneaked in here? [*The man shakes his head again.*] I'll hand you over to the police. [*Noticing something*] But that's what you are! A *fouzdar*. What's a *fouzdar* doing here? What do you take this Sakharam Binder for? A vagabond? Get out! Get out of here! Go out first and then talk. Out! Come on—

[*The man is reluctant to move. Tries to sit down again.*]

No, you just keep standing.

[*He continues to stand looking carefully at him.*]

You are—

MAN [*smiles nervously and half-folds his hands in a greeting*]. Champa's husband. They call me Fouzdar Shinde. I've been sacked.

SAKHARAM. [*losing his temper*] So that's what you are? How did you come here? Who let you in? And where's Champa? Or have you done something to her? [*The man shakes his head sorrowfully,*] Then where is she? Where has Champa gone?

MAN [*shrugging his shoulder*]. I swear to God I don't know. She wasn't here when I came. You were asleep. So I sat down. That's all. [*Again half folds his hands in greeting.*] Glad to meet you.

SAKHARAM. What do you want here? Are you thinking of taking her back? Well, she's not coming.

MAN. But I'm not thinking of that. She's better off here. As long as she's happy.

SAKHARAM. Then why have you come?

MAN. Just to see how she is. Couldn't help myself.

SAKHARAM. You're terribly attached to her.

MAN. She's my wife . . . even though she's left me.

SAKHARAM. Where could she be? Wonder if she's made the tea at least.

MAN. No.

SAKHARAM. What do you mean?

MAN. The tea isn't ready.

SAKHARAM. How do you know?

MAN. There's no tea.

SAKHARAM How do you know that?

MAN. [*slightly scared*] I don't know. I mean I wanted tea. I had a look in there.

SAKHARAM. You searched the house, did you?

MAN. Just looking for some tea.

SAKHARAM. Get out of here! Get out or I'll slit your throat!

MAN. Please don't shout. The neighbours will hear.

SAKHARAM. So what? That's none of your business.

MAN. I'm Champa's husband. Her honour is my honour.

SAKHARAM. She's not your wife any longer.

MAN. She's my wife for life. That was decided up there. [*Folds his hands in a* namaskar *to the heavens.*]

SAKHARAM. She lives with me now.

MAN. I know. That's why I've come here.

SAKHARAM. She won't come back to you.

MAN. I don't mind. So long as she's happy.

SAKHARAM. She doesn't care a bit for you.

MAN. Just my luck!

SAKHARAM. Then what do you want? Why are you here?

MAN [*with a sad smile*]. Just so. No reason. I miss her.

SAKHARAM. Shut up. She walked out on you.

MAN. Yes. But what a woman! Buttocks this size. . . . Breasts so big . . . . Each. . . .

SAKHARAM. I'll break your jaw if you're not careful. Get out of here this minute. That's your own wife you're talking about, you swine! [*Catches him by the neck and drags him to the door.*] Now get out.

MAN. My bag! [*Comes in and sits down.*] I'll wait here, I'll meet Champa; I really miss her.

SAKHARAM [*helpless in the face of such shamelessness*]. Damn! The bastard, he won't even let me wash my face. Just you wait till I have cleaned up, then I'll show you, you damned. . . .

[*Goes to the kitchen. Rinses his mouth out of the window. Splashes some water on his face, meanwhile swearing at Champa. Then he walks to her husband. He is sitting there quietly, after having had another swig from the bottle. He smiles nervously at Sakharam, like an orphaned child.*]

Will you get out of here now?

DAWOOD [*calls from outside*]. Sakharam! Sakharam! [*Enters.*] Where's the bird?

[*Stops speaking as soon as he notices Fouzdar Shinde. Gestures to ask Sakharam who he is.*]

SAKHARAM. The husband. Champa's.

DAWOOD [*looking*]. Just what I thought. So, this is the bird's cage. [*To Shinde*] Hullo!

[*The man smiles nervously.*]

DAWOOD. If the bird comes, its cage is bound to follow. How can he live without her, Sakharam?

SAKHARAM. Don't get taken in by his innocent looks. The damned rascal! You should have heard the filthy way he described his own wife.

DAWOOD. Really? What was he saying?

SAKHARAM. Never mind. He won't even go away, the swine. Just stuck here.

DAWOOD. He goes where the bird goes. [*To Shinde*] Mister, am I right or wrong?

[*Champa's husband again smiles nervously.*]

SAKHARAM [*sarcastically*]. You mean to tell me that he's that fond of his wife! [*To Shinde*] Come on, up! Get out of my sight. You filthy worm! You. . . .

DAWOOD. Sakharam, this time it looks as though you will be looking after the bird *and* the cage. [*Softly*] And if the bird's not around, why're you taking it out on the cage? Eh? Forget it.

[*Champa's husband has another swig and continues to sit there with that nervous smile on his face.*]

SAKHARAM [*clenching his teeth*]. I feel I could tear him limb to limb.

DAWOOD. Cool down. You must learn to put up with such things. But where's the bird gone?

CHAMPA [*outside*]. Hey Baijabai, don't forget to call out tomorrow when you go by, right?

[*Champa enters. Washed and wrung-out clothes are slung on her shoulder.*]

[*To Sakharam*] Are you up? I called out before going down to the river. You didn't wake up. [*Notices her husband.*] Who? What is this clown doing here? [*She tucks the corner of her sari at the waist.*] When did this thing come here?

SAKHARAM. Came in while I was still asleep.

CHAMPA. But why did you take him in? Couldn't you have driven him away from the door?

SAKHARAM. I have no idea when he came here. When I woke up, there he was. After that he just refused to go.

CHAMPA. Refused to go, did he? Just let me see how! [*Moves forward, jerks her husband up by the collar.*] Well, you clod! [*Slaps him violently.*] What do you want, eh? [*Rains blows on him and kicks him.*] Who invited you here, eh?

[*Sakharam and Dawood are watching the scene in shocked silence. Champa lets go of her husband. Picks up a chappal and hurries back to him. Lifts up her husband and again viciously hits him right and left with the chappal. Sakharam and Dawood shudder at the sight. Finally she drags him to the door like a sackful of potatoes and throws him out.*]

Get out. Don't you ever show your mug again if you want to stay alive. And don't ever cross my path! I have nothing to do with you now.

MAN [*somehow staggers up*]. I'll go. I'll go, kill myself. That's what I'll do.

CHAMPA. Yes, do that. Good riddance! But do it quick.

[*The man turns and starts towards the house again. Champa again heaves him out. He falls flat. Gets up. She kicks him again.*]

CHAMPA. Die! For God's sake, die quick.

DAWOOD. But, Champa, at this rate he might really die.

CHAMPA. Oh, no, he won't. He'll never die. But if he does, it'll be such a good thing both for him and for me.

[*Moves forward and slams her fist into his face. Blood streams out of the corner of his mouth.*]

MAN [*staggers up and once again starts towards the house*]. My bag, my bag.

[*Champa makes for him. Dawood holds her back. Her husband stumbles to the wall where his bag is. He slumps down to the ground and rolls about on the floor.*]

Kill myself! I'll kill myself!

[*Somehow pulls the bottle out of the bag and drinks from it.*]

CHAMPA [*pounces on him and kicks again*]. Here . . . here's another one. And another, you corpse. . . .

[*Sakharam pulls her back.*]

SAKHARAM [*to her.*] What kind of a woman are you? Look, what you've done to him! He's your husband. Haven't you a heart?

CHAMPA. No, I don't have a heart. He chewed it up raw long ago. [*Pulls herself free.*] He brought me from my mother even before I'd become a woman. He married me when I didn't even know what marriage meant. He'd torture me at night. He branded me, and stuck needles into me and made me do awful, filthy things. I ran away. He brought me back and stuffed chilly powder into that god-awful place, where it hurts most. That bloody pimp! What's left of my heart now? He tore lumps out of it, he did. He drank my blood. Get up, you pig. I'll stuff some chilly powder into *you* now!

[*She strains forward. Sakharam seeks to restrain her. She tries to break free. She is like one possessed, so that Sakharam becomes aware of the strength in her.*]

SAKHARAM. Dawood, take him away quick. Hurry.

[*Dawood somehow drags her husband out. Champa watches them. Spits in the direction of her husband.*]

CHAMPA. Just you try and set foot here again! I'll roll you in chilly powder, yes! [*For some time, even after he is out of sight*] You insect! You worm! [*To Sakharam*] Let go! There's work to do.

[*Sakharam releases her. Champa goes straight in. Sakharam stares fixedly at her, a trifle scared. She starts on her chores in the kitchen. Dawood enters.*]

DAWOOD [*in a low voice*]. Packed him off. My God, she did give it to him! The very thought of it scares the life out of me! Watch out, this bird is different from the others. God, what a woman!

[*Sakharam stands paralysed. The stage darkens.*]

SCENE III

It is night. A dim light comes up in the kitchen. Champa is asleep on the floor. A shadow falls across her. It is Sakharam's. He's watching the sleeping Champa. Goes out again to the other room. Paces about. Comes in again. He's restless. Bends down to the sleeping Champa. Straightens up again. Unresolved. Sits down beside her. He can't help himself. Undecided. She turns over. He begins to pant. He cannot resist touching her. She reacts immediately and sits up.

CHAMPA [*opening her eyes wide*]. What is it? Who's that? It's you! Same thing on your mind again! I told you, didn't I? Why won't you understand? If I feel cut up, I can turn nasty. [*Straightens her sari.*] Take care not to rub me the wrong way. I don't like it—all that man-woman stuff.

[*Sakharam is standing at a distance.*]

Go, go and sleep out there.

SAKHARAM. We made a deal. The woman I bring here has got to be a wife to me. That's all fixed when I decide to keep her here. There were seven and not one said no.

CHAMPA. Maybe they were that sort. But not me. Now let me sleep.

SAKHARAM. You mean I can't have what's here in my own house!

CHAMPA. I can't do it! Now go out. Or I won't sleep, I tell you.

[*Sakharam hesitates.*]

SAKHARAM. Go to hell!

[*Goes out. Champa remains sitting. Sakharam takes a bottle down from a shelf and puts it to his mouth.*]

To hell with you! [*Drinks some more. Then shouting hoarsely*] Damn you!

[*Opens the door and goes out into the darkness. Champa remains sitting in the kitchen. Still undetermined. Then suddenly she comes to a decision and gets up. Enters the outer room. Goes out. Drags Sakharam in by the wrist.*]

CHAMPA. Shut up. I'll give it to you. All of it. Just hand me the bottle.

[*Sakharam stands still, watching her.*]

Damn you, where's the bottle? Where's the bottle?

[*He takes the bottle down from the shelf. She grabs it.*]

Now sit there.

[*She forces him down. Opens the bottle and gulps down the drink thirstily. He gapes at her. The light is dim. Then darkness descends. Immediately afterwards a dim light comes up.*]

CHAMPA [*in a drunken slur*]. Just a few minutes more. Then you can take me. Do what you like with me. . . .

[*Sakharam is speechless. Darkness.*]

SCENE IV

The lights come up. The morning is well advanced. There's loud knocking at the door. Sakharam staggers up from beside Champa. They are sleeping in the kitchen. He gathers himself together and comes into the outer room. Opens the door.

VOICE [*off*]. Aren't you coming, Sakhya? You'll be late. Damn you, you know how long I've been knocking at the door? You were fast asleep, I expect!

SAKHARAM [*still drowsy*]. Coming. Just a minute.

[*Closes the door and comes into the kitchen. Looks at Champa, who is still fast asleep. Pretending to set her blanket right, he touches her gently. Goes aside and splashes some water on his face. Rinses out his mouth. On his way to the outer room, darts a glance at her. Comes out humming. Puts on his shirt, jacket, cap and chappals, and leaves the house. Carefully closes the door behind him. For a while we see the motionless figure of Champa. She's asleep in the kitchen. Then the stage darkens.*]

SCENE V

The light comes up. It's midday. Champa is sitting by the stove. She is eating. Sakharam comes in from outside. Takes off his chappals and hangs up his jacket and cap on the peg.

SAKHARAM. I'm back!

CHAMPA [*from inside*]. So soon? Half day at the Press today?

SAKHARAM [*comes in*]. No. I thought I'd come home early. Guess why?

CHAMPA. How'd I know?

SAKHARAM. Couldn't fix my mind on work.

CHAMPA. That's not right!

SAKHARAM. But it's true. [*Approaches her.*] Listen—

CHAMPA. Move off. Let me eat. Haven't had my bath yet. I got up late.

SAKHARAM. Last night . . . was great fun.

[*Champa eats in silence.*]

CHAMPA. Don't remember a thing.

SAKHARAM. Rot!

CHAMPA. I'm not lying.

SAKHARAM. It was great fun. All day I could think of nothing else. So I came home.

CHAMPA. Go. Sit out there. Let me eat.

SAKHARAM. No.

CHAMPA. Later.

SAKHARAM. No, 'it' first.

[*He shows her the bottle he has been hiding behind his back.*]

CHAMPA. Let me eat.

SAKHARAM. No.

[*Holds her hand. She snatches it away with unexpected force.*]

Such airs!

CHAMPA. I'm warning you. Don't trouble me when I'm eating.
SAKHARAM. In this house what I say goes, see? You've got to do what I say.

[*Champa continues to eat.*]

My orders have to be obeyed. I can turn nasty otherwise. I'll thrash the life out of you. There's no stopping me.
CHAMPA. You're telling me!
SAKHARAM. You're nothing special. I want you.
CHAMPA. Go out there. I've work to do.
SAKHARAM [*taking her hand*]. Champa!
CHAMPA [*without trying to free her hand but in a tone of voice which is strangely enough, very understanding*]. Listen to me. Don't trouble me so.

[*Sakharam lets go her hand and goes to the outer room and paces about in chagrin.*]

SAKHARAM [*shouting*]. You'll be driven out of here. That'll put some sense into your head. You'll have to live like a bitch then. Sleep with every fellow you meet. Yes, sleep with all of them!

[*Champa is still eating, but now even she is restless. A short pause. Champa stops eating and just sits there in front of her plate. Then in a fit of explosive fury she hurls her plate away. The plate whirls and clatters loudly to a rest. Outside Sakharam stands still, startled by this sound. The noise stops. Champa gets up. Washes her hands and then wipes them on her sari. Picks up her plate and collects all the food leavings. Puts it all by the washing place. Comes out.*]

CHAMPA [*goes to Sakharam*]. Come on. Get me the bottle.

[*For a moment Sakharam stares at the vicious expression on her face.*]

You heard me? Get me the bottle.

[*Sakharam silently hands it over. Clenching her teeth, she uncorks the bottle; then drinks.*]

Here, you have some, too. Go on, drink.

[*Forces it to his lips. Then drinks herself, laughing hysterically.*]

CHAMPA. You'll have your fun. . . . Wait. I'll give it to you. [*Keeps on drinking and making him drink. Laughs uncontrollably.*] Fun for anyone who comes along. A dog. A corpse even. . . .

[*Dawood enters from outside, and stands still. He watches the scene in stricken silence.*]

Who's that? Dawood? Come. You want to have fun? Have it. Take it, you corpse. Come. Why don't you come here? Come, take—

[*Dawood stares at her, dumbfounded. Sakharam stands there stupefied. Champa flings her arm round his neck. She's laughing a drunken laugh. Her clothes are in disarray. Darkness.*]

SCENE VI

The lights come up. It is dark outside. The light from a street lamp finds its way into the room through the kitchen window. Everywhere else it is pitch dark. For a while Champa's faint moans are heard. Half-conscious mutterings.

CHAMPA. Who's there? Come, have fun. You corpse, get away, you . . . [*Drunken laughter, followed by moans.*] I want a drink . . . drink . . . want a drink . . . want a drink. . . . [*Laughter. Moans.*]

[*Darkness.*]

SCENE VII

The lights come up. It is daylight. Champa is not at home. Dawood and Sakharam. Sakharam's face bears the traces of his new life. He looks different.

DAWOOD. But, Sakharam, you can't afford to sit at home. You've got to work. There's the house to run. You haven't gone to work this last week.

SAKHARAM. I'll go when I feel like it.

DAWOOD. And if you're kicked out?

SAKHARAM. Let's see them do it. I'm quite fit and strong. If I lose one job, I can find another. I'll carry loads or break stones. After all, there's no getting away from work, Dawood. Sakharam Binder has never been afraid of work. I've always fended for myself. See! Never called my own father, Father. And as for my mother, to her I was like the son of a wretched *Mahar*, a scavenger. I grew up like a cactus—out in the open. I don't scare

easy. From now on it is going to be Champa, Champa and
nothing more. . . .

DAWOOD. But you know what people say. . . .

SAKHARAM [*bursting out*]. People! What do I owe them or their
bloody fathers. Did they feed me when I went hungry? I lay
dying in the Miraj Mission Hospital. Did anyone bother to find
out whether I was alive or dead? Don't talk to me about people,
Dawood. Run after whores themselves, and carp at others.
Nobody in this place can be cleaner than me. Every single one of
those damned fellows is soiled, filthy. Trying to look clean
outside. Stuffed with dirt inside. Don't talk to me about people.
If there's anyone better than us, it's those whores. Tell me what
they say. Do they call me a drunkard? Do they say women have
caused my fall? Do they say I've gone to the dogs because of
Champa? No. Because they understand. Not much difference
between those whores and your people? Except that the whores
are honest, and your people—they are all fake. That's all.

DAWOOD. But, Sakharam, you must think of yourself at least.
Remember what this house used to be like, and look at it now.
You remember, it's not so long ago. . . . When the other bird was
here, Laxmi *bhabhi*. How it used to be then!

SAKHARAM. Laxmi's gone. She's dead as far as I'm concerned.
What the hell do I have to do with her now? That's all over and
done with. I don't like to rake up old memories. Now it's
Champa. Nothing else. Nobody can match her little finger. You
don't know what fun Champa is.

DAWOOD. Look! It worries me—what I see and hear! That's all I
want to say. It's up to you. Right, I'm off. Time to go to work!

SAKHARAM. Go. And don't worry about me.

[*Dawood goes. Sakharam is left alone. Remains sitting for a while.
Then goes to the shelf. The stage darkens.*]

SCENE VIII

The lights come up. It is day. From far away comes the sound of the
shehnai *and of drums. In the kitchen Champa is doing her chores,*
somehow trying to keep her balance. There are traces of drunkenness in her
steps. Sakharam enters the outer room.

SAKHARAM [*removes his* chappals *and walks towards the peg*]. Champa
. . . Champa. . . .

[*Champa staggers towards him.*]

[*Looking at her*] You've been drinking? So early? It's *Dassera* today. And look at you!

[*Champa laughs a drunk laugh.*]

Drunk so early in the morning? What's wrong with you? This is not right. Champa, you should not drink on a holy day like *Dassera*. What did I tell you before I left for the Press? You haven't even had a bath. And you've been drinking. On a holy day the woman of the house should look all clean and tidy. What will people say? Go on inside. Go. [*Somehow manages to push Champa in to the kitchen.*] Good-for-nothing! Doesn't care for either feasts or fasts. Damn her. Not right for a woman to behave like this. If it had been someone else, I'd have broken her jaw.

[*He closes the outer door. Hangs up his jacket and shirt on the peg. Takes down his* mridanga. *Dusts it and puts it in a corner. Ferrets out the picture of a god and arranges it neatly, after dusting it. Finds a shallow* puja *vessel and goes out to pluck some flowers. He brings them in the vessel. Goes to the kitchen and washes his feet, hands and face. Champa is weaving about, doing her chores. At one point she loses her balance. Sakharam steadies her. She clings to his neck. He tries to push her away. She won't move. Merely laughs drunkenly.*]

Move away, will you? Shove off. I want to do my *puja*. Will you move now, or. . . .

[*Champa continues to laugh drunkenly.*]

Shameless wretch! Get out of my house. Go.

[*Even as he says this, he is roused, watching her intoxicated body.*]

Will you, will you let go? Or I'll kick you . . . you!

[*Champa laughs louder.*]

Go away—get away. Bloody bitch!

[*He pushes her. She crashes against something and falls down.*]

CHAMPA [*agonized*]. Oooh. . . .

[*Sakharam bends down to see if she's hurt.*]

SAKHARAM. Let me see. Are you hurt? Where? Tell me. Where does it hurt? Come, show me. Oh, go to hell!

[*Sakharam remains sitting beside Champa. Darkness.*]

SCENE IX

The lights come up. A dim light in the kitchen. Champa and Sakharam are asleep in the kitchen. Continuous knocking at the door.

VOICE [*off*]. Anybody at home? Sakharam! Sakharam!

[*After some time—silence. Then again knocking at the door.*]

2ND VOICE. Sakharam! Ho Sakharam! You think he's home?
3RD VOICE. Someone's in there.
4TH VOICE. Maybe the woman.
3RD VOICE. Maybe both.
1ST VOICE [*calls*]. Sakharam—are you there?

[*Renewed knocking at the door. Someone stirs in the kitchen. But nobody gets up or answers. The knocking, the calls and the sounds continue at the door at intervals, and then there's silence. The kitchen, too, is quiet, except for the occasional drunken mutterings of Sakharam. Somewhere far away the drums and the shehnai are still playing. A crow caws nearby. Once again the knocking and calling begins. The callers go away. Silence. The stage darkens.*]

SCENE X

The lights come up. It is night. The kitchen is lit by a dim lamp. Far away the dogs are howling in the dark. The crickets are chirping. Repeated knocking at the door.

SAKHARAM [*in a drunken voice*]. Get up.

[*Knocking again.*]

I think someone's knocking at the door. Hey, get up! You heard me? Get up. Look at her sprawling there! Someone's knocking. Go, see who it is. . . .

[*Knocking again.*]

Who could it be at this time of the night? The slut won't get up. Dead to the world! [*Struggles to sit up. Holds his head tight.*] God! What a heavy head I've got!

[*Knocking again.*]

[*Hoarsely*] All right. I heard. Who could it be at this time of night?

[*Staggers up, and comes out, stumbling. Knocks against the* mridanga *kept ready for the* puja. *All the* puja *things scatter on the floor. Goes to the door.*]

Who's there? This time of night?

[*Opens the door. He cannot see very clearly who it is.*]

SAKHARAM. Who is it? [*Rubs his eyes. Then he freezes.*] You? I must be dreaming. [*Rubs his eyes again.*] What are you doing here? How. . . .

[*He stands rooted to the spot. A figure carrying a cloth bundle comes in furtively. Her aspect is terrifying. She's shivering all over. Her sari is drawn across her face. She puts the bundle down. It's Laxmi.*]

LAXMI [*in a flat tone of voice*]. My nephew threw me out. His wife charged me with stealing. Would I steal? Ever? They were going to hand me over to the police. Where could I go? So I came here. The only place left for me.

[*Sakharam stares dumbly at her. He is not sure all this isn't a dream.*]

I'll stay here now. And die here, too. I don't want to go away. I'll live here, die here.

[*Sakharam is still stupefied. Laxmi stands before him, cowering. In the kitchen Champa turns on her side, and mutters drunkenly. Far away the dogs are barking in the dark. Suddenly Sakharam comes back to earth. One swift movement and he grips Laxmi by the arm, pushes her out, shuts the door on her face. He sighs with relief now that there's no more knocking at the door.*]

CHAMPA [*stirring slightly in the kitchen*]. Who's there? Who's come?

[*Silence. Sakharam still can't believe what he has seen. Was Laxmi really there? Did he really throw her out? He doesn't know; and he's in no condition to think about it, since he is still under the influence of liquor. But one thing is certain. There's no more knocking at the door. No other sounds either. Sakharam stands numbly, holding his head in his hands. Then he stumbles into the kitchen and slumps into bed. Soon he's asleep. Champa's drunken muttering continues at intervals. The dogs continue to bark. The stage darkens.*]

CURTAIN

ACT THREE

SCENE I

The lights come up. Morning. Sunlight streams into the house. Champa comes into the outer room with a broom in her hand. She appears unkempt and lethargic. She opens the door. A ray of sunshine shoots in. Absently humming an ovi *to herself, she begins to sweep the house. While she is thus engrossed, a figure appears in the doorway. It is Laxmi. Champa doesn't notice her at first.*

CHAMPA [*now noticing Laxmi*]. Can't keep on giving to beggars all the time! Move on. Go next door.

[*Laxmi remains standing in the doorway.*]

You heard what I said? Are you deaf? I said you'll get nothing here. Now, move on, will you? You're new around here?

[*Laxmi remains where she is.*]

You look quite fit. Why do you go round begging?

[*Laxmi is still standing in the same position in silence.*]

Listen. Are you going to move on or not? How shameless can you be! Get going.

[*Champa makes for her. Laxmi doesn't budge.*]

LAXMI [*in a toneless voice*]. I'm not a beggar.

CHAMPA. Oh, no? I suppose you're some emperor's queen, then!

LAXMI. I used to live here.

CHAMPA [*surprised*]. What?

LAXMI. Yes. That's the broom I used to sweep this house with. I was what you are today.

CHAMPA. So you are. . . .

LAXMI. Laxmi. I stayed here for a year and twenty-one days. He brought me last year in the month of *Shravan*. It was the fourth day of the new moon. I hadn't eaten for six days. I remember it all!

CHAMPA. What made you come here now!

LAXMI. I was at my nephew's in Amalner. They are a young couple. I was in the way. Where else could I go? I came here. I have no one else.

CHAMPA. Your husband?

[*Laxmi sighs.*]

CHAMPA [*begins to sweep the floor*]. He's not at home. The one you want to see. Sakharam. He's gone to the Press.

LAXMI. I know. I saw him go.

CHAMPA. You saw him? Then why didn't you call out?

LAXMI. He was late. Didn't want to delay him further.

CHAMPA. Where were you? It's over two hours since he went.

LAXMI. I've been here all night, sitting there under the eaves. It was raining. Early in the morning I dozed off. I woke up again when he left for the Press.

CHAMPA. You mean you came at night?

LAXMI. Yes.

CHAMPA. And then?

LAXMI. Waited outside. I'd have slept in the yard, if it hadn't been for the rain.

CHAMPA. But why didn't you knock?

LAXMI [*hesitates, and then*]. I didn't think I should have. It was very late. And anyway I don't sleep much; so why disturb you?

CHAMPA. Oh, I was dead to the world. Drunk.

LAXMI [*astonished*]. What? You mean you drink?

CHAMPA. Right. Why?

LAXMI. You'd been drinking . . . last night?

CHAMPA. Right. I drink every day. So does he.

LAXMI [*sorrowfully*]. It was *Dassera* yesterday.

CHAMPA. So?

LAXMI [*pleading*]. You mustn't do that sort of thing on a holy day.

CHAMPA. You're religious, are you?

LAXMI. Yes. I've always been that. Right from the time I was a child. My faith is what gave me strength when life was hard. Another woman would have killed herself. I went on living. [*After a while, and with some curiosity*] When did you come here?

CHAMPA. Must be a couple of months.

LAXMI. Soon after I left?

CHAMPA. How would I know when you left?

LAXMI. In the month of *Bhadrapad*, the eighth day of the moon. I remember exactly. I remember every one of my days here. I could tell you about all of them. Now let me think. Two months ago would be almost immediately after I left. Yes.

CHAMPA. What do you plan to do now?

LAXMI. How can I plan?

CHAMPA. That's true. Since there's nowhere you can go, you'll stay here, I suppose.

LAXMI. That's what I thought. . . .

CHAMPA [*after a pause*]. Come in. I'll make a cup of tea.

LAXMI. Please don't bother.

[*Champa goes into the kitchen. Laxmi is left alone.*]

CHAMPA [*as she goes in*]. I want one myself. Sakharam drives me crazy at night. [*Laxmi reacts immediately to this.*] Can't be bothered to get up in the morning and make the tea. My head and body—just a bundle of pains and aches.

[*Laxmi involuntarily moves in.*]

LAXMI. Why don't you let me make it?

CHAMPA [*promptly*]. Oh, no. You're here for a few days. Can't trouble you.

LAXMI. No trouble at all.

[*Laxmi begins to help without a minute's delay. Champa watches her.*]

Does this not go here, as usual?

CHAMPA. Yes.

LAXMI [*looks around. On an impulse*]. Where are the gods?

CHAMPA. Oh, the gods? How would I know?

LAXMI. How can you say that? Didn't you find them? I left two framed pictures here when I left.

CHAMPA. Maybe.

LAXMI [*worried*]. Where could they have gone to? [*Eagerly*] Does he still do his *puja*?

CHAMPA. Who? Sakharam? He knows only one sort of *puja*!

LAXMI. When I was here, he used to have a bath every morning and offer flowers and sandalwood to the gods. Do you do your *puja*?

CHAMPA. I don't owe God anything!

LAXMI. That's not true! He does everything.

CHAMPA. He's never done anything for me. Here. Drink your tea. [*Puts the tea before her.*] What're you looking at?

LAXMI [*staring into her cup*]. There! Now who asked you to go jumping in here? Eh? Who asked you? There, now your mouth and nose are all filled with tea. That's why you are wriggling, aren't you? You naughty fellow! You mischievous little thing!

[*Chuckling to herself, she puts her finger into the tea and gently lifts up the black ant that's fallen in.*]

A tiny little tummy and he wanted to drink all that tea. Wait a second. Don't run away. Let me wipe you dry. Come here—[*Picks up the ant very gently with the end of her* sari.] H'm. Promise me you won't jump into other people's tea again! Promise! Now run along. [*Lets the ant go.*]

[*Champa has stopped drinking. She sits there wonderstruck, moved by the innocence of the ragged Laxmi.*]

LAXMI. When I used to stay here, there was a big black ant—just like this fellow here. A proud little rascal he was! I used to call him Raja, because he was really like a king. He'd become quite fond of me. And there was a crow too.

[*A crow caws outside.*]

[*Brightening immediately*] There he is! Must be the same one.

[*Runs to the window and looks out. She feels faint. Closes her eyes, leans against something.*]

CHAMPA [*gets up, brings her back, and sits her down again*]. There, drink your tea first. The crow won't fly away. You must be famished. Come and sit here.

[*Forces Laxmi to sit beside her. Both sip their tea.*]

Here. Take this biscuit. [*Gives it to her.*] Dip it in your tea. How long will you stay here?

LAXMI. Who? I? Where can I go? Can't go back to my nephew. Or to my husband either. Their doors are now closed to me!

CHAMPA. Why did your husband drive you out?

LAXMI. Because we had no children.

CHAMPA. And he had children after you left?

LAXMI. How would I know? There's been no news from him. And you . . . what about you?

CHAMPA. Impotent husband! And he was a lot of bother. I walked out on him. Who wants a husband just for the sake of his name!

LAXMI. Where is he now?

CHAMPA. God knows whether that corpse is still alive or dead.

LAXMI [*hurt*]. You shouldn't say such things.

CHAMPA. Then what do you expect me to say about that wretch?

LAXMI. Whatever happens, you are joined to your husband by sacred rites—in the presence of gods and *Brahmins*.

CHAMPA. They don't come and live your hell for you—those gods and *Brahmins*.

LAXMI. But that's part of one's fate. It has to be borne.

CHAMPA. You mean you put up with it like a corpse till you drop dead? I put up with quite a lot. I can tell you that. But when I couldn't take it any longer, I turned my back on him and walked out. Then he brought me here—your Sakharam.

LAXMI [*sighing*]. Not mine. He's yours now.

CHAMPA. Look here. I'm on my own . . . If they're there, well, they're there, for all that they're worth. If not, I'm all by myself, and all alone. That's the way it is!

[*Silence.*]

LAXMI [*curious*]. How are you getting along here?

CHAMPA. Getting along? Once you drink, you get along fine. But your Sakharam, he really takes his money's worth out of a woman. I've managed to last out here. What else can I do? Go out in the streets? Face half a dozen animals every day! Easier to put up with this one.

LAXMI [*sighs, but takes courage*]. Then if I stayed here for good, you wouldn't mind, would you?

CHAMPA [*thinks for a minute*]. As long as you don't push me out! If you try to do that, I can turn nasty. I might as well warn you.

LAXMI. I'd never do that. I won't ask for much. In any case I'm exhausted. I can't cope with things as I used to in the old days. All I want is a roof over my head. I'll do what you want. I am used to hard work.

CHAMPA [*after some thought*]. Stay. You look after the house, I'll look after him. Anyway, I can't cope with both. You stay alive, and I'll stay alive, too.

LAXMI [*very grateful*]. Yes. I—I'll tell him. I promise not to be a bother. I could help out with the work. I don't look it, but I can still get through a lot of work. And I eat very little. A bit of rice and some buttermilk. I'm not fussy. Then there are my fasts. Two *saris* are enough for me—one drying on the line, the other to wear, and not new ones either. Your old ones will do.

[*Sakharam enters the outer room. Removes his chappals. He seems to be in a bad mood for certain reason.*]

SAKHARAM [*to Champa*]. It's me.

[*Champa motions to Laxmi. Sakharam hangs his cap and jacket on the peg.*]

[*Grumbling*] Those swine, they want us to work more and for the same pay! Who'll agree? Who do you think you are? Have you bought us for life? Wait. I'll show them. . . .

[*Laxmi is waiting at the outer door, with a pail of water for him to wash his feet with. Through sheer force of habit Sakharam goes to wash his feet, without noticing her. Then he sees her and suddenly stiffens. For a moment, Laxmi is petrified. She stands before him trembling.*]

SAKHARAM [*viciously*]. You! Why have you come back? Who let you in?

LAXMI [*with difficulty*]. My nephew threw me out. I came here. Where else could I go? They charged me with stealing. . . .

SAKHARAM. Damn it, why here?

LAXMI. Where else?

SAKHARAM. The whole wide world was open to you. I told you, didn't I? 'We'll have nothing to do with each other.'

LAXMI. I remembered this place.

SAKHARAM. I didn't think of you—not once. The minute you left this place you were dead to me. It was all over, done with. That's the rule here. Fourteen years I've followed it. You knew it. I warned you when I first brought you here, didn't I? Well, then?

LAXMI. Everything was over. Where could I go? I came here. I could turn to no one else.

SAKHARAM. No one else to turn to! For all I care you could have dropped dead. What's it to me? Who am I to you?

LAXMI [*almost inaudibly*]. God.

SAKHARAM [*harshly*]. What? Don't you dare say a thing like that again. I'll slit your throat, I will. A link based on a need. The need ended, the link snapped. Why've you come back? Who let you stay? Get out of this house at once! Come on, out with you.

[*Laxmi is trembling all over. Champa, tying her hair in a knot, comes and stands at the kitchen door, watching them. She's not the least bit affected by what she sees.*]

LAXMI [*suddenly puts down the pail of water and the jar and falls at Sakharam's feet*]. Please don't send me away. Nowhere I can go. Nobody to turn to. I'll do everything you want. I'll do all the work. I don't ask for anything just a roof over my head and to die in your lap.

SAKHARAM [*kicking her away*]. Stop this nonsense. Get out this very minute, or I'll split your skull. Get out. Out, this minute.

[*Laxmi is now clinging hard to Sakharam's feet. He cannot free himself. He curses her. Champa is calmly watching the scene.*

Clenching his teeth, he now begins to rain blows on Laxmi. She doubles up in pain, but she will not let go his feet. He swears at her, hits her. Champa is still watching.]

CHAMPA. You'd better stop this now. She'll die otherwise.

SAKHARAM. I don't care. I won't let her stay here.

[*Hits her.*]

CHAMPA. And after you've killed her, what do you plan to do with me?

SAKHARAM. You've got your husband.

CHAMPA. Which woman living with a husband would ever come here?

SAKHARAM [*with a fresh outburst of anger, as he lays into Laxmi with greater brutality*]. You shameless bitch! You leech. . . .

CHAMPA [*pulls Laxmi away and stands between her and him*]. Hit me.

[*He withdraws his hand in a fit of impotent fury. She lifts Laxmi up, forces her hand off her face.*]

Let me see. Just missed the eye. You hurt in the belly? Below? Come. Come on in.

SAKHARAM. Not in. Out.

[*Champa begins to take Laxmi into the kitchen.*]

SAKHARAM. You heard me? Throw her out I said.

CHAMPA. Come on . . . Don't stand there gaping.

[*Champa takes her into the kitchen. He's furious; he feels frustrated, helpless.*]

SAKHARAM. Champa, I'm telling you—throw her out!

[*Champa makes Laxmi sit down.*]

CHAMPA [*to Laxmi*]. Does it hurt where he hit you? It can hurt terribly. Sit here; don't get up.

[*Comes out. Picks up the pail of water and the jar that Laxmi was carrying.*]

[*To Sakharam*] Come on. Let me pour water over your feet.

[*Sakharam is furious.*]

SAKHARAM. She must leave the house at once.

[*Champa is silent.*]

Champa, I'm warning you. Send her out first.

CHAMPA. Who am I to send her out? The house is yours. You throw her out if you want to. I didn't bring her here in the first place.

SAKHARAM. Then why did you interfere?

CHAMPA. Why? Because you'll be hanged for murder, and to fill this belly of mine I'll have to start hunting around every day for a new customer. Instead of having ten beasts tearing at me everyday, I'd rather do what one says to me. You get me? Come, wash your feet now. Your tea's ready.

SAKHARAM. Tell her to go away. I'll have nothing to do with her.

CHAMPA. Why're you so bothered? She can help me in the house. Anyway I can't cope with the house and with you. She'll look after the house. We don't have to give anything except a little food and my old *saris*. Why should that worry you?

SAKHARAM. I don't want to feed two mouths.

CHAMPA. Oh? Then I'll go.

SAKHARAM. No. Send her away. She must go. Damn her! Talks of dying with her head on my lap! [*Shouting*] Laxmi, get out of my house. Get out this very minute. I've no use for you here.

[*Laxmi quakes with fear in the kitchen.*]

CHAMPA. Now are you coming to wash your feet or shall I just leave everything here and go in?

[*Sakharam reluctantly follows Champa out—to wash his feet. Laxmi cowers against the wall of the kitchen, trembling. Outside a crow caws. Laxmi stumbles to the kitchen window and looks out eagerly. Champa and Sakharam enter the outer room. He is wiping his hands and face. Champa comes into the kitchen with the water-pail and jar. Glances for a moment at Laxmi looking out of the window and goes to the washing place to set down the pail and jar.*]

LAXMI [*looking out*]. He didn't shout again.

CHAMPA. Who? The crow or him—your Sakharam?

LAXMI [*as though she hasn't heard*]. This is exactly how he used to call in the afternoons. I'm sure it's the same one.

[*Champa pours out the tea and takes it out. Sakharam is sitting on the mattress.*]

SAKHARAM [*taking the tea from her*]. I hope she's gone.

CHAMPA [*after a pause*]. No.

SAKHARAM [*putting down his cup and saucer*]. No? Why not?

CHAMPA. Drink your tea.

SAKHARAM. How dare you boss over me?

CHAMPA. So? Are you going to beat me?

SAKHARAM. I will when the time comes. You think I won't?

CHAMPA. We'll wait till the time comes. Meanwhile drink your tea. It's getting cold.

SAKHARAM. I won't let her stay in this house. Whatever happens, I won't.

[*Champa puts the tea cup to his lips. He holds it and begins to drink the tea in a huff.*]

Once a thing's over, that's the end. Why did she come back here? I'm not her husband!

[*Laxmi has quietly begun working inside the kitchen. She's limping.*]

CHAMPA. Let her stay for a couple of days. Then I'll tell her to go. Anyway, where can she go?

SAKHARAM. That doesn't mean I'm to take care of her for the rest of her life! Champa, you must send her away. Tomorrow itself. Tomorrow morning. I don't want to see her face again. Shameless wretch. Talks about dying with her head on my lap.

[*He's smouldering. After he finishes his tea, she takes his cup and saucer from him and goes into the kitchen. Promptly Laxmi moves aside.*]

LAXMI [*with diffidence*]. What happened?

CHAMPA. Carry on with the work. Anyway what's to happen to you? What can anyone do for you? But just remember. You can stay, but I don't want a word out of you.

[*Sakharam is still uneasy. He's pacing about. Takes the liquor bottle from the shelf. Begins to drink from it. Then, for some reason, he takes down his mridanga. Dusts it, sets it down. Takes off its cover. Sits down. Starts playing it. In the kitchen Laxmi is thrilled by the sound. Sakharam begins to play the mridanga; he is lost in a trance. Then he begins to play in a frenzy. The two women are working in the kitchen. The drum beats sound louder. Dawood enters. Sakharam is oblivious of his presence.*]

SAKHARAM [*notices him. Very curtly*]. Look who's here! Found time to come today, did you?

DAWOOD. Heard the *mridanga*, and I felt as if the old days had returned.

SAKHARAM. What old days?

DAWOOD. When you had the other bird—Laxmi.

[*Immediately, Sakharam's hand comes to a stop in mid-air. Laxmi, hearing Dawood's voice, comes to the kitchen doorway.*]

LAXMI [*unable to restrain herself*]. Dawoodji!

DAWOOD [*glad to see her*]. Hey? Is this true? [*To Sakharam*] Well, well, two birds in place of one, eh? Or has Champa left?

SAKHARAM [*in a sharp tone*]. Shut up. Or get out. I don't want to hear one more word.

[*Begins to beat fiercely on the* mridanga. *Dawood is silent. Laxmi is still in the doorway. Champa is quietly working in the kitchen.*]

CHAMPA [*to Laxmi*]. Hey, will you come in and do some work? Or are you just going to stand there like a statue?

[*Laxmi starts and goes back to work. Sakharam continues beating on the* mridanga, *Dawood at his side. Darkness.*]

SCENE II

A dim light in the kitchen. The night is far advanced. A cock crows somewhere far away. The dim kerosene lamp has thrown Laxmi's large, black shadow over the entire kitchen. She's clapping her hands softly and muttering 'Sitaram, Sitaram, Sitaram, Jai Sitaram.' Gradually her voice and clapping grow louder.

SAKHARAM [*speaking from the darkness of the outer room*]. What's going on? Stop it at once. In the middle of the night!

[*Laxmi continues her clapping and chanting, but more softly.*]

SAKHARAM. Stop it, or I'll kill you, d'you hear? Damned nuisance.

[*Laxmi still continues with her clapping and chanting but she is barely audible now.*]

Will you put out that light and sleep in peace? Or else I make you vomit blood, I will.

[*Laxmi is quiet after this. She blows on the oil-lamp. It is completely dark now except for some light outside the window coming from an unseen source.*]

Damn her. She won't stop.

[*Quiet everywhere. Except for the crickets. Sakharam rises in bed.*]

[*Grumbling*] Damn her—the bitch.

[*Lies down. Silence.*]

[*From the outer room comes Champa's voice muttering drunkenly. Then slurred sounds. A long sigh. In the kitchen Laxmi is curled up on the rags. Then she sits up in bed.*]

LAXMI [*unable to stop herself*]. Sitaram, Sitaram.

[*Quickly drops her voice. The light from outside the window shows up her figure in silhouette, rocking to and fro like one possessed. And then the stage darkens.*]

SCENE III

The lights come up. It is afternoon. A crow caws. There's nobody in the house. Nothing happens for a moment. Then the bolt of the outer door is hurriedly drawn. Laxmi opens the door and comes in. She is panting heavily, and she looks as if she has just gone through a terrible experience. She stumbles into the kitchen. Comes out again and clumsily bolts the door of the outer room. Goes back to the kitchen and sits before the pictures of her gods. She is still panting. Almost as if her soul is threatening to burst out of her body and she has to hold it in with great effort.

LAXMI [*addressing the pictures, and still panting*]. Do you—do you know? You know about it? Horrible. Just horrible! I thought—I thought I'd faint. Oh, my God, what a thing to happen! I can't understand it. What shall I do? I don't know what. How horrible! *Sitaram, Sitaram.* That Champa—and that Muslim—how horrible! [*Pants again.*] Terrible! Shouldn't have followed her. I couldn't help it. What could I do? [*She slaps her face right and left.*] I don't know why I went. Why did I go? Shall I tell you? I had my doubts. The whole of last week. Where does she go every afternoon? I went for his sake. My misfortune, I couldn't keep the man I married. For me this one was my husband. I worshipped him. Even when I was away, I'd worship him in silence every day. [*Pulls out of her* choli *some black beads strung on a cotton thread. It is a* mangalsutra *of sorts.*] Look at this, I wore this in his name. I belong to him. If I have to be kicked, let him kick me; if I have to die, let me die on his lap—in full glory like a married woman. [*She's overwhelmed with emotion.*] How could she do it to him? This sort of thing behind his back with that

Muslim—Oh, God! [*A lump in her throat.*] I can't bear it. I wish I'd dropped dead the minute I saw it. Evil! Sin! She'll go to hell for this. Let her! What about him? Because of her even he has— [*Shudders.*] Oh, God! Just can't bear it. They're always drinking— day and night. Wasn't so bad when I was here. I wouldn't have allowed it. And now . . . What'll I do now? Oh God, he doesn't know. The thought of it makes me sick.

[*Clamps her hand tight over her mouth.*]

[*Knock at the door.*]

[*Starts*] That's her. What'll I do? I don't know.

[*Hastily touches her head to the floor in front of the pictures. Goes out and opens the door. Starts, turns walking away. Champa's husband, Fouzdar Shinde comes in, haltingly. He is looking even more haggard and uncared for now. His feet are bare. His face is scarred.*]

MAN. Champa! Hey Champa!

[*Laxmi, her back turned to him, stiffens. She is rooted to the spot.*]

Champa, I've come. Beat me—Champa. Today I've come here to die. I won't go from here alive. Death at your hands. I'll drop off. . . .

[*Laxmi turns to look at him.*]

Eh? You're not Champa. You're someone else. Where's Champa? Where's she? Where's Champa gone? Champa! [*Totters down, almost in a faint.*]

LAXMI [*flabbergasted by all this*]. Who're you? Who're you?

[*Hurries in and brings him water to drink.*]

Here. Drink this first.

[*He drinks it in one draught.*]

You related to Champa?

MAN. I'm Champa's husband. Her real husband. The one she married.

[*Laxmi shudders.*]

Where's Champa? I want her. I want her to beat me. I've come to die at her hands. Champa, beat me. Beat me, Champa.

LAXMI. She isn't at home. Where've you come from?

[*Champa's husband shrugs, meaning, 'I don't know.'*]

Where do you live?

MAN. In the streets, in the gutters. In the cemetery. [*Dry sobs.*] Anywhere.

LAXMI [*can't help herself. She goes towards him*]. No, no. Don't cry. Not right for a grown man to cry like this. What's the matter? You running a fever?

[*She touches him and instantly withdraws her hand.*]

No. You hungry? Wait, I'll go and see if there's anything to eat.

[*Goes into the kitchen. Hurries out again with some food in a small bowl. Meanwhile Champa's husband has taken a bottle out of his pocket, has a couple of draughts from it, and puts it back in his pocket.*]

Here. Eat this. [*Puts the bowl before him.*]

[*Champa's husband doesn't move.*]

LAXMI. Wait. Your mouth's dirty. Let me see. [*She quickly brings forward the end of her sari. Then she drops it at once and fetches some water and a piece of cloth from the kitchen.*] Here, rinse your mouth with this water and then wipe it on this.

[*Champa's husband doesn't move.*]

Poor man. You've got nothing inside you! [*She steals herself to wipe his face. Her hands are trembling.*] God knows what sort of creature she is! Now eat. Eat properly. Don't hurry.

[*Champa's husband sits still, without moving.*]

Haven't you strength enough even to eat? Once we get something inside you, I'm sure you'll feel better. It's an awful thing—drink. What's in it? Some horribly nasty stuff, I expect. Ugh!

MAN. Water. . . .

LAXMI. Water? Wait. I'll get it. [*Goes in.*]

[*Promptly Champa's husband takes a couple of swigs from the bottle, and puts it back in his bag.*]

[*Laxmi comes out with a glass of water.*] Here. Drink this. [*Makes him drink the water.*] You're still weak. What a way to treat a body! She's got no heart, but that's no reason why— [*Looks at his face*] where did you hurt yourself?

MAN. She—she hit me.

LAXMI. Who? Champa?

[*He nods.*]

[*Shocked*] You came here, did you? [*He nods.*] And she beat you
and threw you out of the house? She a woman or a fiend? And
you took it from her! You're a man, aren't you?

MAN. No, no. I want her to beat me. Want to die at her hands.
Don't want to live. Why live? No job, no wife, no home—what's
left? [*Sobs loudly.*] What is left?

LAXMI. There, there, someone'll hear you.

[*Involuntarily places her hand on his mouth.*]

She'll come back any moment. You know where she's gone?
[*Hesitates, wondering whether to tell him.*] Never mind. It'll hurt you
more. Go away now. Go before she comes or she'll beat the life
out of you. She's hard-hearted. Shameless.

[*He seems in no hurry to leave.*]

Go on. Go away now.

[*He remains where he is.*]

If she comes back and finds you here, she'll let hell loose. Come
on, get up.

[*He still continues to sit.*]

Get up. Come on. [*She tries to pull him up. He deliberately puts all his
weight on her and finally manages to stand up.*] Go. Come back again
if you like. If you come when she's not around, I'll feed you. But
be sure to come when she's not in. Go. [*Almost pushes him towards
the door. Sees him out. Comes back clenching her teeth.*] Sinner! She'll
pay for this. Walks out on her husband. Lives with another and
carries on with a third. Horrible! To lay hands on your own
husband! [*Goes hastily to the pictures of her gods*] You're watching,
aren't you? [*Closes her eyes.*] Sitaram, Sitaram—

[*Darkness.*]

SCENE IV

*The lights come up. It is evening. Champa is in the kitchen. Laxmi enters
with pots of water balanced on her head and hip. With great difficulty she*

*manages to lower the one on her hip. Then the one on her head. She sighs
with relief. She can't cope with the work. She appears to be in worse
condition than before. Champa barely acknowledges Laxmi's presence and
then she continues with her own work. Laxmi carefully arranges the pots
near the washing place. Then turns to some other work.*

CHAMPA [*without looking at Laxmi, and continuing her work*]. Who's
been coming here in the afternoons?

[*Laxmi stares.*]

LAXMI. Who?

CHAMPA. I don't know. You're the one who's at home.

LAXMI [*trying to evade answering her*]. Who could it be?

CHAMPA. How often has my husband been here?

LAXMI [*confused*]. Husband?

CHAMPA. Look here, don't try a lie to me. Might as well come out
with the truth. Quick.

LAXMI. Three times.

CHAMPA. Why did you let him in?

LAXMI [*with effort*]. He wasn't—sort of—well. How was I to know
who he was? He used to come on his own. Yes. How could I drive
him out?

CHAMPA. How's it he always left before I returned.

LAXMI. He—he used to go. Yes. He'd just go away.

CHAMPA. Why didn't you tell me?

LAXMI. I? [*At a loss to answer.*] I thought—I wasn't sure whether—I
mean if I should tell or. . . .

CHAMPA [*stands before her, hands on hips*]. Look here. Don't double-
cross me. I warn you. [*Laxmi wants to say something, but the words
won't leave her mouth.*] If you act straight, you can stay. You're
here because I let you stay. I'm warning you, don't you dare let
that corpse enter this house again. You'll have me to face, then.

[*Laxmi begins to tremble. She wants to say something, but no words
issue from her lips. Champa goes out. Laxmi looks in her direction. She
is still in the kitchen. She goes to the pictures of the gods.*]

LAXMI [*to the gods*]. Sitaram, Sitaram. You saw that, didn't you?
She's stopped her husband from coming here. Because he found
a friend here. He'd have become strong again. Then she
wouldn't have been able to keep him down. Poor man! She
walked out on him. Walked out on the man she'd been joined to
by gods and *Brahmins*. He still wants her. That's why he keeps on
coming here. But she doesn't want him. He's in her way. She'd

be happy if he died. She's no fool. She's evil. She dared threaten me! What can she do to me? I'm a good woman. Right's on my side. I've always been virtuous. She can't do a thing to me. [*Swallows*] Don't ever forgive her, God. She's evil.

[*As she speaks, the stage darkens gradually.*]

SCENE V

The lights come up. It is night. Laxmi and Champa are in the kitchen. Laxmi sits in front of the framed pictures of the gods reading from a prayer book. Champa is by the stove. She is cutting the vegetables. In the outer room Sakharam is smoking his chilum. *By his side is the* mridanga, *and further away his mattress.*

SAKHARAM. Champa!
CHAMPA [*reluctantly*]. Coming.

[*But she carries on with her work. Laxmi glances in her direction and continues with her reading.*]

SAKHARAM. Champa, what're you doing?
CHAMPA. Getting the vegetables ready for tomorrow.
SAKHARAM. Do that tomorrow. Come and sleep.

[*Champa still continues with her work. Laxmi is conscious of all this but avoids looking at her.*]

SAKHARAM [*in a harsher voice*]. Champa!

[*Champa stops cutting the vegetables, bangs things around, gets up and washes her hands. Wipes them on her* sari *and comes into the outer room.*]

Shut that door and put off the light. Quick.

[*Champa deliberately takes her time doing these things. Approaches the mattress. Laxmi's attention is not on the prayer-book any more—but outside. Sakharam comes to the mattress. Champa is sitting on the mattress.*]

Come on, sleep.

[*Champa remains sitting.*]

Didn't you hear me?

[*Champa continues to sit.*]

Have you gone deaf?

[*She remains seated. He forces her down. In the kitchen, Laxmi shudders.*]

[*Shrilly*] Hey, you, put off the light there!

[*Laxmi quickly puts out the oil-lamp. It is dark. It remains like this for some time. The silence is terrible. Then suddenly the sounds of a struggle in the outer room.*]

CHAMPA [*fiercely*]. No—no—I don't want it—I don't want it today.

SAKHARAM. Be quiet, Champa.

CHAMPA. No. Go away. Move over. Leave me alone or else—

SAKHARAM [*a cry of pain*]. Ooh—you baggage, I'll teach you how to. . . .

CHAMPA. Don't you dare touch me—I'm telling you—Go away. Will you just get away from me! Away. . . .

[*This argument goes on and then Champa lets out an animal cry. In the dark Champa is seen shooting out and moving away. In the kitchen Laxmi's darkened figure stiffens. Now Sakharam's figure is seen leaving the mattress.*]

SAKHARAM [*viciously stalking Champa*]. Come here—All these airs! You were in the streets when I picked you up. I fed you. Come along—this very minute.

CHAMPA. I'll wake up the whole place, I tell you. I can't bear it any more.

SAKHARAM. So what? I'm the master here. My word goes.

CHAMPA. My body can't take it, not any more.

SAKHARAM. Your body can go to hell. I haven't kept you here to pamper your body. Come on now—Come on—

CHAMPA [*resolutely*]. I won't. I didn't mind it as long as you were a man. I won't take you now.

SAKHARAM. Champa—

CHAMPA. Yeah. Can't take it any more—not even with all that drink inside me. If you can't make it, go and lie down quietly. Haven't been able to make it these last few days. A sound from the kitchen and you go cold. That true or not?

SAKHARAM. Champa—

CHAMPA. Stop that 'Champa—Champa—' You're not a man—not since she came. She's made an impotent ninny of you. Don't have the guts to take me before her. You turn into a corpse—a worm.

SAKHARAM. Watch your tongue Champa. I can turn nasty.

CHAMPA. Go away! Who're you trying to scare? Can't frighten even a dog, you!

SAKHARAM. Damn your mother's—

[*In the dim light he is seen pouncing on her. A struggle follows. Laxmi stands motionless in the kitchen. Outside Champa is about to scream. He puts his hand over her mouth. Sakharam's grunting. A bang and a crash. Champa whines like an animal. Sakharam's voice.*]

Drink—drink—drink some more—Open your jaws—don't spit, you slut—Drink, drink or I'll—Drink—Come on, drink.

[*Then the struggle ends. Everything is still. Champa sighs. Silence, Sakharam's indistinct grunts. Laxmi's agonized figure standing inside kitchen door. Then total darkness.*]

SCENE VI

Less dark. A faint murmur from Champa lying on the mattress. Sakharam gets up and comes to the kitchen door. Opens it. Laxmi springs out of bed. Hastily lights the lamp. Sakharam stands in the doorway. Both still.

SAKHARAM [*in a low growling tone*]. Leave this house. This very minute. [*Laxmi trembles all over.*] She says you have made a ninny out of me, you beggar. There wasn't a soul in the world who'd have cared for you. So you got on to my back, did you? Why didn't you die instead? What am I to you? I don't give a damn for you and your God. I'm my own master. I'm a wretched scavenger, a *Mahar* brat born in a *Brahmin* home. Why did you come here again? Why did you stay on here? Get out. Pick up those gods of yours. Pick up all that stuff, and your clothes. Or I'll bring them to you, where you are, but clear out of here. Get out. You hear me?

LAXMI [*inaudibly*]. At least till the morning—

SAKHARAM. No, now, this very minute. I want to lead my own life. I don't want you or your God in my way. Why should I put up with it! Pick up that picture, or I'll kick it.

[*Laxmi hastily picks up the picture and hugs it close to her bosom.*]

LAXMI. Why do this to God?

SAKHARAM. Why did He enter my house? He turned you into a beggar and came into my home under your wing. . . .

LAXMI. You shouldn't talk like that about. . . .

SAKHARAM. You think I'm scared of Him? Oh no! I've lived a clean life. I used my wits to live the way I wanted. I didn't cheat a soul. I'm not scared of anyone, not even of God. So get out. Clear out of here now.

LAXMI [*seeing no other way out, begins to collect all her belongings*]. I could have gone in the morning. [*Sakharam's expression turns brutal.*] No—no. I'll go. I'll go this very minute.

[*She's got everything together now. Comes near him. Suddenly tries to touch his feet.*]

SAKHARAM [*kicks her*]. Out!

[*Laxmi is trembling violently. A terribly pathetic figure. Comes into the outer room, a shrunken figure. Goes to the door. Sakharam follows her. Laxmi again tries to touch his feet. He moves back.*]

No! You have no claim on me. I'll kick you. Make you vomit blood, I will.

[*Laxmi begins to open the door with a trembling hand. Then she stops.*]

LAXMI [*she has found strength somewhere. It is the strength of a cornered animal*]. I'll go—but I've got to tell you something.

SAKHARAM. I don't want to hear a word.

LAXMI. It's for your own good.

SAKHARAM. I don't want to hear.

LAXMI. I . . . I won't wait. I'll go the minute I tell you. It's for your own good.

SAKHARAM [*after a pause*]. All right. What is it?

LAXMI [*pointing Champa*]. She's—she's no good. . . . no good. . . .

SAKHARAM. That's my look-out.

LAXMI. She's unfaithful to you. . . .

SAKHARAM. I don't want to hear it from you. Clear out.

LAXMI. She—she goes to that Muslim—every day.

[*A heavy silence.*]

SAKHARAM. What? Muslim? Which Muslim?

LAXMI. Dawood. To Dawood.

SAKHARAM [*moves forward and slaps her hard*]. I'll break your jaw.

LAXMI. I saw it—with my own eyes—I swear to God—

[*Sakharam pounces on Laxmi like a tiger and beats her right and left. She doubles up in pain. Champa's unconscious and faint muttering.*]

CHAMPA [*faintly*]. Move away, you corpse. . . . Get away. You're a ninny. I can't take it any more.

[*Champa groans in pain. It's an animal sound.*]

SAKHARAM [*flays Laxmi again*]. So! [*Then jerks her up*] Now say it again. Say it once more.

LAXMI [*even though she's being hit all the time*]. It's true—it's the truth—these lips have never spoken a lie yet—She's unfaithful to you—Yes—with Dawood. She goes to him—every afternoon—when you're at the Press. I've seen them—seen them with my own eyes.

[*Sakharam pushes her away with terrible force, and shoots out of the house like an arrow. Laxmi groans. Animal sounds from Champa. Far away the dogs bark. Then darkness.*]

SCENE VII

Less dark now. Laxmi is sitting motionless, against the wall. Before her is the picture of a god. She is moaning. Sakharam comes in. Closes the door. Looks at Laxmi. Kicks her once. She cries out in anguish. Sakharam makes straight for Champa and stands there looking at her. Quickly sits down and puts his hands round her neck. Grunts. Squeezes harder. Her suffocated wail grows fainter. He continues to squeeze. Then sits staring at her motionless body for a few seconds in frozen silence.

SAKHARAM [*shudders and mutters faintly*]. Murder! [*More clearly*] Murder! [*Faintly*] Murder.

[*Laxmi stiffens.*]

Murder, Murder!

[*Laxmi gets up quickly and limps towards Sakharam and Champa. Stands motionless, looking at Sakharam, and then at the prostrate figure of Champa.*]

SAKHARAM [*scared*]. Murdered—I've murdered her—murder—I've murdered—

LAXMI [*summons all her strength*]. Hush! Don't shout. Not a word. [*Continues staring at the lifeless Champa.*] Anyway she was a sinner. She'll go to hell. Not you. I've been, a virtuous woman. My virtuous deeds will see both of us through. I'll stay with you. I'll look after you. I'll do what you say. And I'll die with my head on your lap. Yes. Now don't be afraid. We'll—we'll bury her. Where do you think? Not out there—no. Somewhere here. Inside. And we'll say that she went away. No one will suspect. I'll swear by God. He knows everything. He knows I am virtuous. He'll stand by me. He won't judge you. I'll tell Him to count my good deeds as yours. I'll do everything for you. Yes—

[*Hastily picks up the picture of the god and raises it to her forehead. Then to his forehead. He stands motionless. Then, putting the picture down, she repeatedly rubs her nose on the floor before it. Then closes her eyes and prays.*]

[*Opens her eyes*] Come—come on now. Let's get started. Get the shovel from the garden. I'll clear some space in the kitchen. Don't waste time. Once it is light we won't be able to do a thing. Night is when God rules everywhere. In the day man reigns. And men are sinful. Men are cruel and mean. Like her. Let's finish everything before it is light. He has given me His blessings. [*Pointing at the picture frame.*] Come. Get up. Don't waste time. Don't be scared. I'm a virtuous woman. She was a sinner. I've never harmed a soul—not even insects.

[*Takes her* mangalsutra *out and shows it to him.*]

See—see here—I've worn this round my neck in your name—all these days. The man who tied the first one, broke the bond, himself. I didn't break it. She—she left her husband. She was unfaithful to you. You are a good man. God will forgive you. I'll tell him. He listens to me. Wait. I'll go and get the shovel. You keep sitting—I'll be back—

[*Stumbling and limping she goes out into the dark with a strange kind of courage. Brings the shovel and gives it to Sakharam.*]

Take this. Come. Come to the kitchen.

[*Sakharam stares speechlessly at the lifeless Champa. Laxmi gets up. Picks up a sheet and pulls it over Champa's face.*]

LAXMI. That's better? Now you can't see that unfaithful face. Her soul must be burning in hell. God doesn't take long to decide. [*Looking at the body, with contempt*] Sinner!

[*Holds him.*]

Get up now. Come in. Before dawn breaks everything must be in its place again. Then no one will know. I'll tell everybody that she's gone away.

[*Sakharam gets up, like a frozen statue. Laxmi leads him into the kitchen. Puts the shovel in his hands.*]

Here you are. Dig.

[*Sakharam stands without moving.*]

Dig. Go on, dig, dig. . . .

[*Sakharam is still in the same position. Laxmi now picks up the shovel herself, and mustering all her strength, begins to dig a bit. One after the other the blows fall, followed by Laxmi's grunts. Suddenly there's a knock at the door. Sakharam looks lost. His condition is pathetic. Laxmi stiffens. She is listening to the sound.*]

CHAMPA'S HUSBAND [*knocking at the door and speaking in a heavy drunken voice*]. Champa—Champa—where're you, Champa? Kill me Champa. Champa, Champa, open the door. I'm here. Why don't you beat me, Champa? Beat me, Champa. Champa—

LAXMI [*to the dazed figure of Sakharam*]. It's him. Her husband. He'll knock for a while and go away. Stay quiet.

[*Once again, she begins to dig with all her might. More rapidly now. The shovel rises and falls in quick rhythm. Along with its blows come her muffled grunts. The knocking at the outer door continues. Champa's husband is still calling, but his voice is becoming fainter: 'Champa—My Champa—Where are you, Champa—Champa—please kill me—I'm here. Open the door. Champa, Champa—' Sakharam stands beside Laxmi. All the sap has been squeezed out of him. He's just an empty shell. In the outer room lies Champa's motionless body, covered from head to foot. Outside the door Champa's husband sets up an eerie howl for Champa, a feeble, terrifying and monotonous whimper. It goes on, and on and on. Night reigns.*]

CURTAIN

THE VULTURES
(*Gidhade*)

Translated by
Priya Adarkar

CHARACTERS

PAPPA, Hari Pitale

SAKHARAM, his brother

RAMAKANT [RAMYA], his eldest son

UMAKANT [UMYA], his second son

RAJANINATH, his youngest and illegitimate son

MANIK, his daughter

RAMA, Ramakant's wife

ACT ONE

SCENE I

*Time: any time. The set before you has three sections. The main
section—centre and right—is the interior of a house. A house that reminds
you of the hollow of a tree. A drawing-room full of knotted, worn-out
furniture. In it, a telephone. At its left, the front door, and a staircase
leading up to a concealed door on the first floor. In the centre another
staircase leads up to a platform that suggests the upper floor. This is
Rama's bedroom. In it, a bed and some cases and trunks. In the drawing-
room, a door to the right leads out to a small courtyard, where there is a
tulsi-vrindavan [an altar of sacred basil]. In it grows a feeble strand of
basil. The second section: to the extreme left of the stage, is a small shack-
like structure; the old garage, where Rajaninath now lives. The third
section: a garden passageway that goes between the garage and the house.
It curves and rises so that it can be seen behind Rama's bedroom. When the
curtain rises, the lights on the garage and the tulsi-vrindavan are green.
Those on the drawing-room and bedroom, a dirty grey, almost black.*

*There is light only at the rear, in the garden passageway. And
Rajaninath's table-lamp [in the garage] is on. Rama and Ramakant are
collecting luggage and packages. Rama in the bedroom. Ramakant in the
drawing-room. They both go out, carrying suitcases. Ramakant turns up
his collar. Rama takes the corner of her sari over her head. Ramakant puts
a lock on the front door. They both exit. Ramakant in front, Rama behind.
As they are going. Rama stops suddenly at the door of the garage. And goes
on. Both of them go across the passageway. A fierce wind. They disappear.
While all this is going on, there is a constant sound like wind howling over
a plain. When the two have disappeared, there is a shrill screeching of
vultures for some time. Then the passageway is drowned in darkness.*

*Light in the garage. Rajaninath is sitting writing. He suddenly starts
and looks at the door. There is the noise of a corrugated iron gate opening.
The noise of the wind continues. The sound of the corrugated iron gate
being slammed. Then total silence. Rajaninath sits down again at the desk
and begins to write.*

RAJANINATH. So Rama went away.
  A statue of emotions chilled to stone.
  Alive, she followed after
  That living death, her master,
  With the dogged loyalty

Of a barren beast.
The true companionship
To a leper
Of a mangy dog
On the road to hell.
For both, their future
Is lost, unredeemable,
And there remains to them
Only—death.
As, when a man's nose
Decomposes, and only
A rotting hole remains.
A death unattainable.
Ungainable. Even by prayer.
Their time comes,
But death does not come.
The dragging trail does not end.
The watcher's sufferings
Greater than those of
The living sufferer,
Leave no escape.
From this time forth, at least,
Across the vision
Will obtrude Creation.
Now, at least, that barrier
Of the unknown
Will obscure the hell
Within the brain.
It still remains
To breathe once, freely,
Breathe with freedom—
Such a freedom—
After that living impotence
Of twenty-two endless years.
After that long,
Interminable,
Foul, besmeared,
Most terrible daydream,
Now, only now, at an end.
The skeletons of memory awake.
The skulls of dreams
Begin their laugh.

Those screams that time
Has swallowed, sighs of pain,
Harsh hissings, bursting sobs.
From all, their curse is raised.
And, as you watch them . . . [*he pauses*]
[*Drawn irresistibly*] She was like a doe.
An innocent doe, untouched.
As loving as the earth.
As the first shower of rain
Translucent, hesitant,
Now the ripple of a stream.
Now a rushing flow.
And so, in a moment
Full to the brim, unshed,
A tender, tender-hearted
Idol to adore.
Like the coral flower.
Or the honeyed sweetness
Of dreams at dawn.
—You never wish
To waken from them. . . .
Twenty-two years
Passed by us, didn't they?
Too many years. . . .
Like this was Rama.
Rama. My sister-in-law. Rama.
At her wedding, while playing
The betel-nut game
My lord brother concealed the nut
Where she couldn't find it.
And when guessing, she didn't dare take it out,
Why there, on her shy, confused,
And childlike features,
Rain-clouds slowly filled,
And flooding showers
Ran down the soft slopes of her cheeks
Still stained with the wedding
Turmeric. And then that tall, grown girl,
Hiding her tender mouth
Behind her hand,
Loudly began to cry,
And I,

The immature,
I giggled with the rest,
All pressed by some tickling thought.

[*Carefully controlled*] Return I beg, return.
Go back into your tombs. Fall back
Into your graves. Leave now at least
To this unfortunate, some forgetfulness.
The peace of loss of memory,
Leave it to me.
To me, long dead
Through a million deaths
By memory. Now, at least.
For once, at least. For once.

Then she stepped over
The bridal measure,
And crossed the threshold
Of her new home.
But it was no home.
Not a home, but a hole in a tree
Where vultures lived
In the shapes of men.
A haunted burning-ground
Surrounded by evil ghosts.
Was that a home?

I remember—
Once when I found
No food for my hunger,
Stifling my coming tears
Within a pillow,
Lying there, raging, smouldering.
I'll kill them all!
I'll cut off their heads!
As a goat's is chopped to mince and eat.
In the burning heat of that thought
She came and passed her fingers
Fondly over my head. So—
So gently through this hair.
Scared. But longing to pour out her love.
I lurched and looked around at her.
Jerked, as if a spark had burnt me.
She stepped back a pace.

Straightening her dress,
And with lowered face,
She looked at the floor, and said:
'I've brought some food for you.
From the kitchen.
No one knows. Will you eat it?
Don't tell anyone
What I've done. Or else, I'm afraid. . . .'
She laid on me
The burden of her oath.
Again and again.
It was her oath, and
I kept it. I didn't speak.
I never did speak.
I closed my lips, and just looked on.
Even when that looking on
Became unbearable,
I didn't utter
A single syllable.
Not even in my dreams.
Their torture, their neglect of her,
Their cold despising, her tormented
Struggles, I surveyed.
I stood,
A living corpse, a watchful stone.
Like a worm, I watched and watched her.
For twenty-two long years.
All her hopes, her expectations
Were scorched, uprooted where they grew.
But she only knew
One longing,
Only one. Embraced it to her
Tightly, as one might one's life.
Gathered up all her body, her being,
Grain by grain.
Threw off her chains in her need.
The need to swell with fruit.
A soft fulfilment.
Each womb-bearing woman's right by birth.
A boon granted by life to any bitch.
But on that thirsting vine
There hung no fruit,

There never played a flower.
Instead, a huge and terrible wave
Towered towards the sky.
Came to that final, tender, feeble shoot.
Tore, smashed, uprooted it.
And then passed by.
Left only . . . a little dust.
A crumpled nothing.
Left her a stark insanity of stone
Frozen from her tears.
Empty of pain
And empty of desires.
And, on the swinging branch
Of her rotted hopes,
Five vultures.
On the swinging branch . . .
Of her rotted hopes . . .
Five . . . vultures . . .

[*The lights fade. Spotlight on the passageway at the rear. Pappa is seen, working his toothless mouth. Rama just standing there blinking her eyes. Ramakant and Umakant looking here and there, picking their teeth and ears. Manik scratching her head—laughing. No voice. All silent. Only the loud screeching of vultures can be heard. The lights fade out.*]

SCENE II

Fade-in. Morning. The worn-out house and its courtyard. Smoke coming slowly from somewhere adds to the stuffiness of the atmosphere. At a distance, a cuckoo calls out hopefully. And suddenly ends on a strangled note. Then from some direction, you can hear the sound of people having words—unintelligible—with each other. The voices are male.

Enter Rama. She approaches the altar of basil at the right. In her hands is all the equipment of prayer. Rama is young. She is very thin, but still quite good-looking. In her bearing there is the innocence of a deer. She starts praying devoutly to the basil. She has closed her eyes and joined her hands, when suddenly there is an uproar outside the house, by the front door. 'Ungrateful bastard! Get out of the house. This minute! Comes here at an ungodly hour. Asking for money, the bastard! As if it is your father's money! Get out on the road! Or I'll shoot you!' Rama has unconsciously opened her eyes and is looking in the direction of the voices, or, at least, taking notice of them. Now a second male voice: 'What are you waiting for, Ramya? Kick the bastard in the balls! Give him another! Slam him!' An exchange of shouts. The sound of blows. Of beating.

Then this recedes, Rama can't concentrate on her prayers any more. She somehow or the other hurriedly finishes them. She picks up her prayer things and, climbing the steps, enters the drawing-room. She is about to go on, but just then, Manik enters in haste from the door of the staircase. She is in a great hurry. Her age: about 32 to 35 years. Her body has that withered look of being past its prime. Her eyes are dull; she has got up late. Curlers in her hair. Her clothes are disordered, as if she has come straight from her bed. She appears to be a hysterical type. She is smoking a cigarette. She throws the clothes which were in her hands onto the sofa. Puts a bottle of pills on a side-table, the cigarette in an ash-tray.

MANIK [*seeing Rama before her*]. Fine! I thought as much! I thought you'd do this! I told you again and again last night, wake me at seven! But that's if you could stand to see others prospering.

RAMA. I called out your name. But your door was shut. . . .

MANIK. Ha! So I should leave it open, should I? So you can come and strangle me, all of you? It's because I take care that I've survived in this house! Think it's human beings that live here? The door was shut, says she!

[*Goes to the sideboard. Takes a glass, takes out a bottle of liquor, and pours some into the glass. Leaves the bottle open. Opens a bottle of soda. Pours it in.*]

Is there bathwater in the boiler, at least? Or haven't you kept that, either? I'll go without if there isn't.

[*Rama puts down the tray of prayer things and, coming to the sofa, starts folding Manik's clothes.*]

That old clown of a gardener Jagannath! He's another case! Comes here every day. Asking for money. He and Ramya haggle away. Every morning. Ruin my sleep, the swine! Does money grow on trees here? Or is there a mine of it somewhere? Bloody cheek!

RAMA. But we haven't paid him for the last two months. . . .

MANIK. Oh, what a sin! There isn't enough even for us!

[*Takes the glass and approaches the side-table. Opens the bottle of pills, takes one, drinks. Pulls at her cigarette.*]

The last two months, I've been dying for that latest necklace at Harivallabh's. But I can't bloody afford it! If I ask for money, no one's got any. Just a matter of one thousand. But Pappa comes at me in a fury if I even mention it. The old man's become senile since we divided the estate. As for Umya—that miser, that lickpenny! No use asking him, the bloody ruffian! 'Do you want a kick?' he asks. And Ramya, the hypocrite, he just says your name.

RAMA. But I—

MANIK. You don't have to tell me that! Any witch'll bear witness for the devil! He'll give your name. You'll give his.... It's not as if one thousand's a burden for me. I just thought that for their one-and-only sister—but who wants a sister round here? Since the division, your husband even charges me board and lodging! I suppose I'm lucky he doesn't flourish a knife at me. And get away with my share at night! That much for him!

RAMA. Don't say that....

MANIK. As if I won't! When I had typhoid last year, far from looking after me, you'd all plotted to put poison in my medicine!

RAMA. No, no....

MANIK. I was careful. That's what saved me! I just refused my medicine. I wouldn't even drink water. That's what saved me. I never slept. Even in the dark, I never closed my eyes for a second. That's how I survived. Or you'd have fixed me long ago! I know you all. I know you well. Come on. I'm getting late.

[*Snatches the clothes from Rama. Puts out her cigarette and walks off in a hurry for her bath. Rama goes to the sideboard. She puts back the soda bottle and its cap. Puts away the opener. She puts the bottle and cap on the prayer-tray, to take inside. Enter Pappa, supporting himself on the banisters. The phone begins to ring. Pappa has a habit of working his toothless mouth. A shrunken body. Gold-rimmed spectacles. Totally white hair. He is smoking a* beedi.]

PAPPA [*working his mouth*]. What's happened to Ramya, *Bahu*? I could hear the row from upstairs. [*Goes to the sideboard, and taking a bottle of digestive powder, goes and sits on the sofa.*]

RAMA. Jagannath the gardener had come....

PAPPA. I see. That pimp's a born shirker. Puts off his work all the time. Neglects it. Sits happily smoking away. [*Takes a pinch of the powder and puts it in his mouth. Puts out his* beedi *and throws it to one side. The phone stops ringing.*] If you ask him, then it's no dirt for manure, no this, no that, no bullshit! He'll think of a dozen excuses. I've been watching him for 20 years. A kick in the pants, that's what they need, to get work done, these people! A kick as they rise, and a curse as they sit. That's all these servants can understand. Well, what's happened to my breakfast? Or isn't there permission today from the lord and master? From *your* lord and master?

[*Rama picks up the prayer-tray and sets out towards the side-table. The phone starts to ring again. Rama's attention is on it, but she just fidgets where she is.*]

If you don't have it, you'll starve us to death! . . . What have I been saying, *Bahu*? Where are your wits?

RAMA [*comes to the side-table carrying the prayer-tray. Puts Manik's glass on the tray*]. I was waiting for you to get up.

PAPPA. Mark that. If I don't get up one day, God knows if you'll notice it or not! Or else the old man's corpse will lie rotting up there all day. While his *Bahu* 'waits for him to get up!'

[*The phone, as if fed up, stops ringing.*]

RAMA. The phone. . . .

PAPPA. Who the hell's going to phone me? Must be for your brother-in-law. He always gathers all the darling little boys of the neighbourhood. And plays the Gopi-Krishna game with them! Or else it's for your husband. Every deal of his is a crooked one! He's ruined the whole business. But it's a crime if I mention it! The other day, he raised a flowervase to hit me. Going to kill me, he was! Die, rather! Drop in the ditch! I've just stopped talking to him. [*He goes into a fit of coughing.*]

RAMA [*with lowered head*]. I'll bring your breakfast.

[*Exit Rama.*]

PAPPA. If I die, it'll be a release! They're all waiting for it. But I'm your own father, after all! If I die, I'll become a ghost. I'll sit on your chest! I won't let you enjoy a rupee of it. I earned it all. Now, these wolves, these bullies! . . .

[*He has a fit of coughing. Goes towards the sideboard and swallows a cough-pill. Then comes back and sits on the sofa. Meanwhile, the phone again starts ringing. Enter Ramakant. He is lean-bodied, snub-nosed, small-browed. There is something weak-willed about the set of his jaw. He is wearing tweed shorts. A sports shirt. Canvas shoes. An airgun in his hands.*]

RAMAKANT. Good morning, Pappa. [*Goes and picks up the phone, muttering*] Bloody racket! Even before we're up! [*Leans his airgun against the sideboard. Taking the phone*] Hello. Yes. Speaking. Jaygopal Sheth? What are your orders? You're ringing bright and early. Yes. Cheque for four thousand? Bounced? But that's surprising! It can't happen! Hello. But.... [*Listening*] They must have raised some technical bloody problem. Deposit it again, Shethji. I'll ring the bank. Yes. You know, these banker fellows are all bastards. Who? No, no, *our* dealings are impeccable, Sheth. Business is business. One's bloody reputation *matters*. Without reputation, what've you got? Business'll fold up! Yes. O.K. Bank it. Bank it once more . . . I'll ring them. I'll ring the bank. Yes. Good morning.

[*He puts down the phone. In a little while, enter Rama bringing Pappa's breakfast. She puts it on a side-table. Pappa starts exploring it. Moving his toothless mouth.*]

Bloody old fraud! The bastard! On that cement deal of four thousand last year, he kept a margin of fifteen hundred! Is that business . . . or robbery? How are you, Pappa? Well?

[*Pappa, without answering, goes on with his breakfast.*]

Here's another confounded nuisance! Eats my food, and tries to act smart!

[*Comes and sits on a chair, stretching out his feet to rest on the side-table.*]

Look here, Rama, from now on, don't give an inch to that gardener Jagannath. He was an old servant. He was Pappa's darling . . . that's why I kept him. But he is going too far, now. Give me a salary, says he! A monthly salary. First of each month. As if he's the damned Governor! Came right into my room today. I'd have shot him. But I thought, he's a family man. Wife and children. He'll only die but they'll raise hell against me! So I just slapped him. Blood streamed from the fellow's mouth. Must have lost one or two teeth. Well, they'd have fallen out anyway. It's an *old* beast. Eh, Pappa?

[*Pappa doesn't answer. He sits stirring his tea vigorously, moving his toothless mouth around.*]

RAMA. But what I say is, let us pay his money once and for. . . .
RAMAKANT. There! There, Pappa! See the brilliance of your *Bahu*. I mean, endure the servants' insolence, and pay them for it. Holy alms! And fall at their feet, I suppose. And worship them! It was all right for Pappa. The money market was fluid then. No competition. It rained money. Fine habits he gave to the servants . . . salary, food, betel nuts, clothes!

PAPPA. Not me. It was your mother!

RAMAKANT. Hear that! *Our* mother was no relation of *his!*

[*Exit Rama.*]

PAPPA. My enemy she was! She died. She left you with me!

RAMAKANT. And you with us! A bloody burden to the earth!

[*Snatches the toast out of Pappa's hands.*]

PAPPA. Hold your tongue! I've shared out my property with you pimps. So I've become a burden, have I?

RAMAKANT. Your property! Your millions! There wasn't even bloody ten thousand cash for each of us. And this house between us three. Monthly maintenance: one hundred and twenty-five. A bloody circus elephant would've been better off! And the business . . . a dead horse! The war finished it off! Even beggars and Brahmins shoved into the sand and lime business. A bloody alms-house! Tenders began to be filled at a loss of thousands. How could we make any profit? Sweating blood day and night. And still crying out for lack of profit! Umya was much bloody cleverer! He grabbed the landed property at Lonavla. The shares . . . they were from bum companies, one and all. Wrapping paper . . . nothing more!

PAPPA. So I'm a fool! So now show what great feats you're good for!

RAMAKANT. Hear that! A widow . . . advising her friend to cherish her husband! I'm doing all I need to, Pappa. But let me just inform you of your stupidity.

[*Knocks on Pappa's head.*]

PAPPA. My stupidity . . . yes! to produce bastards like you!

[*The phone begins to ring.*]

RAMAKANT. Pappa, pappa! As the seed, so the tree! Did we ever ask to be produced?

[*Ramakant answers the phone.*]

[*On the phone*] Hello . . . speaking. Morning, Major. What can I do for you? Goods turned out bad? Very surprising! How could they turn out bad? We're not a useless firm of Sikhs! We've some prestige! How many? Fifteen sacks? Fifteen! But it's impossible! [*Listens*] No. Something in your yard, perhaps. . . . [*Listens*] What! No, no. No returnability. No fresh supplies of that item. [*Listens*]

Breach of contract? Go ahead and sue! Oh, yes? We have our
solicitors, too. [*Listens*] There's nothing in the contract. . . .
[*Listens*] Extremely sorry! [*Listens*] Extremely sorry! That's all
right. Keep your military manners for the Border. No, no. This
is business. [*Listens*] Gladly. [*Listens*] By all means! [*Listens*] See
you in court! 'Bye!

[*Enter Rama. She picks up the plate, cup and saucer, and puts them on
the side-table. She puts the stool in its place, then picks up the plate, etc.
Ramakant puts down the phone.*]

Trying to bloody threaten me with a lawsuit! I'll sue his father!
Bloody nuisance, these military contracts. Rama dear, that
Achalanand Swami or what you call'im from Kandivali's coming
this evening. To the Rajadhyakshas', at Linking Road. Let's drop
in there.

RAMA. What is the use?

RAMAKANT. Use . . . what bloody use? You're a fool! So far, we've
kissed the feet of at least twenty swamis. In other words, we
should've had twenty kids, at least! Rama dear, it's all luck, you
know. Man proposes, God disposes. But let's just go, this
evening. Just for bloody fun!

RAMA. It's a waste of money, too. . . .

PAPPA [*sitting moving his mouth*]. Yes, one's father's money!

RAMAKANT. Just watch your words wher you join our conversa-
tion, Pappa. I won't have you butting in when my better half and
I are talking. Old man . . . ought to bloody sit quiet . . . fat chance!
Give him an inch, and he'll swallow us all.

[*Takes out a cigarette-case and lights a cigarette. Then holding the case
out, to Pappa.*]

Smoke?

PAPPA [*loudly*]. No!

RAMAKANT [*closing the case and putting it in his pocket*]. Very well.
Just doing one's duty.

[*Enter Umakant. Flabby. Shapeless. Wears thick-rimmed spectacles.
His appearance is comic and mournful. At the same time, repulsive. A
rather effeminate voice. Puts the towel, underpants and vest, that he is
carrying, by the phone.*]

UMAKANT [*to Rama*]. Who's in the bath?

RAMA. Manik. . . .

[*She puts the breakfast-things which are in her hands on the sideboard.
Mechanically she starts to fold Umakant's clothes.*]

UMAKANT. Why did that cow have to be in such a hurry to block the bathroom? Not a hope now of her coming out for an hour! Thinks herself a beauty queen at the best of times! And now she's after that Raja of Hondur, she's got above herself! As if that sacred elephant would look twice at this poor man's mare! Hopes that lecher'll make her his lawful Queen, if you please.

RAMAKANT. Can't tell, brother. He may, yet.

UMAKANT. Then you may become a millionaire, yet!

RAMAKANT [*affectedly*]. On the day you get married, yet!

UMAKANT [*trembling with rage*]. Shut up! Don't bring my personal life into this, Ramya. If you open your trap again, I'll . . . I'll smash it open for you! [*Catches tight hold of Ramakant.*]

RAMAKANT [*freeing himself*]. Try it and see.

UMAKANT [*retreating*]. Just leave me alone, I'm telling you. For the last time!

RAMAKANT. I'll shoot you! Bloody bugger! You think my mouth's a soda-bottle? Smash it open, says he!

RAMA [*to Umakant*]. Bhaiya, your breakfast. . . .

RAMAKANT. Bugger having breakfast! Never spends a bloody paisa for the family, even at a pinch! My brother—but a lifelong bloody enemy! For ever and for ever! Just take the day before yesterday. Had to settle an agreement worth seven thousand. I said, you pay it. I'll return it with interest. But Mr High-and-Mighty here got on his high horse! I had to slog round a dozen places for it. My brother! Swelling his bank balance! Black-marketing paper! If you're a man, swell a woman's belly for a change! . . .

UMAKANT [*trembling, losing control of himself*]. Ramya . . . shut your trap!

RAMA [*to Ramakant*]. Don't say those things. . . .

RAMAKANT. When he dies, he'll spread bundles of money on his bier! He'll lie down on them. And they'll cart him off to the cemetery. No heir to his name!

RAMA [*heartwrung, to Pappa*]. Please, won't you, at least. . . .

PAPPA [*moving his toothless mouth*]. What'll I tell'em? They're devils, both of them, the pimps! If I'd had millstones instead, 'twould have been better!

UMAKANT. A mangy dog would have made a better father!

RAMAKANT. That's right! Bravo, brother!

[*Exit Rama with the breakfast things.*]

UMAKANT. It's because we're here that you're still alive, Pappa. Know that?

RAMAKANT. Otherwise they'd have had to bloody bury the old man long ago!

PAPPA. Shut your foul mouths, you scoundrels! Bury me, will you! Talk of burying me while I'm still alive, will you, you bastards?

RAMAKANT. If you prefer, we'll discuss our life after you're over and done with. Eh, brother?

PAPPA. If I decided to, I could throw you all out! [*Ramakant and Umakant laugh.*] The property's mine! I earned it! I sweated for it! When we started the business, there wasn't even a capital of fifty rupees.

[*From this point, total indifference from Ramakant and Umakant. All this has been repeated to them frequently.*]

Sakharam and I went hungry day and night. We sweated tears. We scraped and scraped for lunch. That's how such a huge business grew up. [*Ramakant rattles his airgun.*] The Hari Sakharam Company's name became famous in the contracting business. We got an office . . . a phone. This property grew up out of it. And now, go ruin it, go ahead, both of you! Rub it in the dirt, you pimps, and *then* repent! Airs like emperors!

[*Umakant takes some pill or the other from a bottle on the sideboard. He admires himself in the mirror.*]

And not wits enough to make a rupee! You're after my life! You're talking of my funeral. But remember this. I'll see you dead first! I'll see your pyres burning, you pimps! [*A fit of coughing.*]

UMAKANT [*suddenly remembering*]. Go and see if that cow's had her bath yet! Goes and rolls all over town, the cow! And then sits scrubbing herself. Just when one's in a hurry! [*Shouting*] Manik! Come out quick! Or I'll break down the bathroom door!

RAMAKANT. I'll tell you what. There's a mirror in the bathroom, isn't there? Sits and looks at herself.

UMAKANT. I'll smash it! Then there won't be any lingering.

RAMAKANT. Your father's bloody legacy, is it? Whose bloody share was the mirror in? And who's talking of smashing it?

UMAKANT. I've an appointment at one fifteen. Now I'll have to go out without a bath. All because of this cow!

[*Enter Manik. She has had her bath. A towel is wrapped round her shoulders. For the rest . . . she is wearing a blouse and a petticoat.*]

MANIK [*catching hold of Umakant's neck*]. Who you are calling a cow,

Umya? You're not worth four paise yourself! Mind your tongue,
I'm telling you. Don't run away because I'm a woman!

RAMAKANT [*freeing his neck and hitting her on the buttocks*]. You . . . a
woman?

RAMAKANT. What is the evidence?

MANIK. You bastards! You've no shame! Bloody ruffians!

UMAKANT [*mincing about like a woman, one finger on his cheek*]. *We*
don't go for *picnics* with anyone. . . .

RAMAKANT. Or stay the night with them, either!

UMAKANT [*picking up the bottle from the side-table*]. Nor do we keep
those pills in our purse.

MANIK [*snatching the bottle out of Umakant's hands*]. You've been
dipping into my purse, you swine!

RAMAKANT. So? Is it only that Hondur fellow who's allowed to *dip*
into things? Eh, brother? How's that?

MANIK [*turning towards Ramakant and pushing at his face*]. Worms'll
rot your mouths, you bastards!

UMAKANT. The whole town's shouting it! Didn't you two get
drunk the other night? In that room at the Majestic Hall? And
make a scene?

[*He pulls at her towel. She screams.*]

MANIK. An absolute lie! We didn't! You're slandering us. Bloody
beasts! You want to ruin me! You'd like to kill me!

[*She starts to exit. Umakant trips her up. She falls.*]

RAMAKANT [*to Umakant*]. Brother, we are beasts! [*They both laugh.*]

MANIK [*hiding her face and crying*]. Oh-h! These bastards'll burn
me alive one day! They'll poison me, they'll slit my throat.

[*Crying loudly, she goes upstairs to her room.*]

RAMAKANT. Hear that, brother?

UMAKANT [*giving a cigarette to Ramakant, and lighting one up
himself*]. We're going to slit her throat! That's why she goes into
town daily . . . and falls round that idiot's . . .! And that worthless
Hondur's only a third-class Raja!

RAMAKANT. She's bloody thirty-five years old . . . and couldn't care
less for the family's name!

UMAKANT. But I'll tell you one thing. If I were in her place, I'd
have got at least twenty-five thousand out of him, for sure!

RAMAKANT. Who knows? Maybe she will, too! She's a smart girl
that way, our little Manik! *Experienced!*

UMAKANT. Good victim she's spied out this time! Before this . . .
that cycle-shop owner. The film-company cameraman. And, in
between, that stallkeeper from the Market. Used to roam round
town with him. On his motorbike. Arms round his waist! To hell
with it all . . . I'm getting late . . . I'll go for my bath.

[*He hurries off. Rama comes out of the kitchen with a cup of tea and is
about to go out of the house.*]

RAMAKANT. For whom is this extra one? Aha! For our poet-
brother? Go on . . . take it to him! That's another bottomless pit!
Hogs all that's in the house. And sits writing those filthy poems.
Modern poetry! Not worth a bloody paisa! Sheer waste of ink!

RAMA. He didn't ask for a share of the property, so. . . .

RAMAKANT. Obliged to him, I'm sure. A kept woman's bloody
son! A bastard! If he'd come here begging for a share, I'd have
shot him with my rifle. I'd have blasted him! And if he was so
proud, then why does he come begging for food and tea?

RAMA. He doesn't ask for it. I make him take it. It's many years
since he stopped eating and drinking tea here.

RAMAKANT. I know! You've always been on his damned side!
Observe your *Bahu*, Pappa. Likes her brother-in-law better than
her husband. She'll take him tea. Even if he says no to it. She'll
force it on him! And if he won't drink it, she'll feed him too.
They're all bloody obliging us . . . by eating our food! Gimme that
. . . .

[*He takes the tea from her and starts drinking it.*]

Of course, it *tastes* excellent, Pappa! First-class tea-maker, our
Rama!

PAPPA. He's better than you are, you pimps! *He* doesn't try to
murder me!

RAMAKANT. Who? Oh, Rajaninath? He wouldn't have the guts. A
poet! What's he got for a sword? A pen! Supposing he throws his
bloody pen. Who'll it kill? Not even you!

PAPPA. Go on, say it. Say all you want! Kill me . . . that's all you
bastards want. But I won't die! I shan't! If I die, I'll become a
ghost! I'll trample on your chests! Who d'you take me for? I'm
going to dance on your chests. Trample on them!

[*Goes off heatedly, leaning his body on something as he does so.*]

RAMAKANT. Why d'you say such futile things, Pappa? If you
become a ghost we'll be bloody arch-ghosts! Become a ghost!

Bloody nonsense! [*Seeing Rama*] Yes, Rama dear? Why're you standing here? Go . . . go inside. Do your work. Work's important. [*She starts to exit*] And look here . . . remember this. From today, that poet's tea is *out!* Let him drink ink. I-n-k ink! A cupful, morning and evening. Excellent for the health. A tonic. No joke! . . . And you know, Rama dear, I've got a deal in hand right now. A big one. Keep it dark. Don't let the old man get wind of it. If it works, it'll end our lifelong bloody misery! A house, a car, a chauffeur, the club, a cook, absolutely bloody posh! No bloody airs from anyone, what? You'll get lots of leisure, too. Social work! And by then, we'll have a kiddie also. [*Makes gestures to indicate a child.*] A kiddie! A child! [*In despair, she hides her mouth in the corner of her sari*] I really think so this time. Let's see this evening what miracles the Swami will perform. Eh? Keep some—you know—about you. I mean, I don't have any today. The bloody bank was shut yesterday, wasn't it? Return it tomorrow. What? I know you always have some. That's why I asked. I'll get your necklace out of hock, too. Next week. What's money? Let this one bloody deal come off. And I'll put an end to all our misery. Well, I'm off for a spot of shooting. Not one bloody bird did I get in the garden this morning. All right. 'Bye-bye' Rama darling.

[*Exit taking the gun. Rama picks up the cup and saucer and sets out. The telephone starts to ring. Rama starts and stands still. The phone rings on.*]

[*Fade-out.*]

SCENE III

Fade-in. It is late at night. The drawing-room. Pappa and Umakant seated. Ramakant standing, glass in hand. On the sofa, a horizontal, lifeless figure. The paraphernalia of drinks all around.

RAMAKANT [*in drunken tones, looking the body over carefully*]. Completely . . . bloody . . . had it!

UMAKANT. Look again. May be 'live.

RAMAKANT. Bosh! [*Tries shaking the body.*] He's had it! Look at this . . . abs'lute corpse! [*Laughs*] Uncle Sakharam's corpse. [*Laughs*] Our uncle's bloody corpse. Uncle's hopped it. Look't him. Drunk 'mself t'death, brother. [*Laughs*] To bloody death! Damn bore! Drunk t'death! [*Staggers over to Uncle's body and stands by it.*] Long live Uncle!

UMAKANT. Uncle's out of practice! Has t'scrape for food. Where could he get . . . y'know!

RAMAKANT. Poor Uncle! Used to down the whole bottle, brother. Straight.

UMAKANT. How'd Uncle . . . get here, Ramya? Pappa . . . Pappa cut his—er—throat! Pushed him out'f business! Ruined'm! Turned'm out of house. Fifteen years ago.

RAMAKANT. Poor, poor Uncle! I pity him! I love him! Sleeping like an innocent bloody kiddie, damn him. . . . [Pats him.]

UMAKANT. Why did Pappa . . . cheat Uncle? D'y' know?

RAMAKANT. Oh, yes. You tell.

UMAKANT. Simple. Uncle was going to . . . hmm! . . . clean Pappa out. But Pappa found out first. And then. . . . [Sits on the stool.]

RAMAKANT. Poor Uncle! They're both equal bloody swindlers, brother. Pappa'n'Uncle.

UMAKANT. No. Pappa's worse. Ask why.

RAMAKANT. Won't ask!

UMAKANT. Ask. 'cause Pappa won! Uncle lost. Pappa swallowed the lot! Put Uncle in a fix! Uncle cursed like fury. He raged. He said we wou'n't see his face again. Said worms'd rot us!

RAMAKANT. Poor Uncle!

UMAKANT [laughing and hiccuping]. And this's how he came back! [Pointing his finger] Like this!

RAMAKANT [totally drunk voice]. They're all bloody swindlers! Feel like crying, brother! Feel like weeping. Feel wretched, brother! Absolutely bloody wretched! No bloody kiddie! Sleeping like a kiddie, damn him! A child! [Pats him.]

UMAKANT. I envy Pappa. I envy him!

RAMAKANT. Pappa dear! Dear, would you like to . . . one more peg? One? Peg?

PAPPA [with closed eyes]. 'On her brow the . . . crescent moon, oh! On her brow the crescent moon. . . .'

UMAKANT. Leave'm. Give't t'me. With soda.

[Pappa swaying as he sits. The doorbell rings harshly. Pappa comes out of his stupor a little. And goes back into it. Umakant and Ramakant start looking suspiciously at the telephone. Enter Rama from within. She goes to the front door of the house. Then re-enter Rama followed by Manik. Who is tired. Dishevelled. She puts down her purse on the sideboard in order to fill a glass. Goes to the side-table. Exit Rama.]

RAMAKANT. Who's that? Oh! Dear Manik! Manik dear, how was today's picnic?

UMAKANT. 'd'you sleep well?

RAMAKANT. That Hondur fellow didn't *pester* our little Manik, did he?

UMAKANT [*hiccuping and laughing*]. . . . Money's worth!

MANIK [*noticing the horizontal figure on the sofa*]. Who's he? [*Going up to him, says in alarm*] Uncle Sakharam! How did *he* get here?

[*Enter Rama. She puts a shawl over Uncle.*]

RAMAKANT. Magic! Now I'll make'm dis'ppear. Look! One . . . two. . . .

MANIK. When'd he turn up, Pappa? [*Pappa is in a stupor. To Rama*] When *did* he?

RAMA. At dusk.

MANIK. Why'd you take the fellow in?

RAMA. The bell rang. So I went to see. I didn't recognize him. His beard was long. His clothes were dirty. He looked as if he had gone hungry for many days. He just pushed his way in. I thought he was a thief or a burglar. I was going to scream . . . but just then—

RAMAKANT. I came in! I said, H'lo, Uncle. How're you? Very glad to see you after such a long time, dear Uncle! [*winking*] Manners! Bloody etiquette! But Pappa got bloody furious. . . .

UMAKANT. He cou'n't speak clearly. Just stood and shook! With rage!

RAMAKANT. Pappa said . . . Pappa said . . . Why've you come here, you pimp? I *like* our Uncle, y'know. Uncle Sakharam! Poor . . . poor. . . .

UMAKANT. Uncle said, Cough up my money! My money!

RAMAKANT. But our Pappa . . . Y'know . . . perfect bastard. *Great* bugger, our Pappa! He said, Haven't a paisa! [*winks.*] A trick, dammit!

UMAKANT. Uncle said—he said—You're lying! Give me my share! My share! Or I'll—I'll stay right here for it! Won't go! [*Exit Rama.*] He said, There *is* money. You've got it. Spit out my money!

RAMAKANT. But our Pappa was—smooth, y'know. Private Conference! Pappa'n'Uncle!

MANIK. What happened then?

RAMAKANT. No use.

UMAKANT. Uncle stayed on. [*Points to him.*]

RAMAKANT. No, no, no, no, no! Not dead. Brother, he isn't dead. Uncle isn't dead. Had too much, that's all. Out of practice! Out, you know! Absolutely bloody out! I fed it t'him. My own uncle, y'know. Only uncle.

MANIK. You mean this old wreck's going to live here too? With us?

RAMAKANT. Y'know . . . can't help it! He's out! Can't walk on's own! Can't sit up. Can't even open his eyes. Absolutely bloody . . . *newborn* . . . y'know? A kiddie, damn him . . . a tiny little baby. . . .

MANIK. Then throw him out! He'll writhe to death with cold all right. On his own!

RAMAKANT. Y'see, brother? Poor, poor little Manik! I mean, where's there cold enough to kill him? B'sides, his belly's full of drink! He . . . will . . . not . . . die.

MANIK. But where'll we keep *this* bloody nuisance? There's hardly enough for us all. . . .

RAMAKANT. . . . And Uncle's got into the stall! A bloody dead horse, dammit!

UMAKANT. Ramya, Manik's right! Let me—hmm!—chop him! And you—dispose of him. One piece here—one piece there. . . .

[*Manik starts walking slowly towards the record-player, thinking about something.*]

RAMAKANT. Aha! No, no, no. Sorry, brother! I am extremely sorry. He's . . . y'know . . . our *uncle!* Father's brother! Our own uncle!

UMAKANT. Damn him. Our own. . . .

RAMAKANT. Let's—let's take him off the sofa. Before he ruins it. Put him down! It'll get bloody dirty for nothing, the sofa!

[*Umakant staggers to his feet. The two of them, with great effort, drag Uncle's body down onto the ground.*]

That's it.

[*Manik puts on a record, very loud.*]

Ssh! Let him sleep, poor Uncle. Let him have a sound sleep. [*Pats him*] Poor, poor Uncle! [*Sits there drunkenly, gently patting him.*]

MANIK [*shaking Ramakant*]. Ramya, this isn't a good sign, I'm telling you.

RAMAKANT. What isn't?

MANIK. Come here a minute.

UMAKANT [*suspiciously*]. Is't about me?

MANIK. You come, too! [*When they've come up to her.*] There's something fishy going on—it's Pappa! [*Pappa has slumped to one side as he sits.*]

RAMAKANT. You mean it's Uncle! Our uncle!

MANIK. No, no, Ramya! It's Pappa!

UMAKANT. Manik's right.

MANIK. He said Pappa had money, didn't he? Uncle said so. To Pappa.

RAMAKANT. Oh, yes. Yes. Oh, I see.

MANIK. In that case, I'm telling you, Pappa *has* got something! Hidden away. Somehow. Somewhere. So we can't find a trace of it.

RAMAKANT. Bloody prove it!

MANIK [*indicating Uncle*]. *He* wouldn't turn up for nothing! I know the fellow well. He's smelt something out. Definitely.

RAMAKANT. You mean . . .?

MANIK. And that 'Private Conference'? Just for the two of them? It isn't just today I've got to know Pappa. I've had my suspicions all along.

RAMAKANT. Very, very wise girl, Manik! Don't you think so, brother? Don't you?

UMAKANT. Manik's clever . . . whatever else she is. [*Hiccup*] Must be thousands at least!

RAMAKANT. Who can bloody tell? Millions, may be!

MANIK. We must look sharp when we make our plans. It's good from one point of view that Uncle did turn up.

[*She sits on the stool. Umakant stands, leaning a hand on her shoulder. Ramakant leans a hand on his shoulder.*]

RAMAKANT. Brother, I love Uncle! Uncle Sakharam. Poor, poor Uncle.

MANIK [*tipsily*]. Poor, poor Pappa.

UMAKANT. Absolute scoundrel!

[*The harsh screeching of vultures begins to be heard softly from somewhere.*]

Look how fast he's sleeping. . . . Absolutely bloody tight. Old man, when he sits and sleeps, looks quite bloody dead! Bloody funny, y'know! Pray for'm, dammit!

UMAKANT. Ramya, let's—y'know—finish Pappa off!

RAMAKANT. Bugger off, Umya. Are you bloody mad? Pappa— he's our Pappa after all, y'know. Got any sense of the proprieties, or not? Our—begetter! [*Joins his hands.*] Sin to touch him! filial piety!

MANIK. And, besides, what's the point? How would you find the money?

RAMAKANT. Wise, wise girl, Manik. Wise, wise y'know, brother. Let's take Pappa for a ride tomorrow. On a dead horse! Flatter him . . . to the bloody hilt . . . right up . . . and then . . . wham! Eh?

End of the game! [*Laughs, banging his teeth.*] The money . . . in our hands!

MANIK [*in great glee*]. Then my thousand-rupee necklace. . . .

RAMAKANT. Oh yes. Oh, yes. Dearest Manik. Poor, poor, Pappa. Poor Uncle. . . .

[*The screeching of vultures grows louder.*]

[*Fade-out.*]

SCENE IV

Fade-in. Morning. The twittering of birds. The part of the stage by the garage. Rama enters hurriedly with a cup of tea hidden under a corner of her sari. The garage door is closed. She knocks on it once or twice. The door opens.

RAJANINATH [*with half-open eyes*]. Who's there?

[*Seeing her, he rubs his eyes in confusion. Adjusts his shirt.*]

RAMA [*slipping in*]. Please take this quickly.

RAJANINATH. Why've you brought it?

RAMA. Take it, I said. [*He holds out his hand in pique.*] Rinse out your mouth first. How can you drink before that? The tea'll get cold. Rinse your mouth. Quickly.

[*Rajaninath still looks at her with annoyance. Then he brings a vessel of water and rinses out his mouth outside the garage. Splashes water on his face. Uses his shirt as a towel to wipe with. Sits down on his rolled-up mattress. Rama stands glancing continually towards the house. He comes in front of her.*]

RAJANINATH. Useless bother. [*She is silent.*] One can buy tea at a teashop, too. [*She is still silent.*] One could order a tray. Make the tea the way one wants it. No obligations.

[*She is still standing holding the cup of tea. He snatches it from her.*]

And if there isn't any tea, so what? Many things one doesn't have. Doesn't kill one. Last night I went to a *tamasha*. [*Glances at her.*] These days I go daily. And I do many other things, too. If anyone objects, let them cover their eyes. Day before yesterday, I went to a woman. She wasn't a decent woman. But then, was my own mother decent? I understood that day how my mother must have lived. How and where she met my father. This woman also had a son. Tiny. Just skin and bone. Given opium—to put him to sleep. Whose son he was, God only knows. But perhaps, that's good. It's better not to know your father. Your father, your brother. So cruel they'd put the wolves to shame. [*Stops and looks at her*.]

RAMA. Drink it quickly, do. Someone'll wake up.

RAJANINATH. I don't want it.

RAMA. You're grown-up now. But still you want to torment your sister-in-law.

RAJANINATH [*looking her over*]. You've grown up, too.

RAMA [*pulling her sari about her*]. Enough of your nonsense!

RAJANINATH [*getting up abruptly, turning his back on her, and putting the cup and saucer on the table*]. Don't bring me any tea from tomorrow.

RAMA. You've left off eating; you've stopped your breakfast. . . .

RAJANINATH [*turning*]. Have I stopped it, or have you? [*Abashed*] I mean him.

RAMA [*hurt*]. I understood. [*She is dejected. Then suddenly*] But I used to bring it anyway.

RAJANINATH. On the sly. Like alms to a beggar.

RAMA [*hurt*]. There wasn't any shortage of beggars at our door . . . that I should bring it as alms to you!

RAJANINATH. Then you should've brought it openly! In front of everybody. In front of him!

RAMA. I haven't that courage.

RAJANINATH. That's why I don't want it. Don't bring me tea, either. [*He can't help adding*] And don't come here yourself.

RAMA. You are right. I shouldn't. But I can't help myself.

RAJANINATH. There is no point in it. I'm no one to you.

RAMA. Just saying it won't make it true.

RAJANINATH [*turning suddenly*]. Your husband is *not* my brother! It humiliates me to call such low people my brothers! And such a corrupt man, my father.

RAMA [*after a pause*]. Finished? And what did that achieve?

[*He angrily gulps down the rest of the tea, and hands her the cup and saucer. An innocent smile on her face.*]

RAJANINATH. What's there to laugh at?

RAMA. Nothing.

RAJANINATH. Then you won't get back this cup and saucer.

RAMA. Don't do that! Someone'll wake up.

RAJANINATH. So early? Day never dawns in this house before nine o'clock.

RAMA. Give me the cup and saucer. Your uncle came yesterday. I must go and cook something sweet for him.

RAJANINATH. He's Pappa's brother, all right. The same type. A vulgar man! I saw him in the grounds yesterday. Looking like a beggar. It made me feel good to see it.

RAMA. The cup and saucer!

RAJANINATH. Tell me why you laughed.

RAMA. Uh . . . huh.

RAJANINATH. Tell me, why, I say. [*She is silent.*] Shall I smash this cup and saucer?

RAMA. What are you doing? . . . I laughed because . . . because you drank that tea . . . as if it were castor oil! [*She laughs again as she remembers it.*]

RAJANINATH [*putting back the cup and saucer on the table*]. It's my fate to find everything without savour. Insipid. Tasteless. No colour to anything. No beauty.

[*She has grown serious. She picks up the cup and saucer.*]

RAMA. That's all right for people like me. But how will it do for a poet to feel like that? How will you become great? How will you be well-known?

RAJANINATH. I myself don't know who I am.

RAMA. I must go. I'll come again tomorrow.

RAJANINATH. Don't.

RAMA. And if I do?

RAJANINATH. I won't drink the tea.

RAMA. Will you speak to me, at least?

RAJANINATH. Only because I have to.

RAMA. Nevertheless, I will come. [*She exits hurriedly.*]

RAJANINATH [*tormentedly, to her vanished figure*]. Why? [*There is no answer.*]

[*Fade-out.*]

SCENE V

Fade-in. Evening. The drawing-room. A record of Western music is playing. Manik and Ramakant are dancing. Western style, with uncertain steps. Umakant is filling a glass for Pappa. The old man is enjoying himself.

RAMAKANT [*as the record ends, stops dancing and claps his hands. Drunkenly*]. Splendid! Beautiful! Excellent!

[*One can hear the needle scratching away on the record which has ended. Manik goes over, still unsteadily, and puts on another record.*]

[*to Umakant*] Now you dance, brother! Your turn!

[*The record starts. Umakant starts to dance with Manik. Suddenly the phone begins to ring. Ramakant goes over and takes the receiver off the hook and puts it down, muttering curses.*]

[*Coming towards Pappa*] Dear, dear Pappa. How are you, by the way? Carrying on all right? Happy? Like to have some more? English stuff, y'know! Not now? A'right. [*Looks at Umakant, who is watching, and gives him a meaningful wink.*] Not now. Later. Later, y'know. Later.

PAPPA [*speaking with an effort*]. It was bloody fun today. It was fun. [*Laughing in his throat*] It's amusing! Very, very amusing. Sakharam's gone. Gone for good. [*Trying to caress Ramakant*] Ramya my child . . . you worked wonders. You did a good day's work today. One *needs* cleverness. Like yours. Bravo!

RAMAKANT. As long as you're happy, Pappa, everything's fine! Filial debt. Must repay it.

MANIK [*as she dances*]. Our Pappa's ever so wonderful, isn't he, Ramya?

RAMAKANT. Pappa's grateful for what's bloody done for him.

UMAKANT [*as he dances*]. It gladdens my eyes to see Pappa smiling.

MANIK. Yes, indeed! For so many years now, Pappa hasn't smiled at all! Has he, Ramya?

RAMAKANT. Dear, dear Pappa! [*Salutes him with joined hands.*]

PAPPA [*to himself*]. Sakharam's cleared out of the house!

[*He sits swaying. The record ends. Manik takes her glass and goes to fill it. Umakant takes his glass and sits on the stool.*]

MANIK. What fun it was, Ramya, wasn't it? As I came down this morning, I just peeped into the room upstairs. And my—our Uncle just wasn't there! I looked again. Carefully. But I couldn't see him. Not even his slippers! I hunted. Under the terrace room. All through the garden. Every single corner. But Uncle wasn't there at all.

RAMAKANT. Last night, for every bloody four we boozed, Uncle guzzled eight. And fell down drunk. Dead drunk! We had to lift him by his noggin. And his shanks. Just to get him to his room upstairs. Think it was a small weight?

PAPPA [*swaying*]. '. . . moon, oh! . . . crescent moon, oh!'

RAMAKANT. Pappa's in the seventh bloody heaven tonight.

UMAKANT. What else? Uncle'd worn him raw since yesterday. Put
down my share of the money! Put it down! Put down a thousand.
Give me five hundred at least. [*In Pappa's manner*] 'What money
shall I give? What money do I *have*?' [*winking at Ramakant*] Our
Pappa. [*Imitating him*] 'I kicked you out of the business quite
legally, I did. Why'd you lose all the court cases you brought?
Threw you out by law, I did. Won't get a bloody *paisa*, you pimp!
Asking for my money! Where is there any money now? I haven't
got any at all.'

RAMAKANT [*looking vaguely at Pappa*]. Dear, dear Pappa. Poor
Pappa. Poor rascal Pappa.

PAPPA. 'Crescent moon, oh! . . .' [*He is swaying.*]

RAMAKANT. Inseparable brothers. Like Ram and Lakshman,
Uncle and Pappa. Both absolute swindlers. [*In Pappa's manner*]
'Where is there any money? Where is it?' Early this bloody
morning, I took my airgun and stepped out to shoot birds. Day
was dawning. I thought, let's go and enquire after Uncle. He was
tight last night, y'know. I went upstairs. The door was shut. So I
went in. Uncle was lying flat on his back with his eyeballs turned
up. I said, Let's see what's up. Yes! Or else Uncle could've
hopped it in his sleep. We'd be left saying, why isn't dear Uncle
up yet? So I shook him. At that, Uncle woke up. He opened his
eyes. And what a bloody yell he gave! God knows why! I thought,
Pappa was bloody up all last night. And dear Manik probably has
to get up early. To go again to that Hondur chap of hers. So I just
pushed dear Uncle's mouth shut a bit . . . so! Like this, that's all. I
pressed it shut, Umya, I said, Dear Uncle, don't yell for nothing!
At that, Umya, Uncle bounced out of bed. Like a bloody rubber
ball! He stumbled to the door and then . . . flight! Uncle Makes
His Getaway! I *tried* to bloody prevent him. I rushed after him.
With my rifle. But Uncle ran like a bloody deer. Gone! Uncle
disappeared who knows where!

[*Manik laughs throughout.*]

UMAKANT. Great man, Uncle! Cheers to Pappa's father! And
mother, of course.

RAMAKANT. Of course. Need a mother as well, brothers.

[*They drink.*]

Happy birthday to Uncle!

UMAKANT. Happy birthday! [*He laughs drunkenly.*]

RAMAKANT. Uncle's a bloody mannerless brute, brother. Not even
a simple bye-bye as he left. No bloody courtesy!

UMAKANT. You made him run, Ramya.

RAMAKANT. No, no, no, brother. 'Nonviolence be my creed.' Your Uncle means your father's bloody brother. Almost your father himself!

PAPPA [*swaying*]. 'Moon, oh!' . . . 'Fell down' . . . right now, right now, we need some dancing . . . *chhunak chhun chhun . . . chhunak chhun chhun!*

RAMAKANT. Should've arranged it, Pappa. But didn't have the bloody time.

PAPPA. It was here they all danced. That Hira Pandarpurkar . . . that lovely Vitha Satarkar. Oh, the . . . coyness of her! Didn't notice when night ended. When morning flickered in. . . . On this knee . . . right here! . . . 'Crescent moon, oh! moon, oh!'

MANIK [*yawning*]. Ramya, Umya, how much longer is it going to be? I'm getting sleepy, I can tell you. Now what're you waiting for? Eh, Umya? Finish it once and for all. Eh?

[*She points to Pappa who is swaying.*]

RAMAKANT [*to Umakant*]. Brother?

[*Umakant shrugs his shoulders.*]

[*Preparing himself and raising his voice*] Enough! We're going to have some dancing here, Umya. Folk dancing. The whole night. *Chhunaka chhun chhun!*

UMAKANT [*getting up off the stool and raising his voice*]. I won't let you have it, Ramya!

[*Manik goes and locks both the doors. She takes the phone receiver off the hook.*]

RAMAKANT. What d'you bloody mean? Eh? Pappa's word is bloody law!

UMAKANT. Pappa's and his father's too! No *tamashas* in this house! I won't let them take place . . . that's flat!

RAMAKANT. Why won't you let them, eh? Drink . . . drink some more. Then you won't talk such nonsense. . . . Drink.

UMAKANT [*making a show of drinking*]. Who's talking nonsense? Me? Or you?

RAMAKANT. Mark that, dammit! Does it himself . . . and makes me answer for it!

UMAKANT. Shut up! Not one word! I'm drunk, Ramya.

PAPPA [*drunkenly, from where he is sitting*]. 'Crescent moon, oh! . . . King . . . Oh, a trump card! . . . I'm finished!'

RAMAKANT [*winking*]. Bloody swine, damn you! Saying no to Pappa's bloody wishes, you bastard! Manik, one more glass. [*Winks. Manik goes through the motions of pouring him a drink. Taking it*] Ha! My head's throbbing dammit! Who says no to Pappa's wishes?

[*Manik fills her glass. Picks up a tin opener.*]

MANIK [*putting her glass and the tin opener on the side-table as arranged*]. Umya . . . Ramya . . . stop, both of you! We've gathered here to celebrate Uncle's departure. And just look at the two of you! What *will* Pappa think?

UMAKANT. Manik, you stay quiet. Or I'll tear out your guts. I'm drunk.

RAMAKANT. Bloody drunkard! Why d'you put on airs?

MANIK [*looking all around*]. Umya! Umya! I'm telling you, don't! [*She signals to Ramakant.*]

RAMAKANT [*going to the sideboard, taking an empty soda bottle and smashing it, shouts*]. Umya! Come on . . . if you've got the bloody nerve! I'll finish you! Saying no to Pappa's bloody wishes! [*Winks at him.*]

UMAKANT [*picking up the tin-opener from the side-table*]. Let go of me, Manik! Let go! [*She is only pretending to hold him back*] I'll knock the bastard's block off! I'll crack him open like a cockroach! Let go of me! Let me go! I'll kill the pimp! Let go!

RAMAKANT. Fine one you are to come and kill me! I'll bash your bloody brains out! Filthy bloody bastard! Let him go, Manik. Let go of him!

UMAKANT. Manik let me go. . . .

[*Umakant goes towards the chair on which Pappa is sitting. He catches hold of Ramakant who is behind the chair. Putting Pappa between them, Ramakant makes his chair topple. Ramakant, Umakant, and Pappa, all three fall to the ground. Pappa becomes invisible. Some moments pass.*]

PAPPA [*bellowing like a bull*]. Let go of me! Help me! Help! Quickly! Murder! They're murdering me! Run! Mother! Ah! Ah!

[*Ramakant and Umakant raise Pappa to his feet. There is a gash on Pappa's head, from which blood is streaming. The old man is half-dead with fear. He is trembling violently. Manik sets the chair upright. The two men support Pappa to the sofa.*]

RAMAKANT [*seating Pappa on the sofa*]. Oh, dear, dear! You're badly hurt, are you, Pappa?

UMAKANT. Sorry, Pappa. Look, make him lie down.

RAMAKANT. Lie down, Pappa. [*Holds Pappa's throat.*]

PAPPA [*flinching, he leaps up and stands on the sofa*]. No! Never! You're devils, you pimps! You're going to kill me! You're going to murder me . . . murder! I don't want to die! don't want to! I'm not going to! I'll become a ghost. I'll sit on your chests! Murderers! Call the police! Police! [*He runs to the phone and picks up the receiver.*]

RAMAKANT [*going near him, in a wheedling tone*]. Pappa, Pappa. Softly!

[*He takes the receiver out of Pappa's hand and puts it down. Pappa backs away.*]

UMAKANT. I didn't mean to do this. . . . [*to Ramakant*] You're a bastard!

RAMAKANT [*leaping at him*]. And you're a double bastard!

[*Pappa once again tries to pick up the phone. Manik snatches it away.*]

MANIK. Enough! [*Slight anger*] Don't make such an unnecessary fuss, Pappa! It's only a tiny cut.

PAPPA. You get away from me too, you she-devil! You're like the rest of them! You've plotted this. You're going to kill me! You're going to take my life. Murder me! You'll rob what little money I've got left . . . I know it. . . . [*Pappa is shocked suddenly into silence. They are all startled into silence, too.*]

RAMAKANT [*swiftly*]. What money's that, Pappa?

UMAKANT. You mean, there's still some left?

RAMAKANT. Bravo, Pappa! You're a crafty old swine, it seems!

UMAKANT. He's cunning, the old bastard! Hides money from his own children!

RAMAKANT. So? Of course he will. And what'll you bloody do? What'll *you* do? You bloody miser! [*Picks up the broken soda-bottle and the tin-opener. Gives the opener to Umakant.*]

UMAKANT. Shut up, you bastard! [*Points the tin-opener towards him.*]

RAMAKANT. Mind your tongue, Umya. . . .

[*Getting Pappa between them, they feign a fight.*]

PAPPA [*screaming*]. Oh! Oh! Oh! No, no! Don't kill me! . . . Don't kill me! Don't kill me . . . don't kill me. . . . [*On his face, in his body, there is immeasurable fear. He sits trembling violently.*] Don't kill me, all of you. I beg you not to kill me . . . *please* don't. . . .

RAMAKANT [*to Umakant*]. Get to one side there! [*To Pappa*] Well, how much money is there, dear Pappa?

UMAKANT [*going near Pappa*]. Which money are we going to rob, did you say?

RAMAKANT [*shouting at him*]. Shove off, or I'll tear you lengthways! [*To Pappa*] Tell me, Pappa . . . [*Pappa runs towards the door.*]

MANIK [*obstructing Pappa, to Umakant and Ramakant*]. You're devils, the two of you! [*To Pappa*] Pappa, you tell me. Which money did you say we were going to rob?

PAPPA [*his trembling hasn't abated yet*]. Money . . . in the bank . . . the bank! [*He tries to go towards the front door.*]

RAMAKANT [*catching him*]. Which bank? [*Pappa is not willing to speak. He just trembles away.*] In which bank, Pappa? Speak up. Or this bloody Umya here may murder you for nothing . . . the bloody bastard! Tell me. In which bank is the money, Pappa?

UMAKANT [*shouting*]. Are you going to tell us or not, you old swine?

PAPPA [*hastily*]. Punjab . . . the Punjab Bank . . . don't kill me, you pimps!

UMAKANT [*shouting*]. What name's the account in?

RAMAKANT. In whose name is it, Pappa? Tell me quick.

MANIK. Go on, Pappa. Tell it all.

PAPPA. You won't get away with this, you pimps! You won't get away! [*He is still trembling.*] 'Pitale Plumbers. . . .'

RAMAKANT. 'Pitale Plumbers.' [*To Umakant*] It seems an old account. [*To Pappa*] It is an old one, isn't it, Pappa? That's what Uncle Sakharam got wind of. He didn't come here for nothing.

PAPPA. It's old . . . but don't kill me!

MANIK. How much is there in it? Money? [*To Ramakant*] Ask him.

PAPPA [*with an effort*]. Seven thousand.

MANIK [*unconsciously*]. My word!

PAPPA. She-devil! You'll die a whore!

RAMAKANT. We don't need *you* to tell us that. Go on . . . tell us more. Where's the cheque-book?

PAPPA. No! . . . It's . . . with me.

UMAKANT [*casually displaying the tin-opener*]. What other places do you have money at, Pappa? Just so's you won't have needless anxiety.

[*Rama comes and stands by the* tulsi-vrindavan *outside.*]

PAPPA [*shouting*]. There's no more, you devils! There isn't! That's all there is, really. Please don't kill me! I'm your father, you pimps! Your father!

RAMAKANT. A father . . . and hiding money from his children!

PAPPA. Don't kill me . . . Let me go, I beg of you! Let me go!

[*Ramakant, Umakant and Manik make signals to each other.*]

RAMAKANT. Pappa, will you just quietly transfer the account to me? The seven thousand . . .?

PAPPA. No. . . .

[*He gets up. Ramakant leaps onto the sofa. He from the back, and Umakant from the front, both catch hold of Pappa.*]

Yes, I will . . . I will!

MANIK. Let him go, you two.

[*The two move away. Manik holds up Pappa and helps him to sit down.*]

Sit down, Pappa, do. Calm down yourself now. Just write a cheque, Pappa. [*Brings him a pen.*]

[*Pappa, in the grip of unbearable strain, and of whatever intoxication still remains, starts crying loudly and monotonously. He takes out the cheque-book and writes.*]

UMAKANT [*snatching the cheque*]. Damn blood's still flowing!

RAMAKANT. Wait. I'll bring some iodine.

PAPPA [*shouting*]. No! You're going to kill me. [*He cries*] Bahu! Where are you, *Bahu*! They're killing me, they're killing me! *Bahu*!

[*Rama runs from the vrindavan to the back door. It is locked. She remains in constant turmoil, against the locked door.*]

MANIK [*after signalling to Ramakant and Umakant*]. Wait, Pappa. I'll fetch her.

[*She first goes and puts the telephone receiver back on the hook. Then goes and opens the door. She sees Rama in the doorway. There is scorn on Manik's face. But she keeps her voice soft.*]

Listen, Pappa's calling you.

[*Rama runs in. Seeing him, she is thunderstruck.*]

Why're you gaping like a fool? There's been an accident. Get some iodine at once . . . go on . . . get it. . . .

[*While this is going on, Pappa runs out of the other door. Fade out. Light only on the passageway at the rear. Pappa runs along it, holding his dhoti clear, looking backwards. The harsh screeching of vultures can be heard.*]

[*Black-out.*]

SCENE VI

Fade-in. Light only on the garage.

RAJANINATH [*sitting on a rolled-up mattress, hugging his knees*].
This is the story of the venerable
Father-vulture's hallowed end.
Of the epic song of Rama
And her tortures,
Just one part.

The oldest vulture,
That stubborn ghost
With death in his desires.
Hiding his ugly maw,
Trailing a wing,
Departed from the hollow of a tree
Where he lived,
Drawing tracks of hopelessness
Upon the dust,
With the dragging
Of his corpselike,
Hideous,
Dangling limbs.
After him went his tears,
Spilling upon the ground
Like the disgusting
Droppings of a bat.
The foul odour
Of those lust-infested tears may still endure.
It still pervades the air,
Somewhere, perhaps.
Here. Or maybe there.

For vultures' tears are never dry
Though human tears dry up
While still they fall,
And leave behind them only shrivelled
Sobs for a sign.

Here . . . here there trailed
My father's crooked,
Staggering,
Dragging limbs.
And I didn't stop them

The oldest vulture's own born son!
Instead, I prayed
For one more kick,
Just some more blood.
I wished and wished for
A wound less shallow
That it might swallow
The inmost part
Of that rotting brain.
And in its train, might cool
The burning issue.
For once. For all.
Of the five vultures,
The father-vulture's
Story thus ended.
Of the tormented
Tale of Rama's sufferings,
Just one part.

[*Fade-out*]

CURTAIN

ACT TWO

SCENE I

Fade-in. It is day. The drawing-room. Ramakant, Umakant and Manik.

RAMAKANT. I'll finish off each bloody one of you. Pick up your cards, Manik. Pick up yours, Umya. My rummy this time! [*Picks up his own cards. Discards one.*] Play on! Pick one, Manik. You too, Umya—been putting on bloody airs for too long—pick one! And I'll finish you! I'll make you vomit out money!

[*Umakant serenely picks up a card. Throws down another, and places his cards on the table. Game of rummy. Manik quietly puts down her cards. Ramakant is shocked and crestfallen at this.*]

Rummy? Let me see, dammit—show me your cards. [*Looking at them*] Huh! Tactical bloody blunder this Manik made. Doesn't understand the game at all! These women—they just hold their cards in their hands, and throw them down. That's all their game is. No bloody brains. Or else my rummy was assured this time. Missed by a bloody inch!

[*Umakant is calmly counting up the points against the other two.*]

UMAKANT [*to Manik*]. Put down one rupee and twenty paise. [*To Ramakant*] One and a quarter rupees from you. And four and a quarter left over from last deal. Put down five and a half.
RAMAKANT. Bloody mean you're being, Umya. How's it been your rummy so many times? Bastard!

[*Umakant gathers up the cards.*]

Absolute bastard!
UMAKANT. Your own brother, after all. Come on, cough up. Put out the money first. You too, light-skirt!
MANIK. Don't use foul language, I'm telling you!
UMAKANT. Put down the money, and I won't.
MANIK. I'll give it later.
UMAKANT. Later? When is 'later'? You think I'm that Hondur fellow? Cash down! Goods after! Put the money down.
RAMAKANT. What'll you do if we don't?
UMAKANT. What'll I do? I'll make you puke it out. Your tongue'll hang out by the roots!

MANIK. We aren't going to run away anywhere. It's just one rupee and twenty paise, after all.

UMAKANT [*grabbing her neck*]. Put down the money!

RAMAKANT. Don't give it, Manik! Let's see what bloody happens!

MANIK. Ohh! You're twisting my neck—so tight! Ahh! Let go! Let go of me, I say! Let me go, Umya. . . .

RAMAKANT. Don't bloody let her go, Umya! Drag the bloody money out! Look, how she's wriggling! Squash her bloody neck! Twist it!

MANIK. I've told you . . . I'll give it later! I haven't got the money right now. I've finished what I had.

RAMAKANT. What sort of deal d'you make to get money out of that Hondur chap?

MANIK [*furiously freeing her neck with a jerk*]. Ramya, watch your words! It's nothing to do with money. I'm telling you.

RAMAKANT. Hear that, brother. It's nothing to do with money, brother. Then what *is* it to bloody do with? Is he going to marry her or something? Marriage ceremony? The Senior Ranee of Hondur?

MANIK [*in a rage*]. He is, too!

RAMAKANT. Manik, darling, I pity you. Really! Poor soul! If he's going to keep you, or something, that's a different matter. Not such a bad thing, these bloody days! What times are upon us! Business in the bloody dumps! If anyone keeps you, at least you've escaped beggary for the time being. . . .

MANIK. No! No! No! He's going to marry me!

RAMAKANT. Really, brother. . . .

MANIK. He's in love with me. You understand?

RAMAKANT [*laughing*]. That's finished me! Do you hear that, brother? [*Puts out his hand to Umya, who claps it with his.*] His Highness the Raja of Hondur . . . and our little Manik! Love affair! Romance! Romeo and Juliet! Laila and Majnu! That bloody Hondur has six brats from his two previous wives—six! [*Bursts out laughing.*]

UMAKANT. Still a bit naive, our little Manik.

MANIK. I don't care! He's given me his word. What do *you* know about it?

RAMAKANT [*laughing*]. Ha! That's too much! His word! The Raja of Hondur gives little Manik his word! It's bloody love, it is! Going to bloody marry her! I can't even laugh any more.

UMAKANT. It's not absolutely impossible, if Manik plays it cleverly.

RAMAKANT. What's not impossible? Marriage?

UMAKANT. If her belly swells out—
MANIK [*bursting to her feet and pushing his face aside*]. Shut your mouth, Umya! This minute!
RAMAKANT. Oh, I see. Get him in a fix, eh? Scandal or marriage! Blackmail. Then it's possible.
MANIK [*gets up, fuming*]. I'm clearing out of here!

[*She goes hastily up and out of the door to the stairs.*]

UMAKANT [*following her, sticking out his stomach, and then holding out his hand*]. Shake, Ramya! It's definite.
RAMAKANT. What did I tell you? I wouldn't guess wrong.
UMAKANT. She even walks differently.
RAMAKANT. There's something cooking.
UMAKANT. For sure!
RAMAKANT. There is something cooking, brother. The bloody Raja of Hondur seems a total blockhead!
UMAKANT. Yes.
RAMAKANT. Brother, our little Manik's a blockhead, too. [*Puts one finger to his temple.*] No brains. That's all that's lacking. But what about us, brother? Eh? After all, we are her brothers. Her real brothers! We must help her. Must give her a hand, what?
UMAKANT. Go on.
RAMAKANT [*going up to him*]. Why shouldn't we blackmail that Hondur chap? Ourselves?
UMAKANT [*scornfully*]. Into marrying Manik?
RAMAKANT. Oh, no, no, no! Not that, brother. Hear me. 'She's pregnant. If you want her fixed, put down the money. Cash down. Twenty thousand, what? More, if you like. Otherwise, bloody publicity! Uproar in the bloody newspapers!' Let's have a go!
UMAKANT [*pacing about*]. There's sense in what you say.
RAMAKANT. Sense? It's a windfall! A bloody windfall! What times are upon us! Impossible to get money by the sweat of your bloody brow! Suicide to work hard, dammit! It's not a good man's world any more. But how's my idea? Eh? Grand?
UMAKANT. But look here. Won't do for little Manik to know anything of this. Only if you take it into your head. . . .
RAMAKANT. Ha! Who's going to tell her? Let her make *love!* Romance! Picnics! I tell you, in any case, sooner or later, this Raja's going to give her the slip! Bloody bet you he will! Men aren't what they bloody used to be, are they? The whole race of 'em's crooked, dammit! Bloody frauds, the lot!

UMAKANT. But suppose we go to him, and she keeps going too. He may trap us, perhaps, with her support.

RAMAKANT. Oh, forget it, brother. That's very simple. Lock Manik up, we will. Eh? Won't let her out during that time.

UMAKANT. Then she'll find out.

RAMAKANT [*thinking a little, and then snapping his fingers*]. Accident! How d'you like that, brother? We'll manage it. Supposing Manik breaks her arm . . . or her bloody leg? Then how'll she go out? Not with a leg in plaster! If her shank's in plaster, how can any—romance—take place? Eh? Then it's agreed? It is, isn't it?

UMAKANT. Let me think it over.

RAMAKANT. Oh . . . yer-mother! Wants to think it over! Go on. Think. You'll come to an end thinking. Bloody ruin yourself! Action's what we need. [*Looks at him.*] Think, go on, think. Eh? You'll never get another chance like this. That's for sure. Aren't many Rajas left these days. But the twenty thousand is a must. Ten for you. Ten for me, what? Fifty-fifty. If you're willing, we'll fix it up now. We'll call her down. . . .

[*Exit Umakant, pondering. Ramakant stands for some time totally entranced by this new idea. Then, suddenly, in stagey, loving tones*]

Rama! Rama! . . . Rama darling. . . .

[*Enter Rama.*]

Come here. Sit down a little. Sit. You have too much work to you. You tire yourself. No bloody cook in the home right now. And that servant. Said he was going to his village. No trace of him, either. And that gardener turned out a bastard. Their eyes on money, the lot of them! If there's no money, off they march! Any bloody honour or loyalty left? They'll count the beams of the house that's sheltered them! By the way, Rama, I interviewed a cook just yesterday! Absolutely first-class! Experienced! From a big man's house. Now, it'll be a little expensive . . . but if you want to live respectably, you can't keep counting the money. Can you? We should buy a car, too, y'know, Rama. Must have a car. Cheap, dammit. There's a transaction on right now. If it comes off, we buy a car. Then our Madam Rama sits in the car. And off she goes—to the Club! Social work! Rama dear, you've really grown haggard recently. Take some milk and ghee, what? Must have rest as well. Change of climate, that's the best. Change of weather! As for a child, we'll have one any day. Some day. If not today, then tomorrow, what? I mean, it isn't in our hands, is it?

Some people have bloody twelve of them. And others can't have one. There's no logic in it. What a thing luck is, dammit. . . .

[*He get absorbed in thought.*]

Go away now, Rama. Get to work, what? How will it do to leave off working! Work must be done. We'll talk later. All right?

[*Exit Rama. Ramakant shuts the interior and front doors after her. He takes the phone receiver off the hook. Then, going to the sideboard, he smashes a soda-bottle. Enter Umakant and Manik. Umakant following her. As he comes, he picks the tin-opener off the sideboard. Manik comes right up and bumps into Ramakant. She starts at the sight of the broken bottle in his hand. She turns. Behind her, stands Umakant. Words just won't come from her mouth. She backs slowly.*]

[*Fade-out.*]

[*The sound of heavy objects crashing to the floor.*]

SCENE II

Fade-in. Morning. The twittering of birds. Rama comes towards the garage with something hidden under the corner of her sari. She knocks gently on the door. She waits for some movement. There is none inside. She knocks once more. Still it is quiet. Then she stretches up her hand to knock again, when the door suddenly opens. Rajaninath appears, the top of his body bare. He is heavy-eyed. His hair is rumpled. Rama starts. She stands for a while, aroused, glancing stealthily at his bare chest. She looks at his face. She falters.

RAJANINATH. Do I have to say come in?

[*She slips inside.*]

Go on, live your whole life in fear and trembling. People like you infuriate me! Who've you got to be afraid of? Those cowards?
RAMA. What's the matter with you today?

[*It is obvious from her voice that it's her there is something the matter with.*]

RAJANINATH. There's a lot the matter with me. All the time. My blood's corrupt. It's in the family. First your blood rots. Then your brain decays. And then, throughout the body, it's as if a wild animal's rampaging. Thirsting for blood. Your humanity itself gets destroyed.

[*He locks the garage door.*]

RAMA [*suddenly*]. Don't! Don't shut the door! [*He is startled.*] I mean—why must you—lock it, that's what I say.

[*She looks at the floor. Now the change in her is quite apparent. She looks continually and stealthily at Rajaninath's bare torso.*]

RAJANINATH. It seems there's something the matter with you, too.

[*He goes and stands by her. He looks at her. She is dejected.*]

What's the matter?

RAMA [*confused, indistinct*]. Why, what should there be? Nothing . . . nothing, really . . . nothing at all. [*Unconsciously her gaze is on his bare chest.*]

RAJANINATH. Then give it to me. Whatever you've come to give.

RAMA [*starting genuinely*]. What? . . . to give?

RAJANINATH. The tea, you know! You've brought some, haven't you?

RAMA [*remembering it, brings the dish out from under the corner of her sari*]. How silly of me! I quite forgot. Here. They're sweetmeats. I made them.

RAJANINATH [*putting a sweetmeat in his mouth, and putting the plate she hands him down on the table*]. If you took mud in your hand, it'd turn to sweetmeats.

RAMA [*becoming utterly bashful*]. Go on . . . what nonsense!

[*She stands playing with the corner of her sari. He is, for the moment, enjoying the change in her. He puts a piece of the confection happily into his mouth.*]

What's it like? But I forgot. I mustn't ask you. In your lot, everything is tasteless. Nothing has colour, nothing has beauty. . . .

RAJANINATH [*chewing the sweet*]. Everything is tasteless, without savour, insipid . . .

RAMA. Now make a face like that once again! Why don't you? As if you'd swallowed castor oil!

RAJANINATH. An excuse for you to laugh!

RAMA. As if you'd give one to anybody. You'd sooner make them cry!

RAJANINATH. I'm your husband's brother, after all.

RAMA [*with a sudden air of determination*]. Let's forget that subject. Let's talk of something else. There are lots of other things.

RAJANINATH [*sitting down on his rolled-up mattress*]. Aren't you in a hurry today?

RAMA. If hurry becomes a way of life, how long can it remain a hurry?

[*Her gaze constantly turns to his bare body.*]

RAJANINATH. What are you looking at?

RAMA [*starting*]. What? N-nothing!

RAJANINATH. All night long it was so boiling hot I nearly died. There was no breeze. And what's more, I couldn't sleep. So I stripped and sat scribbling away on some paper. Because you came I at least put on my trousers. Or else I'd have been in my underpants.

RAMA [*she can't help herself*]. You don't have to act like *that* in front of your big sister-in-law . . . For many years that's all I saw you in!

RAJANINATH. True. You, however, started wearing a nine-yard sari too soon. At an age when you should've been in a little girl's skirt! I don't remember ever getting a really good look at you.

RAMA [*disturbed*]. You shouldn't talk like that . . . recite me your poems. [*She sits on the ground.*]

RAJANINATH [*in wonder*]. To you! Why to you? You're the kind of person who keeps pictures of chubby gods . . . Ganesh, Datta. And for how many years you'd treasured that picture of a completely spherical baby! No proper proportions or anything to its arms and legs! Its body looked stuffed with cotton. What you women'd call *cuddly!* And it was so—glossy! [*Forcefully*] Real babies aren't like that . . .

RAMA [*sadly*]. How would I know what they're like? [*There is a lump in her throat.*]

RAJANINATH [*acknowledging his error*]. I didn't mean it like that . . .

RAMA. You did. Why deny it?

RAJANINATH [*getting up from the mattress and sitting near her on the ground*]. I've told you I'm sorry! Must I fall at your feet?

RAMA. Once you people say that, there's an end to it. Freedom to forget! [*He is silent, helpless.*] But *one* doesn't have that either. Every day, a new death. Every minute, a thousand, million deaths. A pain like a million needles stuck in your heart. Blinding you, maddening you with pain. [*She presses her bosom. She gets up and goes to one side.*] You can't endure them. But you can't pull them out. You can't support them. But you can't throw them away. Not even for a little. Not for a tiny bit. A million, million needles like that, each second. Endless seconds like that each day. And endless days like that each long, long, unending, endless, never-ending cruel year. So many years like this I've endured. So many. A lifetime. Do you know that? Without one word! [*He is silent.*] Not one tear. Not a single weakness. I didn't complain. I didn't even show displeasure. But . . . but how long is this to go on? [*She kneels by him, putting her hands on his shoulder.*] How much more must I endure? How long must I carry these needles in my heart? How long must I dam up my tears? [*She controls herself. She pulls away her hand with a jerk; she moves away. He is silent.*] I'm afraid that one day, I may lose control. For even one second. And then streams of blood will flow from my eyes. Shreds of my guts and fragments of my heart will fall from my mouth. Then nothing will remain. Nothing at all! And . . . and still if it all doesn't end . . . doesn't end at all. Then what? What'll become of me? [*With a single movement, she goes near him.*] What'll happen to me, *Bhaiya*, what'll become of me? Every day a new mystic, a swami, an astrologer, a doctor—rubbing your head at the feet of every lump of stone he tells you to. Stretching out a begging hand to them. Asking them the same, same question. Quietly enduring whatever sacred ash, ash of incense, talisman, performing whatever useless vows or diets they may give you. And the truth . . . that's known to my heart alone, and to God. Trying to tell him, my husband . . . steeling myself to fling off the reins on my speech for one moment! But even telling wouldn't help. It wouldn't bring understanding, or comprehension. There still remains that same monstrous reassurance you can't shame into changing. Those consumptive hopes. Those efforts more terrible than leprosy. And that she-devil invoked to bless his birth . . . drink! *Bhaiya*, can all the liquor that this world contains, ever be finished? Even though you drink and drink it? Will that thought never occur to him? I wish and wish that all the learned men, healers, doctors, saints and sages of the world would vanish from this earth! At least for two weeks! It's a foolish thought, perhaps. But I think it. I feel, then at least he'll see, for one moment, how things really are. It's not the fault of doctors, of learned men, of saints and sages! It's not even my fault! This womb's healthy and sound, I swear it! I was born to become a mother. This soil's rich, it's hungry. But the seed won't take root. If the seed's soaked in poison, if it's weak, feeble, lifeless, devoid of virtue—then why blame the soil? And if still the soil should cherish that seed—should with god as its witness make efforts—beyond life itself—to guard that seed, to nourish it? Should sew a little bonnet and dress of dreams by day, by night—should stitch them with the threads of wild hope? And then, if that seed should constantly shrivel, should decay? If all those dreams, these hopes, should just—flow away one day? Not once, not twice, but many, many times, the same, the same thing! That the soil should be on fire with thirst . . . and should have to endure a fast without water! The same thing, all, all the time. Tell me honestly, *Bhaiya*. If there should be a raging thirst, and it should meet with a fast of harsh drought? Day after day? Month after month? Year after year, season after season? What's to become of a person? Tell me, what's to happen? What's each breath of yours then except a death?

[*Rajaninath suddenly takes hold of her shoulders and turns her to him. She frees herself and turns aside.*]

Those women long ago who used to commit *sati*, we're all praise for them. They used to burn themselves alive—in loyalty to their dead husbands. But only once. Once they were burnt, they escaped. But I, *Bhaiya*, in this living death of my wifehood—I commit *sati* every moment! I burn! I am consumed! And do you know something?—I wouldn't lie to you—recently—for the past several years—I've felt every day like—like getting out of this! Getting free of this once and for all! In any way whatever. Let the world say what it wants. I don't care! I mean, perhaps one should set oneself on fire. Or else give *him* something—I mean poison—something fatal—like bad women in stories and novels give to good men. So he'll never get up again. So he'll never again show me to any new *swami*, astrologer or healer. So he won't make disgusting drunken love to me. Won't look at me with drooling lips—and talk to me of babies! So that hunger of mine will never blaze up. Nor be starved by fasts! I'd be spared a lot. It'd be a lot easier. I know what to do. But not how. And I don't have the courage to find out! I don't have the luck for it. I feel, let me keep intact whatever wifehood I own. If the joy of being a mother isn't to be mine, then let me at least live as a good wife. I am weak. I am timid. Despicable. Useless. Quite, quite useless. [*Pushing the corner of her sari into her mouth.*] Not good enough to live—I'm going . . .

[*She gets up. Rajaninath stops her suddenly. Holds her. She is expecting this. She avoids his eyes.*]

Let me go. Let me go. Someone will wake up. I have to go.

[*He does not let go of her. He is looking at her, thinking of something. She makes a feeble attempt to free herself.*]

Let me go, I said. Let go. I've troubled you for nothing.

[*She is looking at his bare body.*]

I've been talking nonsense. Talked too much. Forget it . . . all of it. It was all a lie. None of it was true. I—I'm very happy. Honestly! Really! I—

[*Her glance meets and is held by his. She seems under a spell. They are both breathing heavily. She clings to him, resting her head on his chest. He takes her into a tender embrace.*]

What are you thinking of? I'm getting late . . .

RAJANINATH. What are *you* thinking of?

[*She remembers herself and moves away. But he grips her shoulders.*]

Then why did you vomit out all this to me? Why today? Why . . . when you knew I knew it already? Answer me!

[*She casts down her eyes.*]

Why did you tell all this to someone whose own life's a burden to him? Someone as barren as yourself? What were you hoping for?

[*She doesn't answer.*]

I'm a failure myself. A worthless rhymester. I understand it well, that torment of your empty womb. I know the sorrow of a womb that won't bear—no matter how you're gathered up to make it! That's what I myself go through. It burns me. That very same thing. [*He lets go of her, and turns away.*] Day and night. For the same reason. The seed's diseased. All else is good. But the vital core that takes root, that's rotten. A curse has infected it. A curse that's on us . . . On us all. If you at least can escape that curse—why shouldn't you? [*He turns to her again. Holding her.*] If I can be used for that, why should I say 'no'? Why? Virtue and vice are for other people! For us on whom this terrible curse has fallen, there is nothing but this curse. And a burning body. A burning mind.

[*He embraces her fiercely. She puts her arms around him with equal passion. He holds her face with both hands and gazes straight into her eyes. Then he puts her away from him, and turns aside. He hides his face in his hands in shame. She slowly comes towards him. Embraces him. And rests her head on his back.*]

[*Fade-out.*]

SCENE III

Fade-in. Late at night. The drawing-room. Umakant and Ramakant are both dead drunk. Drinks and bottles about them.

RAMAKANT. Cheers for the bloody Raja of Hondur!

UMAKANT. No, no! For the bloody *son* of a Raja of Hondur! Cheer him! Cheer the bitch!

RAMAKANT. Cheers for the son of a Raja of Hondur. [*Drinks*] Dear little Manik. Dear, dear little Manik. The Raja's going to marry her! Great. The Raja of Hondur's going t'marry the mother of that son of a Raja of Hondur! Great!

UMAKANT. Yelled her head off last night . . .

RAMAKANT. You know! She was terrified. Y'know, brother, she thought we were going to—hmm! [*Laughs*] Natural, y'know. She thought we were going to murder her.

UMAKANT. Murder my foot! Waste of time.

RAMAKANT. The bloody bonesetter didn't turn up till the afternoon. What negligence, brother! Bone broken at night. Bone-setter nowhere to be found. Not till the afternoon.

UMAKANT. And when I tried first aid—how she screamed, the bitch!

RAMAKANT. Brother, she was scared, y'know! Natural!

UMAKANT. I know. Scared of her own brother, but that Hondur fellow can . . .

RAMAKANT. Natural, brother, natural.

UMAKANT. Natural, my foot!

RAMAKANT. But, brother, the work was very well done. Little Manik can't go out now! Leg fractured! Plaster! Baby in her belly! Brother, now that son of a Hondur's right in our clutches. Twenty-five thousand at least. Definitely. Bloody blackmail, Umya!

UMAKANT. Blackmail, my foot!

RAMAKANT. 'Put down your money! Or else—publicity in the papers! No money? Then publicity! That's all!' Brother, he'll puke out money! He won't get away now, brother. Ten for you, fifteen for me. [*Umakant gets up even in that state.*] Oh, all right, all right! Twelve and a half, and twelve and a half. All right? Satisfied? You're never bloody satisfied!

UMAKANT. Satisfied my foot! I'll make you puke out twelve and a half. It was I who pushed Manik. No joke, that . .

RAMAKANT. But who gave you th'chance, brother? Who gave it to you? Otherwise—simple! I'd have pushed her myself. Simple. I gave you the chance, brother. Real brother, y'know. Ram and Lakshman. Brother, who came in little Manik's way? Look! Bit my hand, the bitch!

UMAKANT. I'll count them, Ramya. I won't leave you, you son of a . . . No joke! I'll count the twelve thousand five hundred . . . [*The phone starts to ring.*]

RAMAKANT [*holding Umakant and starting to dance*]. Tra—la—la—la—la—la—blackmail—Money, or publicity—fun—great fun—bloody blackmail! [*The phone rings on.*]

UMAKANT. Phone, my foot! Ramya . . .

RAMAKANT. Let it play, brother! 'Play on, play on, thy flute' . . . Fun, dammit, blackmail—bloody posh! car, house, lady secretary—let it play!

UMAKANT. No joke, Ramya, y'know. I'll make you puke it! No joke! [*To the phone*] You shut up! [*The phone goes on ringing.*]

RAMAKANT. Won't bloody stop! Wait, brother. I'll fix the bloody— [*Gets up and, staggering over to the sideboard, puts down his glass and picks up the receiver*] H'llo! You rascal! Bastard! Bloody—late't night, why the bloody—not now! Not later! Get out of it! Get off, I said! Put down the phone. Get off it. Not now! I said, not now! Not—now—[*He goes on listening. His face begins to alter.*] No. What? No! [*Again*] What? Bloody never! No! No! [*He mutters as he listens.*] No! . . . Bloody . . . Heart! [*He is listening, his face white as a sheet. At some point, the receiver falls limply from his hand. He is managing, somehow, to keep himself upright.*] No, dammit! Bloody—how can this—it can't be. It's a lie!

UMAKANT. I'll make you puke it, Ramya! Twelve and a half. Won't take a rupee less, you swine! I pushed Manik—I!

RAMAKANT. It can't be! [*As he comes forward, he collapses at Umakant's feet. Drumming his hands and feet, he shouts*] Shoot it! Shoot the bloody phone!

UMAKANT [*getting off the stool and squatting on the floor by him*]. Twelve and a half! Not less, you swine!

RAMAKANT [*gripping Umya's collar and getting up*]. Umya, the Hondur fellow's dead. The Hondur fellow's dead! His damn heart failed! Yes, he's hopped it! He's hopped it, Umya! The Hondur fellow's dead! He's finished—finished! [*Gets up and goes to the phone again.*] Bloody bastard! [*Looks unbelievingly, wretchedly at the phone.*] The Hondur fellow's slipped off—he's dead!

[*Umakant, with an expressionless face, gets up and sits drinking on the stool. Ramakant picks up his glass and collapses onto the sofa.*]

RAMAKANT. Our bloody luck's a bastard! Absolute bastard! The rascal! Must—shoot it. Brother, that Raja's a bastard too.

UMAKANT. No, he's not a bastard. He's dead. Heart attack. How one can help it if he lost is life?

RAMAKANT. Why'd he lose it? Why now? Why t'day? A plot, dammit! . . .

UMAKANT. No plot. Accident! Heart attack. Lost life, lost all. Nothing left. Got t'die.

RAMAKANT. Don't give me that! It was a plot. He had't in for us. Everyone's got it in for us, brother. Everyone.

UMAKANT. We've got it in for us, too. Since before we were born.

RAMAKANT. I bloody feel like a bitch, dammit! A bloody pig! A bloody swine!

UMAKANT. Our father's a swine! [Gets up and over to Ramakant.]

RAMAKANT. A double swine! He got us.

UMAKANT. And brought's up.

RAMAKANT. That was nurse who did. She was another bloody whore! Y'know, brother, when I was small, she used to tell me, go and play. And d'you know what she used to do with the watchman? Bloody bitch! And I was nursed up on her milk! They're all bastards. All the same. Shoot the lot of 'em!

UMAKANT [going to fill both their glasses]. Should shoot ourselves. Should shoot you!

RAMAKANT. And marry you off!

UMAKANT. Shut up! Pappa did all the marrying. Nothing left for me. [Laughs in his throat and hands one glass to Ramakant.] Haven't got anything left!

RAMAKANT. Never fear, brother. We'll marry you off. To a betel nut.

UMAKANT. Then I'll have babies. Baby betel nuts. [Laughs in his throat.]

RAMAKANT. But you will! You will, brother. So bloody well will I! One. A son, you know. A boy. A lad!

UMAKANT [sitting down]. You'll have a monkey. With a donkey's ears. And three legs. [Laughs in his throat.] And it'll be born dead.

RAMAKANT [smashing the glass in his hand]. No!

[Then suddenly falls silent. Hides his face in his hands. Then takes it out from behind them, gets up, takes another glass and fills it.]

Brother, is little Manik dead or alive?

UMAKANT. Little Manik's committed sati . . . With the Raja.

RAMAKANT. Bosh, How'd she commit *sati*, after her leg was broken? Couldn't sit down . . . on the funeral pyre.

UMAKANT. She'll sit on the baby. The one in her belly.

RAMAKANT. Brainwave! First class scene! 108th Week of Amazing Crowds! Our Little Manik—sitting on the brat in her belly—Commits *Sati*! In bloody Technicolor! Flames leaping to the bloody Sky!

UMAKANT. Watch the scene from a Plane! Bird's Eye View! [*Laughs in his throat.*] Here, have some more.

RAMAKANT. Technicolor! We'll sell tickets for it! Make money, dammit! Pay off our debts. A house, brother, a car . . . bloody posh!

UMAKANT. But you won't have a child!

RAMAKANT [*grabbing Umakant's collar*]. Shut up! You bugger! You son of a . . . You . . . you . . . swine! Bloody bastard! I'll shoot you!

UMAKANT [*calmly shaking him off*]. Shoot, my shoe! Going to bloody shoot me, the bastard! Have another drink.

RAMAKANT. They're all bastards. Absolute bastards. Luck's a bastard too, dammit!

UMAKANT [*making a drunken, enquiring gesture with his hand*]. Manik's Raja's dead. Finished!

RAMAKANT. The bloody bastard!

UMAKANT. A bastard, but dead. Expired.

RAMAKANT. Brother, come here a minute.

UMAKANT. You come here.

RAMAKANT. Come here, I'm bloody telling you! [*Umakant stumbles over to him.*] Listen here! [*Umakant leans towards him.*] The Raja's alive. In little Manik's belly. The bloody bastard, damn him! Bloody enemy! The traitor! I'll shoot him, brother.

UMAKANT. Shoot, my shoe?

RAMAKANT. No joke, brother! He's our enemy, dammit . . . a bloody traitor. A bloody bastard!

UMAKANT [*drawing him close*]. Let's knock him out! The Raja in little Manik's belly! One kick—that's enough!

RAMAKANT. An idea, dammit! Let's abort him! Let's knock him bloody out! Let's kick him out. A bastard breed, dammit—come on, brother. Come on! Let's finish off the Raja's bloody offspring. First come on! Let little Manik scream till she bloody bursts! How she'll scream, dammit. What a bloody riot! Knock him out! Hides the Raja in her belly, bloody Manik! Come on!

[*They both start to make a weaving exit.*]

Bastard bloody breed! Traitor's brat! Knock him out! Finish him!

UMAKANT [*stopping him forcibly*]. Stop. [*Drinks a little.*] I've no football practice. *You'll* be able to kick. [*Laughs in his throat.*]

RAMAKANT. Come on. I'll give such a kick, he'll fly up to the bloody skies . . . Come on . . .

[*They exit, weaving about, muttering, drunkenly calling out to Manik. You can hear them raving off stage. Then there is a rapping on a door—kicks and blows on it. 'Manik, open the door! Open, the door, Manik!' All this rises to a crescendo. Then, in a moment, a horrific scream from Manik. In another moment, Manik, screaming terrifyingly, comes half-crawling down the stairs. One leg in plaster. Her white sari is soiled with blood. Pressing one hand to her abdomen, writhing in pain, looking back constantly, she exits through the front door. She is then seen going through the passage at the rear. At the other end of the passageway, stands Pappa, laughing.*]

[*Fade-out.*]

SCENE IV

Fade-in. The bedroom. Rama reclining on the bed. In the drawing-room stands Ramakant, his back to the audience. He stands there for a little while, and then climbs the stairs and goes and sits by Rama. In the drawing-room, are three men in khaki. Two of them pick up the sofa and carry it away. The third takes the phone and record-player. While this is going on, Ramakant takes a pill from a medicine-bottle and gives it to Rama. She takes it. Ramakant puts back the vessel of drinking water in its place, and comes and sits by Rama. His expression is anxious. After a while, he gets up to go. Rama, who is lying down, at once sits up and, catching hold of him by the shoulder, says:

RAMA. Don't go away from me. Don't move. I'm terrified.

RAMAKANT. Either you're simple, or you're mad! Why be afraid? What's there to be frightened of? You should go right off to sleep! Or else think pleasant bloody thoughts. You've got two lives to think of now, haven't you? You must stay well. It's just a few days now.

RAMA. I can't sleep. Not for a second. If I do, I see terrible things.

RAMAKANT. Hallucinations, those are!

RAMA. I see lots of things. I hear them too. I feel so very, very scared.

RAMAKANT. You're a scared bloody creature to begin with. What do you see? Imagine it's a free cinema. And forget about it!

RAMA. I see . . . [*She tries to get up.*] . . . I see them carrying my child out . . .

RAMAKANT [*making her lie down again*]. Quite, quite stupid. What has astrologer Karve said? What's more, yesterday I brought some sacred ash from Shirdi. Every day, there are doses. There are injections. At least ten rupees are spent every single day. The pills themselves cost bloody seven rupees. What more can a man do?

RAMA. Don't leave me alone.

RAMAKANT. Very fine! How would that do? Who'll look after the business?

RAMA. This house is devouring me. So is this room. And through this window—this window—I sometimes see them. Those two.

RAMAKANT. Those two? Which two?

RAMA. Father-in-law and sister-in-law. They keep looking here . . . with eyes like live coals.

RAMAKANT. Is that all you see? Nothing else? You're bloody seeing things. And getting frightened of them. Even if you see more of them, what's so bad about that? Bloody coward! Those owls! Who's got the nerve to set foot here? I'll shoot them one by one!

RAMA. All the time there's a weight on my chest. I feel suffocated. I feel my life's going . . .

RAMAKANT. Your life's going nowhere! It's just a few more days now. The four months will pass by in a flash. What's there to it! Then Her Majesty'll be in ecstasies. Playing with her little prince! You won't know how the time passes. Then even a bloody husband isn't welcome to a wife. The baby . . . the baby . . . and the baby! That's all!

RAMA. I'm going to become a mother. Am I really going to be a mother?

RAMAKANT. What does that mean? The mid-wife and the nurse, that cradle I looked out . . . are they for me, or something? I was going to get a new cradle. But they said you should use an old one. In which lots of children've played. That's why I bloody took it out of the mess inside. Had it painted and repaired. We all bloody grew in it.

RAMA. I'm going to be a mother. [*She starts to laugh. Going to be hysterical.*]

RAMAKANT. Enough! Enough of laughing. Stop it at once! It's not good to laugh too much right now. One has to be very very careful—with pregnancy. And the bloody fifth month's a bad one!

RAMA [*in frightened tone*]. Is it really bad?

RAMAKANT. By 'bad' I didn't mean to say really bad. But you've got to look out. Lie as quiet as you can. Take lots of rest, what? No one tells *me* to bloody take rest! And when one tells you, there you sit, crying! Because you're 'seeing things'! Because you 'can't breathe'!

RAMA. I won't cry again.

RAMAKANT. That's a good girl. [*Rising*] Shall I go, then?

RAMA. May I ask something?

RAMAKANT [*growing uneasy*]. What d'you want to ask?

RAMA. Who were those people who came to see you downstairs? Just now?

[*He gets up abruptly.*]

I heard voices and movements. They were talking very loudly. You raised your voice, too. I thought, something awful's going to happen. I got up. I started downstairs. But you'd locked my door from outside. [*He is struck dumb.*] Who were they? What were they saying? What did they want? They were calling you such terrible names!

RAMAKANT [*somehow, with an effort*]. Too many useless bloody questions from you women—won't let men do a thing, you people—the slightest thing happens, and in you stick your nose! What's this, what's that, dammit!

[*She turns on her other side, turns her face away.*]

I didn't mean it like that . . . there are lots of complications to business, there are . . .

RAMA. But why at home?

RAMAKANT. Then what am I to do? Where do I get the time for important talks at the office? People coming and going all the time. And phone calls . . . and outside work. Have to visit construction sites. Rainy season's come upon us . . .

RAMA. Then why didn't you go to the office today?

RAMAKANT [*he is in a fix*]. Dammit—one gets tired of it some bloody days! Business! It's a bloody torture! Dealing with labour. Head-splitting work!

RAMA. Don't do it, then . . .

RAMAKANT. And what'll I do?

RAMA [*in anguish*]. Take a job somewhere! Whatever you can get. Never mind if it doesn't pay well. We'll live in poverty, if we have to. Really. You, me, our baby. The three of us. We'll make a feast of crumbs. We'll eat once a day. We'll endure whatever we have to. I'll slave as hard as you want. Gladly. But let's finish this death by imprisonment. Let's end this dreadful play-acting. Stop this murderous deceit. Honestly! Put an end to it. Let's get out of this overpowering house. Go far away. No one, no one at all can live happily here. Not at all . . . never at all. Will you listen to me? Listen, for once? I won't ever tell you to do anything again. Not anything! I'll stay just as I have till this day. Mouth shut, head bent.

[*She sees the alteration in his face. And she is struck silent with fear. As he listens, he at first shrinks. He collapses. Then he stiffens. When she is silent, he gathers up all his strength, and stands up.*]

RAMAKANT. Look here, Rama! In this house, we're not accustomed to listening to any smartness from women! No man in our family's been a bloody henpecked husband, what? I know very well indeed what to do, what not to do. No need for a woman to teach me sense. Can I go now? Have a good rest. Relax. Don't think stupid thoughts. Your husband's still alive, you know. [*He lovingly makes her sit down on the bed.*] Drink some milk, morning and evening. Fruit's excellent too. I'll tell the fruit-seller to send some. O.K. I'm off. I've got an appointment with whatsisname . . .

[*He goes down the stairs. Takes out a bottle. She lies with her face pressed into her pillow, sobbing.*]

[*Fade-out.*]

SCENE V

Fade-in. The same place. Ramakant has drunk too much, and fallen asleep. In an easy chair. The bottle and glass are near him. Spotlight on him.

RAMAKANT'S VOICE [*recorded*]. I tell you, Rama, our kid'll bring us luck! No more hardship, what? I've got a transaction on right now. If it comes off, then what d'you know? A bloody car. A chauffeur. A total bloody renovation for the house! We'll have it done. We'll put down new bloody flooring. Make the house bloody posh. We will! A cook, a chef, a watchman at the gate. Eight or ten servants. All under you. Dinner daily at the Radio Club! Don't have any kind of worry, Rama! It'll all work out right. We'll put the kiddie in a bloody convent-school, what? From there, straight to Rajkumar bloody College at Delhi. Yes! Then Oxford, if he likes . . . After all, hq *is* going to be Managing Director of the top-ranking construction firm in India! That's no joke! Must be absolutely up-to-date. Don't you worry, Rama. Hold on a while. Take rest, what? Fruit's excellent. Ought to drink milk. Morning and evening. That's good for the bloody health, too . . .

[*Now little by little it grows light throughout the drawing-room. The recorded piece fades away. Umakant sitting in front of Ramakant, smoking a pipe. We see him for the first time. For some time, he sits still. Looking at Ramakant. Smoking his pipe. Ramakant unconscious of it. Then suddenly, he wakes up with a start and sees Umakant sitting in front of him, like a nightmare.*]

RAMAKANT [*recovering himself*]. Hello . . .
UMAKANT. Why's the phone gone?

[*Ramakant can't understand. To his newly-recovered consciousness, this question doesn't register at all.*]

RAMAKANT. I fell asleep for a while . . .
UMAKANT. When's the sofa coming back? From being repaired?
RAMAKANT. The sofa . . . the sofa . . . [*The questions aren't really making sense to him as yet.*]
UMAKANT. And the radiogram, which you lent for a wedding? Why haven't you brought it back?

[*Ramakant is trying desperately to bring his brain back to normal.*]

Why? You've a new excuse every day!
RAMAKANT. New . . . no, but brother, that's my affair, you know. Mine alone.
UMAKANT. Where are Mother's jewels? Or is that also your affair alone?
RAMAKANT. They're in the bank. Safe deposit. Useless bloody risk keeping them at home. Who'll look after them all day?
UMAKANT. Without my permission? Is it your father's estate? We've both got a share in them!
RAMAKANT. Who's saying you bloody haven't?
UMAKANT. When am I getting my share of Manik's money?
RAMAKANT. I'll give it to you, dammit! Why're you making such a song and dance about it?

UMAKANT. Who's making a song and dance? And what about that matter of Pappa's separate account? Manik's share's got to be divided between us. Fifty-fifty.

RAMAKANT [*laughing theatrically and standing up*]. Is today your day for bloody stock-taking or something, brother? You're reading out a bloody inventory!

UMAKANT. Don't try to wheedle me! I've known you since my birth! Is it true or not that you've lost your office?

RAMAKANT. Maybe . . . how are you bloody concerned?

UMAKANT. Is it true that there is a double mortgage on the house?

RAMAKANT [*Ramakant makes an annoyed face. He leans back*]. I'm not bound to tell you that!

UMAKANT. What's there to tell . . . you cretin! It's all finished. You won't last two days!

RAMAKANT [*jolted*]. What do . . . what do you bloody know about it? Acting high-and-mighty!

UMAKANT. What you know, I know. But one can't get anything into your empty head. If you allowed it to get in, you'd poison yourself this minute!

RAMAKANT. Poison's no joke, Umya. [*Grabs Umakant by the collar. Umakant shakes him off.*] Get out of here! Trying to bloody frighten me. You bastard! Bloody gnat! Half-cocked bastard! I'll look after my own bloody affairs!

UMAKANT. What've you got left to look after? Double mortgage on the house. The office has gone already. The bank'll attach the account. The creditors'll fall like jackals on the rest of the property. Pappa's account's cleaned out. Manik's share's all gone. So what've you got that's yours, you good-for-nothing? What're you going to look after? Your bloody ill-starred face?

RAMAKANT [*sitting down on the stool*]. So what do you advise me to do, brother? I'll do what you bloody say, brother.

UMAKANT. Fine time it's occurred to you! Now who's going to pull you out, and how? Time's running out. The meeting of your creditors must've ended over there. The bank's got the information, or been sent it! Cheques'll start bouncing thick and fast now . . .

RAMAKANT [*hiding his face in his hand*]. Brother, you must suggest some remedy. You'll do something. Because you're my bloody brother . . . surely . . .

UMAKANT [*puffing at his pipe*]. Where's the profit?

RAMAKANT. Profit? Brother, are you and I different or something? Eh? My bloody profit's your profit, and . . .

UMAKANT. Will you transfer this house to my name? Then I'll redeem it.

RAMAKANT [*shouting*]. Brother, the house is my bloody share . . .

UMAKANT. Your share's going into the Multani moneylender's throat! Are you going to change the house to my name? Tell me!

RAMAKANT. But when everything's going, why're you just talking of the bloody house?

UMAKANT. I won't go into mourning if the rest goes. But I want this house.

RAMAKANT. But brother, it's a matter of bloody life and death to me. Family man. Wife and child.

UMAKANT. Go ahead and die. I want this house.

[*Ramakant gets up unhappily from his seat. He goes to the sideboard and fills a glass.*]

RAMAKANT [*in stiff tones*]. I was going to tell you something too, brother. Lucky I remembered in time. *Meant* to bloody tell you. But where's the time? I *am* in difficulties, I know, brother. Everyone's bloody luck comes tied round their neck from the start. There's no help for it, what? Where'll you make a complaint? God Almighty's in his own heaven. Celestial nymphs! This . . . [*He mimes a drink.*] He hasn't the bloody time either! Absolutely busy, what? Those who've taken a fall, they've got no one. So why should you have the nuisance of my bad luck, eh? I mean, your luck's on the go. You're making money. And you'll make still more. You'll get everything. Money bloody tells! Pretty soon you'll get bloody married, too! You'll have five or ten children, what? Money can do anything. So what I'm saying is, if you're bloody prospering, why have us to put a hex on you? Go where you like. Buy a first-class house. Independent. A car, a chauffeur. A cook, a bloody chef. Who'll question you? We'll stay put in this hermitage of ours. We'll exist bloody somehow. Or we'll go away somewhere, what? Become coolies. Or else beggars. But why all this trouble for *you*, don't you agree? So what if you're my bloody brother! So, brother, goodbye! Get your bad rubbish out of here as quick as possible. Now, if you can. Today! . . . And . . . a happy life to you!

UMAKANT [*really dazed by all this*]. You mean, you're not prepared to think . . .

RAMAKANT. How bloody *can* I? I mean, have I got the head for it? Or the wits? Fool, that's what one is. But you're bloody smart. Intelligent. You do the thinking. About getting out! When d'you go?

UMAKANT. You'll regret this! You'll say later on that . . .

RAMAKANT. But *you* won't be there to hear it!

UMAKANT [*in a fury*]. First settle our account! Then I'll move! Pappa's hidden hoard. Manik's money, Mother's jewels . . .

RAMAKANT. Ask from outside! Then you'll get them! All after you've got out! Out!

UMAKANT [*in an uncontrollable rage, grabbing Ramakant by the nape of his neck*]. Go on. Wait. As if I'm all ready to leave. I'll quit when I've got every single paisa, you bastard! I won't let you get away with it! I'll sit on your neck. I'll make you puke it out! Bloody animal! Swindler! I'll see you in the gutter!

RAMAKANT [*freeing his neck*]. Don't shout. It'll disturb Rama.

UMAKANT. I know about the brat your wife's having. As if no one's ever had one before! If you were such a man, why'd she keep dropping them before this? At two to four months? And how d'you know this brat's yours?

RAMAKANT [*confidently, slyly*]. Then whose is it?

UMAKANT. It's that bastard Rajaninath's! That enemy at your gates! It's your half-brother's! Your bastard brother's! That son-of-a-whore's!

RAMAKANT [*raging suddenly*]. You bastard, Umya. Shut your mouth!

UMAKANT. Your wife used to go to him on the sly. Take him tea, and things to eat.

RAMAKANT [*trembling*]. Shut your trap, I said!

UMAKANT. She used to go daily. I've seen her. They used to sit inside, the two of them. With the door shut. Ask her, if you've got the guts, you coward!

RAMAKANT [*raging with fury from the very core, he catches hold of Umakant's hand and twists it*]. You . . . you're lying, you bastard! You're saying it on purpose. You . . . you know it's all a lie! You know it! You're spreading poison on purpose, you bastard . . . spreading it on purpose! You just want revenge, do you? Stupid bloody bastard! Bloody swine! Muckworm!

UMAKANT. Call the brat your own, go on! Put him on your head! Lick his piss! Let that smart-arse have fun. You be the bloody father. Bloody fool. Not a paisa's worth of sense. Bloody dupe! . . . Bringing shame on all of us!

[*Umakant goes straight out of the house, Ramakant in a pitiful state for a moment. Then calling out inquiringly.*]

RAMAKANT. Rama!

[*Enter Rama from within. As she stands there, her condition, her swollen abdomen, look extremely pitiful. In her hands is a metal plate on which she is cleaning uncooked rice.*]

RAMAKANT [*looking at her*]. So that's it, eh? Why've you got up and come down? What've you bloody decided? Want to die or something?

RAMA [*avoiding the true answer*]. I got tired lying there all day. So I came down.

[*The answer seems to have been thought over in advance.*]

RAMAKANT. Got tired, she says. Convenient bloody tiredness! How'd you sleep last night? Soundly? Or did you have those hallucinations of yours? Your cinema!

RAMA [*sorting the grains of rice*]. The moment my eyes ever closed I'd wake up with a jerk. I didn't feel like sleeping. Right till dawn I kept hearing the hours strike on the clock next-door. Then, at some stage, I fell asleep.

RAMAKANT. I see.

RAMA. I really suffer, from loneliness. There was a light on the whole night in Brother-in-law Rajaninath's garage, too. Looking at it, I managed somehow to pass through the night. It seemed my only company.

RAMAKANT. Ah! I see. Your younger brother-in-law. He must have stayed awake the whole night.

RAMA. Or slept with the light on. He does sleep like that sometimes.

RAMAKANT. Oh, is that so? I had no bloody idea.

RAMA. There's lot that goes on in his mind. Who knows what? He won't let anyone else find out. And he's angry with the whole world. All the time.

[*She is happy while she is saying all this. She has no idea at all of the suspicions in Ramakant's mind. And she has no feelings of guilt at this moment.*]

He sleeps if he wants to, eats if he feels like it. Or else he'll go without. I used to force him to eat meals. But that stopped. And he also stopped eating the snacks I took him. He used to drink tea, at least. But you stopped that. It's a motherless soul. And from such a tender age, he's lived outside the house. No one to care for him.

RAMAKANT. Oh, but there is! There's you . . .

RAMA. I *am* there. But how long can I last him? Not his whole life. Surely. I sometimes think, who'll worry about him then? Who'll ask him to eat, to drink? Who'll ask him, '*Bhaiya*, did you sleep well? Have you dined?' And suppose there's no one left to care? Then what'll happen to his mind, so tormented already? Tell me honestly. What'll happen?

RAMAKANT. The same that bloody happens to me! What else? Don't I have thoughts? Like bloody scorpions, they are . . .

RAMA [*still in her own thoughts*]. At this age, it's good for a person to have someone to call his own. But if I so much as suggest he marries, it's a crime! He comes at me so violently . . .

RAMAKANT. Quite right. If all your *needs* are being satisfied, why get entangled?

RAMA [*not understanding*]. What did you say? Did you say something?

RAMAKANT [*controlling himself*]. No! Where'd I say anything?

RAMA. How stupid of me! What were you discussing with Brother-in-law Umakant just now?

RAMAKANT. What? Oh, Yes . . . yes. That. He says he's leaving. Going to stay elsewhere. He's fed up here.

RAMA. He's had a lot of inconveniences recently. What with me like this, just now . . .

RAMAKANT. Yes, indeed. And no servants, either. No phone!

RAMA. Why has the phone gone?

RAMAKANT [*this question is unexpected*]. It went because, because I myself told the bloody telephone wallahs to take it! Useless bloody headache, dammit! 'Hello, hello' a hundred times each bloody day! And going on all the night. Pick it up, and it's the wrong bloody number. If someone wants a Ratnakar Sheth, then someone else wants a Doctor Bardanwala. Useless bloody headache to us! Took it out! Bloody out!

RAMA. Where is he going to stay?

RAMAKANT. In Hell! . . . [*controlling himself*] What'd you say? Where's he off to stay? If he'd tell me, that'd be the bloody day! He said . . . I'm off. I said . . . 'Your pleasure!'

RAMA. You should have asked him all about it . . .

RAMAKANT. You get upstairs first! Go on! Give you an inch of bloody freedom—and you'll take a mile! Go on. Go. Don't come down again. Bloody headache, dammit!

[*She is silent. Then, steeling herself, she goes upstairs. Ramakant is alone. He goes to the sideboard and fills a glass.*]

[*Fade-out.*]

SCENE VI

Fade-in. Dusk. The interior of the garage. Rajaninath is writing something on a piece of paper, whistling indistinctly. He suddenly stops whistling and gets moody. Continuous writing, doodling, crumpling up of paper and tossing it away. His mood keeps getting worse. Enter Pappa, stealthily. Exhausted. Haggard. He opens the garage door, and slips inside quickly. He shuts the door, and stands with back to it. Live coals still glow in his eyes. Rajaninath doesn't notice him at first.

PAPPA. Rajani . . . [*Rajaninath starts, and looks at him.*] It's me. Pappa.

[*Rajaninath's eyes begin to smoulder. He starts to his feet in a rage. Wishes to say 'Get out'. But the words won't come clear. And as he looks, he weakens.*]

I'll come in. If you'll ask me to.

[*Rajaninath asks him in with a movement of his neck alone. Then goes and stands aloof. There is still anger in his expression.*]

PAPPA [*making a place for himself by the rolled-up mattress, and sitting down, moaning and groaning*]. You must be surprised that I'm here.

[*Rajaninath stands there silent.*]

You are my child after all, aren't you?

[*Rajaninath controls himself by biting his lips.*]

You're not a traitor to your father, like those pimps! I regret the day I ever had such bloody children! Children! Bloody sins of my previous birth! You're the only one who's come out different . . . sonny . . .

[*Rajaninath stands as silent as a statue, leaning on the table, his back turned.*]

What other news? Is everything going all right? For you? Seems all right. You've been a good boy from the first. Not like those pimps. Blocks of stone, either bloody one of them! Only fit to tie round your neck, and kill yourself. No skill in studies. No skill in any art. Just tell the pimps to drink liquor, that's all. That Umya. The pimp's been drinking on the sly since his twelfth year! Same with Ramya. The son-of-a-whore hasn't the wits to make a paisa.

[*Rajaninath stays silent with a fierce effort.*]

You're the only true son to me, Rajani. I used to feel such a . . . respect for you. Even when I saw you from far off. My chest used to swell. You've stood on your own two feet. Ever since you were a child. You've lived with dignity. You're not afraid of anyone. But look at them! Kicked out of the house the very one off whom they lived, the pimps! If they don't end in a mess, my name's not Pitale!

[*Ramakant has come and hidden outside the door, scenting something.*]

RAJANINATH [*with a great effort, in a calm voice*]. Why have you come here?

PAPPA. Good you reminded me! Old age's come upon me. And at this age, the headache of those pimps! I burn up so much just bloody remembering it. I can't tell you! Worms'll rot the hands of those pimps! Beat me, they did, the pimps.

RAJANINATH [*with a slight harshness*]. Well, what've you come to tell me? Tell me just that.

PAPPA. I *am* telling you. I can't endure this, Rajani. Nor would you. This must be changed. Not by anyone else.

RAJANINATH. Will you please tell me why you came here.

PAPPA. Just that! So see here, sonny, you're the only true child I have. Your poor mother . . . she too was a saint. She died far too soon! The poor soul. She didn't even see your face.

RAJANINATH [*growling*]. Tell me what it is . . . hurry up!

PAPPA. I'm telling you. So you're my true son. You stayed in this garage, rotting away like a beggar. My mistake, really, that . . . And those pimps grabbed the house. They've made a gutter of their ancestral home, the pimps. Made a cesspool of it! See what blight's come over the house! My bile rises to see it.

RAJANINATH [*with slight harshness*]. Well, what've you come to tell me? Tell me just that.

PAPPA. I *am* telling you. I can't endure this, Rajani. Nor would you. This must be changed. Not by anyone else. By us. Listen to what I'm telling you. I'm behind you. If you want, I'll raise the money. I've got some credit still. I've made a new will. A back-dated one. I've got hold of a lawyer for the seal, too. In this will, I've divided the whole estate between you and Manik. So you file a suit. Say the will's genuine. Say the deed of division of the property was got by threats. I'm there to back you up. I'll say it in court. Get it all changed! Teach those pimps a lesson. Let them go and beg, either one of them! We'll rub up writs, and slam 'em with 'em! Eh? Once this much is done, I can close my eyes in peace.

RAJANINATH [*pointing outwards*]. Get out of here!

PAPPA. Don't say no, sonny. You're my only true son! . . . [*He starts caressing Rajaninath's cheeks and his chest.*] You're the only one who cares for your father's shame! You'll take revenge for that horrible insult! My boy! . . .

RAJANINATH. Get out of here, I said! Get out!

[*He takes both Pappa's hands and throws them off. Pappa starts to back away.*]

PAPPA. I came to bring you luck for the rest of your life . . .

RAJANINATH. Clear out of here! Clear out. Don't dare set foot here again! Get out! Or I'll throw you out!

[*As the old man backs out, meekly and humbly, but with haste, he bumps into Ramakant, who has entered and is standing there.*]

RAMAKANT [*confronting him by the door*]. Greetings. Pappa!

[*Pappa starts violently from the core of his being. He runs off hurriedly with a thudding heart. Looking back repeatedly. Rajaninath has turned his back, and is standing with his face to the wall.*]

[*seeing him*] Go to bloody do someone a good turn . . . and you'll get no bloody thanks for it. Poor Pappa. You should've done what he said, Rajani.

RAJANINATH. I know well what I should or shouldn't do.

RAMAKANT. You don't feel any bloody pity for the father that begot you?

RAJANINATH [*unexpectedly*]. I feel pity for you!

[*Ramakant in confusion at this. Suddenly, from the house, Rama screams. Both of them start violently. Ramakant starts running towards the house. Rajaninath comes to, and realizes he should run as well, when Manik enters, almost colliding with him. On her face there is a terrible and hysterical joy.*]

MANIK. I've done it . . . I've done as I planned . . . I cut the lemon . . . I rubbed the ash. Seven times, on my loins and stomach! It's going to abort—sister-in-law's baby's going to abort—Ramya's brat's going to abort—it won't live. It won't live!

[*She stands laughing loudly, madly. Rajaninath, terrified, moves to one side. Exit Manik, still laughing. Rajaninath bewildered. Rama's room. Enter Ramakant running. He kneels on her bed. Rama is sitting there trembling, her clothes in disarray.*]

RAMAKANT. What happened? What happened, Rama? [*Looks here and there*] Who came here? More hallucinations! Who knows how much you're bloody going to get scared! Bloody headache the whole day! Useless bloody nuisance! Lie down properly. Go on.

[*He tries to push her into a lying position. Saying 'No! No!' she remains sitting bolt upright.*]

At least tell me what's happened!

[*Words won't come from her mouth.*]

Speak, I'm telling you! Or I'll bash you one . . . tell me quick!
RAMA [*with a great effort.*] Sister-in-law. She came.
RAMAKANT. Who? Manik? That whore? Because she saw I wasn't here? What was she saying? Tell me quick!

[*Rama shudders in terror. A surge of tears comes from her.*]

I said, what did she say? Tell me . . . or to hell with you!

[*Holds her knot of hair and pulls her head back.*]

What did she say, that whore? Tell me . . .
RAMA. She . . . she'd cut lemon . . . and . . .
RAMAKANT [*harshly*]. She had?
RAMA [*saying 'yes' forcefully with her head, she stands up*]. Ash . . . she rubbed it here . . . and she said . . . she said . . . [*Bursting*] . . . your brat's going to abort! Your brat's going to abort! Your brat's going to abort! . . .

[*She sprawls on the bed, and starts to cry loudly and with abandon. Ramakant, for a moment, as wretched as a child that's lost its mother.*]

RAMAKANT [*shouting suddenly*]. Stop crying! I tell you. Stop crying! No one's bloody died! Stop that crying! One bloody torture after another . . . Lie there quiet! This minute! And don't you dare utter another word! Quiet! Or I'll murder you!

[*Rama quietens, terrified. Like a corpse.*]

My child won't ever die. Not because of that bitch's curse. If it's mine, that is.
RAMA [*starting*]. What did you say? What was that you said?

RAMAKANT. You know very well what I mean. Lie down quiet. Not a murmur.

[*Turns sharply and exit. Rama sitting like a stone.*]

[*Fade-out.*]

SCENE VII

Fade-in. Night. A stormy rain is pouring down. Lightning. Thunder. The drawing-room. Ramakant is sitting there; drinking. His face is sluggish, ugly. His rifle is lying beside him. The doorbell rings. Ramakant becomes alert. It rings once, twice, three times. Ramakant does not get up. 'Go on. Ring it!' he says. Then there are blows on the front door. A sharp rap. The bell rings again. And suddenly stops. Umakant's profuse curses can be heard, indistinctly. Blows. Shouts. Calls of 'Sister-in-law.' Ramakant, from where he is sitting, says 'Wait. She's coming.' An ugly smile on his face. After this, to every blow and kick, to every kick that follows in quick succession, his only words are a calm 'Go on!' or 'Harder!' He is drinking all the while. Then the knocking stops. The cries cease. There is only the sound of rain. After some time, there is a noise at some other door, at the rear. Ramakant's reaction is the same as before. The noise at the back door ceases. The rain continues to pour down. Then again . . . a heavy blow at the front door. Umakant can be heard indistinctly, saying 'Ramya, you bastard! Just wait and see!' Then the blows lessen. There is one last one. Then silence. Only the pouring rain. At a distance, a rain-drenched dog howls piercingly.]

RAMAKANT [*heavily, with a sluggish tongue*]. Bye-bye, brother. Best of luck to you! And a happy-happy life. [*Drinks.*] Brother, you bloody thought you were the only bastard. But no! No, brother. I'm a bastard, too. We're all bastards. Each one more than the other. No one's bloody less of one! I know, brother. I know why you wanted this house. This bungalow. This haunted house. You didn't tell me. But I know, brother, I know. Shall I tell? Because there was a ghost in it. That gave you bloody prosperity. A ghost. A spirit. One that was all for you. And had it in for us. Right, brother? The day after one new moon, I found a lemon, a coconut and red powder, in the bloody grounds. You did that. That lemon and coconut business. My revered brother! The ghost was in your bloody control! And was sucking me dry. I know, I know, brother. Bloody humbug. All humbug. No ghost. Nothing. Bloody ghost . . . Me, that's the bloody ghost. Who else?

I'm the bloody ghost. But, brother, you wanted that ghost of yours. That's why you wanted this house. So you wanted me out. Right, brother? So all could be bloody yours. Bloody prosperous, dammit! Bloody fun! Tons of bloody money! Heaps of money. Bloody ghost. But brother, you guessed wrong. Ramakant's no fool. Won't go on my ownsome. To hell with everybody . . . bloody hell! The nether regions! I know, brother, I'm going to hell! Air of Hades! Father, brother, sister, wife, kiddie—no, he's not mine. He's my stepbrother's kiddie. Not mine! His! That son of a whore's bloody brat. Bloody traitor! Bloody bugger! Son of a bloody kept woman! [*Groping for his rifle.*] Bloody shoot him! I'll—bloody kill him! Bloody bastard!

[*Gets up suddenly holding a bottle like a gun. The liquor starts to spill out. He catches as much as he can in the cupped palm of his left hand, and laps it up. He puts up the bottle down on the side-table.*]

Oh! Oh!

[*He moans in some sort of anguish.*]

I'm a useless fellow, brother. Absolutely bloody good-for-nothing. Futile. A bloody bitch. Son of a swine! I—I let my wife . . . go . . . go . . .

[*Raises his head.*]

Not my kiddie, brother! The child's not mine. The brat's bloody his. Nothing. Useless. Bloody pig. I'll shoot myself, brother.

[*Gropes once more for his rifle.*]

Bloody rifle . . . my bloody gun!

[*His hand touches the rifle.*]

Isn't that so, brother? I've had it. Sucked to the core. Bloody stumped! Creditors . . . bank . . . bloody court . . . have to go to jail . . . five bloody years. Seven years . . . Hard labour! Ramakant Pitale: hard labour for life! Bloody stumped. No wife. No kiddie. Knocked out, knocked bloody out! Going to have to serve time. In jail, dammit . . . Oh! . . . Oh!

[*He puts the barrel of the rifle under his chin, his finger on the trigger.*]

But you know, brother. I won't give you your ghost. Won't give you the bloody house. Won't give you bloody prosperity. Give my life. But won't give the house.

[*He puts the rifle on a chair. His mood changes.*]

Tra la . . . la . . . la . . . la . . . Tra la . . . la . . . la . . . Tra la . . . Radio
Club, brother! The Khyber! Mongini's! The Taj! The Venice!
Dance . . . music . . . beauties . . . Tra . . . la . . . Tra . . . la . . . Society
bloody ladies! How do you do? Glad to meet you! Oh, how *sweet*
of you! Bloody kick you! Fun, dammit! Fun!

[*He gives a kick into the air and overbalances. He falls down.*]

Lame, dammit! No feet. Give a paisa to a poor lame man! For the
love of God! A poor beggar! For the love of bloody God! A poor
lame man.

[*He crawls over to the side-table. Sits up and drinks quickly two or three
times in succession. He hiccups.*]

Feel better now, brother. Now I feel fine. But my head's a little . . .
a little . . . [*Shouting suddenly. Harshly. Hoarsely.*] The child isn't
mine! Not mine, not bloody mine, not mine! It's his, that bloody
son of a whore's! Nursed up my stepbrother's bloody offspring . . .
brought it up in my bloody house. Brother, I'll shoot him! I'll
shoot him!

[*Gathers himself up like a wounded beast of prey. One hand thrust hard
against the back of the chair. Then in the deepest of voices.*]

You know, brother, I'll abort him. He's not mine. He's my
enemy's bloody son. My enemy. I'll abort him. Get out, you
bastard. Don't want you. Don't want you, son of a swine!
Enough, dammit, I'll finish off the bastard. Push him out of her
belly. Tear him out! . . . [*Shouts, raging*] Rama! . . . [*Suddenly
bringing a terrible sweetness into his voice*] Rama dear! [*Harshly*]
Where are you, Rama? Come here! Rama . . . Come here!

[*He stumbles over to the door of the stairs, calling out indistinctly to
Rama.*]

You're not going to come? You're not coming? Fine! Then I'll
come up! Just wait, I'll come . . . Bloody useless bloody child! . . .

[*Stumbling along, he exits through the door. His shouts. His ravings
become indistinct, and are mingled with the sound of the pouring rain.
And there is a deafening crack of lightning. Cracking sharply, it falls
no one knows where. Then there is the even sound of continuous,
torrential rain.*]

[*Fade-out.*]

[*In the darkness, the shrill screeching of a single vulture.*]

SCENE VIII

Fade-in. Silence. No sound at all. The garage.

RAJANINATH. The tale of the five vultures
  Had this end.
  The story of men accursed.
  Or else of vultures cursed
  To live their lives as men.

  Oh, show them some compassion!
  Show a path to them.
  Hold out to them
  A merciful hand
  That will bring release.
  Point out to them
  The burning-ground and its ghat
  Where the sinful soul
  Burns off its being,
  Takes its first free breath.

  For they have no other
  Future left to them.
  There is no hope.

  And yet, perhaps,
  There is no escape for them.
  No . . . there is none.
  For there *is* no escape
  For them . . .
  Or for anyone . . .

  [*The terrible noise of the wind now grows. Everything before us, in
  comparison, seems trifling, like a child's toy. A sense of loneliness comes
  over us. Rajaninath enters the garage. Dragging his steps. As he goes,
  his body shrinks, as if he is shivering.*]

  [*Fade-out.*]

CURTAIN

ENCOUNTER IN UMBUGLAND

(*Dambadwipcha Mukabala*)

Translated by
Priya Adarkar

CHARACTERS

VICHITRAVIRYA, King

VIJAYA, Daughter of Vichitravirya

ARANYAKETU

BHAGADANTA

KARKASHIRSHA } Statesmen (Ministers)

PISHTAKESHI

VRATYASOM

PRANNARAYAN, Attendant

OTHER ATTENDANTS

TWO 'PEN-BEARERS'

PAINTER

MAID-SERVANT

ACT ONE

The curtain rises.

PRANNARAYAN [*to the audience*]. On behalf of the Kingdom of
Umbugland, I welcome you all. It is our good fortune that you
have shown respect for our invitation, have come to our small
and not very well-known island, have shaken the dust off your
feet upon this little isle. [*Pausing*] All that I said just now was, of
course, conventional and diplomatic. But much of it was the
truth. I mean, we too have three kinds of truth: conventional
truth, diplomatic truth, and the real truth. The truth I spoke just
now was of all three kinds. Conventional it certainly was. For to
play the host and welcome you who have come here as our guests
may be a convention accepted with pleasure. But it is, nevertheless, a convention. Similarly, this truth is diplomatic. For we in
Umbugland behave most submissively and diplomatically towards
all powerful countries. But the fact is as well as these two, it is also
the real truth, that should not be forgotten. It is a matter for
rejoicing that you have presented yourselves here as spectators
of a historic encounter in Umbugland. No encounter has any
meaning without an audience. With no one to watch them,
fighters don't battle with vigour. I am not a fighter. Since I
reached the years of discretion, I have lived in the palace of the
ruler of this island, the Protector of the Umbugite Nation, His
Majesty King Vichitravirya. Today is the sixtieth anniversary of
his coronation.

[*Behind the rear curtain, trumpets and horns blow and there is a sound
of cannon. Shouts of 'Long live King Vichitravirya!' Two men enter,
one from each wing, wielding huge pens like sceptres. They stand facing
the audience, and bang their pens on the ground thrice.*]

THE TWO [*together*]. Victory! Victory! Victory!
An unforgettable gathering
To congratulate our glorious king
On his sixtieth coronation anniversary!

[*Turn by turn*]

The people's homage in the Palace's Hall of Audience!
An auspicious toot from the sixty major musical instruments!
Of sixty cannons sixty times the thunderous detonation!

Sixty begging priests will give the King their benediction!
Sixty married women will salute the King with light!
Then sixty songs that sixty children somehow managed to write!
Our glorious King will personally let loose sixty pigeons.
Sixty officials will be promoted to the highest divisions.
For sixty men of learning, sacred fruit from the royal hand.
In royal form, fulfilment of all the dreams of Umbugland.
May the King live to be a hundred years old!
May the King live for ever and ever!
May the King be immortal!
Long live the King!
[*Together*] Victory! Victory! Victory!
An unforgettable gathering
To congratulate our glorious King.
On his sixtieth coronation
Anniversary!

[*They bang their pens three times like royal sceptres and exit into opposite wings. Loud shout of 'Long live King Vichitravirya!' from within accompanied by trumpets. This dies down.*]

PRANNARAYAN. During the King's reign, I have lived here as a member of the harem. For I am of the—er—third sex of man. People such as I are appointed attendants in the harem. These days I am in the service of the Princess Vijaya, the only daughter of His Majesty.

VIJAYA [*offstage*]. Prannarayan!

PRANNARAYAN. It seems that the princess has remembered me. I must go.

[*Enter Vijaya. On her hand, a white pigeon.*]

VIJAYA. And where were you rotting, Prannarayan?

PRANNARAYAN. I was on my way.

VIJAYA [*mimicking him*]. 'I was on my way.' The usual servant's answer! Look! This beautiful white pigeon just fluttered down into my garden. I liked it so much I thought at once of you. Isn't it lovely? Do look!

PRANNARAYAN. Is the pigeon beautiful? Or rather, are those hands that hold it, beautiful?

VIJAYA. I'm asking about the pigeon—just tell me about that. Or these beautiful hands will scratch your back till it bleeds! Tell me, where did this snow-white pigeon alight from so suddenly in our garden?

PRANNARAYAN. From the Hall of Audience in the Royal Palace.

VIJAYA. But how did it get there?

PRANNARAYAN. In accordance with custom.

VIJAYA. What custom?

PRANNARAYAN. Has Your Highness forgotten again? The custom of releasing white pigeons. Princess, today is the sixtieth anniversary of your royal father's coronation, is it not? One of the ceremonies in that connection is the release of sixty white pigeons. One year ago, fifty-nine were made to take wing. This one, that has alighted in your garden, must be one of the sixty that were released today. It must be hard even for pigeons to leave the palace precincts.

VIJAYA. If I had wings, I would have left them ages ago—gone so far away, I wouldn't know how to return! Prannarayan, where could the other fifty-nine have gone?

PRANNARAYAN. Somewhere nearby, no doubt. Just like the human race, this race of pigeons, wherever it may go, still returns to the same place in the end. Its familiar pigeonholes seem far dearer to it than freedom.

VIJAYA. Then why should they be freed?

PRANNARAYAN. Even freedom itself can be a diplomatic convention. Let us go, Princess. You must get ready to give your royal father ceremonial congratulations on this day.

VIJAYA. I won't go today!

PRANNARAYAN. Every year, the same stubbornness. Your Highness knows it is useless to be obstinate.

VIJAYA. I won't go there today at all! I don't want to become a diplomatic convention for Father's birthday. I am not a pigeon, Prannarayan. I can think.

PRANNARAYAN. Many have happily spent all their lives in this abode of luxury without bothering to think at all.

VIJAYA. They hadn't met you! You force me to think. You put questions in my way, and when it comes to answering them, you escape with just saying something lively and hard to understand. Something that makes me laugh.

PRANNARAYAN. I make serious efforts to answer Your Highness's questions.

VIJAYA. You're very sly! But you're tender, too. Why are you not cruel, like Father?

PRANNARAYAN. Because I am not a father. I am an attendant. Come, Your Highness must bathe and attire yourself in your new robes for today's ceremony.

VIJAYA. Will you bathe me today?

PRANNARAYAN [embarrassed]. Your Highness is now almost grown-up.

VIJAYA. So?

PRANNARAYAN. A grown-up's bath is an intensely private thing.

VIJAYA [clapping her hands]. But the water sees it all! Never mind about that. You wash my hair. Then I myself will have that intensely private thing, my bath! [Waiting] I warn you! If you won't, I'll stay just as I am! Father will call you and want to know why! Perhaps he'll even punish you!

PRANNARAYAN. It's no use being clever with Your Highness. Proceed.

[She makes a triumphant gesture. Exit followed by him.]

[The rear curtain rises. An apartment in the royal palace. The experienced statesmen, Vratyasom, Bhagadanta, Karkashirsha, and Pishtakeshi are standing in it. All are old; all are bored. In addition to them, Aranyaketu, also a statesman, a middle-aged man who looks old before his time, stands at one side.]

KARKASHIRSHA. Since we got that message from His Majesty, exactly [consults his watch] one full hour has passed.

[He makes a gesture of annoyance.]

PISHTAKESHI. As usual! After completing the anniversary audience His Majesty is sounding forth on his views to a thousand of the populace.

[Aranyaketu has opened a window slightly and is looking out.]

Well, Aranyaketu, where has the sermon got to? Any hope of the end?

ARANYAKETU [turning]. 'The importance of celibacy.'

KARKASHIRSHA. Terrible! It is a matter of shame that in the course of sixty years His Majesty has not once understood the value of his statesmen's time. Does time hang on our hands? Or have we no wives and families? I at least am a family man conscious of my domestic duties. A home-loving man.

VRATYASOM. His Majesty would say, 'If a man is home-loving, great must be his powers of endurance!'

PISHTAKESHI. You too are a home-loving man, Vratyasom. Only it's a different home each time! Ha! Ha! Ha!

VRATYASOM. I make a clear distinction between considering my belly in matters of politics and pleasing myself in all other matters.

KARKASHIRSHA. Your political belly will never be filled. To my reckoning, you have been involved in thirteen acts of official dishonesty.

VRATYASOM. Ha! Don't *you* promote your relations for your belly's sake, Karkashirsha? Apart from that, my slate would have stayed as clean as yours.

KARKASHIRSHA. These accusations are slanderous!

VRATYASOM. Let us not open our mouths too wide about principles and honesty. To observe these two virtues in politics is as inappropriate and stupid as celibacy after marriage. You and I are politicians and ministers; in blunt terms, what does that mean? Eh, Pishtakeshi? It means we are partners in a most profitable game of skulduggery.

KARKASHIRSHA. I disagree vehemently with all this! In my life, politics is a sacred ritual.

VRATYASOM. Shall I tell what sacred ritual you performed to get your Ministership?

KARKASHIRSHA. Tell them! I won't submit to such blackmail, Vratyasom. And certainly not from an unprincipled, character-less politician like you! No! No! No! A hundred times no! A thousand times no!

[*Stands trembling with rage*]

PISHTAKESHI. Let it go, Karkashirsha. Drink some water. [*Hands him water*] This is Vratyasom's way of amusing himself. It doesn't become your profound experience of politics to go up in smoke each time, in spite of encountering it so often. In politics one should have the hide of a rhinoceros, like Bhagadanta here. Say what you will, do what you will, it's impossible to guess his reaction.

[*Bhagadanta merely smiles briefly.*]

But Aranyaketu, any end to the sermon?

ARANYAKETU [*opens the window, stands shifting his weight from one leg to the other*]. His Majesty is making the assembly do physical jerks.

KARKASHIRSHA. Well, really! This is going too far! Our hair's grown white in the service of the island. And still we're treated in this fashion. What does this man think are we?

PISHTAKESHI. Karkashirsha, before my very eyes we have endured forty years of all this. When we came into politics, we were at the height of our foolish twenties. Then we became Ministers. From that time to this, we have continuously received such treatment from His Majesty. At first we bore it enthusiastically, as our sacred duty. Then we competed with each other in swallowing it all, as a temporary stratagem. After that, we all waited patiently together, as a matter of policy. Now it has become an entrenched habit. And the end to it all is not even remotely in sight. Over the last forty years, His Majesty, having come successfully and safely out of the ordeal of four calamitous accidents, and seven moderately serious illnesses, has managed to cast such a deep spell of infatuation over the people, that there is no public danger to him for at least the next hundred years. After a public speech, he very often gets the populace to play mass hopscotch. Or chant their tables, or recite hymns, in chorus. If he doesn't do it, people write letters of protest to the public opinion columns of the newspapers! Don't you remember what an uproar there was recently during His Majesty's tour of the South? Just because at the last moment, arrangements went wrong. And he didn't throw stones at the public from his chariot according to custom! What is the moral? Let us endure the inevitable, and not lose our balance or peace of mind. Even if you deny it, it's true that for statesmen we are old and ailing. We are not young, like Aranyaketu here. Aranyaketu only completed his fiftieth year last month. Because of his youth, His Majesty feels a greater degree of favour for him. Eh, Aranyaketu?

ARANYAKETU [*looking, puzzled, out of the window*]. The sermon has ended—I mean, the speech.

[*The people's cheers can be heard outside.*]

His Majesty is on his way here.

[*All the statesmen straighten their clothing and become nervously alert. Karkashirsha is still enraged.*]

VRATYASOM. It's convenient for Bhagadanta here. He just has to shake out his round dhoti and he's ready to meet anyone. And his grin flashes as wide as if someone's said 'Open sesame!'

[*Bhagadanta smiles. The King's entry is proclaimed.*]

PROCLAMATION. The Most Mighty Sovereign of Umbugland, the All-Virtuous, the All-Eminent, the Warrior Omnipotent, In all

Knowledge, Arts and Government Most Resonant, the True-Living, the Truth-Inspiring, the All-Knowing, the All-Discriminating, the Ever-Youthful, the Ever-Pure, the Ever-Living, the Remover of All Affliction, the Protector of the Umbugite Nation, the Holder of the Imperial Dignity, our Saviour from Iniquity, the Cleanser of All Sins, His Supreme Majesty King Vichitravirya approaches—ho . . . o . . .!

[*All the statesmen stand upright in a row. Enter the decrepitly old, white-bearded and moustachioed, cunning King Vichitravirya. Together with him enters a humble artist, with the implements of his art. Vichitravirya's dress is garish and strange.*]

THE STATESMEN. Victory to His Majesty!
Long Life to His Majesty!
Thrice congratulations to His Majesty on the 60th Anniversary of his coronation!

[*Vichitravirya leaps up to the throne and sits down on it.*]

VICHITRAVIRYA. Wonderful, wonderful, wonderful! What a wonderful time we had today! Karkashirsha, Bhagadanta, Pishtakeshi, when we started to speak it was on the uses of mixed manure. Thereafter we spoke on the cultivation of the agave plant. Have we informed you of the advantages of its cultivation?

[*They all nod vigorously.*]

No, we have not. Our memory is still tolerably keen. But at the appropriate juncture, we will definitely inform you. In the course of talking of the cultivation of the agave plant, we reached the subject of the dangers created by the use of starchy products. These dangers [*Vratyasom has a severe fit of coughing.*] must be reckoned as very great indeed. But the subject that grew liveliest was—
PISHTAKESHI.—that of greyhounds!
VICHITRAVIRYA. Excellent, Pishtakeshi! Excellent! You may not as yet be able to understand our governmental policies. But you can recognize our subjects of discourse without fail. Yet we cannot say that subject grew really lively. You speak without listening, and thus fall into error. The subject that was liveliest was the importance of religion in our lives. Excellent! Excellent! Quite superb! What a pleasure it was! We just did not realize how the time passed!

[*Karkashirsha is swallowing his rage.*]

The people were overwhelmed. They were agitated. They began to sway in rhythm. We had caught the right strain.

[*Aranyaketu is suppressing a yawn.*]

The people were enrapt, so we grew enrapt. Because we were enrapt, they grew still more enrapt.

VRATYASOM [*hastily*]. That subject of—diet in the alkalis, must have been more interesting still, I am sure.

VICHITRAVIRYA. As usual, Vratyasom, you have committed a blunder. Not 'diet in the alkalis' but 'alkalis in the diet.' Today we just touched on that subject before leaving it. For we had mentally decided, in honour of the sixtieth anniversary of our coronation, to give our populace a lesson on a subject of greater importance. What subject could that be? Do not answer us, Pishtakeshi. Karkashirsha will tell us.

[*Karkashirsha chokes in the attempt to swallow his rage.*]

[*With displeasure*] Karkashirsha, salt-water gargles are most beneficial in cases of uvular cough. Kindly take one in future before coming to meet us. All of you have grown very old these days, eh? There's nothing like youthfulness! Look at our constitution! [*noticing the artist*] Who is that man standing there?

PAINTER. I am a painter, Your Majesty.

VICHITRAVIRYA. We realized that. We are not so stupid as to fail to understand that. But with whose permission have you come here?

PAINTER [*fearfully*]. With Your Majesty's. Your Majesty brought me here. To paint a huge and imposing portrait of yourself.

VICHITRAVIRYA. Who has denied it? But then why are you standing there idle instead of beginning the portrait? It was to ask that that we pretended a lapse of memory. Paint the portrait. This time paint an equestrian portrait of us. The picture must be a magnificent one.

PAINTER. Very well, Your Majesty. [*Starts his preparations.*]

VICHITRAVIRYA. At least twenty thousand were assembled today to hear our speech. It is a very happy thing that in the past sixty years, not only the population of Umbugland, but our audience, too, has been increasing steadily, Eh, Bhagadanta?

[*Bhagadanta gives a smile.*]

Don't mime it. Say it.

BHAGADANTA. It is.

VICHITRAVIRYA. Well, Vratyasom, what new machinations?

VRATYASOM [*glibly*]. Who on this island has the temerity to plot against Your Majesty? The sun of Your Majesty's fortunes rises daily! Does it not, Pishtakeshi?

PISHTAKESHI. Without any doubt. Does it not, Karkashirsha?

KARKASHIRSHA [*swallowing his anger*]. Yes, indeed.

VRATYASOM. All over the island there can only be heard the praises of Your Majesty.

PISHTAKESHI. His Majesty is the sole artist of the island's destiny.

VRATYASOM. His Majesty is Umbugland and Umbugland is His Majesty!

ARANYAKETU. The thought of an Umbugland without His Majesty is unimaginable!

VICHITRAVIRYA. But in order to say so, you did imagine it!

ARANYAKETU [*in confusion*]. No, no, no! I just said the words. . . .

VRATYASOM [*enjoying the spectacle of Aranyaketu's confusion*]. It is the custom of today's young politicians to speak without thinking what they mean.

ARANYAKETU. I did not mean anything untoward. I just said that. . . .

VICHITRAVIRYA. Enough! Even if by mistake, you spoke the truth.

[*Aranyaketu is tense.*]

We have become so much one with Umbugland in these past sixty years, and our people of Umbugland have so identified themselves with us, that the thought of one without the other is impossible. If we so command, our populace plays One-Legged Catch, or says its tables together. We are not our own property, we are the nation's.

VRATYASOM [*clapping*]. Well expressed!

VICHITRAVIRYA. Sometimes, Karkashirsha [*Karkashirsha has not yet controlled his anger*], when we think of the past, we feel that we will live another hundred years . . .

PISHTAKESHI [*swallowing*]. What doubt is there of that? What doubt? Is there any doubt, Vratyasom?

VRATYASOM. Your Majesty may even become immortal!

VICHITRAVIRYA. No, to tell the truth, it is not our desire to become immortal. The time will certainly come to hand the reins of this island's government to you people and retire. But we must consider the future of the island. And, the schemes for general development. We have in the past sixty years only laid their foundation. The island badly needs our leadership for at least another fifty years.

KARKASHIRSHA [*aghast*]. Fifty years!

VRATYASOM [*hurriedly covering up Karkashirsha's remark*]. Seventy!

PISHTAKESHI. Seventyfive!

ARANYAKETU. Two hundred.

BHAGADANTA [*giving a smile*]. Five hundred.

VICHITRAVIRYA. It is a very reassuring thing that all of you feel it so wholeheartedly. This is precisely what we wished to hear from you.

ALL. Certainly! Definitely!

VICHITRAVIRYA [*comes down and walks about in front of all*]. It is a good thing. It is a correct thing. Excellent! But still, thoughts of who is to succeed us go on behind our back.

[*All are tense.*]

Discussions are held. Secret conclaves meet. Astrologers are consulted about our life expectancy. What is more, bribes are offered to our royal physician through the hands of others. The intention being, that if we have contracted any disease, the happy tidings should be given to you at once. But by the grace of God our health is still quite robust. And for the sake of the prosperity of the island, we ourselves are taking extremely good care of it. We receive the most detailed intelligence.

[*All are silent.*]

It was for these reasons that we deliberately summoned you here today. There is not in any of you in the slightest measure the capacity to hold the reins of government in this island after us. Even though the responsibilities of government have been divided amongst you, it is still we who take all the decisions. Besides, there is no unity amongst you. It would be extremely amusing one day to confront you with the various things you have told us from time to time about each other. We can give you detailed information about the discussion that took place before we came here. If we were to send you all home and become the sole official of the Kingdom, we do not feel that anything would go wrong on the island. Let anyone who has a doubt of that speak now.

[*They are all taking it quietly.*]

[*Changing his tone*] Power seems more important to you than duty! Selfish designs have replaced service! Have this island's three fathers of the Nation, four Creators of our Era, Six Divine

Incarnations and Twenty-five Martyrs taught you only this? Power! What is power?

[*A yawn is threatening Aranyaketu, who is suppressing it.*]

We have experienced it for the past sixty years. Power is a crown of thorns. Power is a sword hanging over you! Power is the bread you eat at the stake! Power means responsibility! Power means problems and painful decisions. There is no headache like power. There is no trouble like power. We are always saying that we would not wish even our enemies to be punished with power.

[*Aranyaketu yawns into his handkerchief.*]

We endured it only for our people, through a sense of duty, and only because our father passed away. We looked after our Umbugland for sixty years, so that it should have a place of honour and respect upon the map of the world. Other thoughts did not so much as cross our mind. We have not cherished a lust for power even for one second. Well, Vratyasom? What is power? If that is your only desire, take it, with pleasure . . . take it this minute! We will abdicate, and become a hermit. Wandering the mountains and rivers is more dear to us than power. We express a wish to do so from time to time. But our people will not release us. It is according to their wish, their pleasure, according to what their wish and will shall be that we shall stay in power. With this aim, we have planned to undergo an experiment in rejuvenation. Only today we have received medical advice as a result of which we shall be able to rule for at least a hundred years.

[*They are all dismayed.*]

Vratyasom, Pishtakeshi, Karkashirsha, Bhagadanta, Aranyaketu, serve the people, and let us do the ruling. Serve them with greater honesty and integrity, taking greater pains, allowing no family considerations to enter your minds. And remember this: we receive intelligence on all matters. Go, serve the people with new vigour. Our blessings go with you. Aranyaketu, wait here a while. Karkashirsha, gargle as soon as you reach your home. Health first, government next.

[*Except for Aranyaketu, all make an obeisance and exeunt dragging their feet.*]

[*After all have gone, addressing the painter, his hand to his forehead*]
You there, why are you sitting there looking helpless?

PAINTER. Your Majesty does not sit still. . . .

VICHITRAVIRYA. Who does not sit still? We shall sit exactly as you say.

[*The painter makes Vichitravirya sit on a seat as if he were on horseback.*]

The portrait should be as radiant and distinguished as we are. Do not increase our wrinkles. Come here. Observe our eyes closely. Is there not embodied there the lustre of generations? Do not make our beard and moustache too white. And, most important of all, observe our chest. See how prominent it is! Paint the horse, too, to look equally imposing.

[*Aranyaketu is watching all this with a fixed gaze, like one possessed. He has forgotten himself totally.*]

Aranyaketu, our attention is on you!

[*Aranyaketu starts, and bows to him.*]

You may be younger than we are, but you are very inexperienced too. We like your youth. Similarly, we like your understanding, but beware of your colleagues! They promise no good for you. Keep yourself in our favour. Then only will you prosper. It was with a definite aim that we took an inexperienced man like you into our Cabinet. But your appetite has also increased since you became a Minister . . . take care of it. Once one has power, it grows at an alarming rate. The scope of your vision is something that has to grow. When it mingles with a growing appetite, the prospects are not good. You must fast, you must do physical jerks. Try skipping with a rope; it is excellent exercise.

[*Enter Princess Vijaya. A short space behind her, the attendant Prannarayan.*]

VICHITRAVIRYA. Daughter, come. You must no doubt be well. Stay over there. We are on horseback.

VIJAYA. You are on horseback? Then on whose back is the horse? [*Looks at Aranyaketu.*]

VICHITRAVIRYA [*looking straight ahead, because of the painter*]. Daughter Vijaya, the horse must be assumed to be under us. That painter there is painting an equestrian portrait of us.

VIJAYA. If you ask me, I think you look like a horse yourself.

VICHITRAVIRYA. It is true that we carry in our body the strength of a thousand horses. Aranyaketu, do not take her words to heart.

This one and only daughter of ours is a little childish and half-witted. But she has great respect for us, which is only natural. What is it but her great fortune to have a father like us? Painter, do not omit the resolute arch of our brows. It is most important. Do not look at the daughter—paint the sire! The chest—observe our chest, how prominent it is! Or you will make an error. Child Vijaya, you may leave us at once.

VIJAYA. I have come here to give Your Majesty congratulations on the sixtieth—or is it the fifty-ninth?—anniversary of your coronation.

VICHITRAVIRYA. Painter, a brief pause. [*standing up ceremoniously*] May we live a thousand years to make our people happy! Long live Umbugland! [*Sits down as before.*] Have you finished, Vijaya? Then go.

VIJAYA [*annoyed*]. We have put on new clothes today.

VICHITRAVIRYA. So have we. Aranyaketu, how do we look in this dress?

VIJAYA [*angrily*]. Decrepit! Old!

[*Stamps her foot and exit. Prannarayan follows her.*]

VICHITRAVIRYA [*regaining his poise*]. This daughter of ours is a real problem for us. She is not small. But in understanding she is a complete nought. A real worry for us! Of course the fact that we do not have time to worry is a different matter. Painter, are you still again?

PAINTER [*anxiously*]. Your Majesty is moving, talking. . . . I cannot capture the subtleties. . . .

VICHITRAVIRYA. What? Moving? We are amazed! See how quiet and erect we are sitting. See, Aranyaketu. See what control we still have over ourselves.

[*Sits up erect. Does not move or speak. The painter goes on painting.*]

If you wish, we will sit like this for a hundred years! Aranyaketu, wait. Painter, we will not speak.

[*The painter is now painting on. Aranyaketu stands somehow, shifting his weight from one foot to another, and leaning here and there. The painter paints in double fast motion. Music to denote the passage of time.*]

PAINTER [*after some time*]. Your Majesty may move now.

[*Vichitravirya stays as he is. The painter shrugs his shoulders.*]

ARANYAKETU. Your Majesty, the work of painting is now completed. Your Majesty may arise.

[*Vichitravirya stays exactly as he is. The painter is looking at him. Aranyaketu is looking at him. The painter gets up fearfully. He goes towards Vichitravirya and stays looking at him for some time. Spellbound. Aranyaketu is looking at him, too.*]

PAINTER [*as if a terrible thought has occurred to him, turning to Aranyaketu*]. Does that mean that His Majesty . . .?

ARANYAKETU [*beginning to tremble*]. Eh?

PAINTER [*swallowing nervously somehow, goes hurriedly towards his canvas. Again he looks back at Vichitravirya, staring and astonished . . . then hurriedly gathers up his canvas and materials and starts to run out*]. F-Final Portrait! Unique portrait! [*Then turns again and looks with staring eyes at Vichitravirya.*] Ten thousand silver mohurs! Fifteen thousand! Twenty thousand! [*Exit running.*]

[*The rear curtain falls. The two pen-bearers, attired in black, enter and take their positions. A low drumbeat begins. Behind the two of them, the five ministers walk across the stage in a line as if in a funeral procession, bowed down with grief. Last of all goes Aranyaketu.*]

THE TWO CLAD IN BLACK [*to the beat of the drum*].
Darkness at the height of day.
Umbugland in deep dismay.
Sun sinks into gloom.
Umbugland becomes a tomb.
Man driven to desperation,
Two commit self-destruction.
Worldwide lamentation.
Mighty Father of the Nation.
Most excellent Dictator.
Most eloquent O-rator.
Champion of the humbled.
A mighty sword has crumbled.
Our foundation disappears.
The sea itself bursts into tears.
Official warning:
One month of mourning.
Long live the memory of King Vichitravirya!

[*A tearful chorus from inside: 'Long live the memory of King Vichitravirya!' The drumbeat continues. The five ministers once more cross the stage in a line, this time in the opposite direction. They are now a little less bowed with grief. Exeunt.*]

THE TWO [*together*]. Anyway! Anyway! Anyway!
A man is just a human being.
Long live the memory of the King!

[*A less mournful chorus. The drumbeat grows more emphatic and
continues thus. The five ministers quite unbowed, walk in a great hurry
in the opposite direction, holding their sides.*]

THE TWO [*turn by turn, in time to the quickened drumbeat*].
The King was just an inspiration.
—All the rest was prevarication!
Self was his only consideration.
His love for the country, a mere fabrication!
He made puppets of Cabinet men.
He made a cake of the government!
Of democracy he made a noise.
Threw sixty years dust in our eyes!
Autocratic without exception.
Of Opposition—not a mention! [1]
For sixty years, just one illusion;
Either the King, or rank confusion!
One tradition, one incantation;
'The King is the Administration!'

[*Taking a deep breath*]

Now we must admit our doubt.
Willy nilly the truth will out.
We must utter the words we hate.
History must be accurate.
The King was a sorcerer—our bad luck!
The rest was all a load of muck!

[*In unison*]

Anyway! A man is just a human being.
Long live the memory of the King.

[*The chorus announces this with an air of proclamation, to a still faster
drumbeat. The five ministers enter in line, and stand in a row with their
chests and stomachs well out and their backs to the audience.*]

THE TWO IN BLACK [*turn by turn*].
To the future we must turn.

[*The five ministers turn to face the audience.*]

We must look to what's to come!

The King is dead, the land's undying,
Let's gird our loins, and do something!

[*Together.*]

After Vichitravirya, Who?

[*The chorus inside keep repeating this: 'After Vichitravirya, who?'
From within, four people at a time enter carrying placards with the
names of each minister in turn. These include labourers, merchants,
small children, beggars, thieves, madmen. And among these, wanders
Prannarayan. Each time, he joins a different group.*]

SOME [*loudly*]. **Karkashirsha!**
OTHERS [*loudly*]. **Pishtakeshi!**
STILL OTHERS [*loudly*]. **Bhagadanta!**
YET OTHERS [*loudly*]. **Aranyaketu!**

[*They parade round the minister of their choice, raising clenched fists
and shouting: 'After Vichitravirya, who?' No one around Vratyasom.
He is a little uneasy. Then some disreputable women enter carrying
placards and shouting 'Vratyasom! Vratyasom! We want Vratyasom!'
They keep on circling round him shouting and dancing, taking his
hands in theirs. He is delighted.*]

THE TWO IN BLACK [*against this background putting their hands against
their faces as if scanning the distance*].
After Vichitravirya, who?
After Vichitravirya, who?

[*Now the chorus just goes on chanting this. The drumbeat still
continues. On stage a march begins with each candidate's followers
leading and lording it behind the candidates themselves. They march in
two or three directions on stage turning smartly as if in a drill. As they
confront each other, they compete to proclaim more loudly. Then they
march on. This becomes an uproar by itself.*]

THE TWO IN BLACK [*putting their oversize pens to their eyes like telescopes,
and looking into the distance*]. After Vichitravirya, who? After
Vichitravirya, who?

[*All the crowd, making a chant of the names of the ministers, go inside.
The drumbeat slows. Now on the rear curtain can be seen enormous
portaits of the four older leaders. And, slightly less enormous, the
portrait of Aranyaketu.*]

THE TWO IN BLACK. **Hush . . . !**
Hush . . . !

Saturday night will be unique.
The five Big Brothers will sit in clique!
A great decision will emerge.
Time will stop, the land will surge.

[*Turn by turn*]

Four are senior,
Five superior,
Some are naughty,
Some are crafty.
One is dumb, and one irascible.
To choose between them's quite impossible!
The scales are weighted in this one's favour
But that one's got the bossier behaviour!
This one's going to have a bash!
But that one's going to give him a slash!
Better back this fellow's horse.
His stocks are going down, of course!
That one looks like being the top.
That one's surely going to flop.
That one's likeliest to win.
This one will demolish him!
This one'll be hit, that one'll sink;
T'other will flounder in the drink!

[*Anxiously*]

No one knows what is to come.

[*Happily*]

But Saturday night will go all right!
Saturday night will go all right,
Will go all right!

[*Together*]

Anyway . . .!
A new age of gold is dawning.
Long live the memory of the . . . [*going out as they speak*] . . . *King*!

[*They go in. The drumbeat stops. The rear curtain rises. The hall in the palace. Above is Vichitravirya's portrait. Karkashirsha, Vratyasom, Pishtakeshi, Bhagadanta are all waiting impatiently. Cheers outside.*]

VRATYASOM. That is definitely Aranyaketu approaching. He never changes his habits. He still feels that if he can prove the backing of a thousand-odd members of the public, it'll give him strength in the power struggle!

[*Aranyaketu hurries in.*]

ARANYAKETU. Forgive me. Because of the crowd outside, I couldn't come in earlier. I had to give them an assurance that the welfare of Umbugland would be considered in whatever decisions were taken here. Then alone did they allow me to escape.

VRATYASOM. Although that crowd has gathered at your own express wish, we forgive you, Aranyaketu. For what else can we do just now? Eh, Pishtakeshi?

PISHTAKESHI. At the most we can make you our ruler!

[*He claps Vratyasom on the hand, and collapses with laughter.*]

ARANYAKETU [*not knowing quite what to make of this*]. I have no lust for power, actually. I am a social worker.

VRATYASOM. Do we take this to signify, Bhagadanta, that Aranyaketu wishes to keep out of today's conference?

ARANYAKETU [*hastily*]. That wasn't what I meant.

PISHTAKESHI. I had grasped that.

[*Noise outside. Cheering.*]

Aranyaketu, if you would tell your people outside to go home now, this conference could proceed in peace.

ARANYAKETU. If the council so permits, I will try . . .

VRATYASOM. And if you try, the crowd will most definitely go away!

[*Aranyaketu hurriedly goes to the window. He draws attention to himself by gestures.*]

ARANYAKETU [*in rhetorical tones*]. My good people, it is all right if you now wish to depart to your homes. The ministers gathered for this Council have taken due note of your wishes. I am a hundred times, a thousand times indebted to you for the immeasurable love you have shown for me. I hereby assure you that if I come to power I shall make a great thing of this love. Say with me—Long live the memory of our King!

[*Chant outside. Confusion. It abates gradually. Aranyaketu returns and sits down in the council.*]

VRATYASOM. For roughly how much did you buy this crowd, Aranyaketu?

ARANYAKETU [*angrily*]. I can fully understand why this question should come from you, Vratyasom.

PISHTAKESHI. Vratyasom, Aranyaketu, enough of irrelevant quarrels now. Let us begin the conference. Any objections? What about you, Bhagadanta?

[*Bhagadanta goes to one side, empties a small pitcher of water into his mouth and gives a fiery belch.*]

I will be Chairman for the time being. It is necessary for someone to be Chairman. That's the only reason why I'm doing it. I have no craving for power.

VRATYASOM [*standing up, in the King's old pose*]. Power! What is power? A crown of thorns! [*Looking at the portrait*] Although you have gone, your memory is still with us. Eh, Bhagadanta? Lively old man! Impossible to forget him!

PISHTAKESHI. Vratyasom, silence. First, as the customary salutation to the memory of His Majesty, I suggest from the chair that we all observe one minute's silence. Let us all arise and remain quiet.

VRATYASOM [*standing up*]. This is exactly what we did during the old man's lifetime! What else did we do! The crafty old devil! Never another like him. I hope!

KARKASHIRSHA. Mr Chairman, at least for the sake of custom, let respect be shown to the dead.

ARANYAKETU. I, too, feel that to forget so soon the great acts of His Majesty and his infinite love for this island would be ungrateful.

VRATYASOM. To say nothing of the infinite tortures he used to inflict on us. Those terrible, interminable sermons on stupid subjects! My God!

KARKASHIRSHA. I will staunchly oppose electing you as the future ruler of this island. A man who can utter such ungenerous words, about its late ruler!

VRATYASOM. It wasn't with your support that I stood for election, Karkashirsha. If I'd come to that I would renounce politics totally.

PISHTAKESHI [*in the official tones of a chairman*]. Silence! One minute's silence!

KARKASHIRSHA. If I were faced with the support of your supporters for even one instant, I would rather die! You are a traitor to the island!

VRATYASOM. Ha! Every one of you who for the last forty years has allowed the King's madnesses to go on is a traitor to the island! In short, politics itself is treachery. Treachery to the King, the country, the people. And various other kinds of constant treachery. A true politician can be loyal only to himself.

ARANYAKETU. Mr Chairman Pishtakeshi, I am grieved to see this. How little those who are kindling arguments so unsuited to the occasion have the welfare of the island at heart! And how little respect they have for what is fitting at this time.

KARKASHIRSHA. Your mob must still be waiting outside to applaud you. Disgusting! It really disgusts me to see these hired supporters.

PISHTAKESHI [*in chairmanlike tone*]. Silence! One minute's silence!

ARANYAKETU. Mr Chairman Pishtakeshi, as a mark of deep disagreement with these insulting and careless words from Karkashirsha, I hereby walk out of this council. The people of Umbugland will never endure this. [*Starts towards exit. All are watching him. He stops at the door.*] I'll be back in two minutes. [*Exit.*]

VRATYASOM. Seems to have gone to gather a fresh mob. A walk-out—with the assurance that he'll return in two minutes! I have no objection to our younger politicians seeking out new modes of triviality. But why must they be so childish? Eh, Karkashirsha?

KARKASHIRSHA. Only you are competent to speak on that subject.

PISHTAKESHI. I think we should get the matter of the one-minute silence over with before Aranyaketu's return. Let's not waste further time on that. Eh, Bhagadanta?

BHAGADANTA [*seated*]. I finished my one minute a long time ago. [*Gives a smile. Starts picking his ear.*]

VRATYASOM [*sitting down, to Bhagadanta*]. Could you please finish my minute for me too,. Bhagadanta? The various stupid preoccupations of politics don't leave me a moment to be silent. For example, take this habit of standing silent for a minute.

KARKASHIRSHA. For my part I mean to stand silent for one minute. So the soul of the departed may rest in peace. [*Stands silent.*]

VRATYASOM. Look, Bhagadanta, look! Now what respect do you see, in this practice, for any departed soul, or any live one, for that matter? It smacks to me of hypocrisy! I refer to these customs in general, of course. It seems to me just another of these stupid customs imported from abroad by the King. Is sorrow, do you think, expressed by just standing bolt upright like this? Of course, to stand like this for His Majesty is, in one sense, a just form of knavery to honour a knave. Karkashirsha, the minute's over. You can sit down if you wish.

KARKASHIRSHA. There is no need to tell me that. I'm not a politician who dances to another's tune. I follow my principles.

VRATYASOM. Ha! For a full forty years, His Majesty was the only principle you followed!

KARKASHIRSHA. Everyone was compelled to do that. You were party to it too.

VRATYASOM. But without gabbing of my principles. Just for my belly, that's all!

PISHTAKESHI [*still standing*]. One minute is over. [*Sits down*.] The council will continue. Vratyasom, some customs are better observed. How does it hurt us? The King is dead, after all!

[*Enter Aranyaketu.*]

VRATYASOM. Come in, Aranyaketu. [*Winking at the others*] We've just decided who's to come to power.

ARANYAKETU [*stunned*]. What? It's been decided?

VRATYASOM. After all, you had staged a walk-out, hadn't you?

ARANYAKETU. But in those circumstances, I would have walked out later. Mr Chairman Pishtakeshi, all this is without regard either to custom or decorum. That's what I feel. The people of Umbugland will not rest without an answer to this!

[*Goes towards the window.*]

PISHTAKESHI. Do not trouble your mob unnecessarily. Vratyasom was only teasing you. We observed one minute's silence for you. No . . . for the King! Expecting that by that time you would return!

[*Aranyaketu, pacified, takes his seat.*]

The council will now proceed. Who is going to succeed the King is a matter of great importance to Umbugland.

[*Enter an attendant. He claps lightly to attract their attention.*]

PISHTAKESHI. What is it, attendant?

ATTENDANT. Forgive me. It was only because of some extremely important news which has arrived that I interrupted the Council. The Kadamba tribe have broken into fierce riots in the North, West, East and North-East of Umbugland. They have taken possession of some military outposts. There are fifty dead and a hundred and fifty wounded.

KARKASHIRSHA. Terrible! Shoot the rebels!

VRATYASOM. Go slow, Karkashirsha. You are not in power yet! [*To the attendant*] What are their demands?

ATTENDANT. Although that is not clearly mentioned in the despatches, in general they are shouting angry slogans against certain political leaders . . . so the despatches say.

VRATYASOM. Well! Who are the political leaders?

[*All look suspiciously at each other.*]

ATTENDANT [*looking at the despatch*]. Their names . . .

KARKASHIRSHA [*looking fiercely at Vratyasom*]. Attendant, tell us quickly.

VRATYASOM [*looking back at him*]. Yes, attendant, tell us.

ATTENDANT. Yes, my lord. [*looking at the despatch*] In the East, the drift of the rebellion is against Vratyasom.

VRATYASOM [*to Karkashirsha*]. You see? Satisfied? Don't look at me suspiciously. This looks like your handiwork!

KARKASHIRSHA. I never employ such means. Messenger, tell on . . . against whom is the rebellion in the West?

ATTENDANT. Pishtakeshi.

PISHTAKESHI [*looking embarrassed at first, then with a triumphant expression*]. I expected it . . . [*looks at Aranyaketu*] Attendant, tell us the news from the North. What do the 'People' there say?

ARANYAKETU. There's no need to look suspiciously at me, Pishtakeshi? What has this to do with me?

ATTENDANT. The direction of the rebellion in the North is against—Karkashirsha.

KARKASHIRSHA [*to Vratyasom*]. See! See! Now are you convinced? I am always unpopular with the mob because of my principles.

ATTENDANT. The rebels in the North-East . . . [*taking some time*] are hurling insults against Aranyaketu.

ARANYAKETU. That's it! Because I have risen from the common people, naturally the army can't endure me!

VRATYASOM. What else, Attendant? What else?

ATTENDANT. The names are complete, my lord. The fighting and shooting continue. Your leave, sirs.

[*All scratch their heads.*]

PISHTAKESHI. Attendant, further instructions will be issued when we have considered these events. . . . You may go.

[*The servant bows and exits. All are silent. Now all eyes are on Bhagadanta. He is sitting with his eyes closed.*]

VRATYASOM. Just one name missing in the riots, eh?
KARKASHIRSHA. All the riots start at once . . . .
PISHTAKESHI. All the riots are caused by the Kadambas . . .
ARANYAKETU. Sitting woolgathering in the Council . . . hatching
plots!
VRATYASOM [*saluting Bhagadanta ironically with joined hands*].
Wonderful, Maestro, Wonderful!

[*Bhagadanta opens his eyes. Looks at all of them and smiles. He salutes
Vratyasom in return.*]

You are one ahead even of us! Such tricks—and so quiet about
them!

[*Bhagadanta makes a deprecatory gesture.*]

If I myself were not in the contest for the leadership, I would
have confidently said, bring Bhagadanta to power this minute!
This is what a perfect ruler should be. A man of few words, and a
bastard! Pishtakeshi—in other words, Mr Chairman—there's no
point in wasting further time.

[*A mime of discussion and disagreement among the ministers now
begins. It should continue all through the whole passage. The light
fades out. In front of the stage, the Two with the large pens enter. They
are now dressed in a different colour. Spotlights on them.*]

THE TWO [*in unison*].
SERIOUS CRISIS! SERIOUS CRISIS!

[*Turn by turn*]

No decision.
The scales are equal.
Whom to give the power to?
Each one's a rascal.
New meeting on Monday!
New meeting on Monday!
All eyes on Monday!
All attention on Monday!
What'll happen on Monday?
Which one will win on Monday?
Which one'll put the other at fault?
Which one'll turn a somersault?
And which one'll win it by default?

[*Together*]

Serious Crisis! Serious Crisis!

[*Lights go up on the Council once more. All its members are silent. After a while, the lights there fade. Lights go up in front.*]

THE TWO [*together*].
Meeting postponed!
Meeting postponed!

[*Turn by turn*]

No one's willing to withdraw!
No one's coming to the fore!
Status quo.
We don't know
How they'll go.
Can't tell at all who's going to be
The person in authority!
Fierce rioting!
Fierce rioting!
Who will the new leader be?
Who will the new leader be?

Vratyasom's arguments are reasoned.
Karkashirsha's are well-seasoned.
Pishtakeshi's not deficient.
Bhagadanta's quite proficient.
Aranyaketu is—sufficient.

Whose elevation?
Whose perdition?
Which ones will form a coalition?
Compromise?
Mere delusion!
Behind the scenes?
All confusion!
Values here,
Morals there,
Those conditions,
These accusations,
This struggle,
That muddle!
This one's green!
That one's yellow!
This one's sleepy!

That one's stealthy!
He's a surpriser!
He's a surmiser!
He's coming!
He's going!
He's modern!
He's insecure!
He's behind!
He's before!

The Moving Finger's writing on!
They haven't yet chosen any one!

[*Together*]

New Leader not yet chosen!
New Leader not yet chosen!
Fierce rioting!
Fierce rioting!

New Meeting! New Meeting!
Fresh Formula! Fresh Formula!
New Ray of Hope on the Horizon!

[*They exit. Lights go up on the council. The mimed discussion continues vigorously. Suddenly Vijaya intrudes by mistake, and to her embarrassment, into the council. Behind her is the eunuch Prannarayan. She is quite confused. Stands shrinking from them. All eyes on her.*]

VIJAYA. I—I—mistook the room—I'm sorry . . .

[*All of them stand up, just looking at her, and forgetting their conversation.*]

VRATYASOM. Pishtakeshi! Found at last!
VIJAYA. Who?
VRATYASOM. Found our compromise!
VIJAYA [*confused*]. W-what?
VRATYASOM. Meet our new leader! [*Vijaya shrinks.*] His Majesty's heir! This one in front, five of us behind! She'll be the rule, we'll be the rulers! An excellent plan till we agree on a firm decision!

All slowly encircle Vijaya. They are looking her up and down. She stands in their midst like a startled hare.

CURTAIN

ACT TWO

SCENE I

The curtain rises. Princess Vijaya's apartments.

From the tape-recorder on stage, comes the sound of Princess Vijaya making a speech full of complicated words, in classroom tones, fumbling, stumbling, correcting herself.

Enter Prannarayan. He switches off the tape.

PRANNARAYAN. This isn't the actual speech Princess Vijaya is making at her Swearing-in ceremony. This is just a rehearsal we had here yesterday. Of course the child gave the real speech much better. Right now, in the hall of Audience.

[*Bites his tongue.*]

What did I say? 'Child'? Forget I said it.
'Her Royal Highness Princess Vijaya!' For the past few days, at the mere thought of sitting on the throne, she hasn't felt hunger or thirst or slept soundly. At all hours of the night she's been getting up and practising the Oath-Taking.

[*Enter Princess Vijaya in full coronation regalia. She is somewhat tired by the ceremony. But still, she looks beautiful. Prannarayan stands watching her.*]

VIJAYA. Prannarayan, how do I look?

PRANNARAYAN [*bowing in confusion*]. As the crescent moon while you watch it grows into the fullness of its beauty—that is how you look, Your Majesty.

VIJAYA [*goes in front of a mirror and gazes at herself*]. Today I look beautiful. But I'm tired. Prannarayan, how tight you tied the strings of my bodice when I set out today!

PRANNARAYAN. Your Majesty said—tighter—tighter—that's why I tightened them, Your Majesty. Forgive my stupid mistake.

VIJAYA. The strings kept cutting into me during the ceremony. And I kept on cursing you mentally.

PRANNARAYAN. It is this servant's good fortune that at such a moment Her Majesty remembered him . . . no matter what for!

VIJAYA. It was only when I finally bent down with the excuse of bowing to Father's statue, and the strings loosened of their own accord, that I had any relief at all!

PRANNARAYAN. The mistake won't occur again.

VIJAYA. It's myself I'm angry with. Why didn't you come to the ceremony? How well I read the speech. I read it just as you had taught me, without stumbling, and without a single mistake. And do you know? While I was reading it, I kept looking slyly round to see if I could spot you anywhere.

PRANNARAYAN. I had work here, Your Majesty.

VIJAYA [*annoyed*]. Must you call me Your Majesty all the time?

PRANNARAYAN. One never tires of referring to a most happy situation.

VIJAYA. Then only say it once in a while.

PRANNARAYAN. Yes, Princess Vijaya.

VIJAYA. I'm tired. How unending it all was! To start with, the ceremony just wouldn't get to my oath-taking. The speech of welcome, the recital of hymns, the ministers' speeches—and do you know how long the Oath of Accession or whatever you call it, was? Just saying it before me made the Chief Justice quite breathless. I said to him, 'Never Mind, Grandpa, you can tell me the rest tomorrow if you like,' and there was such a guffaw from the assembly! Why do these oaths at court have to be so long, Prannarayan?

PRANNARAYAN. Probably so that they will at least be kept until one has finished taking them.

VIJAYA. You mean one doesn't have to keep the oath later?

PRANNARAYAN. Promises in love and promises at court are of different species, Your Majesty. Promises in love are made unrestrainedly and have to be kept through restraint. Promises at court are made with restraint, and are usually broken unrestrainedly. That is one's experience. Love's promises are made in secret, and have to be kept publicly. Political promises are made publicly, but usually have no witness but history when they're broken.

VIJAYA. Prannarayan, you're very difficult to understand. So was the Oath. To tell you the truth, I didn't really understand it at all.

PRANNARAYAN. If it's possible to keep it, you'll understand it automatically little by little, after a while. And if it's impossible to keep it, it's best that Your Majesty doesn't understand it.

VIJAYA. Oh, dear! Well, I'll change my clothes.

[*Claps her hands. A maidservant enters.*]

I wish to change my clothes.

MAIDSERVANT. Could Your Majesty please follow me?

VIJAYA. Are you, too, going to stop calling me Princess Vijaya?

MAIDSERVANT [*confused*]. Your Majesty . . .?

VIJAYA. At dawn when I am asleep in bed, aren't you going to stroke my hair lightly and gently and say 'Princess Vijaya!' to wake me up?

[*The maidservant is embarrassed.*]

Come.

[*Both of them go offstage.*]

PRANNARAYAN [*to the audience*]. Her mother died when she was a baby. Her father was the father of all Umbugland, so just didn't come to her portion. What did come to it were the fawning parasites and idlers in the palace. Let me tell you about yesterday. She insisted upon having a rehearsal of the ceremony. Finally the ministers agreed. The moment she sat on the throne she exclaimed, 'This is too high for me! Cut its legs a bit!' The Ministers tried to convince her that there was no such custom, but they just couldn't manage it! She was obstinate! Only if they would cut the legs of the throne would she go through with the oath of office—or else she wouldn't become the ruler at all. Crisis! *Prathamgrase makshita patah.* Obstacles right from the start. That's what happened to the ministers. I tried to persuade her. 'Princess Vijaya, one can't cut the legs of the throne.' She asked, 'Why not?' I said, 'The throne is a sacred thing.' So she said 'Then why would one sit on it?' I answered, 'Only a King can sit on it, because a king is sacred.' She replied, 'Then I, about to become your sacred King, order you to cut the sacred legs of this sacred throne. Cutting a throne's legs isn't cutting its sacredness! When I sit on the throne, my legs don't reach the ground; it looks ridiculous! What'll people think? They'll say I'm not fit for the throne! So the legs must be cut at least a little.' It was only when the legs of the throne were cut slightly in the middle of the night that she calmed down, and was prepared to sit on it. Of course, that it didn't come to anyone's notice during today's ceremony is quite another matter. Who ever notices the foot of the throne? But this affair is hardly to the taste of the Cabinet.

[*Vijaya comes back in different clothes.*]

VIJAYA. How relaxed I feel now! Come on, Prannarayan. Come and play hopscotch with me in the park.

PRANNARAYAN [*embarrassed*]. Your Majesty, it won't look fitting to play those games now.

VIJAYA. Why?

PRANNARAYAN. Power games are rather different.

VIJAYA. Power! Power! Power! For the last eight days that's all I've been hearing. This 'power' can go to h-e-double-l!

[*Prannarayan is very embarrassed.*]

What else! I don't want to play power games! I want to play my own. What has power to do with the games I play? Prannarayan, I'm not as old as my father. How is it you keep forgetting?

PRANNARAYAN. No, Princess Vijaya, I haven't forgotten it. But the queen of Umbugland can't play hopscotch, and least of all with a humble attendant.

VIJAYA. What'll happen if I do?

PRANNARAYAN. It will be a breach of royal custom.

VIJAYA. Who were the people who established these customs?

PRANNARAYAN. Your ancestors, each more experienced and accomplished than the other.

VIJAYA. Had they ever played hopscotch?

PRANNARAYAN. They probably had not.

VIJAYA. Then how did they think of the custom of never playing it?

PRANNARAYAN. Princess Vijaya, hopscotch is not one of the accepted customs of the country. People of royal station must know the value of their high degree and behave accordingly. That is the custom.

VIJAYA. Just show me where these customs are written down. I'll just read them and see.

PRANNARAYAN. They are unwritten.

VIJAYA. Then what proof is there that they're true?

PRANNARAYAN. Three generations of your forebears have observed them.

VIJAYA. Who says even that?

PRANNARAYAN. History says it.

VIJAYA. Who wrote that history?

PRANNARAYAN. Your ancestors, who preserved the customs.

VIJAYA. Prannarayan, since those ancestors were men—and old at that!—they couldn't even have had occasion to play hopscotch. What do you think?

PRANNARAYAN. It's possible. People often play ducks and drakes with the truth.

VIJAYA. I'm going to start a new custom. Let's play hopscotch. Or jacks, if you prefer.

PRANNARAYAN. I think that we'll have to call an emergency meeting of the Cabinet to obtain permission.

VIJAYA. In order to play hopscotch or jacks? But we do it every day!

PRANNARAYAN. The situation today is different. Now you are the ruler of the island, Her Most Virtuous Majesty, the Queen.

VIJAYA. And that means I can't play? I didn't know that! No one told me that, when they made me queen. I thought that becoming queen gave me greater power.

PRANNARAYAN. Your Highness must behave with dignity.

VIJAYA. I don't think I can manage it. I feel like dancing, laughing and singing. I feel like playing and running about! Sometimes, Prannarayan, I even feel like shouting loudly without any reason.

PRANNARAYAN. With all due respect to piety and health, this is just human nature!. But it doesn't do for a ruler to be human. He has to be superhuman, or even divine.

VIJAYA. You mean, like Father? Those people didn't give me any idea of this.

PRANNARAYAN. Now that you've understood it, it'll be useful to both parties.

VIJAYA. It's too late. If I'd known this before, I wouldn't have become queen. Prannarayan, I shall play hopscotch or jacks. And you shall keep me company.

PRANNARAYAN. It won't be considered correct, Princess Vijaya.

VIJAYA. Prannarayan, as the queen of Umbugland, I order you to!

PRANNARAYAN [bowing respectfully at this]. Her Majesty's wish is supreme.

[Vijaya squats on the floor. Prannarayan sits in front of her. The game of jacks begins. Enter a maidservant.]

MAIDSERVANT. [Seeing all this, makes hurried signs]. Attendant, the ministers are approaching.

[Prannarayan tries to stop the game and gets up.]

VIJAYA. Why are you getting up, Prannarayan? This round's only half over.

PRANNARAYAN. Your Majesty, the ministers are coming here to meet you.

VIJAYA [to the maidservant]. Make them wait outside. [She goes on playing.]

MAIDSERVANT [*scared*]. But, Your Majesty . . .

PRANNARAYAN [*realizing the seriousness of the situation*]. Princess Vijaya, if the Cabinet thinks that it is a mark of disrespect . . .

VIJAYA. They're quite used to waiting outside Father's apartments for hours at a time. [*Goes on playing.*]

PRANNARAYAN [*with presence of mind, to the maidservant*]. Say to them that owing to the fatigue of the ceremony Her Majesty is resting a while in her bed chamber. Her Majesty will receive them in two minutes.

[*Exit the maidservant.*]

VIJAYA [*still playing*]. Prannarayan, you told a lie!

PRANNARAYAN. No, Your Majesty. I was diplomatic. Each of them is more important than the next. One must insult them so lightly that their self-importance won't suffer.

VIJAYA [*bursting into laughter*]. Prannarayan, you say such amusing things!

PRANNARAYAN. I was just being diplomatic. Now I feel Your Highness ought to give them audience.

VIJAYA [*gathering up the game, and getting up*]. All right. [*Sits on a chair like any ordinary girl.*]

PRANNARAYAN. Could Your Highness please sit like a queen?

VIJAYA [*changing her attitude*]. Like this, do you mean?

PRANNARAYAN [*controlling his laughter*]. No.

VIJAYA [*changing her attitude again*]. Like this?

PRANNARAYAN. No.

VIJAYA. Then how? Like this? [*Strikes a horribly unnatural attitude.*]

PRANNARAYAN [*laughing*]. That's the pose for dismissing the cabinet! [*Seating her correctly*] Like this! Now Your Highness may summon the ministers. And remember one thing. Insult them, but don't wound their egos. And diplomatic language!

VIJAYA. In other words, lies. The opposite of what one feels.

PRANNARAYAN [*mischievously*]. Hush! [*He claps his hands. Enter the maidservant.*]

VIJAYA [*sitting like a queen*]. Maidservant, send in the bloody Cabinet.

[*The maidservant is shocked to the core. Prannarayan's tongue hangs out with surprise.*]

PRANNARAYAN [*reminding her*]. Diplomatic language!

VIJAYA. All right. Maidservant, call in the most honoured Cabinet.

[*Looks at Prannarayan triumphantly to check how she has said it. He indicates approval and starts to exit.*]

Most honoured Prannarayan, you may remain here.

PRANNARAYAN. But . . .

[*By this time, the ministers enter. For a moment they stand observing Vijaya's queenly attitude and diginity. Aranyaketu stares fixedly at her.*]

KARKASHIRSHA. Princess Vijaya, your fatigue has disappeared, I hope?

[*Vijaya is silent.*]

PISHTAKESHI. There wasn't anything lacking in the ceremony. Was there, child?

[*Vijaya is silent. In the corner, Prannarayan watches tensely.*]

VRATYASOM. Viju really looked perfect in that imposing coronation ceremony, didn't she? Eh, Bhagadanta?

[*Vijaya is silent.*]

ARANYAKETU. One felt as if the goddess Parvati herself had appeared at court.

[*Vijaya is silent.*]

VRATYASOM. We only disturbed you because there are some royal decrees that need urgent publication.

[*Vijaya is still silent. All are perplexed.*]

I hope you have not lost your voice because of the hard speech you had to make this morning. If that is the case, I have the most effective lozenges to take after a taxing speech, right here on me. [*Takes them out and offers them*] Here, take one. Take one, Karkashirsha, take one Bhagadanta—but you don't need them!

[*Vijaya is as silent as before.*]

KARKASHIRSHA [*quietly to Vratyasom*]. All does not seem well.

PISHTAKESHI. Speak, child—has the sacred memory of your sire made your throat choke with emotion?

ARANYAKETU. If only His Majesty were here today!

VRATYASOM. He is with us. When such people die bodily, their souls live on. Karkashirsha, take my example. I see His Majesty in my dreams. Really I do!

[*Karkashirsha silences him with a gesture. In the corner Prannarayan is stunned at Vijaya's behaviour. A brief but total silence.*]

VIJAYA [*after having allowed the Cabinet to become thoroughly uneasy*]. Today we will not speak to the Cabinet.

ARANYAKETU. Why is that?

VRATYASOM. Why indeed?

VIJAYA. The Cabinet has broken the protocol of court by omitting to bow to us. We are the queen of this island.

[*A low murmuring at this among the Cabinet.*]

VRATYASOM. In private, child, you seem to us like our own daughter.

PISHTAKESHI. After His Majesty, it is we who are fathers to you.

VIJAYA. It is the custom that people of royal station should remember the value of their high rank. Three generations of my ancestors have kept that custom. This is history. This was made by my ancestors.

[*The cabinet is dumbfounded. Prannarayan is dumb.*]

As from today, we are Her Most Virtuous Majesty, the Queen of Umbugland.

[*The Cabinet is tense. They mutter to each other. Vijaya is watching them out of the corner of her eye.*]

KARKASHIRSHA [*muttering to Vratyasom*]. Yesterday, that stubborn insistence on cutting the legs of the throne, and today, this!

VRATYASOM [*to Karkashirsha and Bhagadanta*]. One should humour a child's stubbornness. How does it harm us!

PISHTAKESHI. I think so too. What do you think, Bhagadanta?

[*Bhagadanta smiles.*]

At least talk now!

BHAGADANTA. No alternative.

ARANYAKETU. I think we'll have to follow protocol.

[*They all bow.*]

VIJAYA [*abandoning the sternness of a queen, starts pressing her stiff neck*]. Don't do it again. My neck hurts! And there must be an emergency meeting of the Cabinet.

KARKASHIRSHA. What for?

VIJAYA. In order to give the queen—that is, to give me—permission to play hopscotch or jacks in the palace grounds or buildings.

VRATYASOM. Good heavens! Why do you need a meeting for that? If you wish, the Cabinet will agree to it unanimously right now. Eh, Pishtakeshi? Eh, Karkashirsha?

KARKASHIRSHA. I'll have to consider the matter.

VRATYASOM. All right. Consider it. By a majority vote, the Cabinet agrees to the request of the Queen.

VIJAYA. When is the Cabinet going to leave? My round of jacks is still half-finished.

KARKASHIRSHA [to Pishtakeshi]. You see? This is why I wanted to consider it.

VRATYASOM. Vijoo—I'm sorry, I mean Your Majesty—the round of jacks can be completed at your leisure. Just now, the Cabinet has come for an audience with you because there is an urgent need for some royal decrees.

PISHTAKESHI. As soon as Your Majesty has written them, you may with pleasure continue your round of jacks. [To Prannarayan] Attendant, bring a pen for Her Majesty.

[Prannarayan brings one. Pishtakeshi places some papers before Vijaya, and a seal of office.]

Here is the Seal of State. Please write as follows . . .

VIJAYA. Wait. [Takes the pen and sits more comfortably.] Yes, now it's all right.

PISHTAKESHI. Decree Number One.

VIJAYA. Prannarayan, this pen's rotten! Fetch me a good one.

[Prannarayan gives her another.]

Let me see. [She tries it out.] This will do. What shall I write?

PISHTAKESHI [winks at Vratyasom and turns]. Decree number one. 'It is hereby decreed that on the occasion of the coronation . . .'

VIJAYA. Slowly! Slowly! 'Occasion . . . of . . . the . . . coronation' . . . 'O-c-a' or 'O-double-c-a'? What is it, Pishtakeshi? What is it, Karkashirsha? Vratyasom?

PISHTAKESHI. I think it's 'O-double-c-a'.

VRATYASOM. 'O-c-a' isn't absolutely wrong, either.

KARKASHIRSHA. It's 'O-double-c-a'.

ARANYAKETU. Will both of them do, Bhagadanta?

BHAGADANTA [giving a smile]. No education. Illiterate.

PISHTAKESHI. Write 'O-double-c-a' for now . . . 'Occasion of the coronation, amnesty is to be given to 51 prisoners in the royal dungeons.'

VIJAYA. Why 51?

VRATYASOM. Because one needs a good, fair-sized number.

KARKASHIRSHA. Fifty wouldn't have been bad at all. But when I said fifty, you all stubbornly insisted on fifty-one.

VIJAYA. I'll write 'a hundred'.

PISHTAKESHI [*hurriedly*]. Fifty-one. . . . write fifty-one . . . 'to fifty-one prisoners . . .'

VIJAYA. What are these prisoners like? I only once saw some prisoners working in the palace gardens. They looked just like any of us.

VRATYASOM. They are all imprisoned because of some dreadful crime.

VIJAYA. What crime did I commit, that I've been imprisoned in the palace since childhood?

ARANYAKETU. To achieve the happiness of birth in a royal palace is counted good fortune. And to add to that, being fathered by such a sire must be considered . . .

VIJAYA. Then *you* live here instead of me. I'll run away. Shall I?

KARKASHIRSHA. Aranyaketu, we are straying from the subject. The royal decrees have to be written.

VIJAYA [*sticking out her tongue*]. 'The royal decrees have to be written'. Why does the queen also have to write? Is the queen a schoolgirl? What do you take the queen for?

[*The ministers glance at each other.*]

[*With her most queenly air*] If I took it into my head, I could order you all to . . .

PRANNARAYAN [*promptly coming forward*]. Take care, Your Majesty, the pen will break.

VIJAYA. Yes. 'The royal decrees have to be written.' [*To Pishtakeshi*] Yes? Go on. If it's fifty-one it's fifty-one . . . 'amnesty is to be given . . .'

PISHTAKESHI. Stamp it below with the Seal of State, Your Majesty. [*Hands her the seal. She uses it as he instructs.*]

VIJAYA [*holding out the paper in front of Pishtakeshi like a handbill*]. Here, take it. Royal Decree Number One. [*Peering on purpose at Prannarayan, who is at a distance*] Well, Prannarayan, how's the handwriting? Do have a look! Chicken-tracks! [*She laughs and laughs at herself.*] Go on, Pishtakeshi, tell me the next decree.

PISHTAKESHI [*taking the decree in his hand*]. Royal Decree Number Two.

VIJAYA [*sticking out her tongue towards her nose in a concentrated writing pose*]. Yes. Now my handwriting will be a little better. Set me at

least ten Royal Decrees like this to write every day, Pishtakeshi.
Or else twenty-five. Or else 'Fifty-one!' [*Mimicking Vratyasom
exactly*] 'Because one needs a good, fair-sized number.' Don't
make a face, Pishtakeshi. Go on. I'm writing.

PISHTAKESHI. It is hereby decreed that . . .

VIJAYA. I think I'll just prepare lots of documents with the words
already written on them: 'It is hereby decreed that . . .', 'It is
hereby decreed that . . .', 'It is hereby decreed that . . .' How often
can I keep on writing that? [*Writing*] 'Once again, it is hereby
decreed that . . .'

KARKASHIRSHA. Cross out the words 'Once again.'

VIJAYA. I won't cross them out!

[*A tense moment.*]

How can I—when I haven't even written them? 'It is hereby
decreed that . . .'

PISHTAKESHI. 'Our father . . .'

VIJAYA. But he's gone to heaven already!

PISHTAKESHI. It is about that that you must write. 'Our father, the
Most Mighty Sovereign of Umbugland, the All-Virtuous, the
Warrior Omnipotent . . . in all Knowledge, Arts and Government
Most Resonant . . .' [*Softly to Karkashirsha.*] What comes after that,
Karkashirsha?

KARKASHIRSHA. You've forgotten the Address of State? Terrible!
'The True-living, the Truth-Inspiring, the All-Knowing, the
All-Discriminating, the Ever-Youthful, the Ever-Pure—' [*Vijaya
yawns.*]

VIJAYA [*suppressing the yawn*]. Uh-huh. It's gone.

KARKASHIRSHA. 'The-Ever-Living, the Remover of all Affliction,
Protector of the Umbugite Nation, Holder of the Imperial
Dignity—' [*Sees that Vijaya is sitting at ease.*] What's this? You're
sitting idle!

VIJAYA. What? This is all too long and complicated. I've just
written 'Our Father, etc. etc.' That covers everything.

KARKASHIRSHA. It's essential that the entire State Address for the
ruler of the island should be written in full!

VIJAYA. The Queen does not agree!

KARKASHIRSHA. The customs will be deemed greater than the
Queen!

VIJAYA. Then we must write our own royal decrees!

PRANNARAYAN [*bringing forward a goblet to hand to Vijaya, with great
presence of mind*] Forgive me, Your Majesty, refreshment is better
than argument. Have some of this . . .

[*She recovers her poise and takes it. All the Ministers are in one corner.*]

VRATYASOM [*shrewdly*]. Let it go, Karkashirsha . . .

PISHTAKESHI. We must make allowances for her youthful inex-
perience . . .

ARANYAKETU. If she leaves a blank space, that's good enough.
The King's Address of State can be written later. It is only a
formality.

VRATYASOM. The royal decrees have got to come duly into our
hands . . . The uprisings on the island must first be crushed . . .

KARKASHIRSHA. No! I will never endure this insult to the departed
ruler of Umbugland!

[*They all stand there persuading him.*]

VRATYASOM [*at last*]. Very well, Your Majesty. A blank space for
the Address of State may be left in the decree.

VIJAYA. The next decree may then be dictated.

VRATYASOM [*gesturing 'I'll dictate it' to Pishtakeshi and Karkashirsha*].
'Our Father King Vichitravirya—a large blank space—having to
our sorrow died, some destructive elements in the island, taking
unfair advantage of the situation, have in all parts made armed
uprisings against the esteemed Cabinet as well as the seat of
power. This being treason—'

VIJAYA. What does 'treason' mean?

VRATYASOM. Rebellion against the King.

VIJAYA. But that's what Karkashirsha did just now.

KARKASHIRSHA. I protest . . . I am a most loyal subject!

VIJAYA. You are most hot-headed! Go on, Vratyasom. Let me get
this written and over with. All right. 'Treason. . .'

VRATYASOM. 'Strong measures should be taken against this, and
the treasonous elements should be rooted out from the base.'

[*His gaze is on Bhagadanta.*]

VIJAYA [*finishes writing, stamps the paper with seal, picks it up in her
hand and lets it fall*]. Royal Decree Number Two.

[*Vratyasom picks up the paper and gives it to Pishtakeshi.*]

VRATYASOM. One last one. Royal Decree Number Three. [*In a
drawl*] 'It is hereby decreed that for the convenience of administration, the powers of the Cabinet should be increased, and
hereafter all decisions must be made with the full agreement of
the Ministers.'

[*Vijaya quickly writes it all down, places the seal on it, and picking up this document too, lets it fall down. Pishtakeshi catches it adroitly before it falls.*]

Today's royal decrees are complete.

VIJAYA. Royal Decree Number Four. It is hereby decreed that only those who are going to sit down and play a round of Jacks may remain here now. All the rest may now depart.

KARKASHIRSHA. Vratyasom, that is an insult to the Cabinet.

VIJAYA. That is an insult to the game of Jacks!

[*Vratyasom and the other Ministers exit, trying to pacify Karkashirsha.*]

[*When they have left, to Prannarayan*] How did I behave?

PRANNARAYAN. If Your Majesty will not be angry, I will tell you. You went a bit too far!

VIJAYA. It was you yourself who said that I must insult them without wounding their egos.

PRANNARAYAN. But Karkashirsha was very angry.

VIJAYA. The rest were all dumb, however.

PRANNARAYAN. To hiss when you're stung is one kind of behaviour. To bluster when you're stung is a politician's behaviour.

VIJAYA. I'm the Queen. How dare that useless old monkey teach me the customs?

PRANNARAYAN. Age has some unfair advantages.

VIJAYA. So should becoming a queen.

PRANNARAYAN. One should take stock of the situation—give some advantages, and get some. Politics means sweetly-smiling enmity and the experience of sacrifice. A show of sacrifice is always profitable in politics.

VIJAYA. All right, all right, I understand—my head's begun to swim with these politics of yours. Prannarayan, why don't you become queen instead of me? I'll become your attendant.

PRANNARAYAN. These are gifts from God.

VIJAYA. You understand so much.

PRANNARAYAN. This is also a gift from God. Being different gives one understanding. I am different. To any two kinds, I am a third. In any three, I am a stranger. I am different. I am not an actor. I am purely a spectator, an onlooker. I am just a bird on a boat of life. I am on the boat, but not of it.

VIJAYA. I feel like lying down with my head on your lap.

PRANNARAYAN. Why just think of it? You may command it.

[*Vijaya lies down with her head resting on Prannarayan's lap.*]

VIJAYA. I am very tired. I'm just exhausted. Prannarayan, I feel as if this lap is the only support I have got in the world. I feel as if it's only here I can relax unafraid. All the rest is a dense forest. All around me are gathered beasts of prey. Above me a terrifying ghost is laughing aloud . . . the ghost of my father. Prannarayan, I'm scared! What's going to happen to me?

[*Prannarayan gently strokes her head.*]

PRANNARAYAN. I'll stroke your head a little. You'll feel better. Even in the densest forest, butterflies flutter, deer run, birds build their nests. Lionesses give suck to their helpless cubs and make fierce males out of them. From dead matter there constantly arises a new creation. The force that creates, protects, and makes to grow, reaches its influence even to this forest. And as there are ghosts, so is there the dazzling light of day. To absorb strength from that bright light and endure through the night of ghosts: that is the law of the forest. Night follows day; a new, light-filled day follows night. This is the forest's daily truth. Nothing in this forest is unprotected; nor is anything fully protected; that is the secret of its ways. In the forest, each one is the devoured, and each the devourer. He who is hunted, if he escapes and lives, becomes the hunter. Nothing here is permanent, nothing everlasting. No one is forever the conqueror, or forever the conquered. This forest is paramount—[*He looks at Vijaya. She is asleep.*]—and so is this peaceful sleep that takes away all sorrow and care. Your Majesty, may such peaceful sleep be granted to you without fail, in the life of storms that is brewing for you.

[*Claps lightly. Enter a maidservant.*]

[*Softly*] Make a couch here for Her Majesty.

[*Exit the maidservant. Prannarayan sits there as he is, lost in nothingness, with Vijaya's head on his lap. Darkness.*]

SCENE II

THE TWO [*together*].
Great Day! Auspicious Day!
Day of Nectar! Golden Day!

[*Turn by turn*]

Let it be written in letters of gold.

In official histories let it be told.
A day like this only comes once a millenium.
May it be remembered for twenty-eight aeons.
What a day! What a day!

[*Together*]

Day of Nectar! Golden Day!

[*Turn by turn*]

Queen Vijaya the Divine enthroned as Umbug favourite!
Queen Vijaya in the front, from Left to Right, the Cabinet!
The Royal Lady of Umbugland at her coronation!
The Darling of the Umbugites speaking to the Nation!
The Mascot of the Country's Luck receiving an ovation!
The Most Excellent Umbug lady making her affirmation!
Right to Left
Left to Right
Right to Left
Left to Right
Bottom to top
Top to bottom
Top to Top
Bottom to bottom!
The Cabinet of Ministers!
The Cabinet of Ministers!
The Cabinet of Ministers!

[*Together*]

Queen Vijaya the Divine, enthroned as Umbug favourite!
Great Day! Auspicious Day!

[*While this is going on, the noise of a band. Enter the Ministers and
Queen Vijaya walking in that order. They go offstage. Now a drumbeat
begins.*]

THE TWO [*together*]. Great Day! Auspicious Day! Day of Nectar!
Golden Day!

[*Turn by turn*]

In Her Majesty Queen Vijaya's honourable presence ·
All-Umbugland Women's Council hold their conference.
Gracious hands of Umbugland's first Queen to reign
Open Mosquito Eradication Campaign!

Her Majesty Queen Vijaya's victorious reception
Given by Washermen's Association.
Queen to receive most loyal citation
Presented by Tailor's Confederation.
Academy of Literature meets under her direction.
Question of the Blind to get her Personal Attention!
Message to Scientists who make Peaceful Inventions.
Advice to Industrialists with Patriotic Intentions.
Meeting with Umbugland Wrestlers' Convention.
Industrial Dispute Calmed by Royal Intervention.
Impassioned Speech by Queen Vijaya.
Intimate Interview with Queen Vijaya.
Successful Tour by Queen Vijaya.
Slight Touch of Cold for Queen Vijaya.
Huge Crowd out to see Queen Vijaya.
Queen Vijaya's triumphant smile.
Queen Vijaya's Excellent Speaking Style.
Who's Engaged with the Queen in Intimate Talk?
A Watermelon Grown in Queen Vijaya's park.
Queen Vijaya here—
Queen Vijaya there—
Queen Vijaya like this—
Queen Vijaya like that—
—The kneecap you see on the left is Pishtakeshi's.
The elbow on the right is Karkashirsha's.
The stomach you see behind is Vratyasom's.
And the ear sticking out *must* be Bhagadanta's.
In every corner it's Queen Vijaya.
Day of Nectar! Day of Gold!
Great Day! Auspicious Day!

[*While this is going on, a cut-out of a motor-car comes onstage to the noise of drums, trumpets and cymbals. Queen Vijaya is standing in the car. She waves her hand, joins her hands to salute an imaginary populace. Exit the motor-car complete with Vijaya.*]

SCENE III

The Council Chamber. Karkashirsha, Pishtakeshi, Vratyasom, Aranya-ketu, Bhagadanta.

KARKASHIRSHA. Terrible! Dreadful! This is too much!

ARANYAKETU. There is no doubt that the Queen's action must be judged immature and unworthy of respect. Let me once more make it clear, however, that, it was not precisely that action to which I object, but rather to the manner in which—

VRATYASOM. You're unnecessarily creating confusion where everything's clear. I just don't understand how you can make a distinction between her behaviour and the manner of it. All told it was a barefaced, laughable and childish stunt. That's all. There's an end to it. What actual need was there for the Queen to step outside the programme arranged for her tour? The programmes are always arranged with her full consent. It was extremely dangerous for her to halt her motor-car where she did, in that Kadamba settlement. For we had just crushed that tribe's treasonous rebellion upon the island. If anything dreadful had happened, who would have borne the responsibility? Eh, Aranyaketu? You must give it most serious consideration. Of course, it's true that the women and children of that area came in the way of the Queen's motor-car. But suppose I myself were in that car—no, just suppose it—I would not, in any circumstances, have stopped it there. What is your opinion, Karkashirsha?

KARKASHIRSHA. I would have driven it straight over those traitors' dead bodies.

PISHTAKESHI. All right—let's assume for a moment that the driver, brought to a halt by the crowd, stopped the car. Even so it was quite unsuitable to commit the lunacy of getting out of it, at that time, in that place. It was just an open invitation to the savageries of that tribe. Anything could have happened. And all because of the Queen's behaviour. Thank God nothing happened. Even the thought makes my hair stand on end!

VRATYASOM. The stupid girl ignored the advice of the senior security officer who was with her. She got down. No, as I am older than she is and a colleague of her late father I am entitled to call her that. Aranyaketu I feel I can even twist her ear if necessary.

PISHTAKESHI. So can we all.

VRATYASOM. Was our security officer mad, when he advised her not to get down?

KARKASHIRSHA. Or were we blockheads, who drew up her programme for her? I for one say, this is an affront to the Cabinet. We must take an extremely stern view of this, Pishtakeshi.

PISHTAKESHI. I agree with you totally. There can be no two opinions about it! We leave aside the question of the danger.

What happened later was completely inconsistent with the ruler's dignity. And extremely ridiculous! Her majesty wandered about through the huts in the Kadamba area!

VRATYASOM. She kissed the children in the settlement!

KARKASHIRSHA. She enquired after the families of men killed or imprisoned in the riots.

PISHTAKESHI. She took some refreshments!

VRATYASOM. And made a speech! [*Puts on his spectacles, and takes out a piece of paper*] A word-by-word account of the speech has come to my hands from the security officer. It is on—thirteen, fourteen, fifteen—fifteen subjects, from the problems facing the island to the dirtiness of the Kadamba tribe's huts! Once again—Vichitravirya! And to top that, she gave an assurance that there would be an impartial and personal enquiry into the causes of the riots! Ha! While all this was going on, the next part of her programme, a function organized by the Industrialists' Association, had to be cancelled. Because the Queen did not reach!

KARKASHIRSHA [*rising*]. Depose her!

VRATYASOM. Don't be so agitated, Karkashirsha. We must make our decision thoughtfully. As seasoned statesmen, we must placidly give a calm answer to no matter what kind of childishness. We musn't lose our balance.

PISHTAKESHI. Today the photographs are in the newspapers. 'Queen Vijaya in Kadamba Settlement' It's tiresome! Where will it all lead? That's my question.

KARKASHIRSHA. While we're here, where else could it go? How could it go further? I say—depose the Queen! I feel that the harsh responsibility of protecting the pristine purity of the monarchy and our traditions is the prime duty of the Cabinet, including myself.

ARANYAKETU. All I ask is that a reprimand should be given to Her Majesty—

VRATYASOM. A reprimand? This occurrence is not the first, Aranyaketu. A reprimand is given for the first, second, or at the most, third offence. But what has been going on for the last seven months has, in my view, begun to appear harmful to the welfare of the island. And, to speak even more clearly, to our welfare. I am not like Karkashirsha, who talks a lot of rot about purity and traditions. I am a politician interested in his own belly. I feel the pranks Vijaya has been up to recently are a challenge to the authority of the Cabinet. A spurning of that authority. In a way, an attempt to strike at the roots of our status. Eh, Pishtakeshi?

PISHTAKESHI. Without any doubt! The speech to the industrialists cancelled! And instead—a visit to the slums! Calamitous!

VRATYASOM. It doesn't seem according to our earlier expectations. She isn't prepared to confine herself prudently to the framework we've prepared for her. Let's put it in unvarnished terms. We placed her on the throne, and now she wants to plant one foot firmly on it and the other on us! Eh, Pishtakeshi? Aranyaketu here has met her personally several times. And given her several presents. But he has failed to bring her round. He can report more authoritatively on the situation.

ARANYAKETU. I did indeed meet her. But I didn't do so with the motive you mention. Not at all—

VRATYASOM. Personally, I don't believe people act motivelessly in politics, Aranyaketu. I don't think you're such a simpleton.

ARANYAKETU. We discussed the development of the island—

VRATYASOM. Quite right. But that was at Viju's instance. She just didn't allow you to bring up other subjects.

PISHTAKESHI. The royal decrees we suggest to her have recently tended to lie untouched by the seal for months on end—owing to the 'Pressure of Work.' If we give her a reminder, we are told that contact with the people is more important than royal decrees.

KARKASHIRSHA. I regard a woman who feels that making an exhibition of herself is more important than matters of State as—woman though she may be—a hundred times, a thousand times too contemptible for words!

VRATYASOM. These days I avoid gatherings and ceremonies. Who knows? There may be a speech by the Queen.

PISHTAKESHI. Take the day before yesterday. A photograph was published of her together with a foreign ambassador. I have never seen such a parade of shamelessness in my life! Her sari had fallen down a good three to three and a half inches! I lowered my head with embarrassment, Aranyaketu. What must the world be saying? [*Sighs.*]

VRATYASOM. The meaning of all this is clear. This brat of Vichitravirya's is not ready to be persuaded, or to become wise or mature. Or perhaps we should say for Aranyaketu's sake that she hasn't the capacity for it. Yes, let's not give her false blame. But say what you wish there is no longer any room for doubt. In the past seven months, she has proved vain all the high hopes we had when we planned to put her on the throne.

KARKASHIRSHA. Depose her!

VRATYASOM. And who'll be the ruler?

KARKASHIRSHA. Who? I will!

VRATYASOM [*clapping*]. Ha! No praise is too great for your temerity, Karkashirsha! What do you think we're going to say—'Go on, become the ruler, do!'—is that it? May the Almighty preserve the island from each of your many obstinacies! I don't feel at all that we have as yet agreed about it. Who should be ruler after Vijaya? Eh, Pishtakeshi?

PISHTAKESHI. There will have to be a detailed discussion on the subject. I am a democrat. I also have some rights in the matter. I definitely have the authority to contest by lawful and democratic means. And I have no intention of surrendering it. The decision must be unanimous.

VRATYASOM. It can't be. Because even your grimmest efforts have not yet succeeded in loosening my grip on the governmental machine. So I do not think that I will happily give up hopes of a still more important position. In other words, of all of you, I am the politician with the utmost regard for his belly. My opinion is that the time for this decision has not yet come. We should confine ourselves today to giving Viju a blistering idea of our strength . . . Of a kind she will understand. It is only practical to make an honest effort to chain her disloyal endeavours. I feel that if all of you bear this in mind, it should not be at all difficult. Eh, Pishtakeshi?

PISHTAKESHI. It is possible.

KARKASHIRSHA. If this is a step in the direction of deposing her, I agree to it. The indication we give her must be blunt.

ARANYAKETU. Apart from deposing her, I am amenable to any other lawful remedy.

VRATYASOM. What is Bhagadanta's opinion of all this? Since the uprisings of his Kadamba tribe on the Island against every one of us here except him, were crushed by royal decree, he has looked a little depressed at Cabinet meetings. Eh, Bhagadanta?

BHAGADANTA. Weather's bad—decision accepted.

VRATYASOM. So then it's agreed?

ALL. It's decided.

VRATYASOM. With one accord, and at the first opportunity, we give the Queen a strong reminder of our existence, one that she'll really understand.

KARKASHIRSHA. We must extinguish her totally!

PISHTAKESHI. When she's understood that she can't achieve a single thing by putting off the Cabinet, our work is done.

ARANYAKETU. I agree to everything except deposing her.

VRATYASOM [*rising*]. Thanks to Providence, even that necessity may arise quite soon. If necessary, we can give Providence a share of the power later on—eh, Pishtakeshi? Ha! Ha! Ha!

[*All stand.*]

[*Fade-out.*]

SCENE IV

Accompanied by crowd effects, an aeroplane stairway is rolled on stage, and placed against the rear curtain. At the foot of it, stand two smart bodyguards with their backs to the entrance.

A door in the curtain opens, and Queen Vijaya steps out of the plane and stands on the stairway, saluting the crowd. Cheers for her. She steps down the ladder and goes offstage. The cheering continues. The guards turn towards the audience. They are the earlier Two who form the Chorus.

THE TWO [*together*].
SUCCESSFUL FIRST YEAR!
SUCCESSFUL FIRST YEAR!
HER MAJESTY QUEEN VIJAYA'S
SUCCESSFUL FIRST YEAR!

[*Turn by turn*]

She filled the vacuum left behind when His Majesty had gone!
She raised the status of Umbugland to match that of Hindustan!
She managed to keep the Price Index firmly in hand!
She fixed the productivity of agricultural land!
Unemployment only went up 1½%!
The war against Malaria was fought from strength to strength!
Infant Mortality was remarkably reduced!
Three times the normal number of bananas were produced!
Foreign Aid statistics showed no fresh reduction!
Beggars were subjected to intensive legal action!
Ten new committees were hatched,
Five delegations despatched!
Two commissions established,
Seven commissioners dismissed!
Twenty-five new grants-in-aid,
A hundred and sixty-three promises made!

Far more oration,
But less opposition!
Yet plenty of dissatisfaction managed to appear!
HER MAJESTY QUEEN VIJAYA'S
SUCCESSFUL FIRST YEAR!
SUCCESSFUL FIRST YEAR!
SUCCESSFUL FIRST YEAR!

SCENE V

Queen Vijaya sitting alone, absorbed in writing something. Some changes in her are noticeable. More confidence. She suddenly calls out delightedly for Prannarayan. He enters.

PRANNARAYAN. What is it, Your Majesty?

VIJAYA [*slapping him on the back*]. Princess Vijaya!

PRANNARAYAN [*rubbing his back*]. Princess Vijaya! But why this affectionate compulsion? Some one will hear it, and this poor pauper will lose his job.

VIJAYA. Prannarayan, you—poor? Then the rest of us are just beggars! For past several days, as you know, I've been preparing a plan for the uplift of the Kadamba tribe. Now I've got the plan exactly as I want it. I'm very pleased with myself today—I'm very happy! If this plan of mine comes into operation, then in the next five years this original tribe of our island will become economically stable and self-supporting. Its exploitation, its wretchedness will come to an end. Do you know in what proportions this tribe exists on our island? It isn't a small figure. It's twenty per cent of the population. Fifty years ago it was thirty per cent. This ratio has been reduced constantly by hunger, poverty and diseases. In the riots after Father's death, hundreds of its people were killed. Hundreds were made refugees. Hundreds more are in prison. This tribe is very very honourable, very brave. It will endure death, but it won't be enslaved. It will not surrender. And Father totally ignored its misery. Opportunists grew rich by exploiting this tribe, they became masters of this island. Have you seen the people of this tribe, Prannarayan? I have seen them. They came and stood before my car to commit suicide. Women, children, the young, the old, all. With heads held high, as if they were saying, with no conceit, kill us. I made the driver stop the car. I got down. I mingled with them, I stayed with them, I ate with them. These people are incredible. They are just skin and bone, their bellies have sunk against their spines, their ribs stick out, their hair and beards are long and unkempt, they don't have enough clothes to cover themselves. But their eyes, Prannarayan, their eyes are like explosions of light! Their necks are straight. Their heads won't bow before anyone. Their words are measured. Their naked little children seemed to me like lion cubs. I tell you Prannarayan, to give battle to bad luck and neglect, generation after generation, to lose, to put your eyes out almost, watching for the final holocaust, and yet to keep your head erect and your lips tight, all this isn't easy, it isn't easy at all! This is something great, Prannarayan, it is something amazing, something priceless! I stayed with them, but they didn't ask anything of me. They gave to me instead. They made me take. As if they were the kings, and I the suppliant. I was tortured by their misery, my eyes swam with tears. But their eyes didn't blink for a second. Prannarayan, I am going to save this glory of the island. I am going to cherish it. Going to give it the right to live a life of respect.

PRANNARAYAN. You haven't eaten anything since morning. You haven't even taken your milk. What shall I bring you?

VIJAYA. I'm not hungry.

PRANNARAYAN. Plans won't fill your hunger.

VIJAYA. They have filled mine.

PRANNARAYAN. First drink the milk I fetch.

[*Goes out.*]

[*Bringing the milk, and handing it to her.*] In one moment you'll be ready for your dinner.

VIJAYA [*drinking*]. Why do you torment me? Take this, eat this, do this, do that—who are you, anyway?

PRANNARAYAN. Your servant.

VIJAYA. No, no! Sometimes I think of you as my mother. Prannarayan, how can a man be such a mother to anyone?

PRANNARAYAN. By not being a man.

VIJAYA. But at some moments you seem more manly than any man. No one else could give me the initimate knowledge of the world you sometimes so cruelly give. At such times I get very very angry with you—and I like you.

PRANNARAYAN. At such times, I count myself fortunate.

VIJAYA. Very often your words are those of a man, but your viewpoint is a mother's.

PRANNARAYAN. Each belongs to his kind. I am of a different kind.

VIJAYA. Who did this to you?

PRANNARAYAN. I myself don't clearly know. But the story I once heard was that I was selected for employment as a eunuch in my early childhood, and was castrated on purpose.

VIJAYA. What!

PRANNARAYAN. It is the custom of the court.

VIJAYA. In early childhood.[*shuddering*] Prannarayan!

PRANNARAYAN. I don't remember it at all. It's best not to think about it. I am as I am, and I will remain so. A man to the touch, but a woman in appearance. A being of flesh and blood, and yet a shadow. Besides, it has its advantages. Like a bat hanging from a branch, I get an upside-down but complete view of the world. And the funny thing is, that from this upside-down position, one sees the truth of the world the right way up! But let it go. Your Highness was talking about your plan.

VIJAYA. I am going to get the Cabinet's approval for this plan today.

PRANNARAYAN. Shall I bring you some more milk?

VIJAYA. Do you take me for a fool? Have I no sense?

PRANNARAYAN. Sense is a scarce commodity, which grows every moment, yet eternally falls short.

VIJAYA. This plan will raise my stature on the island. I will get the credit for achieving what has never been achieved before. This plan will make everyone understand that I am not just my father's daughter, nor a puppet ruler. From now on I plan to rule in earnest.

PRANNARAYAN. 'From now' means a voyage into the mysterious unknown. Who can tell with assurance what will be there, what will happen. Or to what destination it will lead.

VIJAYA. My confidence, my mind gives me that assurance.

PRANNARAYAN. The mind is like a lizard, it sometimes chirps the wrong note.

VIJAYA. What is your opinion, Prannarayan? Is my dream not going to come true?

PRANNARAYAN. To say it will, only after it actually does, would be more realistic.

VIJAYA. Prannarayan, I'm getting angry with you!

PRANNARAYAN. Punish me, Your Majesty.

[*Vijaya takes a tight grip on his hair. They both look at each other, and slowly a smile comes onto their faces. Enter a maidservant.*]

MAIDSERVANT. The Cabinet is approaching.

VIJAYA [*letting Prannarayan go*]. Go. Just see what I'll achieve now.

[*Enter Karkashirsha, Vratyasom, Pishtakeshi, Bhagadanta and Aranyaketu.*]

VIJAYA [*bowing to them*]. Come in, Karkashirsha! Come, Vratyasom, Pishtakeshi, Bhagadanta. [*To Aranyaketu*] Come in. Do sit down all of you. [*They sit*]. Well, Uncle Karkashirsha, how's your blood pressure? Uncle Pishtakeshi, I've been seeing you since my childhood, but you're still exactly the same as you always were. Vratyasom, too, hasn't changed a bit, except for his thinning hair. And don't you think that lately Bhagadanta has started talking a little more? Usually he's silent whenever you notice him! Well, Aranyaketu, you haven't been to see me for several days. All of you must have received copies of the memorandum I sent to you about my new plan. Now I've prepared a preliminary draft in full detail. It's come out very well.

[*They are silent.*]

What will you take? Uncle Karkashirsha? Vratyasom? Bhagadanta? Pishtakeshi? No, no, you must drink something.

KARKASHIRSHA. Nothing, thank you.

[*They are all silent.*]

VIJAYA. This won't do! It's so many days since all you colleagues have come to see me together.

[*She claps. Enter a maidservant.*]

Bring something to drink.

[*Exit the maidservant.*]

I was talking about my plan.

[*Vijaya is serious. Pishtakeshi starts to cough. All the others are silent.*]

[*Waiting for the coughing to stop*] You must have got a fair idea from the memorandum. Have a look at the detailed draft if you wish.

[*She hands some pieces of paper to Aranyaketu. The papers are circulated among all the Ministers. Pishtakeshi starts coughing once more. This time it doesn't stop. Vijaya takes a glass of the lemonade brought by the maidservant and gives it to him. After he has drunk it his cough subsides. All are once more silent.*]

I invited you here to discuss this plan. You will all notice that the rehabilitation of Kadambas . . .

[*Pishtakeshi goes into the attitude of coughing. Vijaya waits for him to cough. The cough does not come.*]

Take something for your cough, Pishtakeshi. I have prepared this plan in order to rehabilitate the Kadambas.

VRATYASOM. What?

VIJAYA. This plan. That is what I am talking about.

[*Vratyasom gets up and goes out. Vijaya stares at him.*]

Why has he gone out?

[*Pishtakeshi begins to cough. All the rest look on slightly amused. Vratyasom returns.*]

VRATYASOM. Your pardon. Please repeat it for me, from the beginning.

VIJAYA. I haven't told much as yet. The plan is for the rehabilitation of the Kadamba tribe—the one I gave into your hands just now.

[*Bhagadanta gets up and starts to search high and low.*]

What are you looking for, Bhagadanta?

BHAGADANTA [*giving a smile, and starting to search once more*]. The plan.

VIJAYA. Here it is, with Karkashirsha.

KARKASHIRSHA. Who said it wasn't?

VIJAYA. This tribe is the original tribe of our island.

VRATYASOM. Which one?

VIJAYA. The Kadambas, of course. It is about them that we're talking.

VRATYASOM. I thought you meant the tribe of rats.

[*Looks at Aranyaketu.*]

VIJAYA. Rats? What have rats to do with this?

VRATYASOM. It seems they were here on the island before the Kadambas.

VIJAYA. We are talking of human beings.

KARKASHIRSHA. Then let us not mention the Kadambas.

VIJAYA. Why?

KARKASHIRSHA. They are not men, they are traitors.

VIJAYA. I think this conversation is growing very strange. Firstly, to say that traitors are not human beings, is—

[*Pishtakeshi starts to cough again.*]

—is not true, moreover, to say that the whole tribe consists of traitors also—

VRATYASOM [*to Pishtakeshi*]. Take a deep breath, and it'll stop. Go on, take a deep breath. I tell you, take one.

[*Pishtakeshi's cough ceases.*]

And it is unforgiveable that you shouldn't think of putting two cloves in your pocket before coming to this council.

PISHTAKESHI. But I didn't have a cough then.

VRATYASOM [*to Vijaya*]. Excuse me. Do go on. [*to Pishtakeshi*] To wait till you have a cough before you keep some cloves ready is in itself an error of judgment. Who knows when a cough will start? [*to Vijaya*] Forgive me. Do go on. I'm attentive. Something about the 'complete tribe'—

KARKASHIRSHA. I think it was about the 'complete truth.'

PISHTAKESHI. Because of my cough, I didn't hear it clearly, but I think it was about 'complete treachery'—

VIJAYA [*patiently taking a deep breath*]. I was saying how unjust it was to regard an entire tribe as traitors.

KARKASHIRSHA. Don't tell me anything about the Kadambas. They drink liquor!

VRATYASOM. We drink liquor too, Karkashirsha. That is, I for one drink it openly. Of course, I drink only high-class stuff.

PISHTAKESHI. I only take it like a medicine at political assemblies. [*Handkerchief over his mouth.*]

VRATYASOM. Don't speak! Your cough will start up again. What happened so suddenly to cause it the moment you got here?

[*Bhagadanta hunts out a clove and gives it to Pishtakeshi.*]

Now that is foresight! Bhagadanta keeps cloves with him even when he doesn't have a cough—mark that! [*This to Vijaya.*]

VIJAYA [*insincerely*]. Yes, of course. Well, some time ago, when I was on tour, I acquired an intimate knowledge of the condition of the tribe.

VRATYASOM. Which one?

VIJAYA. We're talking about the Kadambas!

VRATYASOM [*to Bhagadanta*]. Did I mention anything about rats?

VIJAYA. Vratyasom, we are now going to talk about the Kadamba tribe.

KARKASHIRSHA. By we you mean yourself. Personally I can't bear to hear that tribe mentioned! Filthy people!

VIJAYA. They're filthy because we've kept them so.

VRATYASOM. [*to Pishtakeshi*]. I myself have a bath every day.

VIJAYA. For cleanliness, you need certain amenities. Sometimes in an entire settlement of the Kadambas there isn't a single lavatory; can you imagine it?

PISHTAKESHI. Before I became a Minister, the place where I stayed had only one lavatory for every three families.

VIJAYA. Pishtakeshi, what is one lavatory for three families compared with no lavatory at all in an entire settlement?

VRATYASOM. A lavatory is a luxury that comes with cultural progress. In our village, there isn't as yet a single lavatory. Come there with me; I'll show you. For years together my village has existed without a lavatory. And yet you won't find one example of treason there! That's the village I come from. I call theirs true patriotism, Karkashirsha.

KARKASHIRSHA. Vratyasom, what connection is there between loyalty and a lavatory!

VIJAYA. That's enough! That is not the subject in hand. We are talking about the condition of the Kadamba tribe.

KARKASHIRSHA. In other words, Your Majesty is talking about it.

[*Pishtakeshi holds his handkerchief to his nose and mouth.*]

You are about to cough again, aren't you, Pishtakeshi?

PISHTAKESHI. Who says I am?

VIJAYA. Now look here! You had better listen carefully and without interruption to what I have to say. Why this sad condition—of the Kadamba tribe—came about, it is fruitless to discuss now.

BHAGADANTA [*smiling to Aranyaketu*]. King Vichitravirya, that's why!

ARANYAKETU. There is no point in picking that bone today, Bhagadanta. Let's proceed.

VIJAYA. On seeing the state of the tribe, I was extremely disturbed. I felt that something must be done about this—some remedy—some plan—

[*Pishtakeshi starts to cough.*]

[*A little angrily*] Pishtakeshi, you can go out till your cough is better, if you wish.

[*Pishtakeshi rises and goes towards the door, coughing.*]

KARKASHIRSHA. I disagree with this! May I know for what crime Pishtakeshi is being sent out?

VIJAYA. He is not being sent out. There is no objection to his returning once his cough is better.

KARKASHIRSHA. I regard a cough as a natural reflex beyond human control—

VIJAYA [*losing her poise*]. I don't mind, but will you please shut up!

VRATYASOM [*standing up*]. That was dictatorial! I will not sit calmly and watch all this! To tell a Cabinet Minister to shut up is a blow struck at freedom of speech! Eh, Aranyaketu? Eh, Pishtakeshi?

PISHTAKESHI [*standing, his handkerchief still over his mouth*]. This is undemocratic.

BHAGADANTA [*standing up and smiling at the others*]. A walk-out?

VIJAYA. Look here, this is a lot of foolishness—

VRATYASOM. Ha! 'Foolishness'! Now it's slander against the Cabinet! I've reached the limits of my patience!

KARKASHIRSHA. This is a sign of no confidence in the Cabinet.

PISHTAKESHI. We weren't shown such disrespect even by the late King! 'Foolishness'!

VIJAYA. Look, it wasn't at all my intention to insult the Cabinet—

VRATYASOM. This is an attempt to salvage what's gone!

KARKASHIRSHA. An insult is an insult!

PISHTAKESHI. Today is the limit!

VRATYASOM. No, Karkashirsha, there is only one way to wash away the smear of this slander—

PISHTAKESHI. Resignation!

KARKASHIRSHA. I'll hand mine in first!

PISHTAKESHI. Mine too—and yours, Aranyaketu?

ARANYAKETU [*in a dilemma*]. I don't wish to stay apart from you—

BHAGADANTA [*smiling*]. Are we to give it? Our resignation?

VRATYASOM. There is no other alternative at all for us! The very dignity of the Cabinet has been undermined!

PISHTAKESHI. And an attempt has been made to undermine the foundations of democracy!

KARKASHIRSHA. The Murder of the Constitution!

[*Prannarayan enters and stands behind Pishtakeshi, with a bow.*]

PISHTAKESHI [*to Prannarayan*]. What is it?

PRANNARAYAN. Lozenges to help you cough. Excuse me—lozenges to cure your cough.

[*Pishtakeshi puts one in his mouth.*]

VIJAYA [*keeping sight of the draft plan at the root of all this uproar, says in changed and stagey tones*]. As I have unwittingly insulted the

Cabinet, I am prepared, if you wish, to express my apologies for the error.

[*They all sit down, glum again.*]

This plan is very important. I am not important but the plan is. Look at it. It is essential that it should be approved. I am confident that the Cabinet will be in accord with me over this.

KARKASHIRSHA
VRATYASOM   } [*glumly*]. No.
PISHTAKESHI

VIJAYA. But—there is a fundamental and historical need to redress the wrongs endured by the Kadamba tribe for centuries. It is not only in the interests of progress on the island, but in order to raise its stature internationally—

[*Karkashirsha, Vratyasom and Pishtakeshi look blankly at each other.*]

How is it that you can't understand such a simple thing? The terrible exploitation of the Kadamba tribe for so many years is a very great stigma on humanity. And on the traditions of this island. It is a stain on you, on me—

[*Karkashirsha, Pishtakeshi and Vratyasom shrug their shoulders, as if they can't make head or tail of it.*]

VIJAYA. While this stigma is in existence, we do not have the right to enjoy one taste of comfort.

KARKASHIRSHA. On account of my gastric trouble, I have tasted nothing but bread and milk daily for the past twenty-one years.

VRATYASOM [*to Pishtakeshi*]. No one can come between me and the taste of comfort. I eat only once a day, but to my heart's content!

PISHTAKESHI. In spite of equal opportunity, the Kadamba tribe fell back in the race for progress, that's all. Why should others consider that a stain on themselves?

KARKASHIRSHA. Besides, this tribe is immoral! They drink liquor, their women have two husbands at a time! Their way of living is totally disgusting! And to top it all, treason! There is no forgiveness for rebellion against constituted authority. If I had a gun, I would gladly destroy the whole tribe, Vratyasom.

VIJAYA. I am amazed that you can talk like this! Those starved but proud faces, those mouths tight-lipped with suffering, those bellies sunk against spines—those skeletons—

VRATYASOM. Ha! This is the doctrine of Universal Love! I don't believe in that rot! The problems of a nation can't be solved by

Universal Love. They need prompt action. A certain tribe is being destroyed because it has no share in the national progress, isn't it? I say, let it be destroyed! Pity is unpragmatic. First think of the other, more developed section of our society—think how it can be given greater conveniences and comforts, how more and more modernity can be brought into its life, how its standard of living can be brought into line with that of the developed nations. Think of that! Let a tribe destroying itself, be destroyed!

[*Pishtakeshi and Karkashirsha start clapping.*]

VIJAYA [*Her endurance sorely tried*]. You are entitled to a different opinion. I may disagree. But it is absolutely vital that this plan of mine should receive the assent of the Cabinet. In my view, this plan is a very important one. Behind it, is the promise I have made to those people. I wish to wipe away the terrible injustice that has been taking place from the time of my father and other kings. I wish to be released from my mental anguish. I have prepared this—this plan—after a lot of thought. My whole prestige is bound up with it. I so—so badly want it to be passed. It is my hope that the Cabinet will consent.

[*They are all glum. Aranyaketu is restless.*]

As soon as the Ministers have signed the plan, it is my desire to take immediate steps to have it put into operation. If it is not accepted, I—I will consider it a challenge to my honour. If this happens, we cannot ignore the adverse consequences that may possibly result. I feel sure that the plan will be approved.

[*Explosive silence. All glum. Aranyaketu fidgets about and whispers to the others.*]

As soon as the Ministers have signed the plan, it is my desire to take immediate steps to have it put into operation. The pens are over there.

[*They are all glum. Aranyaketu is in a fix. Bhagadanta's smile, however, is constant. Then they all rise. They bow to Vijaya, and walk out. Last of all goes Aranyaketu. As they walk out, Vijaya, in a fury, smashes the glass in front of her.*]

VIJAYA [*choking with rage*]. Bastards! Swine! Inhuman wretches! Misers! Muckworms! 'A tribe's being destroyed, isn't it? Let it!' As if it's their own bloody property!

[*Spits in the direction of the door they have gone out of. Her rage is still not relieved. She is in a total fury.*]

Pigs! Jackals! Mangy dogs! Slimy muckworms!

[*Enter Prannarayan. He pauses.*]

PRANNARAYAN. Did Your Highness call me?

VIJAYA [*with her back to him fiercely*]. No!

PRANNARAYAN [*noticing her mood*]. I await your punishment.

VIJAYA. Why are men so wicked, so low, so horrible, so mean, so miserly? Why?

PRANNARAYAN. Because they are.

VIJAYA. But why are they?

PRANNARAYAN. Because they are men.

VIJAYA. It's disgusting! It's horrible!

PRANNARAYAN. It is.

VIJAYA. This has to be wiped out! Prannarayan, my blood's just boiling!

PRANNARAYAN. When one's pride is ablaze, the blood does boil.

VIJAYA. What? Pride!

PRANNARAYAN. Which everyone has, and through which everyone gets hurt. Men and nations live by pride alone.

VIJAYA [*angrily*]. My motives are pure! I want to give status to the poor people of this island.

PRANNARAYAN. Perhaps thereby Your Highness wishes to increase your own! The motive of improving your own position on this Island may also be hidden behind this pure motive—

VIJAYA. Prannarayan!

PRANNARAYAN. Your motive may also be an obstinate desire to make what hasn't happened, happen in the end . . .

[*Vijaya has begun to smoulder.*]

The ambition to rule in earnest and without restraint . . .

VIJAYA. Prannarayan, have you considered carefully before saying these words?

PRANNARAYAN. No, I was just remembering them. The words are Your Highness' own; the interpretation is mine. Your Highness yourself said sometime ago, while talking to me, that you wish to have the credit of achieving what had not yet been achieved. You wish to show that you are not just your father's daughter, nor a puppet ruler. Your Highness said, 'I am going to rule in real earnest from now on.'

VIJAYA [*remembering*]. Even so, the motive behind this plan of mine isn't selfish, really it isn't!

PRANNARAYAN. I am not a Minister. It's not the slightest use convincing me. Now calm yourself, Your Highness.

VIJAYA. It is hardly over yet.

PRANNARAYAN. It has touched a tender spot—Your Highness's pride.

VIJAYA. I'll be revenged for this, Prannarayan!

PRANNARAYAN [*proffering a glass of cordial*]. First drink this—it's a cool herbal drink. Sprinkle a little coolness on your inflamed temper.

[*She drinks the cordial and hands the glass back to him.*]

VIJAYA [*still restless*]. Prannarayan, how do men become so base?

PRANNARAYAN. In the same way that ambitions arise. In the same way that I am what I am. Through an unseen justice which is beyond their knowledge.

VIJAYA. Something in me is changing greatly, Prannarayan. I feel afraid of myself, very afraid.

PRANNARAYAN. One should not look inwards too much. One should always look outwards. That way one retains ambitions.

[*Vijaya clutches his hair tight. Looks at him fiercely. Then a smile comes over her face. A smile of comprehension comes over his face, too.*]

CURTAIN

ACT THREE

SCENE I

The curtain rises. The Two are standing on stage holding giant pens.

THE TWO [*together*].
GRAVE EMERGENCY!
SERIOUS PREDICAMENT!
ENCOUNTER NOW BEGINS BETWEEN
 HER MAJESTY AND THE CABINET!

 [*Turn by turn*]

First Round!
First Round!

Her Majesty's plan for Kadamba rehabilitation
Rejected by the Ministers. Her Majesty's declaration
'Serious Consequences' [Intended to denote
'Beginning of Emergency'—*Editorial Note.*]
Ministers get together for important collocution.
Details unavailable. Queen holds the solution.
Ministers give interview. 'WE'RE FULL OF RESOLUTION'.
Depending on which side displays most determination
Will emerge the consequences of this anxious situation.

All eyes centre upon the Encounter!
All eyes centre upon the Encounter!

Unique Confrontation!
Historic Confrontation!
The Ruler of the Palace
and the Leaders of the Nation!
Constitutional Crisis!
—Our Mortification!
Terrible Calamity.
Shattering of Unity.
Dark Tribulation.
Disaster for the Nation!

 [*Together*]

GRAVE EMERGENCY!
SERIOUS PREDICAMENT!
ENCOUNTER NOW BEGINS BETWEEN

HER MAJESTY AND THE CABINET!

[*Turn by turn*]

First Round!
First Round!
By refusing their respect
They gave the plan a kick!
By refusing to have the plan
They gave respect a kick!

Who's winning?
Who's sneezing?
Who's losing?
Who's humbled?
Who's tumbled?
Who's rising?
Who's technically succeeded?
Who's morally defeated?

Our Foundation subsides.
Our Importance landslides.
A Blow to Our Prestige.
A Danger to Our Image.
Worthy of our mention!
Worthy of attention!
Most Appetizing!
Most Agonizing!

Behind the Scenes News!
Under-the-Carpet News!

Everything depends on—
Everything suspends from—
We must be more vigilant—
We must be observant—

[*Together*]

That's all for now. More in our next edition.
GRAVE EMERGENCY!
SERIOUS PREDICAMENT!
ENCOUNTER NOW BEGINS BETWEEN
HER MAJESTY AND THE CABINET!

[*Drums begin to beat. Ministers and the Queen enter with cross*

expressions and march separately. They do not come face to face at all.
Behind stage, all are cheered turn by turn. They go offstage.]

THE TWO [*together*].
   GRAVE EMERGENCY!
   SERIOUS PREDICAMENT!
   FIRST ROUND OF ENCOUNTER OVER!
   SITUATION TENSE!

   [*Turn by turn.*]

   What's the Queen stewing?
   What are the Ministers brewing?
   Queen's significant vacation!
   Ministers' mystery expedition!
   Most important knot combed out of one of Her Majesty's tresses!
   Spot of gloom observed upon the Cabinet Ministers' faces!
   Karkashirsha's silence daily growing grimmer.
   Garlic in increased amounts in Pishtakeshi's dinner.
   Vratyasom has had the barber newly trim his pate.
   Aranyaketu and Bhagadanta have had a tete-a-tete!
   Queen refuses interview to all correspondents.
   Spokesman states the coming month is sure to be important.

   Queen loses First Round!
   Ministers win First Round!
   Five triumph in First Round!
   Queen down in First Round!
   It appears to us that—
   There is no reason to doubt that—
   We logically infer that—
   We emphatically state that—
   We unequivocally note that—
   We firmly opine that—
   It is irremediable that—
   It is unavoidable that—
   History has made it sooth that—
   It is an enduring truth that—

   The occupation of Politics is totally without reason!
   No one knows what's going to emerge in the coming season!
   Read our Next Edition! Meanwhile one understands
   The trump cards are all in the Ministers' hands!

   [*Exit the Two.*]

SCENE II

The Ministers have gathered. They are celebrating a birthday. Funny hats on their heads. Decorations. Food. Music. All five are dancing around in tune to the music.

BHAGADANTA [*suddenly, to the others, pointing to Prannarayan*]. Messenger.

VRATYASOM. He can wait a little while. Dance!

KARKASHIRSHA [*stopping, to the bowing Prannarayan*]. What is it?

PRANNARAYAN [*holding out a letter*]. A letter from Her Majesty.

PISHTAKESHI. Her Majesty is well, isn't she?

PRANNARAYAN. Thanks to your good wishes, yes. [*Bowing in front of Vratyasom*] Your servant's congratulations on your lordship's birthday.

VRATYASOM [*accepting*]. Thank you, thank you. Karkashirsha, open the letter. What does Viju have to say?

[*Claps, and says to the servant who enters.*]

Give this messenger some refreshment and some remuneration to celebrate my birthday.

[*Exit the servant. Karkashirsha, who has opened the letter, and is reading it, stiffens suddenly.*]

KARKASHIRSHA [*biting his lips*]. So?

ARANYAKETU. What's in the letter, Karkashirsha?

PISHTAKESHI. Is it notice of a new Cabinet meeting?

VRATYASOM. Some new plan?

KARKASHIRSHA [*reading the letter*]. Horrible!

VRATYASOM. What's horrible? [*Takes the letter.*] I see.

PISHTAKESHI. What's happened? What do you see? [*Reads the letter.*] So she's beating the same old path. [*Hands it to Aranyaketu.*]

ARANYAKETU [*reading it*]. It doesn't bear thinking of! [*Gives it to Bhagadanta.*]

BHAGADANTA [*looking at it and giving it back smiling*]. Can't read. Illiterate!

PISHTAKESHI. She's not going to wait for the assent of the Cabinet. She is going to put the plan into operation on her own authority!

VRATYASOM. This is humiliation for the Cabinet!

KARKASHIRSHA. Insolence!

VRATYASOM. The same mad enthusiasm!

PISHTAKESHI. The meaning of this is absolutely clear. She hasn't learnt a thing from what has happened.

ARANYAKETU. This is a grave blow to me!

VRATYASOM. This is rebellion on the part of that bitch!

KARKASHIRSHA. This is high treason!

PISHTAKESHI. Does she think she can throw our opposition out with the rubbish?

ARANYAKETU. I was not opposed to the plan in principle—but the way in which—terrible!

VRATYASOM [*reading through the letter again and again*]. Ha! A Royal Decree about the plan, already issued!

KARKASHIRSHA. We are only informed about it after the fact!

PISHTAKESHI. Don't we count?

VRATYASOM. We do, Pishtakeshi! But after this, we will have to prove it. Honeyed words are not going to make that bitch any wiser.

PISHTAKESHI. She's a born dictator!

KARKASHIRSHA. Even if my head's cut off, I won't let this brat born yesterday stamp on it.

VRATYASOM. Is this the reward for sixty years of political drudgery? I won't accept it!

ARANYAKETU. The letter is genuine, isn't it? A forgery, maybe?

VRATYASOM [*giving him the letter*]. Read it yourself, Aranyaketu! Horrible, horrible! This bitter blow had to come on my birthday!

PISHTAKESHI. This is a public insult to the Cabinet!

VRATYASOM. This royal decree is tantamount to proclaiming that we are a puppet Cabinet!

KARKASHIRSHA. We will never endure this!

PISHTAKESHI. We must tackle this squarely!

BHAGADANTA [*rising, with a smile*]. Our resignations?

VRATYASOM. No, confrontation. Let's go at it!

PISHTAKESHI. Yes, we must.

VRATYASOM. Aranyaketu, Bhagadanta, it's no good surrendering meekly now. This is a terrible insult! We must not ignore this. We must not let the time come when a brat born yesterday can teach us lessons.

KARKASHIRSHA. If it comes it'll overwhelm us.

PISHTAKESHI. We must kill this insolence at its source!

VRATYASOM. Yes, we must!

KARKASHIRSHA. Messenger, go this instant and tell the Queen that—

PRANNARAYAN [*bowing*]. Forgive me, but the moment Her Majesty had put the letter in my hands, she went to her bedchamber to lie down—

VRATYASOM. She went to lie down?

PRANNARAYAN. Slowly and surely, she fell into a deep sleep.

PISHTAKESHI. She fell asleep?

PRANNARAYAN. She had already written the Royal Decree. It has already been promulgated all over the island.

ARANYAKETU. It's been promulgated!

PRANNARAYAN. Yes, tomorrow it will be put into operation.

VRATYASOM ⎫ Put into operation? Ha! Horrible!
KARKASHIRSHA ⎬ Unspeakable! Vengeance!
PISHTAKESHI ⎭ Give her a strong answer!

VRATYASOM. Messenger, move on. We are coming immediately to meet the Queen.

PRANNARAYAN [*bowing*]. Forgive me, together with this letter, Her Majesty left a strict command that she was not to be woken before dawn.

VRATYASOM. Her Majesty, Her Majesty! Who is this Majesty of yours? She's just a brat born yesterday!

PRANNARAYAN. Forgive me, it is your privilege to say so. But this humblest of servants regrets it.

KARKASHIRSHA. It was the Cabinet that made you Chamberlain of the Queen's apartments.

PRANNARAYAN. While he is that, it will be this humble servant's duty to obey the Queen's orders.

VRATYASOM. Ha! You're fired!

PRANNARAYAN. Her Majesty considers that, according to the new arrangements, that is Her Majesty's own privilege.

PISHTAKESHI. 'Her Majesty considers'! What do you consider?

PRANNARAYAN. Forgive my frankness, but until I receive an order from Her Majesty to the contrary, I consider myself the Chamberlain of her apartments.

KARKASHIRSHA. You know the punishment you'll get for insulting the Cabinet, don't you?

PRANNARAYAN. The thought of insult never crossed your humble servant's mind. You are all mighty Ministers. Your servant just knows the facts of the situation.

VRATYASOM. It's all right, let him go. Dawn is not far off.

PISHTAKESHI. Go.

PRANNARAYAN. Any answer to the letter?

KARKASHIRSHA. At dawn.

[*Prannarayan bows and exits.*]

VRATYASOM. Ha! Executing the plan without the approval of the Cabinet. A direct decree!

KARKASHIRSHA. Murder of tradition!

PISHTAKESHI. Abandonment of principle!

VRATYASOM. Experienced ministers thrown out with the rubbish!

BHAGADANTA [*gets up smiling*]. Confrontation?

VRATYASOM. Yes, confrontation. This insult will not be tolerated!

KARKASHIRSHA. We must answer a thug with thuggery!

ARANYAKETU. This entire affair is lamentable!

VRATYASOM. We must cut short our lamentation and get ready for
battle, Aranyaketu. There is no time for sorrow! That little brat
has given us blow after blow. Now the only answer is a still
stronger blow.

PISHTAKESHI. We must decide our policy.

KARKASHIRSHA. We must draw up a plan of action!

[*They all come together hurriedly.*]

PISHTAKESHI. I will take the chair. Not that I crave for any power,
but—

VRATYASOM. Pishtakeshi, now no delay any further. The enemy is
at our door.

ARANYAKETU. This was against all our expectations.

PISHTAKESHI. I declare this meeting open.

VRATYASOM [*standing up*]. We must play our cards carefully. Our
opponent is not a negligible one. At least the answer she has
given us is scarcely negligible.

KARKASHIRSHA. My blood pressure is rising.

PISHTAKESHI. Continue, Vratyasom. Let this meeting hear your
advice.

VRATYASOM. That is what I'm giving. The important point is that
this plan of the enemy concerns the Kadamba tribe. This is its
strength, and this is also its weakness. I mean, now at least, we
must consider the situation dispassionately. This is its strength
because the Kadamba tribe will definitely be on the side of the
plan. And this is its weakness because precisely on this score we
can engineer an uprising against the plan.

KARKASHIRSHA. Don't unnecessarily bring the people into this,
Vratyasom. That creates needless confusion in political matters.

VRATYASOM. But if we use this very confusion skilfully, we can put
a firm, and decisive noose around our opponent's neck, Karkashirsha. Let's use that skill! Ha! So, Pishtakeshi, Aranyaketu,
Karkashirsha, you—Bhagadanta—Vratyasom—I mean myself—
we will make the next round the people's round. We must get rid
of this situation before it spreads. It wouldn't be in our interests
to let her stay on the throne after this. We must gather a mob!

We must incite the people! We must loose upon her the tidal wave of an infuriated mob. That's what'll rock her! She's still raw, she's an inexperienced child. She's calling like a jackal; she hasn't as yet seen the angry roaring tiger of the mob. Brave men tremble when they see this fourteenth wonder of the world rushing towards them, shouting till throats are hoarse, attacking with stones. What's a raw girl going to do? We'll force her to surrender! We'll make her submit! Aranyaketu, you incite your followers. Karkashirsha, the common people are just a headache to a man of harsh principles like yourself. But the times are unusual. You must take on the responsibility of some of the people.

KARKASHIRSHA. I'm sorry—don't know any of the common people in any part of the island, let alone in my own. The unprincipled, defective, spineless, vapid, stupid, and baseborn faces I meet in the road or at political assemblies—

VRATYASOM. Even if the description is somewhat exaggerated, that is what the dictionary of politics calls the common people.

KARKASHIRSHA. I feel it ignominious even to go before this 'People' of yours.

VRATYASOM. There is no need for that. Like any other goods that are available wholesale, the people, too, have their agents. They will sell any stupid idea to the mob. In return, they ask for its anger. Of course, when using this anger for political purposes, statesmen have to give these agents some payment—either money or concessions or protection—because the mob is not a full-time business with some of them. Their business is separate and requires several types of protection.

KARKASHIRSHA. All this does not fit into my framework of principles—

VRATYASOM. If you want yourself and your principles to survive, Karkashirsha, this is what you'll have to do. Do you think I am happy to involve myself with this affair of the mob? It's essential just now, only as a stratagem; that's why we must do it.

KARKASHIRSHA. Very well.

PISHTAKESHI. So this advice is acceptable to everyone? Will those who don't agree please raise their hands.

[*Aranyaketu's hand goes up.*]

VRATYASOM. Ha!

ARANYAKETU. I have only one doubt.

VRATYASOM. I expected as much.

ARANYAKETU. This stratagem of yours concerning the mob—
VRATYASOM. Not mine, *ours*.
ARANYAKETU. Very well, supposing that our stratagem is answered by the Queen with troops, there will be bloodshed.
VRATYASOM. Ha! There will! What's wrong with shedding a little blood? As long as it's not your own!
ARANYAKETU. And perhaps the Kadamba tribe may be maddened by the opposition to the plan, and start burning other settlements or destroying marketplaces.
VRATYASOM. You forget, Aranyaketu, that our mob will answer the Kadambas in the same way.
ARANYAKETU. I think this is all dreadful.
PISHTAKESHI. Aranyaketu, you forget that what has happened is more dreadful still. This is a matter of life and death for the Cabinet. If we stay quiet, we're done for . . .
VRATYASOM. The reply we give to the dreadful things that have happened must be the most dreadful possible.
ARANYAKETU. But the destruction of innocent lives and valuable property—
VRATYASOM. For an experienced politician, you use embarrassing terminology. Destruction brings change. Anyone who cannot watch even the greatest destruction dispassionately is in my opinion no politician at all. Eh, Karkashirsha?
KARKASHIRSHA. Principles are even more important than human lives!
VRATYASOM. And by 'principles' you mean anything worth grabbing! Shake hands on that.

[*Karkashirsha does not shake his hand.*]

Well, Aranyaketu, any other doubts?

[*Aranyaketu, torn two ways, is silent.*]

Then we are all agreed on this plan.

[*Bhagadanta rises, smiling.*]

Eh, Bhagadanta?
BHAGADANTA [*smiling on*]. Not agreed. I'm a Kadamba.
VRATYASOM. Ha! You may be a Kadamba, but you abandoned the Kadambas, and became one of us, when you were made a Minister.
KARKASHIRSHA. You cannot go against the majority decision, Bhagadanta.

PISHTAKESHI. You'll have to fall in with what the Cabinet agrees to do.

VRATYASOM. Think of your Ministership!

BHAGADANTA. For that alone, agreed. But if dangerous to life, then not agreed. Our tribesmen, very cruel. Will stay Minister, if living!

[*Shrugs his shoulders.*]

VRATYASOM. The Cabinet will protect you.

BHAGADANTA. Our tribesmen, still crueller.

ARANYAKETU. Besides, even if Her Majesty's methods are wrong, the plan for rehabilitating the Kadambas is quite good in principle.

VRATYASOM. Ha! 'Quite good'! Why won't it get into your thick skull, Aranyaketu, that this plan is not for the rehabilitation of the Kadambas, but for the destruction of the Cabinet? This is the Queen's political malice! And you're being taken in by it! You have feelings of partiality for the Queen—you remain in the Cabinet and try to stay on her side too—you propitiate her—the Cabinet may at any time decide to take a serious view of all this—

ARANYAKETU [*frightened*]. A mistake! A total error! I only show respect for the throne as a Minister should. And whatever happens I am on your side at this moment—as God is my witness!

KARKASHIRSHA. Please keep God out of political discussions.

ARANYAKETU. I just referred to Him by way of conveying—

VRATYASOM. So we may take it that you are now willing to share the responsibility of the Ministers' decision, Aranyaketu?

ARANYAKETU [*still torn two ways, but nodding*]. Yes. . . .

BHAGADANTA [*smiling*]. Indifferent. [*Stands up, smiling*] Shall I go?

[*Exit Bhagadanta at once, smiling.*]

PISHTAKESHI [*disturbed and worried*]. Bhagadanta's gone . . .

VRATYASOM. Let him go.

KARKASHIRSHA. May his soul rest in peace.

VRATYASOM. Pishtakeshi, we will go forward, definitely we shall, together with whoever will join us, without any who won't and we will knock down those who oppose us. The Cabinet's resolution is firm!

PISHTAKESHI. A battle with the Queen is inevitable.

VRATYASOM. In the cause of democracy—

KARKASHIRSHA. For the sake of principle—

PISHTAKESHI. For Umbugland's glorious future—

VRATYASOM. At least fifty martyrs must sacrifice their lives. Property worth at least five or seven hundred thousand must be wrecked. May the people live for ever!

PISHTAKESHI. Long Live the People!

(Fade-out.)

SCENE III

A marching song begins to play. Some people enter carrying banners etc. They start to march in various formations; their shouts are as follows:

> To the Palace!
> Surround the Palace!
> Suspend the Kadamba Plan!
> Victory to Democracy!
> Long live the Cabinet!
> Long live the People!
> Make the Queen abdicate!

[*Slowly more and more people join them. They start marching around together. It acquires the look of a gathering. The Two of the Chorus now enter and start to march with the rest. The rest march offstage during a pause in the marching song. The Two remain.*]

THE TWO [*together*].
MINISTERS' ATTACK!
QUEEN'S COUNTER-ATTACK!
DRAMA OF ENCOUNTER
GOES INTO ANOTHER ACT!

[*Turn by turn*]

Through the Ministers' Party, Her Majesty Drives a Wedge.
Bhagadanta Splits; Aranyaketu Planning to Renege.
Kadamba Plan to go into Immediate Operation.
Ministers Allege Part Played by Enemies of Nation!
Is Decree Against the Law? Supreme Court Petition!
'Ministers Not Party to Her Majesty's Decision.'
Aranyaketu's Brave Attempts to Play the Middle Man.
Queen gives Bhagadanta Highest Order of Umbugland!
Vratyasom Addresses All the Heads of Industry.
Karkashirsha Plants a Tree Inside a Monastery.

Pishtakeshi Interviewed by UMBUGLAND EXPRESS.
All Three Confident that they will End up with Success.
Kadambas March Out Towards Her Majesty's Residence.
Kadamba Leader and the Queen have Serious Conference.
Bhagadanta Present by a Special Invitation.
Supreme Court Orders Stay on Plan for Rehabilitation!
News of Order Reaches Queen. Her Majesty's Policy Stable.
Plan will Start to Operate According to Time-Table.
Queen Presented Scroll by the Kadamba Federation.
Read all about encounter in our Sunday Edition!

The Queen's going to lose!
The Queen's going to win!
The Ministers will lose!
The Ministers will win!

Aranyaketu's mediation promises to succeed!
Aranyaketu's mediation ending in defeat!

Queen's party jubilant.
Ministers' party triumphant.

In principal, Her Majesty's actions are legitimate.
In honesty, the Ministers' doings are of benefit.
The Queen is sometimes partly wrong.
The Ministers' case is sometimes strong.
We cannot say this one is worthless.
We cannot say that one is useless.
That has something sooth in it.
This has a grain of truth in it.
This is thought-provoking.
That must be accepted.
That must be rejected.
But this is stimulating.
This offers plenty of room for hope;
That promises a pact.

**DRAMA OF ENCOUNTERS
GOES INTO ANOTHER ACT!**

SCENE IV

*An apartment in the royal palace. Vijaya is aiming at a target. Beside her
sits Bhagadanta, smiling.*

VIJAYA [*taking aim at a demonic face on the wall*]. Bhagadanta, who's this one for?

BHAGADANTA [*smiling*]. Vratyasom.

VIJAYA [*throws, then*] Missed!

BHAGADANTA [*smiling*]. You'll hit him!

VIJAYA. Who are we, Bhagadanta?

BHAGADANTA [*smiling*]. Benefactress of the Kadambas.

VIJAYA. And?

BHAGADANTA. The Ever Victorious.

VIJAYA [*taking aim again*]. Now who's this one for?

BHAGADANTA. Karkashirsha.

VIJAYA [*throwing*]. He's down!

BHAGADANTA [*smiling*]. Of course he is.

VIJAYA. Bhagadanta, what is Vratyasom?

BHAGADANTA [*smiling*]. A breaker of homes!

VIJAYA. Karkashirsha?

BHAGADANTA. A quarrel-pusher!

VIJAYA. Pishtakeshi?

BHAGADANTA. Mighty fishy!

VIJAYA. Aranyaketu?

BHAGADANTA [*smiling*]. One who'll placate you!

VIJAYA. Who's this one for?

BHAGADANTA. Aranyaketu?

VIJAYA. Will he be hit? Or won't he?

BHAGADANTA. As bad as being hit, even if he isn't, or as bad as not being hit, even if he is.

[*Enter Prannarayan.*]

PRANNARAYAN [*bowing*]. Aranyaketu is here.

VIJAYA [*turning her aim in that direction*]. In person? Send him in.

[*Enter Aranyaketu. Seeing where she is aiming, he stops. In confusion, he makes a bow.*]

[*In the same pose*] We are pleased with you, Aranyaketu. We are going to kill you.

ARANYAKETU [*a little frightened, but gallant*]. Death from the Queen's own hands is the height of good fortune!

VIJAYA. Bhagadanta, what does one call this?

BHAGADANTA. Diplomacy.

VIJAYA. At whom shall I aim?

BHAGADANTA [*smiling*]. At someone with no aim.

ARANYAKETU [*frowning*]. Shut up, Bhagadanta.

BHAGADANTA [*shrugging his shoulders, smiling*]. I am bound by the Royal Decree.

ARANYAKETU [*ignoring him, to Vijaya*]. My motive in coming here—

VIJAYA. Be seated. [*She throws.*] As before, it cheated us, Bhagadanta.

BHAGADANTA [*with a smile*]. Deceit will always find a seat.

[*Aranyaketu, who has sat down, hastily gets up.*]

ARANYAKETU. Please ask Bhagadanta to leave the room, Your Majesty.

VIJAYA. Why? He is a member of the Cabinet.

ARANYAKETU. I feel it's improper to speak while he is here.

[*Vijaya makes a sign. Bhagadanta goes off stage, smiling.*]

[*to Vijaya*] Your Majesty, I have come to make a last attempt at mediation.

VIJAYA. But your mediation hasn't ended yet. You made two final attempts like this yesterday. Today's programme by the Ministers, of besieging the palace with a mob—

ARANYAKETU. I will not give up hope.

VIJAYA. Give *them* up instead.

ARANYAKETU. In all honesty, as God is my witness, I am on your Majesty's side.

VIJAYA. Well, you can stay on their side in all honesty, and come over to ours in fact.

ARANYAKETU. That is difficult.

VIJAYA. Compromise is difficult.

ARANYAKETU. But then the siege will be laid as arranged.

VIJAYA. Yes, it will.

ARANYAKETU. I have a new formula.

VIJAYA. The old ones weren't bad, either.

ARANYAKETU. Then if you can choose one of those, perhaps—

VIJAYA. All unpleasant. Unacceptable.

ARANYAKETU. If I may be so bold—this is a critical time. To give importance to a quarrel, and to give second place to the welfare of the island, may in the end prove injurious to us all.

VIJAYA. Teach *them* all this—teach your friends. They're the ones who wish to quarrel. We are engaged in government, Aranyaketu.

ARANYAKETU. The unity and efficiency of the government must be maintained.

VIJAYA. That is why we are running it alone these days!

ARANYAKETU. But I honestly feel that the government is a chariot pulled by many hands.

VIJAYA. But the hands must all pull in the same direction.

ARANYAKETU. If some compromise could be found, this is not impossible.

VIJAYA. Some people are in fact trying to stop the chariot, to bring it to a total halt, to break it up!

ARANYAKETU. Face-to-face meetings can often dispel a misunderstanding. I have hopes yet that if your Majesty and the Cabinet were to meet, then—

VIJAYA. We are ready to meet them at any time.

ARANYAKETU. Not just meet them—some assurance, perhaps—of thinking over everything afresh, with an open mind—

VIJAYA. We will require a promise from them—

ARANYAKETU. What promise?

VIJAYA. That they will give free scope to our plan for the Kadambas.

ARANYAKETU. But that seems to them the main cause of the quarrel.

VIJAYA. And that has seemed to us, from the very beginning, the first condition of any compromise.

ARANYAKETU. Then successful mediation is impossible. That is what this means.

VIJAYA. We have no need of it. When you came to us yesterday in your last and final attempt, that's what we told you.

ARANYAKETU. But this can't be allowed to happen!

VIJAYA. We understand your situation.

ARANYAKETU. Even if Your Majesty were to express some formal regrets, it would be enough. I've scribbled a few lines, and brought them.

VIJAYA. Regrets? What about? Aranyaketu, we are the queen. It is for them to apologize for their conduct towards us. [*Laughing*] This is impossible.

ARANYAKETU [*wiping his brow*]. It's my nature to keep trying.

VIJAYA. We feel sympathy for you, Aranyaketu.

ARANYAKETU [*disappointed*]. Then I suppose this effort has gone waste too.

[*He sets out with a heavy tread for the exit.*]

VIJAYA [*stopping him with a gesture*]. Aranyaketu, we suppose you are taking part in that programme today of besieging the palace with a mob?

ARANYAKETU [*with bent head*]. I plan to fall ill at the last moment, if possible. I honestly disapprove of these extreme measures; I prefer the middle of the road.

VIJAYA. You prefer to have two roads, Aranyaketu; in other

words, you make the most determined efforts to put one foot on each of two totally opposite roads, and to walk on both at the same time! Very, very pitiable and terribly amusing! Fifty years old—and still trying to walk in two opposite directions at once. Just for a seat in the government!

[*Laughs to her heart's content. Aranyaketu bows hastily, and departs.*]

BHAGADANTA [*entering and looking smilingly in the direction of his departure*]. Persistency!

VIJAYA. Today we are going to order you to go out and meet the huge crowd that will gather around the palace, Bhagadanta.

[*At first, his smile wavers a bit. Then he smiles, and shrugs his shoulders.*]

BHAGADANTA. No orator. Illiterate!

VIJAYA. An enraged crowd doesn't want speeches, it wants blood.

BHAGADANTA [*still smiling*]. My blood, very common.

VIJAYA. Your blood is a politician's.

BHAGADANTA [*still smiling*]. Maybe not blood. Maybe just water. Sweated in the service of the government.

VIJAYA. Or maybe it's blood—sucked from the common people.

[*Bhagadanta smiles and shrugs his shoulders.*]

Go, Bhagadanta. Be ready when we call you. Do not attempt to escape. We need you. We have given instructions to the guards. You will not be able to get away.

[*He goes off indecisively. Vijaya claps her hands. Enter Prannarayan.*]

PRANNARAYAN. Your orders, Your Majesty?

[*Going up to him wilfully, Vijaya clutches his hair, and holds him still in front of her.*]

VIJAYA. How's my new game going? Tell me.

PRANNARAYAN. It may be a game for Your Majesty, but it's killing me.

VIJAYA. That game of killing is going to take place outside the palace today.

PRANNARAYAN. All the arrangements have been completed according to Your Majesty's command. Armed guards are already hidden in every window of the palace. More guards are concealed in convenient houses near the palace square. Famished criminals in Kadamba costume have been stuffing their bellies with food behind the palace for the past two days. And a host of burglars, thieves and pick-pockets, disguised as the common people, have been let loose in the palace precincts on daily wages. Their misconduct has sorely harassed the genuine populace. Of course, our spies, disguised as servants, have penetrated the households of each of the Ministers. Going through the huge bundles of reports they have turned in—on the most unimportant and finicking details of the Ministers' movements—has given me a bad headache. Reading the reports, I've begun to think that the Minister is the most boring, illogical and commonplace animal in the world. He even sings in his bath!

[*Vijaya starts to laugh.*]

Besides, he takes laxatives. And pinches his wife's cheek when his grandchildren aren't looking. Of course, these are all private matters, but I had to *read* those reports—

[*Vijaya is still laughing.*]

—which is a clear injustice to someone like me.

[*Vijaya laughs even more. She tires of laughing.*]

To talk of the more significant matters reported, they are all in Your Majesty's style. Thugs, thieves, robbers, guns and spies have been gathered in great numbers. In short, one sometimes wonders whether one's reading a report of the Ministers' activities, or Your Majesty's. Similarly, it was discovered that some thieves and government officials were in both camps at once.

VIJAYA. Like Aranyaketu! Prannarayan, why is it all like this?

PRANNARAYAN. I am just giving a report on the reports. Inside information about the common people is even more serious, and such as to cause anxiety.

VIJAYA. For example?

PRANNARAYAN. Feelings of dissent against Your Majesty are being voiced aloud by the common people.

VIJAYA [*biting her lips*]. I see.

PRANNARAYAN. By encroaching on the authority of the Ministers, Her Majesty has encroached on this island's democratic rights.

VIJAYA. But I am a queen! I am not a puppet!

PRANNARAYAN. I am not stating my own opinion; I am telling Your Majesty the universal opinion of the people as given in the report that has reached me.

VIJAYA. 'The opinion of the people!' Ha! That only means that my propaganda machine is useless.

PRANNARAYAN. It wasn't easy for it to compete with Your Majesty's actions.

VIJAYA. Meaning?

PRANNARAYAN. The propaganda machine fell far behind.

VIJAYA. My plan was for the benefit of the Kadamba tribe, for the common people.

PRANNARAYAN. It was for your ambition.

VIJAYA. Ambition for someone's welfare is not a sin. It is the sacred duty of a queen.

PRANNARAYAN. And ambition is greater than duty.

VIJAYA. No, a plan for the welfare of a whole society is any day greater than one's personal ambition.

PRANNARAYAN. And the plan is even greater than their welfare.

VIJAYA. Speak plainly, Prannarayan; don't stab from the side.

PRANNARAYAN. That's my nature. In all that is happening I can see the plan quite clearly, but welfare isn't clear at all!

VIJAYA. The two are one and the same thing, Prannarayan!

PRANNARAYAN. But the Kadamba tribe don't realize that. They hear a lot of drumbeating about the Plan, but they don't get a sniff of their welfare in it. On the contrary, because of this strict insistence on the Plan, the question of this tribe has come to everyone's attention, and caused rioting and attacks against them. So the reports say. And they are on the Queen's side, so they tell only the pleasanter facts. Yet the Kadamba tribe's situation, on account of the stubbornness about the plan—my mistake, on account of the plan—has for the time being at least, become very difficult. The tribe is gravely alarmed.

VIJAYA. This is news to me. But after the present political emergency has been settled and the Plan has begun to run smoothly, I'll be able to think about it. For the Plan, it's important that I should get more power into my hands first, Prannarayan. Why can't these people understand that?

PRANNARAYAN. It's because they can't that they need politicians to worry for them!

VIJAYA [suddenly contemplative]. Prannarayan, if the crowd that gathers round the palace today catches hold of me and kills me, what'll happen then?

PRANNARAYAN. One person at least will be heartbroken.

VIJAYA. Only one?

PRANNARAYAN. I'm talking of real grief. To speak conventionally, black grief will of course spread over all Umbugland, and—if enough clouds gather—nature itself will weep.

VIJAYA. How do I know that even that one person will be really heartbroken?

PRANNARAYAN. Because he is not a politician. Because his tears do not as yet flow at a command. And because he does not choke with emotion to order.

VIJAYA. But why will he be unhappy?

PRANNARAYAN. There is no reason behind grief—at least, not behind simple, unpolitical, spontaneous grief.

VIJAYA. Spontaneous! Then perhaps an advance estimate of it would be wrong, Prannarayan. Perhaps—perhaps, when the time comes, there won't be any grief at all!

PRANNARAYAN. It is possible.

VIJAYA [*angrily*]. 'It is possible!' How is it possible? My death— and not grieve a single person? No, Prannarayan, no! I order that people should grieve for me!

PRANNARAYAN [*laughing*]. That is a Royal Decree! Grief only obeys God's decrees.

VIJAYA [*overcome by emotion, flinging her arms around Prannarayan's neck, and rubbing her head on his chest*]. Prannarayan, I don't want to die. Not even if you're going to be really sorry. I want to live. I want to live long!

PRANNARAYAN. I know that. Why else have all these thorough arrangements been made against today's besiegers?

VIJAYA. That is to beat down the Ministers' malice.

PRANNARAYAN. This is the life of people with ambition. To beat down something, or to take advantage of the beaten down and build on it.

VIJAYA. Prannarayan, I don't just want to live, I want to rule as well! I want to rule a hundred years, a thousand years. I want to thumb my nose at these Ministers, and give my Umbugland whatever shape I wish. Who are these old dodderers to stop me? I am young! I've hardly begun my work! There are so many problems, so many dilemmas and obstacles and wants. Umbugland has to develop yet! If I'm not here, how will it? If I am not on the throne, what will these useless old men do to the island? I must look after everything, do everything myself. I will have to do it. [*Taking aim and throwing at the demon's face on the wall*] I'll do everything! Let these ministers come! Let their mob come! Let it happen! Some final decision will be taken today, Prannarayan. Today is my supreme test!

[*Darkness*. CURTAIN. *Enter the Two with pens in their hands.*]

THE TWO [*in unison*].
EXTRA EDITION! EXTRA EDITION!
NEWS OF REVOLT! EXCITING EDITION!

[*Turn by turn.*]

From youngest to oldest,
From good to dishonest,
From rich to oppressed,
From east to west,
From south to north,
From top to bottom,
From bottom to top
From there to here,
From far to near
Subversion in the atmosphere!

The cry of the moment:
Democratization
Throughout the government
Organization!
The power of the Ministers
Must be maintained!
The whims of Her Majesty
Must be restrained!
The Kadamba Plan—
Leave it defective!
The siege of the Palace
Must be effective!

Victory to Democracy
To Umbugland be Victory!
To the People,
To the Cabinet,
To Vratyasom,
To Karkashirsha,
To Aranyaketu,
To You,
To us,
To these,
To those,
To Felines,

To Flutterers,
To Flatterers,
To the Long-legged,
To the One-Legged,
To the Bow-Legged,
To the Deaf,
To the Blind,
To the Ill,
To the Well,
To Painters,
To Poppas,
To Sofas,
To Prayers,
To Sticks,
To Stones,
To Bones,
To Slicksters,
To Tricksters,
To Etc. Etc.
[*Together*] Victory! Victory! Victory!
TO THE PALACE! FOLLOW US OUT!
POLITICAL ENCOUNTER—FINAL BOUT!

[*Behind the curtain, there is the sound of a crowd in procession. The noise fills the stage. The curtain rises. The Ministers Karkashirsha, Vratyasom, and Pishtakeshi are standing in a room in the palace, sticking out their bellies instead of their chests. The noise of the crowd dies down. Vratyasom opens the window. Suddenly the noise enters through it.*]

VRATYASOM. Ha! [*Quickly closes the window*] Excellent arrangements. Pishtakeshi, Karkashirsha, I must congratulate you! Aranyaketu has played the rogue as usual. He's got 'flu, if you please! Ha! But there couldn't be a better sight than this. At least twenty-five thousand, definitely! A dazzling sight!

KARKASHIRSHA [*angrily*]. Even so, Her Majesty hasn't yet arrived. We've been hanging about here for the last half-hour. [*Looks at his watch.*] Thirty-seven minutes!

VRATYASOM. You must remember one thing, Pishtakeshi. One must not forget it even at this moment to victory. As far as the Queen is concerned, we have no connection with that crowd; we have no idea how it gathered. We are devoted servants of the Crown. Eh?

KARKASHIRSHA. But bear one thing in mind, Vratyasom: I have the first right to power. I have served the Crown longer than you have. Let there be no argument about that later.

VRATYASOM. Everyone will have to agree to the majority's decision. Eh, Pishtakeshi?

[*Opens the window, looks out, and at once shuts it again.*]

Good heavens, one feels terrified! Viju's stocks are going to tumble. Defeat for her, definitely! What an uproar!

PISHTAKESHI. In a little while will come the stones!

KARKASHIRSHA. The decision to destroy palace property is yours, however. Let me state right now that I do not agree to it. If the decision were in my hands, I would have shot anyone who did such things. I'm only on your side as a matter of principle. Your methods are highly distasteful to me. How is it that no stones are being thrown yet, Pishtakeshi?

PISHTAKESHI. The arrangements are perfect. They will come. Instructions have been given to burn some vehicles if possible. Vratyasom, see if you can spot smoke anywhere.

VRATYASOM. You have a look. Ha! Are you scared to peep through the window, Pishtakeshi?

PISHTAKESHI. I am nonviolent and a sensitive man. I expect at least ten or twenty corpses today.

VRATYASOM. There must be martyrs in every agitation. What are ten or twenty, Pishtakeshi? I hope that fifty or sixty will be killed. The world must realize it. This golden page in Umbugland's history must be inscribed in blood! Let me see how it's going on—

[*He opens the window a trifle. Sounds of shooting, stone-throwing and shouting outside.*]

[*Shutting the window*] My God! Shooting! [*Wipes away sweat.*]

KARKASHIRSHA. Why are you scared? For me the sound of bullets is the very symbol of law and order! I firmly believe they must be used from time to time! You have shut the window properly, haven't you?

[*A bullet comes in through the window and goes into the ceiling.*]

[*Clinging to the wall*] A b-bullet! Vratyasom, this is t-too much! Who fired into this room?

VRATYASOM. Wait! I'll have a quiet look. [*Looking out through a crack in the window*] I can't see it properly, but it's a most violent spectacle. Well done! Fight on, my friend! Don't retreat! Ignore the bullets! It's better to die! Death to the Queen!

[*Vijaya, dressed in slacks, has entered and is watching all this. In her hands is some knitting.*]

PISHTAKESHI [*behind Vratyasom*]. Oh, well done! How well he threw that stone! Smashed that window totally! Here's another! The crowd isn't moving! Brave people . . . Karkashirsha, please don't keep pushing me forward!

KARKASHIRSHA. I'm only trying to see the crowd. Don't push backwards all the time! Look, there's one killed! Bright red blood! Look, another's fallen! Just move aside a little, Vratyasom.

VRATYASOM [*looking out*]. Death to the Queen! Death to the Queen! Forward, all of you! Victory to the People! Victory to the Martyrs!

[*A stone strikes the window and falls inside. All three of them twist and bend in alarm to look at it. They notice Vijaya.*]

VIJAYA. Arise, Vratyasom, Karkashirsha, Pishtakeshi. We guarantee your safety.

[*All three at once jerk upright. They move to a safe distance from the window.*]

Finished watching the show outside?

KARKASHIRSHA. Lamentable!

VRATYASOM. Pitiful!

PISHTAKESHI. Infuriating!

KARKASHIRSHA. I scorn this bestial behaviour!

VRATYASOM. I wish to announce my dissent from this uncivilized behaviour. I mean the behaviour of the crowd.

PISHTAKESHI. As soon as this despicable affair is over, I must publish a leaflet, Vratyasom. This stone—this stone did not just hit this window, it—

VIJAYA. It could have hit your head!

PISHTAKESHI. No, no! I was going to say—that is, I still say—this stone has struck the heart of every thinking man, of everyone who truly cares for Umbugland.

VIJAYA. If it was looking for such a person when it entered, it must soon have realized he wasn't here!

VRATYASOM. Why not? It might have hit Your Majesty's own heart!

VIJAYA. You've guessed wrong again, Vratyasom. The shooting outside is going on at our command. And if necessary we will shoot the last survivor of that crowd—shoot him like a dog! We are just calculating whether or not there are enough bullets. That's all.

VRATYASOM. Terrible! Absolutely dreadful!

VIJAYA [*reminding him*]. 'Death to the Queen! Victory to the People! Victory to the Martyrs! Fight on!'

VRATYASOM. I was only saying that sarcastically. Wasn't I, Pishtakeshi?

PISHTAKESHI. We too.

KARKASHIRSHA. Permit me to declare that I disagree with all this rioting.

VIJAYA. Don't do it here. Go outside and declare it to the people!

KARKASHIRSHA. It would be madness at this moment. The crowd is quite enraged. It's paying no attention to bullets. What use would words be?

VRATYASOM. I don't think that the crowd will disperse before its demands are accepted. Eh, Pishtakeshi?

[*A window breaks somewhere else.*]

Another stone!

PISHTAKESHI. Perhaps Her Majesty would be able to calm the crowd.

VIJAYA. In other words, Pishtakeshi, you mean to say that the crowd which won't listen to you, will listen to us?

PISHTAKESHI. I just say that it is possible. Isn't it, Vratyasom?

VRATYASOM. There's no harm in trying.

KARKASHIRSHA. In short, if any effort is possible to prevent further killing, it should be made. I say it as a loyal servant of the Throne.

VIJAYA. Then, Karkashirsha, it is a decree from the throne that the Cabinet sould go out and try to pacify the crowd.

[*Karkashirsha in confusion.*]

KARKASHIRSHA. The crowd's demands are addressed to the Throne.

VRATYASOM. Without any doubt.

PISHTAKESHI. The appeal is against the Throne. There's no doubt of it.

VIJAYA. We decree that you should go as our representatives and discuss with the crowd what their demands are.

PISHTAKESHI. We know them already.

VRATYASOM. We have heard them.

KARKASHIRSHA. They are quite clear.

VRATYASOM. 'Stop the Kadamba Plan!'

PISHTAKESHI. 'Give the Ministers back their power!'

KARKASHIRSHA. And 'Abdicate!'

VIJAYA. Are these the people's demands?

ALL. So we have heard.

VIJAYA. 'So we have heard!' Karkashirsha, Vratyasom, Pishtakeshi, we are Father's daughter; we have grown up in the crowd and with the crowd—don't forget that! Does the crowd make these demands, or the Ministers?

ALL [*with hesitancy*]. The crowd.

VIJAYA [*clapping her hands*]. All right, then. We'll show you what the crowd wants.

[*Enter Prannarayan.*]

Attendant, turn Bhagadanta loose before the crowd.

[*Exit Prannarayan. Vijaya is calm. Determined. She sits and knits. The Ministers, unable to contain themselves, rush to the window. A huge uproar outside. The uproar subsides. The Ministers close the window and turn. Their faces show unbearable emotion.*]

VRATYASOM. What happened, Pishtakeshi?

PISHTAKESHI. Bhagadanta's done for.

VIJAYA. Use your words more precisely. One of the crowd's demands was fulfilled—blood! Someone's blood!

VRATYASOM. Terrible!

VIJAYA. Now the rest of the Ministers will go before the crowd one by one.

PISHTAKESHI [*hiding his face*]. No!

KARKASHIRSHA. This is inhuman!

VRATYASOM. The Cabinet does not consent to this!

VIJAYA. But the Cabinet does consent to gathering this crowd, inciting it to come here, and to creating this spectacle, doesn't it?

VRATYASOM. This is a slander!

PISHTAKESHI. It's untrue!

[*Enter Prannarayan. All are frightened. Prannarayan bows.*]

VIJAYA. What is it, attendant?

PRANNARAYAN [*looking at the Ministers*]. Your Majesty's further commands?

VIJAYA. What does the crowd want?

PRANNARAYAN. Attempts are being made to burn down the palace. A wild chase is going on between the soldiers and the crowd. The mob is uncontrollable.

VIJAYA [*putting down her knitting and getting up*]. Attendant, we ourselves shall go before the crowd.

PRANNARAYAN. Princess Vijaya!

VIJAYA [*suppressing a smile*]. Say 'Your Majesty'.

PRANNARAYAN. Forgive me—Your Majesty. But you—

VIJAYA. It is the wish of our Cabinet—no, of the remainder of our Cabinet—that we should go before the crowd. We are agreeing to the Cabinet's request according to our democratic customs. Come, attendant.

[*They go out, Prannarayan in front, and Vijaya behind. The Ministers are consumed with impatience. With delight. The lights fade. Darkness. The noise of the crowd swells and becomes deafening. Shouts. Roaring. Bullets. Cracking. Screams, then slogans, chanted indistinctly but deafeningly. Gradually the noise lessens and dies away. The Ministers are still where they were. They have long faces. Fade out.*]

PISHTAKESHI. Long live the memory of the Queen!

KARKASHIRSHA. This is called devotion to duty. Vratyasom, open the window. Now there's nothing to fear from that direction.

PISHTAKESHI. Still, we must take care.

[*They open the window and look out. Huge uproar from the crowd. It is deafening. A stone flies in. Vratyasom shuts the window.*]

VRATYASOM. Really! The crowd is mad with fury!

PISHTAKESHI. The Queen committed a grave error in going before them.

VRATYASOM. After Bhagadanta, the Queen. Tut, tut, tut. She was like a daughter to me.

KARKASHIRSHA. What courage! Whatever you may say, it was still His Majesty's flesh and blood!

PISHTAKESHI. She was not very old.

KARAKASHIRSHA. I saw her when she was a tiny thing.

VRATYASOM. Why are you telling us about yourself, Karkashirsha? I tell you, once when she was playing horsey-horsey with the late King, I happened to enter. She stubbornly insisted that I should be the horse for a while. I remember it as clearly as if it happened yesterday! Pishtakeshi, why is the crowd so silent?

KARKASHIRSHA [*his ear to the window*]. Why, here they are, shouting again!

PISHTAKESHI [*sighing*]. Oh, dear, Kingship is a Bed of Nails. I had better prepare my pamphlet.

VRATYASOM. Pishtakeshi, the mob is a terrible thing. We must prepare pamphlet upon pamphlet. We mustn't forget Bhagadanta, either.

KARKASHIRSHA. Dutiful man! Risen from a backward tribe!

PISHTAKESHI. Illiterate, besides. Really amazing!

VRATYASOM. Patriotic character!

[*Enter Vijaya. After her comes Prannarayan. All stand stock-still.*]

ALL. Your Majesty!

VIJAYA. Why? Is the Cabinet surprised? [*They are horrified.*] Attendant, a glass of water.

[*Prannarayan pours out a glass of water and brings it to her. She drinks it slowly and deliberately, while the Ministers wait, consumed with impatience. Vijaya is totally cool and unconcerned. She hands back the glass to Prannarayan and finally turns to the Ministers.*]

VIJAYA. I expect you would like to know what happened? As soon as we went before them, our people, incited against us, demanded our life. Three times. In a loud voice. One or two stones were thrown in our direction. We were afraid. But it was impossible to hide. So we stood there. Just then some of our attendants formed a cordon around us. One of them had his head cracked. Then we shouted, 'Enough of this foolishness! First stand still and be quiet!' For a moment, it was all silence. So as not to frighten that silence away, we began to speak. We just said whatever came to our lips. We were not listening to what we were saying. But the crowd were listening. In surprise. We swore at the crowd. There was a rattle of applause. We scolded the crowd. They began to cheer. We asked the crowd to explain themselves. The crowd hung their heads and stood silent. Then for the first time we looked at the crowd. They stood there in that gathering, enormous as a giant, waiting for something. They wanted something more. We felt pity for the silence of that enormous crowd. We said, we will strive for the welfare of our people. Even then, their silence persisted. We said, taxation is hereby abolished. Yet they were silent. We said, 'We shall institute a public enquiry into the private property of our Ministers, who have today gone against the interests of the people.' At that, the crowd brightened up. We said, 'Those Ministers who are found guilty will be severely punished'. The crowd brightened up still further. We shouted, 'Down with the Cabinet'. The crowd shouted it back louder than us. Didn't it, Attendant?

[*Prannarayan nods his head.*]

It was a thrilling moment. We saw that the crowd was getting what it wanted. Then, someone with a whining voice shouted from behind, 'The Kadamba Plan must be scrapped!' Four weak voices repeated it. We realized that something had to be done at once. The crowd was still unsated. We shouted, 'Down with the Plan—*and the Ministers who made it*'! It was a thrilling experience. Again we shouted, again and again we shouted it, and the crowd each time shouted it back at us. They shouted it deafeningly. Death to Vratyasom! Death to Karkashirsha! Death to Pishtakeshi! Death to Aranyaketu! Bhagadanta was already done for. While the crowd were shouting your names, we promised to hand you over to them, and to meet them from time to time hereafter. And then we left to the sound of cheering.

[*Karkashirsha, Vratyasom and Pishtakeshi are petrified.*]

We have returned. Now it is our Cabinet's turn.

[*All three are terrified. They can't get out a single word. As Vijaya opens the window, the tremendous uproar of the crowd comes in.*]

The Cabinet should proceed to meet the crowd. Attendant, escort them there.

KARKASHIRSHA [*somehow*]. This—this is dreadful!

VRATYASOM. I don't wish to go! I won't go!

[*Pishtakeshi has actually collapsed into a chair.*]

VIJAYA [*enjoying the state they are in*]. The Cabinet seems terrified. If there is a delay. the crowd will not hesitate to make its way into the palace. It is greatly enraged. Isn't it, Prannarayan?

[*He nods.*]

The Cabinet should set out.

KARKASHIRSHA. The C-Cabinet does not wish to go!

VIJAYA. The Cabinet that talks of the virtues of a people's democracy, afraid to face a gathering of the people? Tut, tut, tut! This is hardly a credit to our Cabinet. Rise, Pishtakeshi. The mob is calling you. If you don't go out, it will come in to meet you.

PISHTAKESHI [*helplessly*]. Save me, Your Majesty!

KARKASHIRSHA. I was a patriot—from the very beginning. All this is Vratyasom's mischief.

VRATYASOM. A mistake! I only gave the ideas. The decision was unanimous.

PISHTAKESHI. Y-you were the leaders. I w-wasn't in total agreement.

VRATYASOM. You're lying!

KARKASHIRSHA. You're a liar!

VRATYASOM. Both of you have stabbed me in the back.

VIJAYA. The Cabinet has no time for discussion. Make haste.

KARKASHIRSHA. I fought for my principles. Otherwise I am a devoted subject.

PISHTAKESHI. I just wasn't involved.

VRATYASOM. I was struggling for the honour of the entire Cabinet. It isn't a question of myself alone.

[*Pishtakeshi gently opens the window a bit. As the roar of the mob comes in, he hastily shuts it again.*]

PISHTAKESHI. My God! The protection of the Cabinet is hereafter the d-duty of the Throne!

VIJAYA. Very well. We must do our duty. Attendant, give them disguises. Quickly. Go!

[*Pfannarayan takes the three of them off stage. An individual totally veiled in a burkha enters.*]

ARANYAKETU [*throwing off the burkha, in agitated tones*]. Three cheers for Her Majesty! As soon as I got the news of your victory, I rushed here, uncaring for my life or for the mob. Victory to Your Majesty! Three cheers for the Kadamba plan! I was only opposed to it in detail. In fact I was on the side of the plan from the beginning. I said from the first that it was only Your Majesty's leadership that could save the island. I was never really on the side of the Cabinet. It was only a gross misunderstanding, my being one of their party.

[*Vratyasom, Karkashirsha and Pishtakeshi enter in disguise in women's clothes. They are now much more controlled.*]

Who are those? Karkashirsha? Pishtakeshi? And Vratyasom? It's hard to recognize you!

KARKASHIRSHA. When did you arrive?

PISHTAKESHI. Late as usual, in fact at the right time.

VRATYASOM. Yes, you can look down your nose at us again! We're the fools!

PISHTAKESHI [*listening carefully through the window*]. The situation seems to have calmed down, Karkashirsha.

VRATYASOM. Besides, we now have these disguises. So there's no need to worry.

KARKASHIRSHA. The danger to our lives has been averted, Vratyasom. Terrible! Most terrible it was!

VRATYASOM. Such occasions do come in politics, Karkashirsha. It's no use for a born politician to tremble. You two were frightened out of your wits just now!

PISHTAKESHI. Yes, and I suppose you weren't!

VRATYASOM. I'm all right.

[*Aranyaketu opens the window.*]

ARANYAKETU. The crowd is dispersing and going home, cheering the Queen.

[*Bhagadanta comes limping in, smiling, in tattered clothes.*]

THE FOUR OTHERS [*joyfully*]. Come in, come in, Bhagadanta. You are still in one piece! Our congratulations!

BHAGADANTA [*smiling*]. Hidden injury. [*Turning to Vijaya*] Three Cheers for Her Majesty!

VIJAYA. We are delighted to find that our Cabinet is alive. [*Suddenly in harsh tones*] ATTEN-TION: CLOSE—RANKS! [*They all stand in a line*]. RIGHT. ABOUT—TURN!

[*They turn and stand with their backs to the audience. Vijaya starts walking round them like a ring-master, after the manner of Vichitravirya, and giving them a visible sermon. That is what it looks like, and that is what their attitudes are like.*]

PRANNARAYAN [*coming to face the audience*]. On behalf of the kingdom of Umbugland, I wish you all a thousand years of peace, prosperity and plenty. It is you who give life to the Encounter. I am not a fighter. From the time I could understand anything, I have grown up in the women's apartments, in the palace. For I am of the—er—third sex. A bat hanging on the tree of life. I only saw the world upside down. And the amusing part is, that from upside down the people of this world seem the wrong way up, but I see the truth straight! I see you upside down, a formless, characterless, lifeless, existenceless gathering. The blind, deaf and dumb spectators of the whole encounter—who allow men to become politicians, politicians to become statesmen, statesmen to become cunning, and cunning men to become robots, mechanical men. You are a force that claps its hands, makes strange noises with its mouth, an amazing untiring force—

[*Enter The Two from either wing. They are carrying giant pens, and stand facing the audience.*]

THE TWO [*holding their pens before their mouths and making a sound like trumpets, together*].

THREE CHEERS FOR THE QUEEN OF THE LAND!
MIRACLE IN ISLE OF UMBUGLAND!

[*Turn by turn*]

Ministers' Stratagems Finally Come to Nought—
Turn to Page Six for our Exclusive Report!
We had made the prediction that—
We'd made the calculation that—
We had made the deduction that—
We'd made the implication that—

[*Together.*]

Anyway!
The big reception they're going to give Queen Vijaya will be grand.
AMAZING MIRACLE OCCURS IN ISLE OF UMBUGLAND!
MIRACLE IN UMBUGLAND!
MIRACLE IN UMBUGLAND!

[*Prannarayan stands behind them smiling. Behind him a tableau of the Queen haranguing the Ministers.*]

CURTAIN